Rethinking Nasserism

Copyright 2004 by Elie Podeh and Onn Winckler. This work is licensed under a modified Creative Commons Attribution-Noncommercial-No Derivative Works 3.0 Unported License. To view a copy of this license, visit *http://creativecommons.org/licenses/by-nc-nd/3.0/*. You are free to electronically copy, distribute, and transmit this work if you attribute authorship. *However, all printing rights are reserved by the University Press of Florida (http://www.upf.com). Please contact UPF for information about how to obtain copies of the work for print distribution.* You must attribute the work in the manner specified by the author or licensor (but not in any way that suggests that they endorse you or your use of the work). For any reuse or distribution, you must make clear to others the license terms of this work. Any of the above conditions can be waived if you get permission from the University Press of Florida. Nothing in this license impairs or restricts the author's moral rights.

Florida A&M University, Tallahassee
Florida Atlantic University, Boca Raton
Florida Gulf Coast University, Ft. Myers
Florida International University, Miami
Florida State University, Tallahassee
University of Central Florida, Orlando
University of Florida, Gainesville
University of North Florida, Jacksonville
University of South Florida, Tampa
University of West Florida, Pensacola

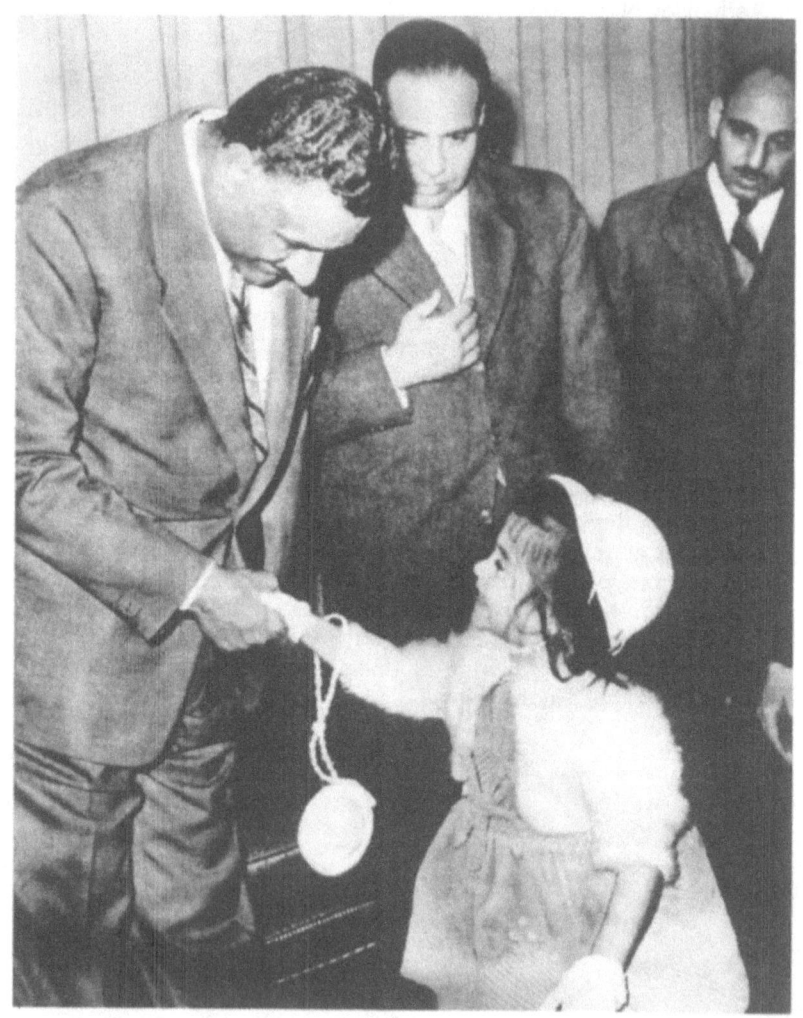

Gamal 'Abd al-Nasser greets a little girl. From *Al-Musawwar*, Cairo, 1959.

# Rethinking Nasserism

Revolution and Historical Memory in Modern Egypt

edited by Elie Podeh and Onn Winckler

University Press of Florida
Gainesville · Tallahassee · Tampa · Boca Raton
Pensacola · Orlando · Miami · Jacksonville · Ft. Myers

Copyright 2004 by Elie Podeh and Onn Winckler

All rights reserved

09 08 07 06 05 04  6 5 4 3 2 1

Library of Congress Cataloging-in-Publication Data
Rethinking Nasserism : revolution and historical memory
in modern Egypt / edited by Elie Podeh and Onn Winckler.
p. cm.
Includes bibliographical references and index.
ISBN: 978-1-61610-130-5
1. Egypt—History—Revolution, 1952. 2. Nasser, Gamal
Abdel, 1918–1970. 3. Egypt—Politics and government—
1952–1970. 4. Arab nationalism—Egypt.
I. Podeh, Elie. II. Winckler, Onn.
DT107.83.R45 2004
962.05'2—dc22      2003070525

The University Press of Florida is the scholarly publishing
agency for the State University System of Florida, comprising
Florida A&M University, Florida Atlantic University, Florida
Gulf Coast University, Florida International University, Florida
State University, University of Central Florida, University of
Florida, University of North Florida, University of South
Florida, and University of West Florida.

University Press of Florida
15 Northwest 15th Street
Gainesville, FL 32611-2079
http://www.upf.com

Contents

List of Tables   vii
List of Figures   viii
Foreword by Gabriel Ben-Dor   ix
Preface and Acknowledgments   xiii
List of Abbreviations   xvii

Introduction: Nasserism as a Form of Populism   1
   *Elie Podeh and Onn Winckler*

### Part I. Images of Nasserism

1. Gamal 'Abd al-Nasser: Iconology, Ideology, and Demonology   45
   *Leonard Binder*
2. Demonizing the Other: Israeli Perceptions of Nasser and Nasserism   72
   *Elie Podeh*
3. History, Politics, and Collective Memory: The Nasserist Legacy in Mubarak's Egypt   100
   *Meir Hatina*

### Part II. Political and Social Aspects of Nasserism

4. Nasserism's Legal Legacy: Accessibility, Accountability, and Authoritarianism   127
   *Nathan J. Brown*
5. Sports, Society, and Revolution: Egypt in the Early Nasserite Period   144
   *Yoav Di-Capua*
6. Nasserist and Post-Nasserist Elites in an Official Biographical Lexicon   163
   *Uri M. Kupferschmidt*

### Part III. Nasser's Foreign Policy

7. 'Abd al-Nasser's Regional Politics: A Reassessment   179
   *Avraham Sela*

8. 'Abd al-Nasser and the United States: Enemy or Friend?  205
   *David W. Lesch*

9. Nasser and the Soviets: A Reassessment  230
   *Rami Ginat*

**Part IV. Nasser's Socioeconomic Policies and Achievements**

10. An Assessment of Egypt's Development Strategy, 1952–1970  253
    *M. Riad El-Ghonemy*

11. Nasser's Egypt and Park's Korea: A Comparison of Their Economic Achievements  264
    *Paul Rivlin*

12. Nasser's Family Planning Policy in Perspective  282
    *Gad G. Gilbar and Onn Winckler*

**Part V. Cultural Aspects of Nasserism**

13. The Nightingale and the Ra'is: 'Abd al-Halim Hafiz and Nasserist Longings  307
    *Joel Gordon*

14. Nasser and Nasserism as Perceived in Modern Egyptian Literature through Allusions to Songs  324
    *Gabriel M. Rosenbaum*

Selected Bibliography  343

List of Contributors  355

Index  359

Tables

10.1. Shares of Consumption, Savings, and Investment in GDP, 1950 and 1970   258
10.2. Investment, GDP Growth, Inequality, and Poverty Estimates in Agriculture, 1952–1970   260
11.1. Population, Total GDP, and GDP per Capita in Egypt and South Korea, 1960–1998 (current prices)   265
11.2. Primary Educational Enrollment Ratio in Egypt and South Korea, 1960–1997   267
11.3. Literacy Rates in Egypt and South Korea, 1960–1997   268
12.1. Egypt's Rates of Natural Increase, 1907–1998   283
12.2. Demographic Variables for Egypt and Several Middle Eastern, Asian, and Latin American Countries, 1960–1998   288
12.3. Selected Socioeconomic Data for Egypt and Tunisia, 1960 and 1998   295

# Figures

11.1. Total Population and GDP per Capita in Egypt and South Korea, 1960–1998   265

12.1. Egypt's Crude Birth and Death Rates, 1907–1998   284

# Foreword

Gamal ʿAbd al-Nasser appears to some pundits as a towering giant but to others as a leader who may have been a good manipulator and a successful demagogue and nothing more. These conflicting assessments are the result of the difficulty entailed in adopting a proper perspective on the study of political leaders just a few decades after they have passed from the scene. This foreword attempts to present a balanced review of Nasser's achievements and failures. An analysis of these leads to some tentative conclusions, indicating that Nasser should indeed be credited with great accomplishments that can be understood only in the context of his own time. His failures, though, are also characteristic of the legacy he left. Nasser, therefore, has been a towering figure, and it is difficult to think of anyone else to compete with his stature and impact. Hence a study of his politics and socioeconomic policies yields useful insights toward a better understanding of Arab and Middle Eastern political issues and systems. Looking back upon the age and deeds of Nasser, even in retrospect of three decades, evokes very strong emotions. It was impossible to be indifferent toward Nasser. One either loved him or hated him. Nasser belongs to the category of distinguished names and figures. He tried to do great things for his country and the Arab world, and his successes were as resounding as his failures.

Nasser strove to bring about massive change in both domestic politics and international relations. This unity of his actions came late, ultimately resulting from his practical experience in the rough and tumble of the political arena. Nasser was not, by nature, an ideologue, despite his rhetoric, which often seemed to indicate otherwise. Rather, he was a true pragmatist who believed in trial and error and who changed ideologies not exactly rapidly or easily but without too many strong attachments or qualms. In this, he may be representative of a broad spectrum of leaders who seemed ideological but who came to ideology late in their careers, mixing and changing all the while. However, he was not great in building political institutions, which was one reason for his difficulties in forging a viable political party. He did not enjoy the kinds of political activities in which party apparatchiks excel.

At the same time, by way of contrast—great leaders are often men of great contrasts!—Nasser was an eloquent speaker and a supreme charmer as well. In fact, theoreticians quote him as a prototype of charismatic leadership not only for his generation but in a broader sense as well. Even now, it is hard to pin down what made him so "charismatic." But clearly it was a combination of general personality, phenomenal rhetorical ability, physical appearance, and sensitivity to the nature and needs of the constituency. While this list may be only partial in its explanatory power, in any case we do not really know what makes a charismatic leader "charismatic." In fact, it does not even make much sense to speak of charisma as if it were a personal attribute of the leader in question. Rather, it is better to speak of a charismatic relationship between leaders and followers.

It is no coincidence that so many of us speak of the age of Nasser, of the generation of Nasser and so on, including Nasserism and Nasserist ways of thinking and approaches to politics. Nasser did dominate and define the politics of an entire generation. He was able to evoke their enthusiasm, their loyalty, and their obsessive devotion. He managed to speak to the masses of Arabs in other countries, even going over the heads of their own leaders. This is something that no other Arab leader has been able to accomplish on any considerable scale. Since everything that Nasser did was so very personal, it was just as difficult, if not outright impossible, to imitate him. What this means is that while Nasser left behind him an impressive legacy, it is not one that can be coherently transferred as a system. It had to do with the man at the center of it all, and once that man was gone, the entire "system" no longer made sense and therefore had to change drastically. Because so much of what Nasser did was really a matter of political psychology, many of his achievements were precisely in this realm. To name a few: the restoration of pride in being Egyptians; the immense increase in the status of Arabism and Arabs throughout the region and the world; the confrontation with imperialism and the West, while building pride and confidence in doing so successfully; the mobilization of the masses in the political process as participants, at least in demonstrations, elections, and other forms of involvement; the creation of a sense of optimism about the future by building on the symbols of the Revolution and its slogans.

This is no mean feat. Even practical steps taken along these lines were successful and partially enduring, among them the development of a more or less universal Arabic language, at a level somewhere between the lofty literary Arabic and the local dialects of the spoken Arabic in the various countries around the Arab world. Some of the other steps made a big difference not only psychologically but also socially and economically, yet they failed to resolve the problems that they were intended to tackle. For instance, the famous Agrarian Reform or the building of the Aswan High Dam were of enormous importance, and they have left lasting marks. Nevertheless, they have not resolved the basic structural problems of the Egyptian society, economy, or even agriculture.

Here are some additional thoughts about trying to assess the role of Nasser in Egyptian and Arab politics with the hindsight of three decades. First, there are many dangers and pitfalls on the way to thinking clearly and coherently about such passionate political issues. The distance of time is not that great, and passions still run high in this part of the world. The dangers and pitfalls are many and varied. At times, they represent the two sides of the same coin. There is the danger of nostalgia, of looking back at the past with a measure of romantic longing, with a yearning to be young again or to remember the good things, inasmuch as the present looks so bad. This happens often, but so does the opposite. By this I mean that people at times, for various reasons, choose to remember only the bad things about the past, perhaps because they would like to believe that the present is so much better. What is needed is a sense of balance and realism.

In practice, this means that we need to be knowledgeable about Egypt and the Arab world in the middle of the twentieth century, if we wish to understand what Nasser was trying and able to do. Most of us are aware of the importance of analysis, theory, and generalization as dominant modes of modern science. But it will not suffice to engage in this process historically. No amount of theorizing will explain the man and his work if the explanation is devoid of concrete and specific historical content. Furthermore, an exaggerated tendency toward generalization and theorizing might lead to underestimating the role of the person in question. While political history is not about the heroic chronicles of selected individuals, it is not justifiable to read politics out of political science or people out of history. History and politics are about people, and how people think and act makes a huge difference in the annals of the human race.

Finally, there is politics, pure and simple. Opponents of Nasser might want to make him look bad, while Nasserists of the day might want to make Nasser look good simply because that would be a way for them to score a few points at the expense of their putative opponents. This kind of political polemic is all too evident in historical assessments, often conducted with surreptitious sophistication. It means that one can overcome these dangers and fallacies if one is aware of them. In the case of Nasser, it makes sense to take into account his admirers as well as his critics, in which case one arrives at a general assessment that is more or less balanced. Ultimately, the decision to either admire Nasser or merely criticize him is upon the criteria one uses to make an assessment, that is, what one expected of him or would have expected of him had one lived during his time. Thus, to say that Nasser did not deliver the goods raises the question of what goods and whose expectations.

Today, it is possible to defend both sides of the argument. One might give credit to Nasser for accomplishing what he tried to do, and add that his agenda may have been wholly, or at least partially, wrong. This need not even be considered a devastating criticism of any sort, because the argument may stem from the assumption that what Nasser was trying to do at the time may well have been correct in the context of that period. The opposite may also be true. It is possible to argue that Nasser may well have been ahead of his time and ahead of his critics. He may have had a better agenda, if there is such a characterization, than even many of his later critics. He may have had closer touch with political reality and with the ambitions and needs of the people than did others, who may have been intellectually his superiors but were less politically realistic and more detached from mass politics in the region. I suspect that to a large extent this was indeed the case. Nasser's acute sense of what the people wanted and needed allowed him to communicate with them better than practically anyone before him or since. This is a rarity in political history that should be properly appreciated.

Gabriel Ben-Dor
University of Haifa

# Preface and Acknowledgments

In July 2002, Egypt lavishly celebrated the "golden jubilee" of the July 1952 Revolution. In contrast to previous anniversaries, this time Nasser's personality figured prominently in the public discourse, which attempted to dispassionately analyze the legacy of his period. This rather sober public debate only served to highlight the fact that Nasser, the Nasserite period, and Nasserism are important phenomena that should be reviewed and reassessed, perhaps leading to some historical revisionism.[1] This book—the product of an international conference jointly organized by the Harry S. Truman Institute for the Advancement of Peace at the Hebrew University of Jerusalem and the Jewish-Arab Center at the University of Haifa—is the first systematic attempt to rethink the Nasserite phenomenon.

The aim of the conference, held in December 1999, was to reevaluate the period of Nasser and the phenomenon closely associated with him, known as Nasserism. Indeed, on the eve of a new millennium, it seemed evident that Nasser had been the most important Arab leader and that Nasserism had been one of the most influential phenomena in the Arab world in the twentieth century. Surprisingly, however, the quantity and quality of research on that subject have not adequately reflected Nasser's perceived centrality in the annals of Middle Eastern history. Moreover, it seems that since the late 1970s, scholars have lost interest in the subject as a result of growing interest in other contemporary issues: the rise of Islam, the Iranian revolution, the Iraq-Iran war, Iraq's invasion of Kuwait, the Arab-Israeli conflict, and so on.

To be sure, the opening of Western archival material as well as the burgeoning of a wider historical perspective triggered the renewed interest in Nasser and Nasserism. Significantly, the growing use of interdisciplinary methods in Middle Eastern studies has enabled us to concentrate not only on the historical dimension but also on various economic, demographic, social, cultural, and psychological aspects that have hitherto been neglected in the literature. This volume does not pretend to cover all aspects of Nasserism; indeed, the discussions at the conference and the papers written by the participants have raised many issues that were not dealt with in this volume—perhaps calling for another conference and another volume.

In contrast to many other edited works, the introduction to this book does not offer a summary of the articles herein; instead, it offers a theoretical framework that views Nasserism as a form of populism. This interpretation, by all means, was *not* imposed on the other writers in this volume, although most articles certainly point in this direction, as we have tried to show in the introduction. Evidently, the Nasserite phenomenon cannot be framed within one theory alone—be it populism, modernization, or messianism. Based on new archival material and new insights derived from the possession of a broader historical perspective, each writer attempted to "rethink" the Nasserite phenomenon in his own field. What has emerged is a multiplicity of voices that attests to the complexity of the subject matter. Most of the articles in this volume have been written by Western scholars; while perhaps an Egyptian or Arab perspective is missing, its absence should be attributed not to the negligence of the editors but rather to the preferences of these Arab intellectuals themselves. In any case, the complaint made by Hoda 'Abdel-Nasser, a professor at Cairo University and Nasser's daughter, that the Egyptians should not leave their history to be written by foreigners,[2] evidently has yet to be redressed.

It is only natural that throughout such a long journey, we were assisted by many whom we would like to thank. First, we are extremely grateful to the heads of the Harry S. Truman Institute for the Advancement of Peace at the Hebrew University of Jerusalem and the Jewish-Arab Center at the University of Haifa, Amnon Cohen and Amatzia Baram, respectively, for their ceaseless support. We would like to warmly thank the Berta Von Suttner Research Program of Germany, which provided much of the financial support for the conference and the publication of this volume. In particular, we would like to thank Karlhienz Koppe from the institute for his personal interest in this project. We would also like to thank Zvia Haimovitz, the administrator of the Jewish-Arab Center, for her support throughout the project; Sharon Woodrow, for editing the volume; and Eran Shayshon, for collecting some necessary material for the project. We should also thank Meir Litvak of Tel Aviv University, who was instrumental in our decision to analyze Nasserism as a form of populism. Finally, we would like to express our appreciation for the two anonymous referees, whose reviews helped us to improve the quality of this volume.

The scholars who wrote the articles in this volume either belonged to Nasser's generation or remembered the image of him from their early childhood. Indeed, their personal perceptions of Nasser may have colored their interpretation. This differs greatly from the twins Eden and Idan Podeh, who coincidentally came into the world two days before the conference. They and their generation will probably learn about Nasser through history textbooks and academic studies such as this one. Undoubtedly, this joyful event made our preoccupation with a distant past more enjoyable. Therefore, although this book is a joint venture, and not a personal one, we are confident that all the participants will join us in dedicating this book to them!

Elie Podeh
Onn Winckler
Jerusalem and Haifa

## Notes

1. See, in particular, the articles in *Al-Ahram*, 21–24 July; *Al-Ahram Weekly*, July 18–24, August 1–7, 2002.

2. "Safeguarding Nasser's Legacy," Hoda Abdel-Nasser's interview with *Al-Ahram Weekly*, July 18–24, 2002.

# Abbreviations

| | |
|---|---|
| ASU | Arab Socialist Union |
| AUC | American University in Cairo |
| CCPE | Civil Committee for Physical Education (Egypt) |
| CIA | Central Intelligence Agency |
| EU | European Union |
| FRUS | Foreign Relations of the United States |
| GDP | Gross Domestic Product |
| GFETU | General Federation of Egyptian Trade Unions |
| GNP | Gross National Product |
| HCPY | Higher Committee for the Patronage of Youth |
| IJMES | *International Journal of Middle East Studies* |
| IMF | International Monetary Fund |
| ISA | Israeli State Archive |
| KDP | Kurdish Democratic Party |
| £E | Egyptian Pound |
| LPA | Labor Party Archive |
| MECS | *Middle East Contemporary Survey* |
| MEDO | Middle East Defense Organization |
| MEED | *Middle East Economic Digest* |
| NDP | National Democratic Party |
| NGO | Nongovernmental Organization |
| NPUG | National Progressive Unionist Grouping |
| NSC | National Security Council |
| OAU | Organization of African Unity |
| OECD | Organization for Economic Cooperation and Development |
| PRO | Public Record Office (London) |
| RCC | Revolutionary Command Council |
| SCP | Syrian Communist Party |
| SCPFP | Supreme Council for Population and Family Planning |
| SLP | Socialist Labor Party (Egypt) |
| UAR | United Arab Republic |
| UN | United Nations |
| UNSC | United Nations Security Council |
| USAID | United States Agency for International Development |
| USNA | United States National Archive |

# Introduction

Nasserism as a Form of Populism

Elie Podeh and Onn Winckler

### Existing Interpretations of Nasserism

"Egypt gave Nasserism to the Arab world," wrote Fouad Ajami in his celebrated book, *The Arab Predicament*.¹ We may surmise that Ajami, like many other scholars, did not consider it necessary to define Nasserism, since it has become a term commonly used in Arab and Western parlance. Admittedly, several definitions have been offered in the literature, but they all highlight the fact that the term *Nasserism* has been rather vaguely used and its meaning and components have been inadequately defined.² Thirty years after Nasser's death, armed with a wider historical perspective, we may organize existing interpretations of Nasserism into five clusters.

The first interpretation views Nasserism as an ideological movement. Although Nasserism was not considered to be as consistent or comprehensive as other ideologies—such as liberalism, socialism, or communism—it was seen as a system of ideas comprising all or some of the following components: anti-imperialism, pan-Arabism (or nationalism), and Arab socialism. All those adhering to these principles, so it is claimed, constituted part of the Nasserite movement. Taking into account the central role that ideologies had played in politics after World War II, the perception of Nasserism as an ideological movement seemed plausible. The main principles of this ideology, it is argued, are included in three documents: Nasser's *Philosophy of the Revolution*, published in 1953–54, the 1956 constitution, and the National Charter (al-Mithaq al-Watani), published in May 1962; some add the March 1968 Manifesto.³ Nasser's speeches and interviews are also considered important sources for understanding the Nasserite ideology.

Understandably, proponents of this interpretation may argue on the level of the rigor and cohesiveness of the ideology. Nissim Rejwan, for example, admitted that Nasserism as an ideology "remains far from coherent, self-complementary, methodical, or consistent." However, this does not negate the validity of the interpretation, because ideology "is rarely a perfectly defined, coherent, and universally accepted or approved system of values and beliefs." Consequently, his analysis of Nasserism was guided by four criteria: the ideas concerning its structure, internal processes, and position in the world; the way in which a society views its history; the broad outlook on man, society, and the world; and the values and goals of society.[4]

Walid Khalidi offered a more nuanced version of this interpretation, seeing Nasserism as a psychological phenomenon shared by an entire Arab generation. In his opinion, Nasserism was not an ideological movement per se but rather an "attitude of mind" that is "eclectic, empirical, radical, and yet conservative." The appeal of Nasserism, according to his analysis, lay in the fact that "it has transferred, if only partially, to the Arab world itself, the center of decisions concerning the future of that world." This development, Khalidi concludes, gave the Arabs a feeling of confidence in themselves and largely counterbalanced the psychological shock of the loss of Palestine.[5]

The second interpretation revolves around the magnetic personality of the Egyptian leader and his style of rule. A salient representative of this attitude is P. J. Vatikiotis, who claimed that Nasserism, "as the term itself implies, was Nasser himself—his vision, style, and approach to power." In his opinion, Nasserism means an "authoritarian 'leader state' with an administrative apparatus for the execution of decisions which, in the absence of a clear ideology or other objective criteria, were taken by the Rayyis: in short, a despotism on the Nile."[6] According to this interpretation, shared by several Egyptian intellectuals, Nasser's charismatic personality, autocratic rule, direct connection with the masses, and use of rhetoric constitute the essence of Nasserism.[7]

The centrality of the giant-leader phenomenon also gave rise to several attempts to apply the Weberian concept of charisma to Nasser.[8] According to this interpretation, Nasser was considered either a modernizing leader or a patrimonial leader, with a personal and informal style constituting trademarks of his behavior. Naturally, a style of leadership that associates Nasser with modernization signals a break with tradition, the Turkish model of Ataturk being a convincing parallel. In contrast, a patrimonial style of leadership might be regarded as a direct continuation of older Arab or Islamic patterns of rule. Evidently, other interpretations of Nasserism did not neglect this personal dimension, though they did not place it at the center of their argument.[9]

The third interpretation, prevalent among Western social scientists in the 1950s and 1960s, perceived Nasserism as a modernization movement and Nasser as a modernizing leader. In general, modernization denotes "an erosion of traditional authority based on ascription, religion, and heredity and the rise of a new legitimacy formula based on secular assumptions."[10] Egypt was seen as a typical Third World country undergoing a process of decolonization and, under new revolutionary leadership, aspiring to national prosperity through modernization. Thus, Nasserism was perceived as an attempt to transform Egyptian traditional society through the modernization of its economy and society. Nasser was seen as a modern version of Muhammad 'Ali, who would turn Egypt into a modern nation-state in accordance with the Western model. This approach concentrated on investigating overall economic performance, consumption level, political mobilization, institutionalization, and legitimacy—all considered important elements in the creation of a modern political community. In this connection, Nasser's use of pan-Arabism and socialism was interpreted not as a manifestation of ideological convictions but rather as a convenient means for achieving modernization.[11]

The hegemony of the modernization theory was challenged by the Marxist view of Nasserism, which might be regarded as an offshoot of this interpretation (though some would definitely regard it as an independent interpretation). According to the Marxist view, Nasserism was essentially "a product of Egypt's national struggle against imperialism and dependency."[12] In addition, it represented a class struggle between the old landowning elite and the new middle class, represented by the army officers. This struggle led to the overthrow of the monarchy and the old elite, resulting in a new stratification of Egyptian society. Yet, owing to the petit bourgeois nature of the leadership, it was claimed, Nasserism created an inherently unstable regime. As such, Nasser was criticized for interrupting an inevitable process of a proletarian revolution.[13]

The fourth interpretation considers Nasserism primarily as a protest movement against Western colonialism and imperialism, which appeared following a significant period of crisis or disorientation. An encyclopedia of the Middle East defined Nasserism as a "general socio-political outlook, marked by substantial protest against the ancient Arab regimes and Western influence in the Middle East, and Israel as a symbol of that influence."[14] Leonard Binder saw Nasserism as an ideological movement, but he emphasized its tripartite protest nature: against the division of the Arabs into several states; against the existing economic, social, and political structure; and against the polarization in the international system.[15] Similarly, Saad Eddin Ibrahim emphasized Nasser's leadership qualities in the makeup of Nasserism, but he subordinated this element to wider historical processes: "The history of this area," he wrote, "is that of Abraham, Moses, Jesus, Muhammad, the Guided Caliphs, the Saladins, the Muhammad Alis, and the

Nassers. But each of these giants emerged in a society in crisis, confronted a challenge, had a message, and found people disposed to believe in his message and to follow his lead in search of salvation."[16]

Within the boundaries of this interpretation, Shimon Shamir offered a more complex definition, attempting to combine various elements of Nasserism by placing them in wider historical and comparative perspectives. After dismissing the modernization interpretation and discussing the significance of Nasser's personality and Egypt's unique geopolitical conditions, Shamir defined Nasserism as "a messianic response of the Arab-Islamic world to 'the attack of the West,'" emanating from the psychological-cultural crisis that evolved after the first generation of political independence. According to Shamir's interpretation, Nasserism "expresses itself through a system of beliefs, policy lines and institutions of the 'revolutionary regime,' which shares certain characteristics with similar Third World regimes undergoing processes of modernization, and decolonization."[17] In this last vaguely phrased sentence, Shamir was in fact pointing at the more general and comparative nature of Nasserism, which later would be offered by other scholars. Shamir also incorporated in his definition Khalidi's interpretation of Nasserism as an "attitude of mind," stating that its strength was derived from the movement's ability to attack the core components of the crisis—"the insult and embarrassment" of long subjugation to foreign domination.[18]

The fifth and newest interpretation attempts to equate Nasserism with populist leaders and movements, mainly found in Latin America during the first half of the twentieth century. Torcuato Di Tella, a leading expert on Latin America, was the first to suggest, as early as 1965, that Nasserism should be seen as one variant (of four) of populism, termed the "Nasserite" or the "Militarist Reform Parties." The Nasserist model, however, according to Di Tella, was not found in Latin America because the economic, social, and political conditions differed from those of the Middle East.[19] Among Middle Eastern experts, Morroe Berger was the first to equate Nasserism with populism—perhaps the only one to apply this theory during the Nasserite era. Yet, beyond an insightful division of Middle Eastern regimes into prepopulist and populist, Berger did not elaborate on this model.[20]

It was only in the late 1970s that other scholars started to refer to Nasserism as a kind of populism. Mark Cooper, for example, spoke of "bureaucratic populism," which meant that ideologically the regime was defending the individual, politically it was promoting corporatist alliances, and economically it was furthering anticapitalist policies.[21] Fouad Ajami, for his part, suggested that Nasser's "implicit ideology" was populism, meaning that the state "implemented programs that benefited and secured the support of large and influential segments of the Egyptian population." He added, however, that Nasser's populism was diffuse: "In striving to appeal to many groups (medium-sized landholders, landless laborers, bureaucrats, industrial workers, students), the state tried to be many things to many groups."[22] Likewise, Raymond Hinnebusch, who focused on Sadat's "post-populist" regime, attempted to show the nature of the transformation by analyzing the Nasserite "populist" regime. Although Hinnebusch offers a comprehensive analysis of Nasser's regime, his study does not cover all the aspects of his populism.[23]

In the mid-1990s, Nazih Ayubi offered a certain typology of Arab regimes. In his opinion, the "socialist" or "revolutionary" regimes represent a distinct combination of étatist and welfare policies. Since their description as "socialist" suited the needs of domestic elites and the vocabulary of the Cold War, Ayubi preferred the term *populist-corporatist,* which he applied to Nasser's Egypt as well. In analyzing the nature of this regime, Ayubi relied heavily on Latin American models of populism. Rather than a socialist ideology inspiring institutional arrangements, he asserted, it was actually the political quest for national independence and for state building that led Nasser to adopt socialist programs. Moreover, Nasser adopted a tightly planned economy, including the control of foreign trade, mainly as effective technical devices for achieving the tasks of accelerated economic growth and political control. Ayubi claimed that Arab populist-corporatist leaders were opposed to the old oligarchy associated with colonialism. Beyond that, he concluded, "their alliances and orientations were subject to a great deal of contingent change."[24]

Some scholars assert that the term *Nasserism* (al-Nasiriyya) is a Western invention.[25] Others suggest that Nasser's Arab adversaries coined the term.[26] Arab intellectuals and politicians have been reluctant to adopt this term for two reasons: First, the supposedly Western origins of the term caused unease among followers of Nasserism, since it was perceived as an anti-imperialist and anti-Western phenomenon. Second, the term seemed to overstate the personal role of Nasser, thus unjustifiably diminishing other important meanings of Nasserism. Gradually, however, the term *al-Nasiriyya* did enter into Arab discourse, appearing in encyclopedias, books, and articles. With the de-Nasserization process gaining momentum in Egypt and the Arab world in the early 1970s, the term became negative and its supporters were politically marginalized. No wonder, therefore, that the study of Nasserism has been unpopular in the Arab world (and, consequently, in the West in general) since that period. Skimming through articles appearing in *Al-Mustaqbal al-'Arabi,* a leading academic journal known for its pan-Arab orientation, clearly indicates that al-Nasiriyya has been treated as a marginal issue.[27]

Is there an Arab interpretation of Nasserism? A cursory review of Arab literature tends to refute this hypothesis. It seems that all of the interpretations described above are to be found in the Arab literature, with the emphasis on Nasserism as an imprecisely defined ideological movement aimed at struggling against Western imperialism and capitalism. For example, Louis 'Awad, one of Egypt's leading intellectuals, scathingly criticized al-Nasiriyya, which, in his opinion, was based on seven "pillars": the six principles of the Free Officers declared upon assuming power in July 1952, plus the formation of the National Union (later to be replaced by the Arab Socialist Union).[28] A conference, held in 2000 by the Arab World Institute in Paris on the occasion of the thirtieth anniversary of Nasser's death, did not offer new insights on Nasserism.[29] Evidently, the populist dimension of Nasserism has not been entirely overlooked in the Arab literature.[30]

In addition to the existence of various academic interpretations of Nasserism, there were also various political perceptions of it. In Israel, for example, a monolithic image of Nasser and Nasserism emerged during the 1950s and 1960s that largely mirrored the Western image. Most of the Israeli decision-making elite, as Elie Podeh shows in chapter 2, saw Nasserism as an expansionist movement bent on conquering and dominating the Arab world and portions of Africa. Such an enterprise entailed, of course, the liquidation of the Jewish state. An oft-repeated analogy was made between Nasser and Hitler and other vicious enemies in the annals of Jewish history. As a result, incoming information was filtered through these images, constituting an important element in the decision-making process.

Thirty years after Nasser's death and the beginning of Sadat's de-Nasserization, it is possible to look at the Nasserite movement less passionately. It is obvious that some of the interpretations offered in the past were rooted in the current political zeitgeist and guided by Western models and theories. It is also clear that the many failures of the Nasserist movement encouraged scholars to abandon the subject, which had attracted so many during the time of Nasser, when Egypt was considered to be a prototype of a modernizing Third World country. Consequently, only a few studies on Nasserism have appeared since the late 1970s.[31]

This chapter attempts to offer a framework combining most, if not all, of the elements appearing in the five interpretations suggested above, while integrating the Egyptian case study with global historical trends. It seems that by seeing Nasserism from a wider perspective, that is, as a form of populism, we might generate a new, or even better, interpretation of this phenomenon. By elaborating on this approach, we follow the path of several scholars who have pointed in this direction but have not fully developed it.

## Populism: The Theoretical Dimension

The term *populism* has been used by many social scientists in a variety of ways, but its definition remains imprecise. As Torcuato Di Tella recently observed, "This term is useful, though somewhat excessively broad in its meaning, as many different fish can be found in that pond."[32] Populism, as a concept, may be applied to a sociopolitical movement, a kind of ideology, a style of leadership, or some combination of these elements.[33] Historically and geographically, populism has appeared mainly in Latin America, but various types of populist movements have also existed in the United States and Russia, as well as in Asian and African countries. Thus Ervand Abrahamian, discussing Khomeini's form of populism in Iran, offers the following definition:

> A predominantly middle-class movement that mobilizes the lower classes, especially the urban poor, with radical rhetoric against imperialism, foreign capitalism and the political establishment. In mobilizing the "common man," populist movements use charismatic figures as well as symbols, imagery and language that have potent value in their popular culture. They promise to raise drastically the standard of living and make their country fully independent of the West ... in attacking the status quo with radical rhetoric, they intentionally stop short of threatening the petty bourgeoisie and whole principle of private property.[34]

Since most of the theoretical discussion in the literature focuses on twentieth-century Latin American experience—Peronism in Argentina (1943–55) being one such case—the analysis of Third World populism in general and Nasserism in particular will rely on insights derived from Latin American models. It will become evident, however, that despite the existence of similarities, one may discern important differences between Latin American forms of populism and Nasserism. For the sake of simplicity, the discussion will focus on the conditions for the emergence of populism and three of its major characteristics. Bearing in mind that Nasserism appeared only after the consolidation of a military takeover, the following analysis will not discuss the type of mass populist movements that have brought populist leaders into power (such as the Iranian example).

### Conditions Conducive to the Emergence of Populism

Populism is most likely to emerge in a society experiencing the two processes of urbanization and industrialization—a result of rapid modernization. The resultant influx of migrants from the rural countryside to the urban environment, which usually is accompanied by the transition from a traditional to a more modern society, creates stressful socioeconomic conditions. Such drastic changes, according to some sociologists, may lead to a generalized sense of rootlessness and malaise, called "anomie." In addition to this alienation, migrants feel powerlessness, resentment, and frustration due to low wages and the absence of sufficient employment opportunities, limited access to urban amenities and services, and exclusion from the political process. Moreover, the semifeudal socioeconomic structure guarantees that the status quo, which has benefited the traditional landed elite, will remain unchanged.

Modernization, through industrialization and urbanization, may also lead to alienation of the urban working class and the bourgeoisie. The urban working class becomes antagonized by the massive control of the elite over the means of production, the deteriorating standard of living, and exclusion from the political process. The frustration of the middle class might be even greater, since access to higher forms of education does not guarantee the attainment of better employment and higher income. Economically, the ability of the urban bourgeoisie to play an important role may be circumscribed by the existence of a large foreign business community that controls the local market. Politically, the closed nature of the elite and its domination over the political system ensures that the educated middle class, in contrast to its initial expectations, does not have an important impact on politics. Among the various groups of the middle class, army officers and students may play an active role in attempting to change the status quo. Other segments of the middle class, as well as urban workers and rural migrants, may play a more passive role, but they constitute available masses that can be mobilized at any given time in their shared aim to change the status quo.[35]

This complex sociopolitical situation creates a convenient hotbed for the emergence of populist leaders, who attempt to give the new masses a sense of belonging and direction, promising to undertake changes that would improve their daily lives. Thus, the domestic tension between developed and backward parts of the same society, such as that which existed in Latin American countries experiencing rapid modernization during the interwar years, constitutes fertile ground for the emergence of populist leaders promising to change the status quo. Indeed, many populist leaders and movements appeared during the decolonization period, when the tension between these developing countries and the more advanced colonizers reached its apex.

Therefore, it appears that a necessary condition for the emergence of populism is "the contact with forces and ideas associated with higher levels of development than those to be found in the society producing the response."[36] The extent to which this tension is crucial in precipitating the appearance of populism depends on three variables: the nature of the political association between the state and the European colonial power; the level of economic dependency on the colonial power; and the extent of cultural similarity between the colonial power and the local society. A major antagonism on all three levels is likely to cause a confrontation between the state and the colonizer, with the subsequent emergence of populist leaders espousing nationalistic platforms. Significantly, some of these variables were absent from the Latin American case, since most of these countries had been liberated from colonialism at the beginning of the nineteenth century. Moreover, they continued their association with their previous colonial masters. Economically and politically they were linked to the United States, while culturally they were tied to Europe and the Iberian Peninsula.[37]

## Charismatic Leadership and Its Link with the Masses

Socially, populist leaders—either civilians or army officers—have usually come from the middle and upper middle classes. Evidently, all populist leaders have possessed some measure of charisma, forming a direct link with the masses. The Latin American experience suggests that the twentieth century saw the appearance of a breed of "leaders of the people," modern *caudillos,* who came from a military background and were antagonistic to the upper classes. These leaders also typically play a psychological role by transmitting a kind of "father figure" image to the masses—an aspect that is particularly significant to rural migrants uprooted from their traditional neighborhoods.[38]

Max Weber defined charisma as "a certain quality of an individual personality by virtue of which he is set apart from the ordinary men and treated as endowed with supernatural, super-human or at least exceptional power or qualities."[39] Based on theoretical and empirical studies, Richard Dekmejian identified four stages in the evolution of charismatic leadership.[40] The first is the existence of a situation of acute social crisis in society and a breakdown of the existing mechanisms of conflict resolution. This kind of social turmoil is usually accompanied by a political crisis of legitimacy. The second stage is the appearance of an "exemplary personage" endowed with charisma that would initiate a charismatic process. The success of the leader depends on three variables: performance-message, personal qualities, and opportunity to propagate. In relation to the first variable, Dekmejian asserts that the message has to fit the deeply felt needs and expectations of the society, as well as coincide with its cultural ethos. He adds that the leader "may selectively invoke history, myth, and past heroes to reinforce the sanctity of his mission. To capture a mass audience, he propagates the highlights of the message in simple and explicit terms. On the basis of these promises—reinforced by heroic activity—the leader establishes an initial charismatic bond with the masses."[41]

In terms of personal qualities, the charismatic leader is seen as an "outstanding personality, endowed with great dynamism, sensitivity and resourcefulness," traits that are instrumental in imparting his message to his followers. The opportunity to propagate the leader's charisma is often obtained only after achieving a position of power, which allows him to skillfully use the mass media. On the basis of the psychological bond formed between the leader and the masses, the third stage involves "a significant change in the subject's value system." The final stage in the evolution of charismatic authority is its "routinization"—an attempt to rely on rational means of legitimacy.

### The Style of Politics and Mobilization Techniques

The special link forged between populist leaders and the masses—the educated middle class, urban workers, rural migrants, and peasants—facilitates the political mobilization of social groups that had hitherto been largely excluded from politics or left on the periphery. This is made possible by another outcome of modernization—the growth in communication, especially through the press, radio, and television. By using colloquial language and stirring emotions during their speeches, populist charismatic leaders are able to successfully communicate with and mobilize the masses. This rhetoric is typically anti-elitist and anti-imperialist, making frequent references to well-known or newly revived myths and symbols. In this way, populist leaders tend to manipulate their followers in their desire to consolidate their power and strengthen their legitimacy.

Although populist leaders recruit from all socioeconomic strata in an attempt to forge a classless society, they often ignore or exclude some groups, such as the wealthy landed oligarchy that was once associated with the old regime. This populist desire to forge a cross-class coalition is aimed at achieving national integration while providing a wide base of support for the regime. The popular rhetoric, therefore, is naturally focused on such terms as the *people,* the *nation, unity,* and *integration.*[42]

Most Latin American populist leaders have attempted to maintain the existing democratic system in general and the electoral process in particular, despite their largely authoritarian style of politics. Lacking a tradition of some form of democracy, as in Latin America, populist regimes in Asia and Africa have been highly authoritarian, with only a semblance of democratic-type institutions. This kind of rule is deemed "appropriate" for the success of a process of modernization held from above, which logically necessitates or even dictates a strong kind of leadership and the imposition of tight control.[43] Paul Drake, however, offers a more complex explanation:

> Both mobilization and institutionalization constituted double-edged swords for populists. Mobilization raised demands, followers, and claims to a share in political power. It provided legitimacy and a social base for carrying through programs once in power. However, it also threatened to outrun populists' capacity for control and ability to deliver on promises. As mass mobilization gains momentum, it can destabilize populist governments. Institutionalization could cost the movement its protest credentials, its dynamism, and its followers.[44]

Van Niekerk makes a distinction between political mobilization in Latin American countries, where it is conducted through populist movements, and the less developed Afro-Asian countries, where it is conducted through mobilization parties characterized by loose coalition structures.[45] The formation or expansion of existing trade unions has served as another mechanism for widening the popular base of a given regime, however authoritarian.

In their efforts to mobilize the masses, populist leaders raise the awareness of popular culture, reviving interest in popular forms of music, folklore, cinema, theater, literature, and other expressions associated with the "common" people. In the past, these forms of popular culture were contemptuously rejected by the old elite, which was associated with the alien "high" culture of the colonial regime. Populist regimes also tend to promote organized campaigns aimed at reviving, rediscovering, and rewriting the past by referring to local myths and symbols. At the same time, the activation of popular forms of sports (such as football), once scorned by the old elite as well, has been encouraged by populist regimes. This revival of popular forms of culture and sports, coupled with the self-discovery process, facilitate a synthesis between the basic values of the traditional culture and a desire for modernization.[46]

### The Eclectic Use of Ideology

Scholars agree that populism is not a coherent ideology but rather an eclectic amalgam of ideas combined with the aim of attaining independence and national integration. According to Van Niekerk, ideology is not of great importance. Leaders are familiar with current ideologies, which allow them to concoct their own blend. In some cases, it constitutes the real mainspring for political action, but more typically it represents "a pseudo ideology ex-post-facto." In short, ideology is "flexible, opportunist and continually subject to changes in political strategy."[47] It has been argued that given their multiclass composition, populist movements and leaders could not be anything but eclectic in order to satisfy different, even conflicting, constituencies. This is why the most common term for these programs derives from adding *ism* (or *ismo* in Spanish) to their leaders' names (e.g., Peronism, Kemalism, Nasserism, Khomeinism, etc.).[48]

Politically, populism is nationalistic, seeking an end to foreign rule in the form of direct colonialism, military bases, formal treaties, or defense organizations. Patriotic sentiments, in Van Niekerk's view, "are easily extended [beyond the borders] to *Latinismo* and continental nationalism."[49] In certain cases, populism may include elements of ethnicity or religious fundamentalism.[50] Studies on populism have emphasized that populist leaders tend to conceive international and domestic politics through the prism of "conspiracies." Van Niekerk went so far as to claim, "Populism possesses only a thought diagram that does not extend beyond the conspirational theory of power." According to this view, the "innocent" masses are victims of certain malicious forces, such as imperialism, capitalism, and other reactionary influences. Thus, populism is largely characterized by its negativism: anti-imperialist, anticapitalist, anti-Semitic, and anti–status quo.

Economically, populism entails "a reformist set of policies tailored to promote development without explosive class conflict. Eschewing unbridled capitalism or socialism, these programs seek national integration." Often enough, populist leaders devise a diluted version of socialism or some kind of a welfare policy, with an eye toward the urban working class, the peasants, and some elements of the middle class. Naturally, this kind of policy necessitates étatism. While in Latin American populism the state is regarded more as "a protector and an employer, than as the principal promoter of economic development," in Asian and African countries the state is "the principal agent in the development process, relying heavily on government intervention in economic life." The outcome of this policy has been the emergence of a "Third Way" between capitalism and communism. By opting for industrialization, populist leaders aim at reducing dependence on the world economy in general and the former colonial power in particular. In parallel, by carrying out various socialist measures, they aim at creating a more egalitarian society, thus broadening the social base of the regime and, consequently, its legitimacy.

### Nasserism as a Form of Populism

Several scholars have already noted the similarity between Nasserism and other forms of populism, but none have offered a systematic analysis of

Nasserism as a form of populism.[51] This failure is all the more surprising because the terms *people* (*sha'ab*) and *of the people* or *popular* (*sha'abi*) were frequently used by Nasser, as well as by Egyptian intellectuals, and thus may give some indication of the regime's popular nature. The number of times these terms appeared, for example, in the National Charter convincingly illustrates the centrality of the populist dimension in Nasserism.[52]

What follows is an attempt to show the relevancy of the populist theory to Nasserism, using, inter alia, the various articles in this volume. Without discounting the validity of other possible explanations for the rise and endurance of Nasserism, the main argument presented here is that the political and economic crisis Egypt had been undergoing, both internally and externally, since the end of World War II facilitated the rise of a populist leadership. Embodied in the charismatic personality of Nasser, this leadership astutely employed various techniques of control as well as mechanisms of persuasion and mobilization typifying populist regimes in Latin America and elsewhere. In essence, Nasser's goals did not differ from other developing countries: independence, modernization, and national integration. Still, Nasserism, as a form of populism, had its own unique features resulting from the particular historical and cultural characteristics of Egypt and its place in the Arab-Islamic world.

### Roots of Nasserite Populism

The July 1952 Revolution, wrote Hinnebusch, "was a classic case of a Third World movement against imperialism and the delayed dependent development which resulted from it."[53] Politically, Egypt had long been controlled by the Ottomans (since 1517) and the British (formally since 1882). A narrow-based, non-Egyptian, Turco-Circassian elite often served Ottoman and British interests. In addition, Egypt, more than any other Arab territory, was exposed to the uneven cultural confrontation between a domineering West and an insecure Arab-Islamic world, which had commenced with Bonaparte's occupation (1798–1801). Based on religious and ethnic differences, this antagonism served to magnify the acuteness of what has been termed "cultural imperialism" and traumatize the Middle East.[54]

Egypt formally received independence and was admitted to the League of Nations in 1936, but Britain's involvement in Egyptian domestic and foreign affairs remained paramount. In Egyptian eyes, the monarchy and the nationalist Wafd Party have gradually become associated, if somewhat unwarrantedly, with British imperialism, a process that led to their delegitimization and eventual fall. Thus, the coup was not only a rebellion against the regime's Western orientation, its instability, and its inability to avoid the 1942 humiliation (with the British) or the 1948 debacle (with Israel). It was also an attempt to free Egypt from all traces of imperialism. Moreover, it was a reaction, albeit somewhat unconscious, against the feelings of inferiority, insult, and embarrassment prevalent among Egyptians following a long period of subjugation and confrontation with Western domination. Generally, many Arabs in other neighboring countries shared these anti-Western feelings and therefore were amenable to populist policies. For many Egyptians, however, gaining complete independence and changing the foreign orientation was not enough. There was a need to change the political superstructure as well as the socioeconomic infrastructure.[55]

Prior to the revolution, the Palace and a small, wealthy landowning elite dominated the political system. This elite had consistently blocked the entrance of the ever-growing educated middle class, which could challenge its privileged position. This class, termed *effendiyya,* comprised students, professionals, teachers, civil servants, and businessmen—in short, the bulk of the urban middle class.[56] The frustration of the middle class stemmed not only from its inability to climb the social ladder and gain greater access to politics but also from the long-standing control by non-Egyptian minorities over many jobs in the private sector. All of these factors contributed to the increasingly violent atmosphere engulfing Egyptian society since the mid-1930s, as well as the gradual spread of pan-Arabism among members of the effendiyya.[57] Most army officers participating in the July Revolution came from this class. Understandably, the coup raised hopes for political and economic changes in favor of the middle class; similar hopes were raised among other deprived sectors of society as well.[58]

Economically, Egypt had been subjected to British colonial rule, which meant direct dependence on the world economy. Until 1952, according to John Waterbury, "Egypt had been a classic example of an export-dependent country whose foreign exchange earnings rose and fell with the sale of raw cotton on international markets."[59] This situation had significant social and economic ramifications, as Hinnebusch described:

> Western imperialism shaped Egypt to suit its own needs, turning the country into a plantation for Western industry and its landed upper class into *compradors* with a stake in the extroverted economy. Egypt's agriculture developed but her peasants did not, and land concentration and population growth produced a growing and impoverished landless class. Industrial development was stunted and delayed while business and finance fell into the hands of foreigners.[60]

Predictably, British colonialism encouraged the pace of modernization, resulting in growing urbanization. Between 1937 and 1947, there was massive migration of *fellahin* from the rural areas to the cities, especially to Cairo and Alexandria. According to official Egyptian statistics, this process continued with almost 1 million migrants arriving in Cairo between 1947 and 1960, and another 700,000 arriving between 1960 and 1970. More than half of these migrants came from rural areas.[61] Janet Abu-Lughod estimated that by 1960 the number of rural migrants was 7 million, or 23 percent of the total Egyptian population.[62] The first impetus for this rural-to-urban migration, in her opinion, was a selective process that "skims the qualitative cream from the countryside and sends it to the city." The second, and more important numerically, impetus was a nonselective migration, primarily stemming from rapid population growth, which "created a backlog of agriculturalists who were neither needed on the land nor capable of being supported by it."[63] In addition to these "push" factors, the much better chances for acquiring employment and education, particularly at the tertiary level, combined with high subsidies for basic foodstuffs and services, pulled large numbers of peasants into the cities.[64]

Uprooted, however, from their natural surroundings, migrants often felt culturally and socially alienated. It was hardly surprising, therefore, that these newly arrived masses constituted fertile ground for populist leaders. In a period characterized by a high level of social dislocation, a charismatic, populist leader could project a "father" image, thus replacing the patrimonial and religious links that were lost or eroded during the transfer from the village to the city.[65] Indeed, it is a common knowledge that one of Nasser's nicknames, especially among the younger generation, was *baba* (father).

It is reasonable to assume, as Abu-Lughod suggests, that migrants become "politicized" in direct proportion to their urbanization. In other words, as they become more integrated into the city, migrants tend to become more involved in politics.[66] By the mid-1950s, when Nasser emerged as a charismatic leader, many migrants flocking into the major cities were psychologically prepared for the appearance of such a leader. Although their actual political contribution would be rather limited, these migrants would play an active role in demonstrations and other mass political activities.

In sum, the conditions for the emergence of populism in Nasser's Egypt were ripe, given the country's political crisis, coupled with rising socioeconomic discontent.[67] In many ways, the Egyptian scene was even riper than in Latin American countries, which have been independent since the beginning of the nineteenth century. In addition, the cultural similarities between Latin America and the West in general somewhat softened the acuteness of the Western challenge there. In contrast, the Western challenge of the Arab-Islamic identity reached a peak in the 1950s, serving as a reminder to the average citizen of the inferiority of the Arab Middle East vis-à-vis the West.

## Nasser's Charismatic Leadership and the Masses

Although scholars differ on what actually accounts for charisma, all agree that Nasser was a charismatic leader who managed to form a special link with the Arab masses. Saad Eddin Ibrahim equated Nasser's ability to reach people with the famous Egyptian singer, Umm Kulthum. Indeed, the crowded funerals that the two received attested to their enormous popularity and charisma.[68] He was, in the words of the common people, "*habib al-malayin*" (beloved of the masses). Thus, Nasser may be regarded as a typical populist leader.

Hinnebusch asserts that Nasser "seemed to be the right man at the right time."[69] Indeed, taking into account Egypt's multifaceted problems in the political and economic spheres, his appearance was analogous to the descent from heaven of a *deus ex machina* in a tragic drama. As other charismatic leaders, he "emerged in a society in crisis, confronted the challenge, had a message, and found people disposed to believe in his message and to follow his lead in search of salvation in this world or in the hereafter."[70] Nasser's humble origins (the son of a postmaster) made him an authentic native leader, the first in many centuries to rule Egypt. Thus his unique connection with the masses rested not only on his charisma but also on the fact that he represented an entire Arab generation. As noted in the foreword by Gabriel Ben-Dor, Nasser's "acute sense of what the people wanted and needed allowed him to communicate with them better than practically anyone before him or since." The Arab sociologist 'Iyad Bin-'Ashur described this peculiar bond between the leader and the masses:

> The relationship between the *ra'is* and the people is a direct one: immediate, emotional, marvelous, almost "bodily." It forms the backbone of the political system, in a situation where political organizations are no more than tools for mobilization and recruitment for the sake of a plebiscite, populist democracy. The discourse in this democracy is addressed to the "people," in the sense of the needy, the badly-off in terms of money or culture. It is a political discourse full of wishes, promises, and appeals to the joy of life, to progress and equality.[71]

Like other charismatic leaders, Nasser made use of several symbolic manifestations of populism. First, he glorified the values and ways of life of the common man, while lashing out against the previous privileged class. Second, his speeches were delivered in "medial" or colloquial language and punctuated by folksy humor. By addressing the masses in their own language, Nasser succeeded in creating an image of "one of us." In the past, the common people were not accustomed to meeting the king "face to face" and hearing him in their own language. Nasser's messages promised to solve the political and social crisis, or they were interpreted as such. In order to attract all social classes, these messages were broadly and simply phrased, encapsulated in slogans such as "freedom," "social justice," "independence," "anti-imperialism," "anti-Zionism," and "pan-Arabism." By emphasizing the issue of "restoring national dignity" in his discourse, Nasser made a psychological appeal to the emotions of Egyptians and Arabs from all walks of life. The fact that his charismatic leadership coincided with the spread of transistor radios helped Nasser to reach remote places that had hitherto been excluded from the political scene. In his study of an Egyptian village, Harik poetically describes the impact of Nasser's speeches on the villagers:

> Nasser's speeches contained no fiery rhetoric; they were monotonous, flowing slowly and incessantly like the great Nile. His words were pronounced with deliberation; his pauses and repetitions were frequent. His style was not ornate; rather, he spoke in a colloquial, conversational manner. The villagers sat listening as if at a seance. Nasser took them into his confidence, or seemed to do so, by explaining affairs of state in uncomplicated language.... He congratulated himself for what he had done for them, called on their patience for hardships that had to be endured, and lectured them on socialism. The villagers were entertained, moderately enlightened, and above all, flattered.[72]

Third, like other populist leaders, Nasser pointed a finger at the "enemies of the people," be they reactionaries, imperialists, or pro-Zionists. By "discovering" plots allegedly carried out by these agents against the "people," a semblance of unity between all social classes was evoked.[73] Fourth, Nasser used the clever technique of self-criticism in his speeches and interviews, thus "taking the wind out of the sails of the opposition."[74] Fifth, Nasser invoked the memory of historical heroes, such as Salah al-Din al-Ayyubi, Ahmad 'Urabi, Mustafa Kamel, and Sa'd Zaghlul, who also had undergone a process of "Arabization." Such historical analogies were used to form an "inevitable" link in the chain of endless confrontations between East and West. The use of these "cultural unifiers," to use Saad Eddin Ibrahim's phrase,[75] also served to create a link, even if artificial, between the Arab-Islamic tradition and modernity. Sixth, Nasser created new revolutionary symbols, while destroying other symbols associated with the colonial past. Thus, long before it was officially opened in July 1970, the Aswan Hign Dam had already been displayed as a monument built for the benefit of the people, representing a national and economic triumph over the West.[76] On the other hand, the statue of Ferdinand De Lespes, the French builder of the Suez Canal, was removed due to its association with Western imperialism.

Nasser's popularity, legitimacy, and mythology grew dramatically during the second half of the 1950s. In chapter 1, Leonard Binder acknowledges that the heroic image of Nasser was based on the popular response to several bold moves taken between 1955 and 1961. He emphasizes the impact of the British evacuation, the opposition to the Baghdad Pact, the Czech arms deal, the nationalization of the Suez Canal Company, the seizure of foreign properties, the rejection of the Eisenhower Doctrine, the establishment of the UAR, and the adoption of socialist policies. These successes served to solidify Nasser's link with the masses, reinforcing their Arab identity and elevating their self-respect.[77] Moreover, these acts were instrumental in "laying the preliminary groundwork on which future charismatic legitimacy would rest."[78] But since charismatic authority rests on heroic performances, there was a constant need for success. Nasser's foreign adventures can be attributed to this need.

Interestingly, however, all the foreign disasters that followed (e.g., the breakup of the UAR, the involvement in Yemen, the June 1967 War, and the War of Attrition) did not substantially erode Nasser's charisma and legitimacy. When he resigned after the devastating defeat of June 1967, the masses roamed the streets demanding his return, thus demonstrating once again the existence of a remarkable bond with the *ra'is*.[79]

### Nasserism Style of Politics and Mobilization Techniques

Like other populist regimes, Nasser's Egypt was an authoritarian-bureaucratic state, relying on three pillars: the presidency, the army, and the party. Consequently, as Ayubi maintains, a three-layer state was created: a boss-state, a security state (*dawlat al-mukhabarat*), and a party state that dominated most associations in society, while the civil bureaucracy was directed and controlled by all three. The mobilization of the people within the system, Ayubi contends, "was partly charismatic (via the boss), partly ideological/political (via the party) and partly organizational (via the bureaucracy and sometimes the army)."[80] Overall, Nasser's political system, as Nathan Brown observes in chapter 4, promised greater accessibility and accountability, but in fact delivered—in quite a heavy-handed fashion—authoritarianism.

Soon after seizing power, the Free Officers abolished the monarchy and the multiparty system. Instead, Nasser attempted to form a single mass organization (the term *party* was to be avoided because it signaled partisanship) that would become a vehicle for mobilizing, activating, and eventually controlling the masses. The aim of the organization was "melting" (*tadhwib*) all class differences on the road to a classless society. The Liberation Rally (1953) and the National Union (1957) were two unsuccessful attempts to form such a front. The most serious effort was associated with the Arab Socialist Union (1962), which was meant to represent the "national alliance of working forces" consisting of workers, peasants, intellectuals, national capitalists, and soldiers. "While the five parts of the alliance were far more a rhetorical device than an organizational reality," wrote Waterbury, "they served to focus attention on social categories that cut vertically across strata of income and privilege."[81] Concomitantly, the Nasserist regime initiated a propaganda campaign directed at these groups, in order to strengthen their sense of belonging to the Egyptian community as well as to emphasize their important role in the creation of a new socialist society.

The National Charter stipulated that at least 50 percent of all elected seats, at whatever level of political, union, or cooperative activity, be reserved for workers and peasants. This step represented Nasser's determination to mobilize constituencies that had previously remained on the margins of politics and could now be expected to support the regime in its drive for socialist reforms. In reality, however, the Charter did not adequately define these corps, and since they had hardly exhibited any corporate activity prior to 1961, the identity given to them from above had proven to be largely fictitious.[82] Henry Clement Moore claimed that none of the five groups succeeded in acquiring sufficient corporate power to demand autonomy or to attain a bargaining position that would allow influence in decision making.[83] It would seem, however, that this was exactly what Nasser had in mind: to mobilize the support of the common people by adopting corporatist organizational principles without encouraging a concomitant increase in their political power. Nazih Ayubi described this duality thus:

> Because Egypt's experimentation with corporatism has coincided with a populist phase (and often with the leader's charisma), the organizational sophistication of their corporatist arrangements could not exceed a certain prescribed level without upsetting the populist character of the regime and threatening to unravel its coalition. The populist coalition was basically "distributive," and it had therefore mainly incorporated its component classes and groups economically while excluding them politically.[84]

The authoritarian nature of the regime was also reflected in its attitude toward the media in general and the press in particular. The nationalization law of the press in 1960 abolished the relatively liberal system that existed under the monarchy, transforming it into a "mobilization press." This "reorganization" of the Egyptian press turned it, in the words of a shrewd observer, "into a government agency exercising the only freedom available to it—the freedom to justify, support and flatter."[85] Thus, while the regime was investing great efforts in mobilizing the five components of the "alliance," it simultaneously acted to curb the activity of independent organs of public opinion that could threaten the regime's control.

In its attempt to mobilize the workers, the regime substantially improved their standard of living, offering them attractive legal guarantees concerning job security, social security, promotions, retirement benefits, wage increases, and subsidies on basic foodstuffs. In addition, an organized campaign aimed at improving the hitherto negative image of the workers had been launched. Moreover, they were given the opportunity to organize; by 1970, fourteen syndicates (including various professional trade unions, such as journalists and engineers) were in existence and their membership was steadily growing. In 1957, the regime allowed the formation of the General Federation of Egyptian Trade Unions (GFETU). In return, union leaders had to acquiesce to the regime's prohibitions against declaring strikes, inciting class antagonism, organizing work stoppages, trying to overthrow the political system, or using force to recruit union members.[86] These strict terms reflected the authoritarian-populist nature of the regime. In short, as Joel Beinin asserted, the loyalty of union leaders was ensured through "a combination of repression, reform, and appeals to national unity."[87]

Such modes of action became especially relevant during periods of crisis, which necessitated the support of the workers. More generally, the syndicates were highly instrumental in strengthening the regime's legitimacy and widening its popular base. Robert Springborg claimed that the significance of the syndicates did not lie "in their role as organizations articulating demands and recruiting political leaders, but rather in their role as vehicles through which the regime attempts to control the behavior, and in some instances mobilize the support, of the professionals."[88] This policy reflected the state's commitment to provide goods and services for the benefit of the people in return for political docility. According to Waterbury, "there was no call to sacrifice for future generations, no austerity measures other than those dictated by military defeat. Egyptians were promised the fruits of the revolution in their time."[89]

Nasser's instrumental attitude toward the economy made Egypt a classic example of a "soft state," as Gilbar and Winckler claim.[90] Paul Rivlin states in chapter 11 that in contrast to the leadership in South Korea and elsewhere in East Asia, Nasser's regime "failed to give economic issues an absolute priority.... This is not to say that Nasser and others in the leadership did not want the best for their people; indeed, their concern for the citizenry was demonstrated in their unwillingness to impose burdens. They managed to maintain basic consumption levels, and this was enough to keep them in power." Another aspect of Nasser's "soft state" was Egypt's family planning policy, which, in contrast to the Tunisian family planning policy, was based on the voluntary response of the population to a governmental policy that did not entail economic and social restrictions deemed crucial for fertility reduction (see chapter 12). The combination of Nasser's "soft state" with huge security expenditures, particularly since the intervention in the Yemen Civil War in late 1962, and the immense negative economic consequences of the defeat in the June 1967 War, created a severe economic recession in Egypt during the late 1960s—the most severe of the second half of the twentieth century.

The regime also acted in different ways to mobilize the rural middle class and the peasants. Binder claimed that the Free Officers formed an alliance with the second stratum—the rural class of locally influential landowners of moderate means (owners of ten to fifty *feddans*), who were mobilized through the medium of the Arab Socialist Union.[91] Indeed, the September 1952 Agrarian Reform, supplemented by the reform laws of 1961 and 1969, stripped the wealthy landlords of their economic privileges and political power. Instead, an expanded group of rural small landlords emerged, becoming the link between the regime and the villagers. Since the successive land reforms largely did not affect these medium-sized landowners economically, insofar as they retained their share of the cultivated land, the change was more reflected in the social and political spheres, which had been previously dominated by the big landlords. This new position of the rural middle class enabled the regime to use it as an instrument of political and social control in the countryside.[92]

The great beneficiaries of land reform, however, were the poor peasants, owners of less than five feddans, who increased their holdings from 35.4 percent of the total area in 1952 to 54.8 percent in 1964. While the structural change in landownership was indeed impressive, still many peasants remained landless.[93] Overall, however, the common villagers not only perceived Nasser's policies and reforms in the countryside as "positive proof of his concern for the *fellahin*" but also "identified with him and accepted his innovations."[94]

The other three corps constituting the "national alliance of working forces"—intellectuals, national capitalists, and soldiers—belonged to the urban middle class. It was from these groups that the new elite, composed of former officers and educated bureaucrats, was recruited. Nasser's regime acted in a variety of ways to expand its base of support among the educated middle class, targeting the students in particular. In fact, the students had constituted the most restive sector in society, playing a major role in the organization of riots and demonstrations during the monarchy period. By declaring that all secondary school graduates would be admitted to universities (1962), and by decreeing that the state would be obliged to offer employment to any university graduate in the civil service and public sector (1964), Nasser transformed the students into his most ardent supporters. Indeed, during Nasser's era, the increase in the number of students was higher than ever before or after. Whereas in 1950 the total number of university students in Egypt was 33,595, their number reached 233,304 in 1970, representing an increase of sevenfold in only two decades.[95] Although in the long run this populist decision produced a glut of graduates who became a burden on the bureaucratic apparatus and the economic system, in the short run the students refrained from taking part in activities against the regime. In February 1968, when the students went to the streets, Nasser responded with the March Manifesto, which attempted to address their grievances.[96]

In the effort to reach hitherto excluded segments of society, Nasser's regime also acted to acquire the support of women.[97] True, the regime did not have any feminist agenda, and women in general were expected to fulfill their traditional role in the family, but the social and political status of women was considerably improved. The 1956 Constitution provided suffrage rights to women, declared that all Egyptians are equal before the law, and endorsed the equal treatment of all employees in terms of work hours, wages, insurance benefits, and vacations. Although in reality employers often ignored these rights in regard to women, still it was an important turning point in the status of women in Egyptian society. No less important was the fact that female enrollment rose dramatically in primary and secondary education as well as at the university level. One of the major results of the widespread education among women in the Nasserite era, particularly higher education, was the increasing percentage of women in the Egyptian elite thereafter. This is clear evidence from Uri Kupferschmidt's study on the *National Encyclopedia of Prominent Egyptian Personalities,* in which women represented 8 percent of the total entries. In this regard, Kupferschmidt noted, "This may not be an impressive proportion in Western terms, but it is nevertheless remarkable in Egypt" (see chapter 6). It would seem, however, that Nasser's interest in promoting women's rights had a populist dimension. As Mervat Hatem concluded, Nasser appropriated a "state feminism" whereby economic independence was granted to women, who in return "supported the state, embraced its ideology, participated in the modernization plans, and accepted their generally unreformed status in the family."[98]

In his attempt to reach all previously neglected groups in society, Nasser also took some conspicuous measures with respect to children. Since the early 1960s, Child's Day (or Childhood Day, 'Id al-Tufula), has been celebrated on January 15—not incidentally Nasser's birthday. The regime depicted children as the human raw material of the future, for both the Egyptian people and mankind.[99] Emphasis was put on education, with the 1953 law providing for free education between ages six and twelve. At the same time, the new school curricula accentuated Egyptian and Arab national education, including speeches by the president.[100]

A primary mobilization technique of the Nasserite populist regime was the arousal of a new cultural awareness among the masses. "The search for a popular culture," wrote Michael Conniff, "answered an existential need to define the 'people' whose role in national life was expanding, and in whose name the populists campaigned."[101] In contrast to the colonial powers, which projected the ideals of an ordered Western civilization, populism revived interest in native cultures. Yet the confrontation between modernization and the maintenance of traditional culture often led to the emergence of a synthetic approach.[102] According to Jack Crabbs, the revolution "has mounted a frontal attack on all aspects of the ancient regime and has deliberately altered the historical and cultural self-image of society." This had been carried out through a "constantly changing mixture of elements of coercion, persuasion, and patronage."[103] In reality, however, the cultural transformation was based on a reinterpretation of Egypt's past rather than a disengagement from it. Elements of Pharaonic, Islamic, Egyptian, and Arab cultural "unifiers" were eclectically woven into this popular culture.[104]

In January 1956, in accordance with the new constitution, the Higher Council of Arts, Letters, and Social Sciences was set up to coordinate between governmental and nongovernmental agencies. The institution was aimed at directing and supervising artistic activities along the desired goals of the revolution, as well as "accentuating the national character in Egypt's intellectual production."[105] In time, the Council became part of the Ministry of Culture, which was formed in 1957 with the aim of promoting programs in music, cinema, theater, dance, and other forms of popular art. Both the Council and the Ministry invested great efforts in reaching the rural periphery. Most of the sponsored activity was organized for the masses, aiming at popularizing the revolution and Nasser as well as glorifying the common people.

The link between Nasserism and popular culture was nowhere as salient as in the field of music. Gabriel Rosenbaum shows how Umm Kulthum, 'Abd al-Halim Hafiz, and Muhammad 'Abd al-Wahhab, all of whom were personally acquainted with Nasser, influenced an entire generation of Egyptians through their patriotic songs (*wataniyyat*).[106] Of the three, 'Abd al-Halim was particularly considered "the voice of the revolution." Rosenbaum further asserts that although new generations of Egyptians may not be familiar with Nasserite ideology, "they know 'Abd al-Halim's songs, which convey elements of this ideology" (see chapter 14). Likewise, Joel Gordon shows how the younger generation of filmmakers utilized the "Dark Nightingale" ('Abd al-Halim Hafiz) as a symbol of the long-lost Nasser era (see chapter 13). According to the minister of culture, Nasser was personally involved in encouraging these cultural activities:

> He was keen on supporting cultural projects, believing that cultural revival would bring into the intellectual sphere what heavy industrialization brings in the sphere of industry. He was passionately endeavoring to show that the word has a mission in strengthening the forces of the nation no less than the mission of the gun in safeguarding the borders of the homeland.[107]

In the field of literature, the Ministry of National Guidance was responsible for formulating a common collective memory by publishing inexpensive popular booklets that propagated national history, as well as works of a cultural-educational character.[108] The regime attempted—usually unsuccessfully—to harness leading intellectuals to this campaign. Moreover, a school of writing devoted largely to the poor was founded in the mid-1950s, according to Abdel Rahman El-Abnoudi, considered the "most famous living poet of the sixties generation." In his view, "those of us who belonged to the disinherited classes had no choice but to belong to that literary school that endorsed the poor—the classes whose interests the revolution would serve."[109]

The regime's promotion of popular culture was also manifested in the realm of sports, where popular forms of sports were encouraged at the expense of other "elitist" forms associated with Egypt's colonial past, such as golf and polo. In his analysis of the sports revival, Yoav Di-Capua asserts that "sports were perceived as an important tool for the organization and conscription of citizens behind the national movement" (see chapter 5). The most popular form was football, with personal involvement by leading politicians, including Nasser and his minister of war, 'Abd al-Hakim 'Amer, in the competition between al-Ahli and al-Zamalik, the two rival teams from Cairo. The extent to which this issue transcended the playing field was reflected in a statement by the Lebanese journalist Salim al-Lazwi and the Egyptian writer Yusuf Idris to the effect that these two teams were "the only parties in the Arab world."[110] Not incidentally, "sports parties" also dominated the university campuses.[111]

### The Eclectic Use of Ideology

Although one school of thought sees Nasserism as a kind of ideology, it was, on balance, an eclectic amalgam of ideas. In this respect, the assertion of

John Waterbury that "there was an enormous amount of '*ad hocism*' in the Egyptian experiment"[112] truly reflects Nasser's haphazard nature of policy and ideology. Upon seizing power, the Free Officers had only vaguely defined their goals, focusing on three negative aspects—struggling against imperialism, feudalism, and exploitative capitalism—and three positive aspects—attaining social justice, building a strong army, and establishing a healthy democracy.[113] More concretely, Nasserite ideas can be classified around three clusters and roughly divided into three distinct periods: Egyptian nationalism (1952–54), pan-Arabism (1954–61), and Arab socialism (1961–67).[114]

The nationalist aspect of Nasserism was paramount in the early revolutionary years, when the Free Officers focused on the evacuation of British forces. This was achieved with the signing of the Anglo-Egyptian treaty in October 1954, signaling an end to foreign occupation and complete independence.[115] In fact, this move was a source of great pride for many Egyptians. "Lift up your head, brother, the age of subjugation is over" was Nasser's oft-quoted slogan. The completion of British withdrawal allowed Nasser, who had by then emerged as the sole leader of the revolution, to adopt pan-Arabism, a doctrine he had never before espoused. From then until the collapse of the UAR in September 1961, pan-Arabism dominated Nasser's discourse and policy.[116]

Although the exact role of pan-Arabism in Nasser's thought and conduct is still a subject for debate, it seems that he perceived this doctrine mainly as an instrument enabling Egypt to achieve a dominant position in the Arab world. Indeed, Avraham Sela reaches the conclusion that "even after the establishment of the UAR, Nasser's adherence to Arab unity was a matter of pragmatism rather than an ideological commitment" (see chapter 7). Indeed, some of Nasser's boldest moves in the Arab world and in the Arab-Israeli conflict were taken as a reaction to external and internal challenges and not necessarily out of ideological conviction.

In comparison to Latin American models of populism, Egypt's drive for regional leadership based on pan-Arabism constituted a unique feature of Nasser's populism. The concept of Arab identity infiltrated Egyptian intellectual discourse in the early 1930s, slowly becoming an influential political force domestically. This ideology was more attractive to the educated effendiyya because Egyptian territorial nationalism had been promoted by the wealthy elite and associated with Western models of community. For a generation imbued with anti-Western sentiment, the espousal of an identity based on Arab-Islamic indigenous culture was seen as a kind of defense mechanism against Western cultural domination. Moreover, its legitimacy was derived from the authenticity of the alternative, with a potential for elevating the effendiyya's low self-esteem. As Israel Gershoni and James Jankowski asserted, "Even if Supra-Egyptian nationalism was an invented tradition, at least it was a home-made invention."[117]

This process, occurring in tandem with British withdrawal, considerably improved Egypt's maneuverability in Arab politics. For those perceiving the Arab world as Egypt's natural lebensraum, a golden opportunity now presented itself. Undoubtedly, Nasser, in his quest for regional preeminence, was aware of these political-strategic considerations, with his claim resting on the existence of a shared Arab identity not devoid of Islamic undertones. Thus, as Sela concludes, "Nasser's years in power were marked by a constant drive for all-Arab hegemony," but he was in fact "halfhearted in his self-aggrandizement" (see chapter 7).

Nasser's espousal of pan-Arabism was an essential part of his populism. He made use of his charismatic appeal by communicating his message through the mass media and by speaking directly to the Arab masses. All of these attributes were skillfully used for achieving an age-old Egyptian aim—namely, Egyptian hegemony—disguised in a new garb called Arab unity.[118] Essentially, Nasser repeated on the Arab stage what he had done in Egypt. If he could succeed in spreading the pan-Arab message among Egyptian villagers,[119] who for centuries had been Egyptian-centered in terms of their identity, then it was hardly surprising that Arabs outside Egypt would be attracted to his doctrine as well. The success of his populist style of leadership on the Arab stage can thus be primarily attributed to the similarity of historical processes that Egypt and other Arab countries were undergoing. In many respects, Nasser represented an entire Arab generation mesmerized by similar problems, and this is precisely what made Nasserism such a powerful force in the Arab region.[120]

With respect to international politics, populist leaders may search for a middle path between East and West, thus opting for neutralism or nonalignment. This kind of approach characterized Nasser's policy: In his attempt to gain maximum benefits from the superpowers, he fluctuated between them regardless of ideological considerations. Both David Lesch and Rami Ginat, the first in his analysis of Nasser–U.S. relations and the second in his review of Nasser-Soviet relations, show how Nasser's policy exploited the Cold War to his own advantage. Thus Lesch concludes: "Washington could never quite figure out whether Nasser was an asset or a detriment to U.S. interests in the Middle East.... To the end, Nasser was something of an enigma to Washington" (see chapter 8). At the same time, Ginat concludes that Nasser's neutralism was intended to manipulate both the United States and the Soviet Union in order to further Egypt's foreign policy. Ginat emphasizes, however, that Nasser's neutralism was not balanced and that his speeches and interviews were characterized more by their anti-Western tone and less by their anticommunist content (see chapter 9).

The third period of Nasserist "ideology" was characterized by socialism or étatism, which was fully developed during the years 1961–67 with the decline of pan-Arabism. Hinnebusch claimed that "the Nasserist modernization strategy was essentially a populist form of étatism."[121] This meant that the state emerged as the major source of economic activity and employment, while allowing some measure of private enterprise. In order to justify his socialist policy, Nasser described Egypt's social structure before the revolution as "the half percent society," one in which only half a percent of the Egyptian population controlled both the economy and the political system.[122] This situation was particularly visible in the field of landownership, "where some 2,000 individuals representing an even smaller number of families owned almost 20 percent of the cultivated area."[123] In other sectors of the economy, one can find the same income gaps.

Consequently, an expanded public sector emerged, largely responsible for planning, stimulating, and directing development. This kind of policy was connected with populism insofar as a powerful, interventionist state apparatus was needed in order "to change Egyptian society, to promote mass literacy, to shift the country to an industrial footing, and to achieve the rates of growth required to bring about broad-based prosperity."[124] In fact, a somewhat similar kind of étatism has also characterized several other types of populist regimes in the Middle East, such as Kemalism, Khomeinism, Ba'thism, and Bourguibism.[125]

Ayubi questions the applicability of the term *socialist* for the Egyptian revolutionary regime, preferring to use the term *étatist*. He claims that Nasser used socialist slogans, applied social policies, and adopted institutional arrangements reminiscent of Soviet-style European regimes, but that it would be "misleading" to call his regime "socialist." In his opinion, "socialism" was partly adopted as an extension of nationalist concerns into economic spheres. In other words, national independence, state building, mass mobilization, and political control were the primary aims of the regime, while the socialist components were formulated eclectically, often as a response to external or internal challenges.[126] A similar conclusion was reached by Riad El-Ghonemy, contending that the several measures for social justice which were actually implemented did not warrant the exaggerated title of "socialism" (see chapter 10). In this sense, both pan-Arabism and Arab socialism served the same means.

On May 21, 1962, in front of 1,750 delegates to the National Congress of the Popular Forces, Nasser presented the National Charter, the most important document to be published during his era. This statement could be regarded as a logical consummation of Egypt's drift toward socialism.[127] However, it was equally possible that this move was precipitated by the breakup of the UAR and that Nasser responded to internal and external challenges by attempting to broaden the social base of his regime and thereby strengthen his legitimacy.

A textual analysis of the Charter reveals its eclectic nature, with long statements on socialism, democracy, Arab unity, foreign policy, and Islam, as well as an exposé of the revolution's "official" historical narrative. As a major symbol of Nasserism, the Charter undoubtedly reflected the populist nature of the regime, which is strikingly evident in its rhetoric. Moreover, the Charter indicates that the state did aspire "to be many things to many groups," offering disparate promises to workers, peasants, and various groups of the effendiyya.[128]

## Conclusions

Historians of the Middle East accentuate the influential role of the unique Arab-Islamic culture in shaping contemporary history. Without discounting the force of this argument, a comparative analysis may enrich our understanding of Middle Eastern phenomena. By viewing Nasserism as a form of populism that has certain parallels with Latin American forms of populism, one can see the peculiarities as well as the comparative aspects of Nasserism. Such an analysis reveals that populism is more likely to emerge in certain places (Di Tella calls it the "periphery") and at certain times. Arguably, when certain historical and socioeconomic processes coalesce—such as modernization, rapid urbanization, and sometimes decolonization—society and its individuals might be more prone to the appearance of populist leaders. Thus, an analysis of the historical conditions underlying the emergence of Nasserism, which focuses on its regional dimensions, might lead to the conclusion, as has been suggested by Shamir and others, that it constituted an Arab-Islamic protest movement against the West. Though such an interpretation may be sound, it must be understood as reductionist. On the other hand, a comparative analysis, which sees Nasserism as a form of populism, places it as part of a worldwide—or at least a Third World—phenomenon.

Nasserism shares certain features with Latin American populism: the central role of the charismatic leader and the special bond with the masses; the authoritarian nature of the regime, with its various techniques of mobilization among broad stratums; and the regime's eclectic use of ideology. Yet Nasserism differs from Latin American models in three important ways that are somehow connected. First, while populist regimes appeared in Latin America long after nations achieved their independence, Nasserism emerged as an anticolonial movement, aiming to eliminate all traces of Western imperialism. Second, while Latin American elites and societies are culturally tied to their previous Western (Hispanic) colonizers, the Arab-Islamic identity of Nasserism turned it a priori into an anti-Western movement. Raised during what was considered British "occupation," Nasser and his generation viewed with suspicion any association with the West. The adoption of neutralism in world politics was, therefore, a natural choice for this generation.

The same logic, though more complex, motivated Nasser in pursuing pan-Arabism. The adoption of this doctrine could offer several advantages: a counteridentity, a "shield" against Western imperialism, a symbol of independence, a means to achieve Egypt's hegemony over the Arab world, and perhaps an economic opportunity to transfer some of the huge oil revenues of the Gulf states to the benefit of the Egyptian people. It is indeed ironic, as Sela concludes in this article, that Nasserism, "often conceived as the great priest of pan-Arab unity, was in effect a powerful catalyst in the process of state formation" (see chapter 7). But the very instrumental use of pan-Arabism to promote Egypt's leading role in the Arab world constitutes, in fact, the third difference between Nasserism and Latin American populism. Peronism and other forms of populism in Latin America have not radiated beyond state borders in the attempt to assume a leading regional role. In contrast, the regional dimension of Nasserism, one of its major components, stemmed from the existence of an imagined collective Arab identity among societies and individuals all over the Arab world. Similar historical conditions and Egypt's age-old interest in what was perceived as its own natural sphere of influence combined to form this unique feature of Nasser's populism.

Populism does not only offer an explanation for the emergence of Nasserism and its particular characteristics; it can also offer some insight into its spectacular failure. Most scholars are unanimous in their negative appraisals of Nasserism, while indicating some positive elements of it.[129] Instead of repeating these largely accepted assessments, we will highlight several points in regard to its failure as a populist movement.

First, as Samuel Huntington and Joan Nelson have noted, populism can generate its own "vicious circle." The initial gains that lead to the expansion of a regime's support base can become a drain on the economy "as more groups become participants and attempt to share in a stagnant or slowly growing economic pie."[130] In the case of Egypt, so long as the economy grew at a pace of around 6 percent during the First Five-Year Development Plan (1960–65), it was somehow possible to respond to the grievances of the various sectors that Nasserism was aspiring to mobilize. These included urban workers, the urban middle class (including students), peasants, city emigrants, and others. Generally, Egyptian populism made substantial gains among the lower and middle stratums, including increased opportunities in the bureaucracy and an expanded educational system, redistribution of surplus land expropriated from large landholders, and business possibilities opened up by the departure of the "local foreigners."

In addition, there was a substantial infusion of aid generated by Nasser's successful diplomacy in playing off East against West, which eventually led to receiving aid from both.[131] In the long run, however, Nasser's attempt to maintain a nationalist-populist coalition, as Hinnebusch explained, led to mounting imbalance between resources and commitments, supply and demand. These commitments included an ambitious development program, a large army, a bureaucratized elite, and a substantial welfare state. These imbalances were further aggravated in the mid-1960s as a result of several developments. First was the problem of rapid population growth, which was not met by a proper governmental response. Second was an overall decrease in foreign assistance, which included a cutoff of U.S. food aid in the spring of 1965.[132] Finally, there were the disastrous effects of the foreign adventures, first the Yemen Civil War (1962–67) and then the June 1967 War.[133] Thus, by 1965, when the burden of debt had grown so heavy that international banks were no longer prepared to provide new loans, the Second Five-Year Development Plan (1965–70) crumbled.[134]

In Hinnebusch's opinion, the ultimate factor undermining Nasserism was the widening contradiction between Nasser's radical populist policies and the dominant bourgeois segments of the regime's social base. As he stated, "The official ideology was socialist, collectivist, and anti-imperialist, but the 'state bourgeoisie' kept a covert 'counter-ideology,' liberal, pro-Western, and consumption-oriented, alive at the very heart of the state." Even the Free Officers were gradually "embourgeoised."[135] In addition, Nasserism suffered from institutional weakness insofar as large segments of the masses supported and benefited from Nasserism, but remained politically passive because there was no viable party to represent them.[136] Finally, like other populist Latin American regimes, Nasser's internal need to demonstrate constant success pushed him into the Yemen affair and the June 1967 War—two episodes that signaled the death knell of Nasserism. Thus, populism offers important insights into the reasons for the decline and eventual fall of Nasserism.

Perhaps the most striking phenomenon was the gap between what Nasser's populism promised and what it actually accomplished for the people it aspired to represent. As one Egyptian intellectual aptly described this phenomenon in retrospect:

> The past had two aspects: that of the facade, and that of the reality. The facade was splendid: it included the abolition of capitalism, of feudalism, of exploitation and of factionalism, along with the struggle

against imperialism, the strengthening of the military, a fair deal for peasants and workers, the realization of social justice, industrialization of the country and unification of the Arab nation from the Ocean to the Gulf. This splendid facade dazzled us at first, as it dazzled the entire Arab nation. . . . The Arabs believed in this aspect of the past, a belief that had almost become an ideology. The master of past became a demigod: to honor him, statues were erected and sacrifices were made; institutions and organizations were created hailing his name and fostering his ideology. This was the facade. As to reality, matters were utterly different.[137]

In 1933, when the great Egyptian novelist Tawfiq al-Hakim published his acclaimed *Return of the Spirit* (*'Awdat al-Ruh*), he was, to a large extent, voicing the people's yearning for the appearance of a leader who would give expression to their feelings and validate their rights to freedom and life.[138] Seeing Nasserism from this perspective, one may wonder if this movement was not more successful than has commonly been accorded. When Nasser died on September 28, 1970, his biographer, Robert Stephens, tells us, "it was the day of the Egyptian people, the humble millions, who had come to say farewell to the man they regarded as 'the father of the nation.'"[139]

His death, however, was followed by an organized campaign of de-Nasserization masterminded by Sadat, which served to obliterate almost all traces of Nasserism. Moreover, Nasser—or rather his successors—have not left any impressive and lasting physical incarnation to bear his name. But the surprising popular reception of *Nasser 56*, forty years after the nationalization of the Suez Canal Company,[140] may indicate that populism is not yet dead. Indeed, after reviewing the intellectual discourse of the Sadat and Mubarak regimes, Meir Hatina comes to the conclusion that the Nasserist legacy "has survived in the public memory" (see chapter 3). The lively public discourse over the Nasserite legacy, which took place during the July 2002 Jubilee celebrations, indeed validates this assertion. Thus, under the shadow of a harsh reality, the Egyptian people, we may contemplate, are just awaiting another hero-leader. Until then, the spirit of Nasser—or rather what is left of his mythical image—may be resurrected time and again.

## Notes

1. Fouad Ajami, *The Arab Predicament: Arab Political Thought and Practice since 1967* (Cambridge: Cambridge University Press, 1981), 18. Ajami, however, did provide a sketchy blueprint of Nasserism elsewhere that will be followed below.

2. All the following sources used the term *Nasserism* (sometimes even extensively) without defining its meaning: Shimon Shamir, ed., *From Monarchy to Republic: A*

*Reassessment of Revolution and Change* (Boulder: Westview Press, 1995); Paul Salem, *Bitter Legacy: Ideology and Politics in the Arab World* (Syracuse: Syracuse University Press, 1994); James Jankowski, "Arab Nationalism in 'Nasserism' and Egyptian State Policy, 1952–1958," in James Jankowski and Israel Gershoni, eds., *Rethinking Nationalism in the Arab Middle East* (New York: Columbia University Press, 1997), 150–67; Kirk J. Beattie, *Egypt during the Nasser Years: Ideology, Politics, and Civil Society* (Boulder: Westview Press, 1994); Joel Gordon, *Nasser's Blessed Movement: Egypt's Free Officers and the July Revolution* (New York: Oxford University Press, 1992); Leonard Binder, *In a Moment of Enthusiasm: Political Power and the Second Stratum in Egypt* (Chicago: University of Chicago Press, 1978); Tareq Y. Ismael, *The Arab Left* (Syracuse: Syracuse University Press, 1976); Gabriel R. Warburg and Uri M. Kupferschmidt, eds., *Islam, Nationalism, and Radicalism in Egypt and the Sudan* (New York: Praeger, 1983); George Lenczowski, "The Objects and Methods of Nasserism," in Jack H. Thompson and Robert D. Reischauer, eds., *Modernization of the Arab World* (Princeton: D. Van Nostrand, 1966), 197–211. See also Reeva S. Simon, Philip Mattar, and Richard W. Bulliet, eds., *Encyclopedia of the Modern Middle East*, vol. 3 (New York: Macmillan Reference, 1996), where there is an entry on Nasser (1313–15) but not on Nasserism.

3. Kemal Karpat, ed., *Political and Social Thought in the Contemporary Middle East* (New York: Praeger, 1982), 158–61; Hrair Dekmejian, *Egypt under Nasir: A Study in Political Dynamics* (Albany: State University of New York Press, 1971), chaps. 5, 8, 9; Majid Khadduri, *Arab Contemporaries: The Role of Personalities in Politics* (Baltimore: Johns Hopkins University Press, 1973), 43–63. According to Khadduri, Nasser was a prototype of "the ideological school." See also Israel Gershoni, "Rethinking the Formation of Arab Nationalism in the Middle East, 1920–1945: Old and New Narratives," in Jankowski and Gershoni, eds., *Rethinking Nationalism in the Arab Middle East*, 4; "Nasserism," in *Cassell Dictionary of Modern Politics* (London: Cassell, 1994), 200; "Nasserism," in Dilip Hiro, *Dictionary of the Middle East* (Houndmills, Basingstoke: Macmillan, 1996), 216.

4. Nissim Rejwan, *Nasserist Ideology: Its Exponents and Critics* (New York: Wiley, 1974), 1, 6–7, 176.

5. Walid Khalidi, "Political Trends in the Fertile Crescent," in Walter Z. Laqueur, ed., *The Middle East in Transition* (New York: F. A. Praeger, 1958), 125. Similarly, Hisham Sharabi claims that Nasserism is "an emotional trend rather than a regimented and coordinated movement." See his *Nationalism and Revolution in the Arab World* (Princeton: D. Van Nostrand, 1966), 97.

6. P. J. Vatikiotis, *Nasser and His Generation* (New York: Croom Helm, 1978), 297–98, 322.

7. Ibid., 195, 269, 297–98, 342. See also the interpretation of the Egyptian intellectual Fuad Zakariyya (quoted in ibid., 335–36); James A. Bill and Carl Leiden, *The Middle East: Politics and Power* (Boston: Allyn and Bacon, 1974), 149–55; Jean Lacouture, *The Demigods: Charismatic Leadership in the Third World*, trans. Patricia Wolf (New York: Knopf, 1970), 13–31, 81–136.

8. See, e.g., Leland Bowie, "Charisma, Weber, and Nasir," *Middle East Journal* 30, no. 2 (1976): 141–57.

9. See, e.g., Dekmejian, *Egypt under Nasir,* chaps. 4, 10; Sharabi, *Nationalism and Revolution in the Arab World,* 97.

10. Cyril E. Black and L. Carl Brown, eds., *Modernization in the Middle East: The Ottoman Empire and Its Afro-Asian Successors* (Princeton: Darwin Press, 1992), 204.

11. Most of the sources that analyzed Nasserism from this perspective did not use the term *Nasserism* when describing Nasser's attempts at modernization. See in this regard Daniel Lerner, *The Passing of Traditional Society: Modernizing the Middle East* (London: Free Press, 1958), 214–63; Manfred Halpern, *The Politics of Social Change in the Middle East and North Africa* (Princeton: Princeton University Press, 1963); James B. Mayfield, *Rural Politics in Nasser's Egypt: A Quest for Legitimacy* (Austin: University of Texas Press, 1971); Maxime Rodinson, "The Political System," in P. J. Vatikiotis, ed., *Egypt since the Revolution* (New York: F. A. Praeger, 1968), 87–113; Bill and Leiden, *The Middle East: Politics and Power,* 145–55. See also various articles in Benjamin Rivlin and Joseph S. Szyliowicz, eds., *The Contemporary Middle East: Tradition and Innovation* (New York: Random House, 1965); Thompson and Reischauer, *Modernization of the Arab World.* For a summary of the modernization school, see Shimon Shamir, "The Decline of Nasserist Messianism," in Shamir, ed., *The Decline of Nasserism, 1965–1970: The Waning of a Messianic Movement* (Tel Aviv: Mifʻalim Universitayim, 1978), 4–6 (Hebrew). On the significance of the modernization theory in Middle Eastern political science in the 1950s and 1960s, see Lisa Anderson, "Policy Making and Theory Building: American Political Science and the Islamic Middle East," in Hisham Sharabi, ed., *Theory, Politics, and the Arab World: Critical Responses* (New York: Routledge, 1990), 55–60.

12. Raymond A. Hinnebusch Jr., *Egyptian Politics under Sadat: The Post-Populist Development of an Authoritarian-Modernizing State* (Cambridge: Cambridge University Press, 1985), 3.

13. See in particular Anouar Abdel-Malek, *Egypt Military Society: The Army Regime, the Left, and Social Change under Nasser,* trans. Charles Lam Markmann (New York: Random House, 1968); Mahmoud Abdel Fadil, *The Political Economy of Nasserism: A Study in Employment and Income Distribution Policies in Urban Egypt, 1952–1972* (Cambridge: Cambridge University Press, 1980); Mahmoud Hussein, *Class Conflict in Egypt, 1945–1970* (New York: Monthly Review Press, 1973). For a reference to this school, see Hinnebusch, *Egyptian Politics under Sadat,* 3; Saad Eddin Ibrahim, "A Socio-Cultural Paradigm of pan-Arab Leadership: The Case of Nasser," in Fuad I. Khuri, ed., *Leadership and Development in Arab Society* (Beirut: Center for Arab and Middle East Studies, American University of Beirut, 1981), 35; Shamir, "The Decline of Nasserist Messianism," 5.

14. Avraham Sela, ed., *Political Encyclopedia of the Middle East* (New York: Continuum, 1998), 546.

15. Leonard Binder, "Nasserism: The Protest Movement in the Middle East," in Binder, ed., *The Ideological Revolution in the Middle East* (New York: John Wiley, 1964), 198–99.

16. Saad Eddin Ibrahim, "A Socio-Cultural Paradigm of Pan-Arab Leadership," 39.

17. Shamir, "The Decline of Nasserist Messianism," 16 (our translation). See also a similar interpretation in "Nasserism," in Joel Krieger, ed., *The Oxford Companion to Politics of the World* (New York: Oxford University Press, 1993), 613.

18. Shamir, "The Decline of Nasserist Messianism," 10.

19. Torcuato S. Di Tella, "Populism and Reform in Latin America," in Claudio Veliz, ed., *Obstacles to Change in Latin America* (London: Oxford University Press, 1965), 67.

20. Morroe Berger, *The Arab World Today* (Garden City, N.Y.: Doubleday, 1962), 418–23.

21. Mark Neal Cooper, "The Transformation of Egypt: State and State Capitalism in Crisis, 1967–77" (Ph.D. diss., Yale University, 1979), 41–42.

22. Ajami quoted in the introduction to Gouda Abdel-Khalek and Robert Tignor, eds., *The Political Economy of Income Distribution in Egypt* (New York: Holmes and Meier, 1982), 8–9. For the article, see Fouad Ajami, "The Open-Door Economy: Its Roots and Welfare Consequences," 469–516. See also Robert Tignor's article, "Equity in Egypt's Recent Past, 1945–1952," where he observed populist policies in the pre-Nasser regime in Egypt (50).

23. Hinnebusch, *Egyptian Politics under Sadat*, 11–29.

24. Nazih N. Ayubi, *Over-Stating the Arab State: Politics and Society in the Middle East* (London: I. B. Tauris, 1995), 197–201. It would be only fair to mention that Marsha Pripstein Posusney recently stated that "Nasirism resembled Latin American populism," but she did not elaborate on this statement. See *Labor and the State in Egypt: Workers, Unions, and Economic Reconstructing* (New York: Columbia University Press, 1997), 24.

25. This argument appears in Binder, "Nasserism," 199; Shamir, "The Decline of Nasserist Messianism," 1.

26. Sharabi, *Nationalism and Revolution in the Arab World*, 97.

27. For some exceptions, see 'Ismat Sayf al-Dawla, "Tatawwur Mafhum al-Dimuqratya min al-Thawra ila 'Abd al-Nasir ila al-Nasiriyya," *Al-Mustaqbal al-'Arabi*, no. 56 (October 1983): 49–79; 'Abd al-Illah Bilqaziz, "Al-Nasiriyya wa-al-Awda' al-'Arabiyya al-Rahina," *Al-Mustaqbal al-'Arabi*, no. 96 (February 1987): 78–99; Burhan Zurayq, "Hawla Nazariyya 'Amma Taqaddumiyya lil-Din: Qira'a fi al-Fiqr al-Nasiri," *Al-Mustaqbal al-'Arabi*, no. 210 (August 1996): 60–80. See also a report on a conference on Nasserism in December 2000, *Al-Mustaqbal al-'Arabi*, no. 262 (December 2000): 79–111.

28. Louis 'Awad, *Aqni'at al-Nasiriyya al-Sab'a* (Beirut: Dar al-Qadaya, 1975), 61–62. The Translation—"the Seven Masks of Nasserism"—stands for the seven "pillars."

29. *Al-Mustaqbal al-'Arabi*, no. 262 (December 2000): 79–111.

30. Amin al-Mahdi called Nasser's regime "the July Populism" (sha'abawiyyat yulyu); see *Al-Sira' al-'Arabi-al-Isra'ili: Azmat al-Dimukratiya wal-Salam* (Cairo: al-Dar al-'Arabiyya lil-Nashr, 1999), 163. See also Kamal Rif'at, *Nasiriyyun? Na'am* (Cairo: al-Kahira lil-Thaqafa al-'Arabiyya, 1976), 7–9; Salah Zaki Ahmad, *Qamus al-Nasiriyya* (Cairo: Dar al-Mustaqbal al-'Arabi, 1985), 13–18; Magdi Riad, *Hiwar Shamil m'aa Jamal al-Atasi 'an al-Nasiriyya wal-Nasiriyyin* (Cairo: Markaz al-Khadara al-'Arabiyya lil-I'lam wal-Nashr, 1992), 153–57.

31. The latest serious analysis was by John Waterbury, *The Egypt of Nasser and Sadat: The Political Economy of Two Regimes* (Princeton: Princeton University Press, 1983). The author, however, did not use the term *Nasserism* in his book.

32. Torcuato Di Tella, "The Transformation of Populism in Latin America," 2. We would like to thank Prof. Di Tella for allowing us to quote from this unpublished paper, written in December 2000.

33. For possible definitions, see Margaret Canovan, "Populism," in Adam Kuper and Jessica Kuper, eds., *The Social Science Encyclopedia*, 2d ed. (London: Routledge and Kegan Paul, 1996), 646–47; Torcuato Di Tella, "Populism," in William Outhwaite and Tom Bottomore, eds., *A Blackwell Dictionary of Twentieth-Century Social Thought* (Oxford: Blackwell, 1994), 494; Di Tella, "Populism and Reform in Latin America," 47.

34. Ervand Abrahamian, "Khomeini: Fundamentalist or Populist?" *New Left Review*, no. 186 (1991). See also his "Fundamentalism or Populism?" in Abrahamian, ed., *Khomeinism: Essays on the Islamic Republic* (London: I. B. Tauris, 1993), 13–38.

35. For various sources that shortly deal with the historical setting from a comparative perspective, see Di Tella, "The Transformation of Populism," 3–5; John D. Wirth's foreword to Michael L. Conniff, ed., *Latin American Populism in Comparative Perspective* (Albuquerque: University of New Mexico Press, 1982), x; Paul W. Drake, "Requiem for Populism?" in ibid., 218, 223, 238; A. E. Van Niekerk, *Populism and Political Development in Latin America* (Rotterdam: Universitaire Pers Rotterdam, 1974), 24; Val Moghadam, "Islamic Populism, Class, and Gender in Postrevolutionary Iran," in John Foran, ed., *A Century of Revolution* (Minneapolis: University of Minnesota Press, 1996), 194; Peter Worsley, "The Concept of Populism," in Ghita Ionescu and Ernest Gellner, eds., *Populism: Its Meanings and National Characteristics* (London: Weidenfeld and Nicolson, 1969), 239; Michael L. Conniff's introduction to his *Populism in Latin America* (Tuscaloosa: University of Alabama Press, 1999), 8–9; Raanan Rein, *Populism and Charisma: Peronist Argentina, 1943–1955* (Tel Aviv: Modan, 1998), 99–100 (Hebrew).

36. Angus Stewart, "The Social Roots," in Ionescu and Gellner, eds., *Populism*, 181.

37. Ibid., 182. See also Van Niekerk, *Populism and Political Development*, 18–19; Di Tella, "The Transformation of Populism," 10.

38. Di Tella, "The Transformation of Populism," 2–3. On the Latin American experience and connection with the masses, see Conniff, "Toward a Comparative Definition of Populism," in *Latin American Populism*, 21; Drake, "Requiem for Populism?" in ibid., 218, 221–22; Rein, *Populism and Charisma*, 102; Nicos Mouzelis, "On the Concept of Populism: Populist Modes and Clientelist Modes of Incorporation in Semiperipheral Politics," *Politics and Society* 14 (1985): 334.

39. Max Weber, *On Charisma and Institution Building*, ed. S. N. Eisenstadt (Chicago: University of Chicago Press, 1968), 48.

40. The following section is based on Dekmejian, *Egypt under Nasir*, 4–9. His conceptualization is based on Weber and other sociologists; see his sources, 312.

41. Ibid., 5. See also Ann Ruth Willner, *The Spellbinders: Charismatic Political Leadership* (New Haven: Yale University Press, 1984), 61.

42. Di Tella, "The Transformation of Populism," 5; Conniff, "Toward a Comparative Definition of Populism," 15–16; Drake, "Requiem for Populism," 221–23; Rein, *Populism and Charisma*, 100; Di Tella, "Populism and Reform in Latin America," 53; Canovan, *Populism*, 297; Conniff, introduction to his *Populism in Latin America*, 7; Moghadam, "Islamic Populism," 197.

43. See Hinnebusch, *Egyptian Politics under Sadat*, 4.

44. Drake, "A Requiem for Populism?" 225.

45. Van Niekerk, *Populism and Political Development*, 19, 40.

46. Ibid., 20; Rein, *Populism and Charisma*, 102; Moghadam, "Islamic Populism," 195; Stewart, "The Social Roots," 187, 192; Wirth, "Foreword," xi.

47. Van Niekerk, *Populism and Political Development*, 34.

48. Conniff, "Toward a Comparative Definition of Populism," 232; Conniff, introduction to *Populism in Latin America*, 5. Kenneth Minogue claims that in contrast with European ideologies, "these [populist] beliefs have the look of umbrellas hoisted according to the exigencies of the moment but disposable without regret as circumstances change." See Kenneth Minogue, "Populism as a Political Movement," in Ionescu and Gellner, eds., *Populism*, 209; Peter Wiles, "A Syndrome, Not a Doctrine: Some Elementary Theses on Populism," in ibid., 166–71; Rein, *Populism and Charisma*, 101. On populism as an ideology, see Ernesto Laclau, *Politics and Ideology in Marxist Theory: Capitalism, Fascism, Populism* (London: NLB, 1977), 147; Donald MacRae, "Populism as an Ideology," in Ionescu and Gellner, eds., *Populism*, 153–65.

49. Van Niekerk, *Populism and Political Development*, 35.

50. Di Tella, "The Transformation of Populism," 3.

51. See, e.g., Vatikiotis, *Nasser and His Generation*, 198, 342, 349, 352–55; Lacouture, *Nasser*, 387; Waterbury, *The Egypt of Nasser and Sadat*, 10, 313; Moghadam, "Islamic Populism," 194. For works which analyzed Nasserism as a form of populism in a more thorough way, see Di Tella, "Populism and Reform in Latin America," 65–67; Ayubi, *Over-Stating the Arab State*, 196–208; Hinnebusch, *Egyptian Politics under Sadat*, 11–29; Ajami, "The Open-Door Economy," 472–75; Cooper, *The Transformation of Egypt*, 39–60. Youssef Choueiri has recently concluded that "Nasserism was essentially a populist movement linked to a charismatic leader and a set of policies." See his *Arab Nationalism: A History—Nation and State in the Arab World* (Oxford: Blackwell, 2000), 196.

52. For the text of the National Charter, see Rejwan, *Nasserist Ideology*, 193–266. In the introduction of the document alone, these terms appeared fifty-six times (195–201). Ayubi asserts that the terms *sha'ab* and *sha'abi* have connotations similar to the Latin American *el pueblo* and *lo popular*, which are not captured by the English words *people* and *popular*. He also adds that the term *sha'ab* has no singular form and always has to be a collective noun. In contrast, the term *populism* in Arabic (*sha'abawiyya*) was hardly used. See Ayubi, *Over-Stating the Arab State*, 204. For the use of this term in Arabic, see Amin al-Mahdi, *Al-Sira' al-'Arabi-al-Isra'ili*, 163.

53. Hinnebusch, *Egyptian Politics under Sadat*, 11.

54. Saad Eddin Ibrahim, "A Socio-Cultural Paradigm of Pan-Arab Leadership," 42.

55. Ibid.; Shamir, "The Decline of the Nasserist Messianism," 9–11; Hinnebusch, *Egyptian Politics under Sadat,* 11–12.

56. On the meaning and composition of the *effendiyya,* see Israel Gershoni and James P. Jankowski, *Redefining the Egyptian Nation, 1930–1945* (Cambridge: Cambridge University Press, 1995), 7–14. For more on the middle class, see Hinnebusch, *Egyptian Politics under Sadat,* 12.

57. Gershoni and Jankowski, *Redefining the Egyptian Nation,* 14.

58. On the political scene in the pre-July 1952 period, see P. J. Vatikiotis, *The Egyptian Army in Politics: Pattern for New Nations?* (Bloomington: Indiana University Press, 1961), 21–43.

59. Waterbury, *The Egypt of Nasser and Sadat,* 29.

60. Hinnebusch, *Egyptian Politics under Sadat,* 11.

61. Onn Winckler, "The Challenge of Internal Migration in Egypt: Tendencies in Urban and Village Development, 1974–1990" (M.A. thesis, University of Haifa, 1992), 10 (Hebrew).

62. Janet Abu-Lughod, "Rural Migrations and Politics in Egypt," in Richard Antoun and Iliya Harik, eds., *Rural Politics and Social Change in the Middle East* (Bloomington: Indiana University Press, 1972), 316.

63. Ibid., 318–19. It should be noted that Iliya Harik's conclusions were different. After concluding his research in a Delta village called Shubra, he asserted that "one of the basic observations in this study is that modernization under mobilizational and welfare-oriented regimes has had positive rather than disruptive effects on rural communities." See his *Political Mobilization of Peasants: A Study of an Egyptian Community* (Bloomington: Indiana University Press, 1974), 21–22.

64. Abu Lughod, "Rural Migration and Politics in Egypt," 317–20. See also a more general analysis of this phenomenon: Saad E. M. Ibrahim, "Over-Urbanization and Under-Urbanism: The Case of the Arab World," *IJMES* 6 (1975): 29–45.

65. Hinnebusch, *Egyptian Politics under Sadat,* 11–12; Research Team, "Distress among the Popular Classes," in Shamir, ed., *Decline of Nasserism,* 84–86 (Hebrew); Waterbury, *The Egypt of Nasser and Sadat,* 6. A different view, however, is presented by Abu-Lughod, who claims that the migrants do not necessarily suffer from anomie, as they receive moral support from their compatriots and create a variety of institutions whose function is to protect migrants from the shock of anomie. See Janet Abu-Lughod, "Migrant Adjustment to City Life: The Egyptian Case," *American Journal of Sociology* 67 (1961): 22–32.

66. Abu-Lughod, "Rural Migration and Politics," 323.

67. For a similar description of the crisis in Egypt, see Gad Silbermann, "National Identity in Nasserist Ideology," *Asian and African Studies* 8, no. 1 (1972): 74–76.

68. Saad Eddin Ibrahim, "A Socio-Cultural Paradigm of Pan-Arab Leadership," 30; Dekmejian, *Egypt under Nasir,* 302; Michael C. Hudson, *Arab Politics: The Search for Legitimacy* (New Haven: Yale University Press, 1977), 242.

69. Hinnebusch, *Egyptian Politics under Sadat,* 13.

70. Saad Eddin Ibrahim, "A Socio-Cultural Paradigm of Pan-Arab Leadership," 39.

71. Quoted in Ayubi, *Over-Stating the Arab State,* 204. Such an appraisal of the

function of the masses stands in contrast to Malcolm Kerr, who underestimated the role of the huge crowds: "they are not political forces of any kind," he said, "but simply noisy, helpless spectators." In his opinion, Nasser speaks to a limited group of at most 1.5 million Egyptians (out of 29 million) who have enough education to form political opinions. See his "Egypt," in James S. Coleman, ed., *Education and Political Development* (Princeton: Princeton University Press, 1965), 179.

72. Harik, *The Political Mobilization of Peasants*, 141. For similar conclusions on the effect of the media (especially the radio) on the peasants, see Ibrahim Abu-Lughod, "The Mass Media and Egyptian Village Life," *Social Forces* 42 (1963): 97–104.

73. For more on these symbolic manifestations of populism, see Ayubi, *Over-Stating the Arab State*, 208; Hudson, *Arab Politics*, 243–44; Sharabi, *Nationalism and Revolution*, 90–91, 94. For a comparison with Khomeini, see Abrahamian, "Khomeini: Fundamentalist or Populist?" 37–38. For the role of conspiracies in populist rhetoric in general, see Ionescu and Gellner, eds., *Populism*, 3; Stewart, "The Social Roots," 192.

74. Eliezer Be'eri, *Army Officers in Arab Politics and Society* (Jerusalem: Israel Universities Press, 1969), 390.

75. Saad Eddin Ibrahim, "A Socio-Cultural Paradigm," 58.

76. Yoram Meital, "The Aswan High Dam and Revolutionary Symbolism in Egypt," in Haggai Erlich and Israel Gershoni, eds., *The Nile: Histories, Cultures, Myths* (Boulder: Lynne Rienner, 2000), 219–26.

77. See Elie Podeh, *The Decline of Arab Unity: The Rise and Fall of the United Arab Republic* (Brighton: Sussex Academic Press, 1999).

78. Dekmejian, *Egypt under Nasir*, 43.

79. See Hinnebusch, *Egyptian Politics under Sadat*, 13–14; Dekmejian, *Egypt under Nasir*, 39–47, 302; Hudson, *Arab Politics*, 243.

80. Ayubi, *Over-Stating the Arab State*, 203. See also Hinnebusch, *Egyptian Politics under Sadat*, 15–18. Clement Henry Moore offers the following definition for an authoritarian regime: "Technically, what most distinguishes an authoritarian from a pluralist or totalitarian regime is the relative autonomy of the state. In a totalitarian regime the party controls the state, while in pluralist system groups working through the political institutions are expected to control the bureaucracy. In the authoritarian system the state—in the sense of leader or junta plus bureaucracy—is relatively autonomous." See "Authoritarian Politics in Unincorporated Society," *Comparative Politics* 6 (1974): 196. See also the discussion in P. J. Vatikiotis, "Authoritarianism and Autocracy in the Middle East," in P. J. Vatikiotis, ed., *Arab and Regional Politics in the Middle East* (London: Croom Helm, 1984), 148–51.

81. Waterbury, *The Egypt of Nasser and Sadat*, 315. On the Arab Socialist Union, see ibid., 313–14. On the National Union, Waterbury wrote that Nasser "had no clear model in mind, but snippets of approaches of Peron, Salazar, Tito and Ataturk were loosely blended together to produce the National Union" (313). See also Hinnebusch, *Egyptian Politics under Sadat*, 19–20. On the special importance attached to the workers, peasants and students, see Tignor, "Equity in Egypt's Recent Past," 33–37.

82. Waterbury, *The Egypt of Nasser and Sadat,* 325.
83. Moore, "Authoritarian Politics in Unincorporated Society," 207.
84. Ayubi, *Over-Stating the Arab State,* 208.
85. Fauzi M. Najjar, "The Egyptian Press under Nasser and al-Sadat," in George N. Atiyeh and Ibrahim M. Oweiss, eds., *Arab Civilization: Challenges and Responses* (Albany: State University of New York Press, 1988), 335. On the law and its ramifications, see also Sonia Dabous, "Nasser and the Egyptian Press," in Charles Tripp, ed., *Contemporary Egypt: Through Egyptian Eyes. Essays in Honour of Professor P. J. Vatikiotis* (London: Routledge, 1993), 100–121.
86. For more information on the syndicates, see Robert Springborg, "Professional Syndicates in Egyptian Politics, 1952–1970," *IJMES* 9 (1978): 275–95; Robert Bianchi, "The Corporatization of the Egyptian Labor Movement," *Middle East Journal* 40 (1986): 429–44; Joel Beinin, "Labor, Capital, and the State in Nasserist Egypt, 1952–1961," *IJMES* 21 (1989): 71–90. See also Ayubi, *Over-Stating the Arab State,* 207.
87. Beinin, "Labor, Capital and the State," 88.
88. Springborg, "Professional Syndicates," 279. For the same conclusion, see Beinin, "Labor, Capital, and the State," 85.
89. John Waterbury, "The 'Soft State' and the Open Door: Egypt Experience with Economic Liberalization, 1974–1984," *Comparative Politics* 18 (October 1985): 69.
90. A "soft state," a term initiated by Gunner Myrdal, refers to countries in which "policies decided on are often not enforced, if they are enforced at all, and in that the authorities, even when framing policies, are reluctant to place obligations on people." *Asian Drama: An Inquiry into the Poverty of Nations,* vol. 1 (New York: Pantheon, Random House, 1968), 66.
91. Binder, *In a Moment of Enthusiasm,* 36. See also Hamied Ansari, *Egypt: The Stalled Society* (Albany: State University of New York Press, 1986), 6; Harik, *The Political Mobilization of Peasants,* 99.
92. Waterbury, *The Egypt of Nasser and Sadat,* 277. See also Binder, *In a Moment of Enthusiasm,* 376. Binder, however, also claimed—an assertion that Waterbury rejects—that the second stratum does not rule but is "the stratum without which the rulers cannot rule" (*Moment,* 26). On the land reforms and their implications, see Waterbury, *Egypt,* 263–81; Robert Mabro, *The Egyptian Economy, 1952–1972* (Oxford: Clarendon Press, 1974), 56–82; Harik, *The Political Mobilization of Peasants,* 35–38; M. Riad El-Ghonemy, *Affluence and Poverty in the Middle East* (New York: Routledge, 1998), 159–61.
93. Harik, *The Political Mobilization of Peasants,* 36–37.
94. Mayfield, *Rural Politics in Nasser's Egypt,* 7, 12. See also Harik, *The Political Mobilization of Peasants,* 140–41, 146.
95. UNESCO, *Statistical Yearbook,* various issues (Paris). For details on the impressive increase in the number of students in Nasser's era (a process that continued during Sadat's and Mubarak's eras), see Gad G. Gilbar, "The Expansion of Higher Education," in his book *The Middle East Oil Decade and Beyond: Essays in Political Economy* (London: Frank Cass, 1997), 79, table 5.1.

96. Haggai Erlich, *Students and University in Twentieth-Century Egyptian Politics* (London: Frank Cass, 1989), 171–93; Kerr, "Egypt," in Coleman, ed., *Education and Political Development*, 189–90; Ajami, *The Arab Predicament*, 103.

97. The following section relies mainly on Selma Botman, "Women and the State during the Nasir Years," in Selma Botman, ed., *Engendering Citizenship in Egypt* (New York: Columbia University Press, 1999), 50–74.

98. Quoted in ibid., 64.

99. See, e.g., *Al-Jumhuriyya*, January 15, 1965; *Al-Akhbar*, January 14, 1967. The newspapers usually did not make any connection between the two events, but apparently such a connection existed; see *Al-Idha'a wal-Telefisyon*, January 16, 1971, 8–11. The Arab League decided to celebrate this occasion in all Arab countries on that date. We would like to thank Doron Saqqal for providing us with this information.

100. An extensive study of Egyptian education during the Nasserite period has yet to be written. See Daniel Josef, "Changes in the Egyptian Education System since 1952" (M.A. thesis, Tel Aviv University, 1976), 23 (Hebrew); Michael Winter, "The Balance of the Education System under Nasser's Regime," in Shamir, ed., *The Decline of Nasserism*, 114–21 (Hebrew).

101. Conniff, "Toward a Comparative Definition of Populism," 20.

102. Stewart, "The Social Roots," 187.

103. Jack Crabbs Jr. "Politics, History, and Culture in Nasser's Egypt," *IJMES* 6 (1975): 412.

104. Yoram Meital, "Revolutionizing the Past: Historical Representation during Egypt's Revolutionary Experience, 1952–62," *Mediterranean Historical Review* 12 (1997): 69–72. Take, for example, the erection of the statue of "Egypt's Awakening" (*Nahdat Misr*) outside Cairo University. It showed a peasant woman lifting her veil, standing behind the sphinx. See Joel Gordon, "Secular and Religious Memory in Egypt," *Muslim World* 87 (1997): 96.

105. See the memoirs of the first minister of culture, Tharwat 'Ukasha (November 1957–September 1962), *Mudhakkirati fi al-Siyasa wal-Thaqafa*, vol. 1 (Cairo, 1987), 472–73. See also Vatikiotis, *Egyptian Army in Politics*, 126–27.

106. See also Meital, "Revolutionizing the Past," 69–72; Crabbs, "Politics, History, and Culture," 405–6; Louis 'Awad, "Cultural and Intellectual Developments in Egypt since 1952," in Vatikiotis, ed., *Egypt since the Revolution*, 157–60; Harik, *The Political Mobilization of Peasants*, 129–30.

107. 'Ukasha, *Mudhakkirati*, 474–75.

108. Menachem Klein, "*Ikhtarna Laka* (We Have Selected for You): A Critique of Egypt's Revolutionary Culture," *Orient* 38, no. 4 (1997): 677–91.

109. El-Abnoudi's interview with *Al-Ahram Weekly*, 18–24 July 2002.

110. Quoted in Gabriel M. Rosenbaum, "Football, Popular Culture, and Literature in Egypt: The Rivalry between al-Ahli and al-Zamalik," *Proceedings of the First International Conference on Middle Eastern Popular Culture* (September 2000, forthcoming).

111. In 1966, Prof. Fuad Zakariyya lamented that "sports parties" in general, and football in particular, dominate the campuses. Quoted in Erlich, *Students and University*, 181.

112. John Waterbury, "Reflections on the Extent of Egypt's Revolution: Socioeconomic Indicators," in Shamir, ed., *Egypt from Monarchy to Revolution*, 65. For the same argument, see his book *The Egypt of Nasser and Sadat*, 48; Be'eri, *Army Officers*, 374, 389. Some scholars attribute the failure of Nasserism to the lack of ideology (as well as to other reasons). See, e.g., Raymond William Baker, *Egypt's Uncertain Revolution under Nasser and Sadat* (Cambridge: Harvard University Press, 1978), 13.

113. Shamir, "The Decline of the Nasserist Messianism," 3.

114. This mixture was suggested by Vatikiotis, *Nasser and His Generation*, 195, and Silbermann, "National Identity in Nasserist Ideology, 1952-1970."

115. Hinnebusch, *Egyptian Politics under Sadat*, 14.

116. Silbermann, "National Identity in Nasserist Ideology, 1952-1970," 57-68.

117. Gershoni and Jankowski, *Redefining the Egyptian Nation*, 15. See also Ralph M. Coury, *The Making of an Egyptian Arab Nationalist: The Early Years of Azzam Pasha, 1893-1936* (Reading: Ithaca Press, 1998), 278, 327, 418-19.

118. On Egypt's aims and perceived leadership role in the Arab world, see Elie Podeh, *The Quest for Hegemony in the Arab World: The Struggle over the Baghdad Pact* (Leiden: E. J. Brill, 1995), chap. 1; Elie Podeh, *The Decline of Arab Unity*, 27-30; Dekmejian, *Egypt under Nasir*, 105-8. For the same, but more comprehensive, argument, see Carl Brown, *International Politics and the Middle East* (London: I. B. Tauris, 1984), 162-79.

119. See the interesting report of Harik in his study of an Egyptian village, *The Political Mobilization of Peasants*, 178-79.

120. Though phrased somewhat differently, this is the main thesis of Vatikiotis, *Nasser and His Generation*.

121. Hinnebusch, *Egyptian Politics under Sadat*, 14.

122. See Galal A. Amin, *Egypt's Economic Predicament: A Study in the Interaction of External Pressure, Political Folly, and Social Tension in Egypt, 1960-1990* (Leiden: E. J. Brill, 1995), 130-31.

123. Robert Mabro, *The Egyptian Economy*, 216.

124. Waterbury, *The Egypt of Nasser and Sadat*, 260.

125. Ayubi, *Over-Stating the Arab State*, 197; Moghadam, "Islamic Populism"; Abrahamian, "Khomeini: Fundamentalist or Populist?"; Suna Kili, *Kemalism* (Istanbul: School of Business Administration and Economics, Robert College, 1969). On Bourguibism, see a recent article by Carl Brown, "Bourgiba and Bourgubism Revisited: Reflections and Interpretations," *Middle East Journal* 55, no. 1 (winter 2001): 43-57.

126. Ayubi, *Over-Stating the Arab State*, 197-98. A similar view was offered by Waterbury: "There is little evidence that Nasser . . . gave much thought to economics before coming to power and some would say decidedly insufficient thought thereafter" (*Egypt of Nasser and Sadat*, 49). He believes, however, that Nasser had the will and the capacity to "push Egypt much further toward socialism," and he does not believe that Nasser was a "closet capitalist of petty bourgeois origins whose radical rhetoric was only skin-deep" (20). For a different view of Nasser's socialism, see Rami Ginat, *Egypt's Incomplete Revolution: Lutfi al-Khuli and Nasser's Socialism in the 1960s* (London: Frank Cass, 1997).

127. Ginat, *Egypt's Incomplete Revolution,* 9–34.

128. For the text of the Charter, see Rejwan, *Nasserist Ideology,* 195–265. For this argument, see Fouad Ajami, "The Open-Door Economy," in Abdel-Khalek and Tignor, eds., *Political Economy of Income Distribution,* 9.

129. For a few examples of such assessment, see Shamir, "The Decline of Nasserist Messianism," 16–38; Baker, *Egypt's Uncertain Revolution,* 235–39; Vatikiotis, *Nasser and His Generation,* 267–69, 298–99, 315–17, 325–31, 335–68; Lacouture, *Nasser,* 391–94; Waterbury, *The Egypt of Nasser and Sadat,* 423–33; Gad G. Gilbar, "Nasser's Soft Revolution," in *Population Dilemmas in the Middle East: Essays in Political Demography and Economy* (London: Frank Cass, 1996), 92–93.

130. Samuel Huntington and Joan Nelson, *No Easy Choice: Political Participation in Developing Countries* (Cambridge: Harvard University Press, 1976), 23–24.

131. See, e.g., Ajami, "Sadat's Open-Door Policy," 474.

132. See William J. Burns, *Economic Aid and American Policy toward Egypt, 1955–1981* (Albany: State University of New York Press, 1985), chap. 6, 149–73.

133. Hinnebusch, *Egyptian Politics under Sadat,* 34–36. See also Ajami, in ibid., 474–75. See the sources mentioned in note 125.

134. Gilbar, "Nasser's Soft Revolution," 89–90.

135. Hinnebusch, *Egyptian Politics under Sadat,* 29–31.

136. Ibid., 33. The failure to institutionalize Nasserism was emphasized by several scholars. See the sources mentioned in note 129.

137. Salih Jawdat, *Al-Musawwar,* March 15, 1974. Quoted from the English translation in Shimon Shamir, "Nasser and Sadat, 1967–1973: Two Approaches to a National Crisis," in Itamar Rabinovich and Haim Shaked, eds., *From June to October: The Middle East between 1967 and 1973* (New Brunswick, N.J.: Transaction Books, 1978), 205.

138. Tawfiq al-Hakim, *Return of the Spirit,* trans. William M. Hutchins (Washington, D.C.: Three Continents Press, 1990), 273.

139. Robert Stephens, *Nasser: A Political Biography* (London: Penguin, 1971), 557 (quoted from *Al-Ahram,* October 16, 1970).

140. See Joel Gordon, "Film, Fame, and Public Memory: Egyptian Biopics from Mustafa Kamil to Nasser 56," *IJMES* 31 (1999): 61–79. Within this popular and intellectual revival, we should also mention the Arab conference on Nasserism (see note 29), and the decision of the Center for the Study of Arab Unity (*Markaz Dirasat al-Wahda al-'Arabiyya*) in Beirut to establish an award on behalf of Nasser (*ja'izat 'Abd al-Nasir*) in 1998. The first award was given to Haykal. Not incidentally, the ceremony took place on July 26, 1999, the anniversary of Nasser's decision to nationalize the Suez Canal Company. See *Al-Mustaqbal al-'Arabi,* no. 247 (September 1999): 72–95.

I.

**Images of Nasserism**

# 1

# Gamal ʿAbd al-Nasser

Iconology, Ideology, and Demonology

Leonard Binder

## Introduction

Gamal ʿAbd al-Nasser emerged early as the dominant personage in the Egyptian Revolution of July 1952. For many Egyptians and many foreign observers, Nasser appeared to be larger than life—a symbol representing Egypt itself, a new class, an awakening, Arab authenticity, or even the resurgence of the Third World. Despite much solid evidence to the contrary, Nasser was portrayed at first as a charismatic leader, capable of breaking with tradition and of unleashing huge pent-up powers—a danger to the West, a blessing for Egypt and the Arab masses, and a double-edged sword for the Soviets.

This heroic image of Nasser developed throughout the years up to 1961, based on the popular response to Nasser's successes in ending the British occupation of Egypt, defiance of the western monopoly on arms sales to the Middle East, opposition to the Baghdad Pact, the nationalization of the Suez Canal Company, political victory in the brief Suez War of 1956, the seizure of foreign properties and business enterprises, the rejection of the Eisenhower Doctrine, the union of Egypt and Syria, and the adoption of doctrinaire socialist policies in 1961. The conclusion drawn from these events was that Nasser had produced a new strategic model for the achievement of modernization and development—a strategic conception which could avoid dependency while exploiting the Cold War.

After the secession of Syria from the United Arab Republic in 1961, as representatives of the Syrian Baʿth sought a reconciliation with Egypt, Nasserism came to be represented as an alternative ideology.[1] While this usage was developed primarily for polemical (anti-Ba'thi) purposes, it was also employed by Egyptian leftists during and after Anwar al-Sadat's presidency and by various Sunni groups in Lebanon during the Civil War.

But after Egypt's defeat in the June 1967 War, Nasser's image was remade by the events of June 9–10, 1967, when he announced that he would resign as a consequence of his responsibility for the disaster. Despite the emotional popular response on that day, and despite the great affection felt for Nasser among the Egyptian masses, his image suffered a marked decline during the long months that he was unable to regain any of the territory occupied by Israeli forces in the Sinai. The 'Abd al-Hakim 'Amr affair, ending in the death of Nasser's closest colleague, and the conciliatory gesture of the Bayan proclamation of March 30, 1968, further diminished the Nasser image. The initiation of the War of Attrition along the Suez Canal raised hopes, but these were disappointed when it became clear that Nasser could not push his Soviet allies any further and that Soviet medicine could not cure his illness. The huge public funeral that followed his sudden death on September 28, 1970, reinforced the tragic image shaped by the defeat of June 1967 but, nevertheless, reaffirmed the deeply emotional bond of identity between Nasser and the Egyptian masses that was not shared with other Arab communities.

After his death, the "licensed" Egyptian Left, though at odds with Nasser since the mid-1960s, embraced the role of interpreters of the Nasserist legacy in an effort to weaken Sadat and facilitate the seizure of power by a pro-Soviet faction. With Sadat's success in preempting such a coup on May 15, 1971, a "de-Nasserization" program was begun which permitted the publication of books, articles, and movies, depicting the brutal suppression of civil rights under Nasser. These publications painted Nasser as a vicious autocrat whose behavior was antithetical to the warm and empathetic character of Egyptian popular culture. Tawfiq al-Hakim's *'Awdat al-Wa'y* (Restoration of consciousness) and Nagib Mahfuz's *Al-Karnak* (also a movie) were the most influential statements of the harm done to Egypt's civic culture by Nasser. These voices were strengthened by the belated complaints of "the Silent Ones," members of the original Revolutionary Command Council (RCC) who had been relegated to secondary and largely honorary positions because of their liberal or religious inclinations. There were some vigorous rebuttals, from Hasanayn Haykal, of course, but also from the Haditu (Marxist) intellectuals. The critics were joined by the increasingly emboldened Islamic fundamentalists who excoriated Nasser for what they called "the slaughter" of the Muslim Brothers—a policy of suppression that was initiated after an aborted assassination attempt against Nasser in the fall of 1954.

After Sadat's assassination in October 1981, the ideological significance of Nasser as an anti-Sadat and anti-Western icon declined. That reading of Nasser was challenged by the rise of the seemingly more radical anti-Western, anti-Israel, and anti-Sadat force of the Islamic resurgence, relegating Nasserism to the limited ideological potential of serving the secularist Sunni Arab minority in Lebanon. The falling market for Nasserism, as either image or ideology, was related to the alleged decline of pan-Arab nationalism, but the parochialism of would-be heirs such as Asad, Qaddafi, and Saddam Husayn (not to mention 'Arafat) has transformed imitation into parody, accelerating that decline. Outside of Egypt, the Nasserist political model remains the dominant statist pattern except for the monarchies, but Nasser himself, as a symbol of a powerful and persuasive transnational ethnic and cultural force, is increasingly irrelevant to the domestic and foreign challenges facing Iraq, Syria, Libya, Sudan, Yemen, Algeria, and even Egypt itself.

In the Arab world, it appears that the debate over Nasser's legacy has diminished in its intensity and significance without settling the questions of whether Nasser's achievements were squandered by his successors or even by Arab leaders in general, whether his talents simply exceeded his resources, whether his successes were the consequence of bipolarity rather than strategic wisdom, whether his ultimate failure was due to the bankruptcy of the statist, or bureaucratic-authoritarian, model, or whether Egypt would have been better off sticking with the old parties and the nascent capitalism and internationalism that prevailed in 1952.

The polemical tendency to exploit the Nasser image has distorted and exaggerated Nasser's achievements and failures. These distortions impede a balanced assessment and confound the effort to distill a single authentic characterization of Nasser out of the wealth of information available to us. Moreover, the public affairs and scholarly literature on Nasser and Nasserism is quite large. Leaving aside newspaper, magazine, and journal articles, I found some 255 book titles devoted to our subject in the UCLA catalog alone. Obviously, a complete survey of this literature as a means of constructing a retrospective appraisal of the man and his legacy is hopelessly beyond the scope of this article. Instead, the present effort has been limited to demarcating the most promising regions to be further explored. We shall find that partisan reports have given us many Nassers, possibly casting greater light on the period after his death than on his life. In this essay, the most important of these Nassers will be briefly identified.

### Nasser as a Charismatic Leader at Home and Abroad

A full-page photo of a handsome, thoughtful, dreamy, young, uniformed Nasser appears in a volume entitled *Icons of the Twentieth Century*.[2] If memory serves, he is the only Arab leader selected for this dubious honor, but it is clear that he did make a difference. A similar photograph graces the cover of Peter Woodward's 1992 political biography of Nasser.[3] Both pictures are examples of the then popular matinee idol or Valentino image. In the 1950s, most western observers saw him as that dashing, handsome officer who was transforming an ancient society by the sheer force of his personality, his daring, and his informal but earnest rhetoric. His influence over the masses, not only of Egypt but of the Arab and Islamic world, was astonishing and more than a little frightening. Anthony Eden went so far as to compare him to Adolph Hitler, but that bit of political hyperbole cost Eden his reputation for probity and damaged Britain's effort to win the support of its allies in its contest with Egypt.

Nasser conjured up the image of a psychological force that might transcend the limits of normal interest-based political power. For example, Peter Mansfield, writing in the 1960s, opens *Nasser's Egypt* with this statement: "The Egyptians are a docile and humorous people." And in nearly the last words in the book Mansfield writes, "But it is essentially Nasser who has forced the world to reassess Egypt and not the Egyptians themselves. . . . [H]e has succeeded in hauling the Egyptian people on to the world stage by the scruff of their necks to play the role. Most of them still suffer from stage fright."[4]

Indeed, the young Nasser seemed to fit the definition of a charismatic leader offered by Max Weber—and sometimes applied to the vexed question of how to initiate the process of modernization in the absence of both capitalism and the Protestant ethic.[5] Contemplating the enigma of why the Egyptian masses believed Nasser represented their will despite the fact that no valid means of representation existed, P. J. Vatikiotis wrote: "One is left with the impression that a charismatic leader is more important in Arab politics than the mechanisms, checks and balances that loom large in Western political theory, because the type of leadership has always been more important in Arab societies than the type of political institutions. . . . The tradition of centralized authority in Egypt especially breeds charismatic qualities in the ruler, whoever he may be."[6]

The ambivalence of Vatikiotis is suggested by his discussion of charisma as a component of Egyptian political culture rather than as an attribute of the man himself—transcending the prevailing political culture. Besides, Vatikiotis argued that the central phenomenon to be explained was the successful seizure of power by the military rather than Nasser's popularity. In the subtitle of his excellent early work, he asked whether the intervention of the Egyptian army in politics was a "pattern for new nations." And, of course, it was.

It is also surprising to see how many authors describe Nasser as having been indecisive in the early years of the revolution. But Miles Copeland saw him as an intelligent and skilled Machiavellian who took risks.[7] Copeland noted Nasser's willingness to act the demagogue. He actually reserved the term *charismatic* for Nagib, and it is clear from several discussions of the crisis of 1954 that Nagib was far more popular than Nasser (114). Copeland believed that Nasser's brinksmanship was a rational strategy based on weakness, but his ego prevented him from knowing when to quit. Much later, reporting on a meeting with Nasser after the June 1967 War, Copeland wrote:

> I would say that his mental faculties . . . are about what they always were. . . . [H]owever, I would have to assume that what happens sooner or later to all Nasser-type leaders happened to Nasser himself: whatever the endurance of his personality under the assault of sycophancy, blind adulation, uncritical loyalty, and ordinary fear, the barriers between him and the outside world have grown so thick that all but the information that attests to his infallibility, indispensability, and immortality has been filtered out. (92)

Copeland writes that even some highly placed Egyptian officials considered the possibility of moving Nasser up "to the chairman of the board level. . . . Knowing Nasser, however, it is no surprise to me that it did not get anywhere. When Nasser goes out it will not be with a whimper but a bang—*Götterdämmerung*, even" (279). Copeland's prediction of the exit line was obviously wrong.

A similar view of the psychological hazards of charismatic leadership was expressed by Jean Lacouture.[8] Lacouture's work celebrated the multifaceted role of virtually deified dictatorial leaders of newly independent nations that had emerged to sovereignty in the accommodating context of the Cold War. Although he became increasingly critical of these maximal leaders, Lacouture did not seek to demystify the legitimacy they enjoyed. Rather, he presented a confusing and untidy conception of charismatic leadership, drawing on sundry patterns in their profusion and diversity as extravagant variations on a single theme. Nor could he decide whether the charismatic leader would make something out of nothing (20, 23). But, above all, his account of postcolonial charismatic leadership failed to show what the indigenous peoples were thinking in supporting such governments. There is little evidence adduced to support the view that the masses thought of their leaders as demigods, and less that the educated classes did so.

Citing the work of Richard Dekmejian as a prime example, 'Ali al-Din al-Hilal al-Desouki, the eminent Egyptian political scientist, wrote that the exceptionally personal nature of the power wielded by President Nasser was so great that some scholars considered charismatic authority to be the most important characteristic of the system, and they studied Egyptian politics from that point of view.[9] Desouki seemed to believe that Nasserism was more authoritarian than charismatic—and he was not convinced that Nasser's charisma had anything to do with modernization. Desouki wrote that after the transition period that lasted from 1953 to 1956, the proclamation of the constitution in January 1956 introduced the Nasserist stage. He calls it the Nasserist stage not merely because Nasser was the effective ruler but also because the institutional structures employed and policies followed throughout the period reflected the thinking and the opinions of Nasser.

The transitional period had been one of collective leadership where Nasser had been the first among equals, but after 1956 Nasser became the uncontested leader (29). Moreover, the regime gained a good deal of its legitimacy from its association with the personality of Nasser and his direct contact with the people of Egypt and of other Arab states, as demonstrated in the Suez War of 1956, the dispute over the nationalization of the Suez Canal Company, the following tripartite aggression, the unification with Syria in February 1958, and the establishment of the UAR (30).

But the Nasserist stage was also characterized by an elaborate form of authoritarianism, limitation of participation, concentration of power, and the restriction of freedom of expression. Desouki goes on to argue that the most important of the reasons why things turned out so badly in the long run is precisely because of the charismatic or "historical" nature of Nasser's personality and his ability to address the masses directly without the mediation of institutions (39). This charismatic/historical style and the willingness of a privileged elite to exploit its opportunities explains but does not excuse the failure of the revolution to construct a viable and stable political system in Egypt. It is not a question of how mistakes were made. The failure is due to the absence of a political will to establish a powerful and active political organization (40).

Thus does Desouki place the blame for the weakness of Egypt's democracy directly on the political style and predilections of Nasser. His greatest strength was the source of Egypt's greatest weakness. I believe that Desouki is not alone among Egyptian liberal democrats in holding such a negative opinion of the Nasser legacy.

But a limited democratic breakthrough occurred during the early years of Sadat's presidency, resulting in the licensing of several political parties, and Desouki asked which political events were conducive to such a development. He answered that the most important event was the postcharisma syndrome caused by Nasser's sudden absence from the political stage. This absence produced a gap which no individual or group could fill because Nasser's personality had been the major source of legitimacy for the regime and his presence had allowed Egypt to overcome a series of disastrous events and failures (48). Desouki concludes that Sadat's experiments with democracy faced virtually insuperable obstacles, and he blames Nasser for Sadat's failure to democratize post-Nasserist Egypt.

### The Posthumous Socialist Reconstruction of Nasser

Over twenty years ago, in *In a Moment of Enthusiasm,* I wrote at length about the edgy relationship between Nasser and a group of Egyptian Marxists who, at the bidding of the Soviets, disbanded their organization and joined the Arab Socialist Union (ASU), becoming members of the elite cadre organization set up under the National Charter (al-Mithaq al-Watani) of May 1962 and called al-Tanzim al-Siyasi or al-Tanzim al-Tali'i.[10] It is likely that both sides went into this marriage of convenience with some awareness of their respective-prospective costs and benefits. Nasser wanted to create a cadre organization that would help him to mobilize Egypt's human resources without truly sharing power and without creating an organization that might be able to seize power either before or after his death.

In 1970, immediately after Nasser's death, while only too well aware of the legitimate but potentially challengeable succession of Sadat, Egyptian Marxists hoped and planned for a de facto takeover of the Egyptian state and a return to what were for them the hopeful days of the swing to the left as manifested in the passage of the Socialist Laws of 1961, the May 1962 Congress of Popular Forces which produced the National Charter of the ASU, the integration of the Haditu faction of the Communist Party of Egypt into the newly organized ASU, and the creation of a secret cadre apparatus within the ASU. The highpoint of Marxist influence had been reached in late 1966. The disastrous war of 1967 weakened the regime to the point that a Marxist takeover (with Soviet support) became a real threat. Popular demonstrations early in 1968 led to the proclamation of the Bayan of March 30, which committed the regime to a policy of democratization and reform as soon as the effects of the war were remedied. Thus Nasser decisively turned away from the (ambiguous) socialist commitments of the early and mid-1960s.

After Nasser's death, the Tali'a group chose to forget his moves to control the Marxists from 1965 to 1970, and instead portrayed Nasser as steadfast in his commitment to socialism, class struggle, and opposition to Arab reactionaries. Their eulogy of Nasser, published in a special issue of their organ in November 1970, was devoted to reaffirming this anachronistic view.[11]

Among the interesting aspects of this special issue was the diversity of the images of Nasser to be found in its pages. Most fascinating was the depiction of Nasser as an ideological naïf whose development into a practical socialist was the product of the transformation of his consciousness through the first ten years of the revolution by the bitter experiences of the tripartite aggression of 1956, the failure of the National Union, the Syrian secession, the hostility of world capitalism, etc. But Nasser was also depicted as an Egyptian Lenin, a convinced democrat, and a visionary builder of political organizations and institutions.

Nasser was portrayed as one who shared the popular sentiments and experience of the toiling masses of workers and peasants and who was capable, in all sincerity, of arguing that the ultimate justification of the social revolution he was leading was the same social justice (al-'adala) that is the goal of the Islamic Shari'a.[12]

The longest of the dozen articles in the memorial volume of Al-Tali'a was written by Hilmi Yasin and 'Adil Sayf al-Nasir, and it focuses on the question of the most suitable political apparatus for realizing the goals of the July Revolution. The background is, of course, the many changes in political organization which took place over those eighteen years: The prerevolutionary political parties were banned and replaced by the Liberation Rally, followed by the National Union, dissolved by the Preparatory Committee paving the way for the Conference of Popular Forces to adopt the National Charter defining the goals and structure of the ASU, which itself underwent constant reorganization until the goals of the revolution and the methods of political action were redefined by the Bayan of March 30, 1968, culminating in the total reconstitution of the ASU later that year.

One might well ask why this constant change of organization? Was Nasser lurching from one palliative device to another, fending off challenges from the Left, the Right, and the army, or did he have a long-term goal which had to be approached by a winding tactical road? Was he maintaining his popular leadership by keeping out in front of the masses, or was he simply drawing on the power of mass support while skillfully avoiding sharing real power? The answer given by the two authors is that Nasser's genius lay in his capacity to understand the nature of each changing situation and then adapt his organizational defense to that stage of the conflict:

> The ASU and its Vanguard Political Apparatus are examples of the most notable teachings of the leader [qa'id] Gamal 'Abd al-Nasser. . . . The ASU and the Vanguard Political Apparatus bear a continuing responsibility to arm the [revolutionary] combatants and the masses with the revolutionary teachings of Gamal 'Abd al-Nasser and to carefully protect [those teachings] from corruption and distortion. . . .

[T]he responsibility for mobilizing the toiling social forces that believe truly in the teaching of Gamal 'Abd al-Nasser has been placed on their shoulders. (25)

William Sulayman Qallada took a somewhat different approach to the same organizational theme. While Yasin and Sayf al-Nasir thought that the socialist cadre structures in the ASU ought to be preserved, Sulayman sought to build new representative structures based on the Bayan. His article was entitled "Nasser's Legacy: The Preservation of the Political and Constitutional Institutions" (36–40). Sulayman wrote that Nasser always saw himself as a representative of the people and as a leader whose heart beat as one with the heart of the Egyptian masses. But he also insisted that the revolutionary will of the people should not depend upon any one person, regardless of how close he was to the people. The people's will ought to be expressed by the people themselves through fixed and stable institutions. This was the reason why Nasser put such effort into constructing both representative and constitutional institutions. Now, after Nasser's death, more than ever, the Egyptian people have to consider how to perpetuate the Nasserist legacy.

The legendary farewell funeral in which the masses participated was a kind of referendum of popular support for Nasser and his ideas, but from now on, that support and the expression of the people's will must take place through stable, permanent institutions. It is therefore gratifying, wrote Sulayman, to see how the succession was managed in a legal and constitutional manner, thus demonstrating the maturity of the Egyptian people.

Mustafa Tayba contributed a brief article on "Gamal 'Abd al-Nasser and the Intellectuals," in which he described how Nasser skillfully transformed a liberal and fractious intelligentsia into a disciplined state bureaucracy (50–54). Hence Tayba, more than any of the other contributors to this memorial volume, points to Nasser's greatest and perhaps worst achievement and his most lasting legacy: the creation of the Nasserist state.

### Liberal Remorse: Nasser Revisited by Tawfiq al-Hakim

In the mid-1970s, as Sadat gained more confidence, the political, economic, and cultural de-Nasserization of Egypt was increasingly encouraged.[13] In this atmosphere, the publication of a number of books and articles revealing the extent of political repression that had prevailed under Nasser had a considerably negative effect on Nasser's image.[14] Another group of articles and books and even a couple of movies focused on the political hypocrisy of which the intellectuals of both the Marxist Left and the moderate liberals had been guilty. In several cases, most notably in the case of Tawfiq al-

Hakim, debunking the self-serving rhetoric of the Nasser period took the form of a mea culpa, acknowledging that he had supported and believed in the revolution and in Nasser's leadership and had remained silent in the face of obvious and quite horrendous abuses of power. But the defeat in the June 1967 War so shocked al-Hakim that he began a rethinking process that culminated in the publication of a small book completed on the twentieth anniversary of the July Revolution.

That book, *'Awdat al-Wa'y,* is a devastating condemnation of the revolution and especially of Nasserism. Al-Hakim made an effort to separate Nasser from Nasserism, but the message was that the revolution came to an end when Nasser assumed absolute autocratic authority and deprived all Egyptians of any degree of freedom and self-determination. He then called for a reappraisal of the achievements of the revolution, finding them mostly rhetorical, theatrical, or musical.

In his estimation, land reform produced no improvement in agriculture, socialist reforms produced no increase in economic well-being, the drive for Arab unity alienated other Arab states, and the political institutions deprived Egyptians of freedom of any kind. But worst of all, argued al-Hakim, was that Egyptians gradually assumed a kind of false identity, a consciousness produced by the propaganda machine of the state in place of the authentic consciousness of the historical Egyptian people. What was needed was an assessment of the revolution and restoration of the consciousness of the people. What was needed was an examination of the "dossier [*milaff*] of Gamal 'Abd al-Nasser."[15]

In the introduction to the second edition of his booklet, al-Hakim noted that the Nasserists in and out of Egypt had been angered by its publication. "They roiled and boiled as though Nasserism were a holy religion that must not be touched" (3). And among those thus aroused was Hasanayn Haykal, who accused Nasser's critics of cowardice for speaking up only after his death. Haykal (as cited by Hakim) went on to describe Nasser as

> the natural product and true expression of twentieth-century Arab nationalism. Nasserism will remain a method of developing the Arab nation, susceptible of change—it is not rigid. Nor can I see a future for the Arab world, and the whole of the developing world, without Nasserism as a totality of ideas, and the Nasserist achievements and strategic judgments [*ijtihadat*] which must be the basis for anything they undertake.... 'Abd al-Nasser will remain the expression of Egypt and the Arabs at a certain historical stage to the same extent that Napoleon remains the expression of France (99–100).

But unlike Napoleon, who abandoned the revolution, 'Abd al-Nasser's attention from the first day to the very last day was directed at change, the future, and history.... When 'Abd al-Nasser was present, his power and the force of his intensity and his dignity prevented any real discussion of his ideas.... 'Abd al-Nasser embodied the idea of the possibility of change—an idea that presented itself so forcefully that it swept aside a great many things. I believe that, in the end, we will come to be convinced that everything that 'Abd al-Nasser called for, whether principles or ideas, is correct (101).

In addition to Haykal, the editorial staff of *Al-Tali'a* objected to al-Hakim's critique of Nasserism, but they took up his call for a serious discussion of what had been achieved over the twenty years of the revolution. They invited al-Hakim, in the politest manner, to participate in a series of seminars that would extend over many months, and he accepted. But the correspondence between Lutfi al-Khuli and al-Hakim that led up to that agreement demarcated the implicit ground rules for the seminars. Both sides agreed that they respected and admired Nasser as a person. Both agreed that Nasser had made great contributions to Egypt and the Arab nation. Both agreed that Egypt must follow the path of socialism. Both agreed that Nasser had failed to guide Egypt to true socialism. The purpose of the seminars was, therefore, to clarify what went wrong under Nasser and to determine how best to proceed in the post-Nasser period to achieve socialism and democracy.[16]

## The Socialist Critique of Nasser's Good Intentions

It appears that the rhetorical goals of al-Tali'a were to call al-Hakim back to his early, somewhat romantic socialist roots, to blunt the idea that Nasser's failings were caused by his lust for power, to refute the notion that his failures were due to his commitment to socialism, and to assert that Nasser failed because he did not carry his socialist program far enough. If public opinion were to be turned against Nasser, they did not want the socialist baby thrown out with the Nasserist bathwater. The consistent theme of those who called themselves the "Egyptian Left" was that Nasser failed because he engaged in halfway measures.

Khalid Muhi al-Din insisted that Nasser's power was not based on military force or on "brainwashing" those around him. It was based on his popularity and his achievements, which were so great that no one could challenge him. Nasser was a patriot devoted to the masses, but he also refused to be bound by any institutional or consultative arrangement in making decisions. Hence the reason things turned out badly in the June 1967 War and in other matters was because of the absence of efficient structures of planning and decision making. Nevertheless, Nasser's greatest contribution was to demonstrate that the only way in which developing nations could both develop and maintain their independence in a capitalist world was to choose the socialist path (64–72).

In the fourth session, Lutfi al-Khuli steered the discussion toward the key documents of Nasserist thought: *The Philosophy of the Revolution,* the 1962 National Charter, the Bayan of 1968, and the special program for "National Action." Murad Wahba led off with an analysis of the *Philosophy of the Revolution,* stating that Nasser believed that the task of the revolution was to achieve both political and social freedom for the Egyptian people. Nasser knew that the achievement of these twin freedoms required change, and he had a good grasp of the logic of revolution, which can help identify contradictions. But Nasser had little understanding of revolutionary theory, which is necessary for finding solutions that will resolve contradictions.

It follows that Nasser could never come up with the right solution because of his theoretical deficiencies, and it further follows that Nasser could succeed in his efforts only with the aid of those adept at socialist theory. Nasser's theoretical inadequacies were in part due to his dichotomous perception of class conflict. Nasser believed incorrectly that some social conflicts could be resolved within the ASU rather than by means of class struggle.

The fifth session was devoted to the negative aspects of the Nasserist experience, and the most important (and longest) statement was made by Khalid Muhi al-Din concerning the imposition of the Socialist Laws of 1961: "One of Nasser's characteristics was that he paid a lot of attention to the domestic conflict and its dangers. And whenever matters came to a head, Nasser would always choose the progressive solution. I would not say the complete progressive solution, no" (243). "Nasser was not convinced that it was possible to separate experience, or the sociopolitical order, from theory —and that's why he always remained afraid of a complete openness to Socialist thought" (244).

At this point al-Hakim tried to suggest that the reason why Nasser kept theory rooted in political practice was because he preferred to avoid the implementation of the democratic provisions of the various constitutions, charters, and the like. Al-Hakim even quoted Muhammad Sayyid Ahmad as saying that Nasser wanted to avoid a revolution from below (245). But Muhi al-Din steadfastly avoided that issue, arguing that Nasser was essentially a revolutionary pragmatist who refused to set rigid theoretical limits to the evolution of the July Revolution.

Muhi al-Din developed this idea further, asserting that Nasser could never rid himself of the fatally mistaken view that there might be a third way between the capitalist and socialist paths. It was this worst of all of

Nasser's theoretical errors which led him to take halfway measures at critical times when theoretical sophistication would have indicated the correct strategy. Nasser wanted to avoid making the indispensable sacrifices that were needed to accumulate the necessary capital to achieve development in the shortest time without relying on the imperialist powers and without compromising with the Egyptian bourgeoisie. Nasser thought he could find sufficient resources through foreign grants and loans, through land reform, and through the nationalization of foreign firms, and he refused to take the only possible path of self-reliance, which required squeezing the middle class for at least ten years.

Nasser took halfway measures in setting up a Committee to Liquidate Feudalism instead of invoking peasant action. The allocation of 50 percent of all representative positions to authentic workers and peasants had little effect because so many members of the middle class misrepresented themselves. The integration of "nonexploitative" national capital into the Coalition of Popular Working Forces set up under the Charter and the ASU was a failure because, as everyone knows, there is no such thing as "nonexploitative capitalism." Nasser also brought the agrarian revolution to a screeching halt in 1969.

Khalid Muhi al-Din concluded that Nasser's tendency was revolutionary, including hostility to imperialism and capitalism, in general, and a bias in favor of the poorer classes. But he had no idea of how a new society might be structured and was completely mistaken about the possibility of multiple paths to socialism (245–57). He was, however, far more progressive than other members of his social class (264).

### Abandoned Allies: Nasser and the Silent Ones

After the October 1973 War, the political atmosphere in Egypt encouraged more outspoken attacks on Nasser, and one of the most widely read was the book *The Silent Ones Speak Out*, written by Sami Gawhar.[17] The sixth printing, 1976, included a new chapter entitled "'Abd al-Nasser and the Slaughter of the Ikhwan." Gawhar does not identify himself in this book, but he offers fulsome praise of Sadat for freeing Egyptian history from the prison in which it had been held from 1954 to 1970. Gawhar tells us that he relied on notes taken by Rishwan Fahmy throughout the Nasser years. Fahmy had served as dean of the doctors' syndicate three times, and he was an intimate of several members of the RCC before the revolution and met all of them afterwards (8). Fahmy died before he had a chance to publish his notes, which were then passed on to Gawhar. Gawhar was able to interview many of the principals and confirm and amplify the story told in the notes, primarily by 'Abd al-Latif al-Baghdadi, Kamal al-Din Husayn, and Hasan

Ibrahim—all of whom had been members of the RCC in 1952 and were later marginalized or worse because of their opposition to Nasser.

Gawhar describes Nasser as a dictator, a phony hero, a murderer, and a liar who distorted the facts and persecuted the true Egyptian patriots. In relating the story of the conflict between Nasser and Nagib as told to him by the not so silent ones, Gawhar tells us that Nasser hypocritically accused Nagib of dictatorial ambitions, but it was Nasser who hungered to exercise power as the sole leader (14). Gawhar quotes Kamal al-Din Husayn as reporting that Nasser, along with other members of the Free Officers, took the oath of membership in the clandestine military organization of the Muslim Brothers. Nasser committed himself, reaffirmed that commitment on various occasions, including the very eve of July 23, 1952, and then betrayed the organization and its leaders, despite the crucial support they gave him during the revolution, ultimately condemning to death many of those who trusted him (40). After the revolution, Nasser surrounded himself with a number of officers of bad morals who were only out for their own gain and who used drugs and alcohol, while distancing himself from those who were close to the Ikhwan (33).

Nasser tried but failed to induce the Ikhwan to join his cabinet and then to merge with the Liberation Rally, dissolving their own organization. But whenever Nasser heard the word *no,* it would send him into a rage (44). He called his Ikhwan interlocutors "traitors" and berated them for calling for free elections, demanding to know whether they wanted the return of the Wafd (45). At the same meeting, apparently frustrated by the resistance of the Ikhwan representatives, Nasser burst out, "Listen, ya Farid, I'll tell you what is on my mind, and that's it. I have this idea that has possessed me, and I don't know whether it is mistaken or sound. I just want, within two or three years, to arrive at a point where I can press a button and the country will move as I want it to, and when I press another button, it will stop."

Farid answered that the Ikhwan had been working for twenty-seven years to get their members to understand the teachings of Islam, and they could not count on them to dissolve the organization on command. Clearly Nasser was thinking like a military officer, but social change can only come through freedom and democracy. Farid related that he and his colleagues laughed at Nasser's desire to press buttons, but in the end, he was able to realize his pipe dream. Nasser then trumped up charges of treason against them, framing them by planting weapons on the farm of Hasan 'Ashmawi (37).

Gawhar goes on to question whether the attempted assassination of Nasser on October 26, 1954, was a put-up job. Regardless of whether it was organized by the Ikhwan, by Nasser himself, or by a lone assassin, Nasser exploited the incident to achieve three goals: to build up popular support for his own leadership, to get rid of Nagib once and for all, "and to destroy the Muslim Brothers who had helped him at the beginning of the revolution" (57).

As in the case of *'Awdat al-Wa'y,* the Samitun inspired a number of rebuttals and replies. One of the sharpest rejoinders came from Hasanayn Karum, who tried to establish his objectivity by showing that he had actually been a beneficiary of Sadat and had suffered from discriminatory treatment under the Nasser regime. In his book *The Silent Ones Lie,* Karum mounts a vigorous counterattack against the Silent Ones, the Muslim Brothers, and other critics of Nasser.[18] The Silent Ones were bitter because they lost a simple struggle for power. They preferred an oligarchy to an autocracy, and they were poor losers (28). As for the Ikhwan, they themselves decided that they were God's representatives on earth, and they proceeded arbitrarily to accuse anyone who defied their authority of *kufr* (47–51).

Gamal Salim makes a more affirmative case in his book *The Silent Ones in the Balance: For the Truth . . . Confidence . . . and History.*[19] Salim writes that the Silent Ones—'Abd al-Latif, Kamal al-Din, and Hasan Ibrahim—all played secondary roles in the revolution while Nasser was the "maestro" who called the tune and directed the orchestra. His fellow officers followed him because they knew that he spoke the language of the people, and that is the most powerful instrument. The Free Officers were not the leadership. They were the base, and Nasser was the leader who organized them, brought them together, and harmonized their heartbeat and pulse with his own (3–5).

Toward the end of his book, Salim took up the theme of the June 1967 War:

> The Silent Ones said that the popular demonstrations that occurred on June 9 and 10, 1967, were staged like a play [*masrahiyya*], but they did not explain what they meant by that. Did they mean that the whole Arab people were the audience and that Nasser acted out the only role in the *masrahiyya* while the audience applauded because the only thing they could do was applaud? If that is true, then Nasser was the best and most gifted actor who ever lived. But the truth of the matter is that he was not the greatest actor. Unfortunately, he lacked that gift which was enjoyed by those who spoke after having remained silent. The only thing of that sort in which Nasser was gifted was amiability and sociability—in simple terms, not showing what one is feeling or hiding it from people. Nasser was a sort of expert [*ustadh*] in this gift. He would smile, even though pain would be ripping at his heart, and he would appear to be in good health, lively and active, though illness was squeezing out all his strength. (16)

No. Unfortunately, Nasser would not have had that gift of acting had he lived a hundred years . . . though he shook all the various hands stretched out to him, and was pleasant and cheerful [*hash wa-bash*] to all the frowning faces of the crowds around him. Unfortunately, he was bereft of the gift of acting. But as for them [the Silent Ones] they were experts. . . . They excelled at playing their roles. When Nasser was alive, they played the role of revolutionaries during the July Revolution, and the role of enthusiastic supporters during the March [1954] crisis, and the role of fighters during the aggression of 1956, and the role of proponents during the union in 1958, then they played the role of provocateurs advocating a strike against Syria to compel it into the bounds of the union by military force. Then the end came at the Presidency Council when the curtain descended on their *"masrahiyya."* (417–18)

The deceitful "actors" included not only the Silent Ones but also 'Ali Sabri. Salim blames Sabri for abusing his position as *"bashkatib,"* namely, chief of the presidential staff. Using that key position, and his post as head of the ASU, Sabri was able to wield a great deal of power which he used to transform the revolutionary system into a highly bureaucratized and inflexible system. According to Salim, Sabri was in league with the Silent Ones and with 'Abd al-Hakim 'Amr in trying to exploit the defeat in the June 1967 War to get rid of Nasser and seize power.

Finally, Salim insists that Nasser was following the requirements of the Egyptian constitution to the letter when he announced on the night of June 9, 1967, that Zakariyya Muhi al-Din would succeed him as temporary president when he resigned the next day. Salim vigorously denied that Nasser's choice was based on any strategic or political plan. Nasser did not plan scenarios of that kind. His decisions were based solely on what would best serve the interests of the Arab people—not just the Egyptian people (418–31).

## 'Abd al-Nasser and the Muslim Brothers and Islam

Writing in 1960, Nadav Safran concluded his classic work on Egyptian ideology with a cautious approval of Nasser's suppression of the Muslim Brothers, noting that "the dangerous drift toward the emotional Muslim orientation has been decisively stopped, apparently by government fiat, ever since the suppression of the Muslim Brotherhood."[20] Since 1955, little new work has appeared exalting the perfection of allegedly Islamic political, social, and ethical principles and contrasting them with Western-imported ideas and values or implying that the application of Islam to Egyptian life would solve all problems.

Safran thought this was a "favorable development." He also noted with satisfaction that the "revolution eliminated the obstructive power of the religious leaders by submitting all religious institutions to the strict control of the state and canceling the bargaining position which the 'ulama had enjoyed under the previous regime owing to the multiplicity of the centers of power" (255).

Safran believed that the leaders of the revolution had opened new ideological possibilities by breaking "the association of nationalism with the Western-modeled Liberal constitutional regimes by abolishing the old political order," and it fought the Muslim Brothers' hold on the symbols of Islamic reform "by destroying and then defaming that movement" (255). "The final product seems to be a new nationalism, which though it feeds on Muslim emotion, is, nevertheless, intolerant of Muslim tradition whenever that tradition seems to conflict with the course of the desired modernization" (256). In spite of Safran's cautious optimism regarding Nasser's commitment to modernization, he did express some doubts as to "whether the leaders would be able to control the religious impulse that moves the masses" (257).

The suppression of the Muslim Brothers, which took place in 1954–55, was part of the postrevolutionary struggle for power among the several groups and factions that favored the overthrow of the monarchy. The fact that the major religious group—not a part of the clerical institution—lost out may be compared to the alternative outcome in Iran. The Nasser regime did proceed to assert its control over the religious establishment that usually goes by the general name of al-Azhar, by the use of both some fat carrots and a few relatively flexible sticks. The Muslim Brothers organization was not actually destroyed, however. It was gravely weakened, but the word was still preached, books were published, adherents met informally or clandestinely, and evidently a lively intellectual debate was pursued among those imprisoned. In 1965, the various remaining factions of the Muslim Brothers were accused of plotting to overthrow the regime, and trials and executions ensued, including that of Sayyid Qutb. Consequently, and obviously, the adherents of the Muslim Brothers and, to an even greater extent, of the extremist Jama'at see Nasser as a terrorist and a murderer. They accuse Nasser of burning Cairo in January 1952, falsely accusing and framing them, and betraying their trust. They accuse Nasser of despotism, arrogance, and unbelief, and they charge his government with tyranny, oppression, and demonolatry.

According to one of Nasser's defenders, 'Abdallah Imam, the Ikhwan claimed that Nasser had concocted the whole episode of the attempted assassination in 1954. They claim that Nasser even persuaded the would-be assassin to sacrifice his life rather than reveal that Nasser put him up to it.

The Muslim Brothers deny everything, but their claims are obviously preposterous. Thus they say

> that they [the Muslim Brothers] did not blow up families—children, women, and men in the cinemas, or in the Jewish Quarter, or the Sharqiyya Advertising Company, or the Cicurel Department Store, or elsewhere. They never fire[d the] bullets that would lodge in the chest of an innocent judge who had decided against them. They are not the murderers of Counselor Khaznadar in front of his home in Helwan, and they did not blow up the courthouse before or after. Not one of them put on a police uniform and slipped into the Ministry of the Interior in order to kill Nuqrashi, the Prime Minister. And the Society [of Muslim Brothers] did not organize the murder of Prime Minister Ibrahim 'Abd al-Hadi; nor fire the bullets that struck his car and those in it—the driver, and the Speaker of Parliament.[21]

After reviewing the familiar history of the conflict between the Nasser regime and the Muslim Brothers and its offshoots, Imam sums up Nasser's attitude toward Islam in his concluding chapter. He claims that it is not true that Nasser's Egypt was either hostile or indifferent to religion. In fact strenuous efforts and a lot of money were put into strengthening Islam, Islamic institutions, and the Islamic faith under Nasser. Most of these efforts, as we know, were made through the increasingly state-controlled al-Azhar or through various devices intended to establish Egypt's primacy in the sphere of international Islamic affairs.

Imam's purpose is not only to refute the factual claims of the Ikhwan but also to refute their characterization of Nasser as a person and a Muslim. Imam starts out by asserting that Nasser was not a Marxist or communist, and the erstwhile close relations between Egypt and the Soviet Union did not extend to ideology (151). Imam makes an important point of the fact that Nasser did not delegate control over media, information, and propaganda to Marxists or communists. Although he lists many names, he does not mention Lutfi al-Khuli and 'Ali Sabri or *Al-Tali'a* and *Al-Katib,* and he makes light of others like Khalid Muhi al-Din, Mahmud Amin al-'Alim, and Kamal Rif'at.

Imam wonders why some observers thought that Nasser was antireligious, and he opines that their mistake may be due to the fact they misunderstand the nature of his hostility toward the Ikhwan. That hostility was based on politics alone. Nasser had no quarrel with their religious beliefs and their religious practices. But the Ikhwan believe that there can be no separation between religion and the state, the Qur'an and the sword. Their methods included conspiracy and armed violence. It was a question of legitimate authority versus illegitimate authority.

Imam argues that Nasser's most important quality was his understanding of the mentality of the Egyptian people and his ability to communicate with them. He was able to do this because he was one of them in the sense that he shared their culture and sentiments. The people of Egypt are religious. Their culture and values are based on Islam. He describes Nasser's belief and manner as pure and clean, modest, ascetic, and simple in habits of dress, eating, and drinking. Hence Nasser, as one of the people, was also religious and motivated by the same sentiments. It is the Ikhwan who are alien and who want to denature Egypt.

To establish this argument, Imam presents anecdotes of Nasser spending time talking with religious specialists and ordinary people, praying at mosques, lecturing students at al-Azhar, leaving meetings with Soviet leaders to join his staff in prayers—in Moscow, and visiting Sayyida Zainab mosque at night. He tells of a meeting in Bandung with Shaykh al-Baquri, minister of Awqaf, during Ramadan. Nasser had been fasting, and al-Baquri reminded him that he was exempt from fasting because he was on a trip. Nasser replied that he preferred to fast because to do otherwise might leave a bad impression with so many of the political leaders he was meeting at that gathering of Third World statesmen. Imam quotes al-Baquri further:

> In two little words, 'Abd al-Nasser is a man of Egypt for Egypt [*rajul Misr li-Misr*] and a man of the Arabs for the Arabs [*rajul al-'Arab lil-'Arab*]. And I swear to Allah, than whom there is no other but Him, that I do not exaggerate in that statement that Nasser is Egypt. For Egypt before Nasser was not Egypt. It was a plantation for exploiters and the most vicious bloodsuckers and gamblers who used to steal the blood of the peasants to take it to summer resorts in Europe and gamble it away at Monte Carlo. . . . No Egyptian had any say in Egypt until Gamal 'Abd al-Nasser came along with his righteous brothers. (157)

At the very end of the last chapter Imam takes up the delicate issue of Nasser's intellectual conception of Islam. If the Ikhwan did not separate Islam from politics, neither did Nasser. Nasser declared that there was no conflict between Islam and socialism. Islam and all the revealed religions oppose exploitation of man by man, and that is what socialism is all about. Imam quotes the National Charter rather than Nasser: "The essence of religion is to guarantee that all human beings have the right to life and freedom" (163). Quoting Nasser: "It is the religion of justice and equality." "The relations between religion and nationalism are strong and solid. . . . In truth, in the call for freedom, the one comes from the light of Allah, and the other comes from the reflection of that light on the conscience of humanity. . . . In Nasser's thought Islam is a progressive revolution against imperialism" (164). And, most clearly spoken by Nasser in colloquial Egyptian:

> As far as we are concerned, our socialism is scientific [*'ilmiyya*], based on knowledge [*'ilm*]. Our socialism is scientific and not based on disordered thought [*al-fawda*]. We didn't say that we're for socialist materialism; and we didn't say that we're for Marxism; and we didn't say that we're abandoning religion. Rather we said that our religion is a socialist religion and that in the Middle Ages, Islam realized the first socialist experiment in world history. (166)

In these last passages, it is clear that Imam has departed from the sentimental, touchy-feely cultural characterization of Nasser and has embraced a quite different image of an in-your-face, tell-it-like-it-is ideologue. Religious orthopraxis may remain untouched, but the historically defined political aspirations of the Egyptian military elite—regime stability, development, modernization, independence, nationalism, state socialism, social mobilization, and Arab unity—define Islam politically. Islam will serve the Egyptian state, and the Egyptian state will, in turn, see to it that the Islamic establishment prospers.

### Nasserist Iconography: From Valentino to Brezhnev

To this point we have been dealing with verbal iconology presented in the idiom of political discourse. In this section we will deal briefly with the relatively unstudied subject of the graphic iconology of Nasser, and in the next section we will recall some of the best-known literary and film contributions to our subject.

Iconography is commonly referred to as the traditional or conventional representation of saintly personalities and biblical events as imagined by ordinary Eastern Christian believers. The icon is an anthropomorphic representation of theopathic experience that is often purported to transcend speech and reason. The representation, when it is understood and when it works, goes straight to the emotions or the consciousness and may have a powerfully persuasive effect. The images may represent a convoluted and recondite doctrine, but their simplicity and their evocation of the familiar dispense with the need for tiresome explication.

Political iconography aims at a similar bond of solidarity between the leaders and the masses, but its success turns on whether or not it is possible to represent an ideology as a personality or whether the idealized person is simply a king or a tyrant. Victoria Bonnell describes, for example, how Soviet revolutionary iconography slipped away from the idealization of the proletariat to the deification of Stalin.[22] Moreover, the logic of traditional iconography depends upon the recognition that the person portrayed is a sacred person, while political iconography may seek to beatify the profane. In some cases, the method of portrayal may defeat the purpose of inspiring the selfless love of subjects, as in the court iconography of the Qajar Shahs emphasizing despotic power in huge paintings of ornately dressed shahs seated on great thrones, or as in the case of modern Iraq, where the grotesque, gigantesque representations of Saddam Husayn inspired fear more than love.

But the modern understanding of the term *icon* often turns the traditional notion on its head. Instead of inspiring a targeted emotion by invoking a conventional and cathected symbol, the term is often applied to a striking and unusual photograph or painting that comes to represent a new phenomenon, a new generation, a new cultural development, or a new era. For examples of this second type of icon, we can suggest the picture of a grimacing Yitzhak Rabin shaking 'Arafat's hand, or Andy Warhol's painting of Marilyn Monroe, or the picture of the astronauts on the moon.

It seems to me that the Nasserist iconography falls into neither category. Most Western observers, obsessed with what they saw as Nasser's charisma, were inclined to ignore what appears to be the plain meaning of most of the Nasser photos. Their most outstanding feature is their ordinariness—certainly after the first few years. Rather than portraying Nasser as a saint or a knight in shining armor (a modern Salah al-Din), Nasser's standard photos have come to represent an era during which Egypt came of age politically and learned the limits of its capabilities. Rather than leading Egypt out of the wilderness, Nasser reaffirmed Egypt's quotidian destiny.

Lacouture starts out by linking "the cult of the leader" with the search for a collective identity (48). The people "identify spontaneously and enthusiastically with a visible and prestigious human being, who in turn infuses each of them with his glamour and his glory" (49). The leader personifies the nation's power, its destiny, and its independence. He invokes theatrical images such as "vigorous and radiant image," a "purifying portrait," "bold power, blindingly displayed," and "savior." But even Lacouture's infatuation falters when he considers the inevitable failure to maintain the suspension of disbelief. It appears that Lacouture thinks that the initial seizure of power is virtually imposed on the hero by the people and that the role of acting as both symbol and savior is defined by mass adulation or intoxication. But then the performance becomes routine—a mere memory or parody of the great moments of the past. And, referring specifically to Nasser, Lacouture laments in *The Demigods,* "Thus the eloquence that was a source of power begins to wither, and the speaker hears only the sound of his own voice. . . . Going to hear the *za'im* speak is like attending the performance of a great tenor in his most famous role. With every voice shouting the same slogans, doesn't it mean that they are all behind him still?" (65–72).

The iconology of the Egyptian revolution, though it exploited the image of the Egyptian peasant for a while, moved rather quickly to the cult of the personality of Nasser. There was not much that was ideological about the campaign, as opposed to the identitive and representative aspects. The centrality and persistence of the Nasserist iconology was a constant if subtle reminder that both Arab nationalism and Arab socialism were secondary to Egyptian identity and the Egyptian national interest. The images of Nasser diffused throughout the Arab world and beyond had one set of meanings in Egypt and another set elsewhere.

In spite of the highly political character of the Nasserist iconology, Nasser was rarely portrayed as the embodiment of a political ideology or the holder of the highest office. The implicit frame within which his image was manipulated was a biographical and developmental one rather than an ideological or historical one. In perusing collections of photographs, leaving aside, perhaps, the ubiquitous head shots that were hung in every government office, one cannot avoid the feeling of looking at someone's family album. For the most part, Nasser was usually presented in a relatively simple and straightforward manner. Even when he was portrayed in twenty-foot-high hand-painted posters, the drawings were often sloppy and not very flattering or fear inspiring. In the early years, Nasser was photographed in uniform, riding in an open jeep, sitting at a desk, poring over a chessboard, seated on a carpet in prayer. But later he appeared in a double-breasted suit that exaggerated his portliness and made him look like a Soviet commissar or an Egyptian insurance salesman.

During the Nasser years, his photographs were everywhere. Every government office, store, schoolroom, and business was likely to have one. Newspapers usually published pictures of Nasser every day in the usual sorts of ceremonial activity, standing around in his striped blue double-breasted costume. The general feeling that these photos provided was one of familiarity rather than fear or hero worship. To be sure, at least before 1967, Nasser was supposed to represent courage, dignity, independence, strength, wisdom, patience, honesty, modesty, piety, and discipline. Toward the end, Nasser appeared stolid, distant, a wounded lion, more parry than thrust.

But it appears to me that the one consistent theme to be found in the public presentation of Nasser and in the response of the Egyptian masses to him was his ability to represent Egyptian authenticity, whether in triumph or defeat, in retrospect or in anticipation of a brighter future. Early on, he was described as representing what Egyptian authenticity ought to be, but at the end, on June 9, 1967, and at the funeral, there seemed to be little gap between him and the grieving masses. Whatever the lingering sentiments of the masses, the Egyptian intellectuals gradually turned away in disinterest.

## Literature and Movies: The Collective Memory

I think that this rejection by the educated classes may well be the theme of the enigmatic novella *Al-Karnak*, written by Nagib Mahfuz.[23] As I read it, Mahfuz strikes only a glancing and subtle blow against Nasser in his iconic capacity as an emblem of Egyptian authenticity. It is true that in this book, as opposed to *Tharthara Fawq al-Nil* and *Miramar*, Mahfuz attacks the regime directly rather than describing the effect that the failed revolutionary regime has on middle-class Egyptians.[24] But in *Al-Karnak*, written in 1971 or even earlier, there is no direct criticism of Nasser as is to be found in *Amam al-'Arsh*, written in 1983.[25]

Literary critics seem to agree that the existentialist alienation and moral bankruptcy that pervades both *Tharthara Fawq al-Nil* and *Miramar* and leads, in both cases, to the abuse of peasant icons by middle-class stereotypes are to be attributed to the effect of the authoritarian regime. But the causal nexus is never made clear because of Mahfuz's well warranted caution.[26] It isn't clear whether the peasant icons are supposed to represent simple innocence or Egyptian authenticity—bearing in mind that the peasants, who were so much the focus of revolutionary attention, were not central to Mahfuz's aesthetic sensibility.[27]

In *Al-Karnak*, all the action takes place in a small, tidy coffee shop on a central Cairo sidestreet. The story is told by a narrator who learns of the events from conversations with some of the coffee shop's regulars. The café itself is, however, outside of time and in a place where little action occurs.[28] In fact, the narrator stumbles onto the café while "killing time" waiting for his watch to be repaired. He is drawn back to the café again and again by a compelling nostalgia—personified by the proprietress, a striking woman, now past her prime, who was once a famous *baladi* dancer in the days before the revolution.

The narrator tells us the story of how three idealistic and ambitious Egyptian students, members of the first generation of the revolution, are "devoured"—betrayed, humiliated, tortured, exploited, and psychologically destroyed. Two of the students are lovers, and the third is having an affair of sorts with the proprietress. The agent of the revolution responsible for this destruction is a Mukhabbarat interrogator called Khalid Safwan. Mahfuz emphasizes the emotional and psychological impact upon the personalities of the two chaste but betrothed lovers, who are manipulated into denouncing one another to the Mukhabbarat in a sequence evoking O. Henry's story "The Christmas Gift."

The three students are arrested and interrogated thrice, after which Safwan is himself arrested, tortured, and imprisoned for three years in some sort of purge. The two locales are conjoined when an ailing Safwan suddenly turns up at the café, killing time, waiting for the pharmacy to prepare his prescription medicines. We are not told exactly what his ailments are, but we assume they are illnesses of the soul.

In contrast to the café regulars, Safwan is frank, outspoken, cynical, intelligent, and critical. The regulars and a few new patrons are somewhat taken with his observations on the failures of the revolution and the disillusion which has followed the military defeat of 1967. Safwan is virtually welcomed into the group—no hard feelings—all are victims of the same impersonal phenomenon.[29] The prescriptions are delivered. Safwan gets ready to leave and delivers a striking exit speech in which he condemns the hypocrisy of the Nasser regime, insisting that honesty, freedom, and democracy should never be sacrificed on the altar of political expediency. In fact, Safwan emerges as the most articulate and rational character in the novel.

Safwan says nothing about Nasser. In fact, Nasser is mentioned only once in the book, when the narrator asks the now morally and emotionally catatonic couple whether they still support the ideals of the revolution. They answer in a strong affirmative, telling him that they both went out into the streets on the night of June 9, 1967, to protest Nasser's intent to resign and to implore him to stay on. The reader, I believe, is expected to find this sentiment to be self-destructive and even illogical, especially in contrast to Safwan's frank and unalloyed condemnation of the Nasser regime. The reader may even look for some reassurance or consolation from the disconcertingly unmoved and even passive author-narrator. But all we get is a brief conversation that the narrator has with a new student patron of the café, Munir Ahmad. The narrator expresses hope in the new generation and asks Munir about his ideological position. Munir refuses to be categorized, but admits that he respects both religion and the Left. Munir insists that he wants to be himself and that neither the *turath* nor westernization represent the individualism and the authenticity that he seeks. Where, then, will he find this *asala,* asks the narrator. "Here," says Munir, pointing to his heart.

The younger generation would seek its own authenticity within, rather than accept the alterity of a distant political icon that is emblematic of a collective identity. And if the younger generation succeeds in discovering its own authenticity, will it be able to reconnect with the Egypt that existed before the revolution? Well, it seems that the proprietress (symbolizing the charms of prerevolutionary Egypt?) has an eye for Munir, and the feeling may be mutual.

Menahem Milson has provided us with a very helpful summary analysis and translation of key passages from *Amam al-'Arsh*.[30] In that novel, Mahfuz puts Nasser on trial before the mythical and historic heroic rulers of Egypt, and he compares Nasser's achievements with those of Sadat as well. Nasser is praised for his outstanding accomplishments, but he is harshly criticized for squandering every opportunity for consolidating those gains. All the good that he did is undone by the evil that was the consequence of his pride, his ambition, his unwillingness to compromise, and his tyranny. The emphasis is on Nasser's personality and not on the system he constructed and bequeathed to his successors.

*Amam al-'Arsh* is about policy and strategy whereas *Al-Karnak* is about consciousness and authenticity. In 1983, Mahfuz is defending both Sadat's peace policy and his economic policy as adopted by the still shaky Mubarak regime. In 1971, if that is indeed the date of the composition of the earlier book, Mahfuz was arguing that the revolution, or at least the methods adopted to achieve the goals of the revolution, had succeeded only in alienating Egyptians from their own authenticity. Mahfuz rejected the idea that revolutionary change required a break with history and tradition. On the contrary, and despite exaggerated claims such as al-Baquri's equating of Nasser and Egypt, the Nasser regime did not overcome the alienation wrought by imperialism and latifundism. In fact, Nasserist authoritarianism greatly expanded the petite bourgeoisie and, in Mahfuz's opinion, profoundly alienated that class by subalternating it rather than empowering it. Nevertheless, in *Al-Karnak* Mahfuz seems to be echoing the views of Desouki and of Tawfiq al-Hakim in separating the man from the consequences of his policies, leaving room for the preservation of the heroic image, carefully limited in time—as suggested by the film *Nasser 56*.[31]

Donald Malcolm Reid concludes an excellent review of this movie with the following paragraph:

> By its careful selection of theme and time frame, the movie avoids confronting divisive issues of Nasser's legacy—the repression of the Muslim Brothers and other political opponents, the abuses by the secret police, the failures of the United Arab Republic and Arab socialism, and the catastrophic defeat at Israel's hands in 1967. To both the diminishing number of Egyptians old enough to recall the events of 1956 and to the majority who were not yet born when Nasser died in 1970, this film will have a powerful impact on the way he is remembered.[32]

## Notes

1. Malcolm Kerr, *The Arab Cold War, 1958-1964: A Study of Ideology in Politics* (London: Oxford University Press, 1965), 80f.

2. Barbara Cady and Jean-Jaques Naudet, eds., *Icons of the Twentieth Century: Two Hundred Men and Women Who Have Made a Difference* (Woodstock, N.Y.: Overlook Press, 1998), 260–61.

3. Peter Woodward, *Nasser: Profiles in Power* (London: Longman, 1992).

4. Peter Mansfield, *Nasser's Egypt* (London: Methuen Educational, 1965, rev., 1969), 1, 246.

5. See Raymond A. Hinnebusch Jr., *Egyptian Politics under Sadat: The Post-Populist Development of an Authoritarian-Modernizing State* (Cambridge: Cambridge University Press, 1985), 289f.

6. P. J. Vatikiotis, *The Egyptian Army in Politics: Pattern for New Nations?* (Bloomington: Indiana University Press, 1961), 229.

7. Miles Copeland, *The Game of Nations: The Amorality of Power Politics* (New York: Simon and Schuster, 1969). Page numbers are cited in the text.

8. Jean Lacouture, *The Demigods: Charismatic Leadership in the Third World*, trans. Patricia Wolf (New York: Knopf, 1970), 70. This work is described as a translation of a doctoral dissertation supervised by Jacques Berque at the College de France. Page numbers are cited in the text.

9. 'Ali al-Din al-Hilal al-Desouki et al., "Al-Mushkila al-Siyasiyya fi Misr wal-Tahawwul ila Ta'addud al-Ihzab," *Tajribat al-Dimuqratiyya fi Misr: 1980–1981, Al-Qadaya al-Siyasiyya*, no. 2 (Cairo, 1982), 30. Subsequent page numbers are cited in the text.

10. Leonard Binder, *In a Moment of Enthusiasm: Political Power and the Second Stratum in Egypt* (Chicago: University of Chicago Press, 1978), esp. 4f. and 330f.

11. "Turath 'Abd al-Nasser fi Rihab al-Taharrur Wal-Taqaddum," a special issue of *Al-Tali'a: Tariq al-Munadhilin ila al-Fikr al-Thawri al-Mu'asir, Gamal 'Abd al-Nasir . . . , Fikrihi wa-Nidalihi*, 6 (November 1970) 6.

12. "Gamal 'Abd al-Nasir—and the Revolution," ibid., 9; "Who Are 'the People' in the Thought of Gamal 'Abd al-Nasser," ibid., 12.

13. See Hinnebusch, *Egyptian Politics under Sadat*, 61f.

14. For a list of relevant titles and dates, see John Waterbury, *The Egypt of Nasser and Sadat: The Political Economy of Two Regimes* (Princeton: Princeton University Press, 1983), 338, 339 n. 4.

15. Tawfiq al-Hakim, *'Awdat al-Wa'y*, 2d ed. (Beirut: Dar al-Shuruq, 1975), 3, 4, 75–91. Subsequent page numbers are cited in the text.

16. The proceedings of those seminars were published in a book called *Milaff 'Abd al-Nasir* (Beirut, 1975?). Page numbers are cited in the text.

17. Sami Gawhar, *Al-Samitun Yatakalamun*, 6th printing (Alexandria: al-Maktab al-Misri al-Hadith, 1976). Page numbers are cited in the text.

18. Hasanayn Karum, *Al-Samitun Yakdhabun: al-Radd 'ala Kitab "al-Samitun Yatakalamun"* (Cairo, 1976).

19. Gamal Salim, *Al-Samitun fi al-Mizan: min ajl-il-Haqiqa .. wal-Imana .. wal-Ta'rikh* (Cairo: Dar al-Qahira lil-Thaqafa al-'Arabiyya, 1976).

20. Nadav Safran, *Egypt in Search of Political Community: An Analysis of the Intellectual and Political Evolution of Egypt, 1804–1952* (Cambridge: Harvard University Press, 1961), 253.

21. 'Abdallah Imam, *'Abd al-Nasir wal-Ikhwan al-Muslimun* (Cairo: Dar al-Qahira lil-Thaqafa al-'Arabiyya, 1981), 3–4.

22. Victoria E. Bonnell, *Iconography of Power: Soviet Political Posters under Lenin and Stalin* (Berkeley: University of California Press, 1997).

23. El-Enany writes: "Following the military debacle of 1967 and Nasser's death in 1970, Mahfuz's onslaught on the revolution rose to a crescendo in *The Karnak* (1974), a bitter condemnation of the repressive techniques of the Police state and their destructive effect on the dignity of the individual and hence the nation as a whole." Rasheed el-Enany, *Naguib Mahfouz: The Pursuit of Meaning* (London: Routledge, 1993), 26.

24. Ibid., 110–14.

25. Ibid., 44.

26. Menahem Milson, *Najib Mahfuz: The Novelist-Philosopher of Cairo* (New York: St. Martin's Press, 1998), 154.

27. El-Enany tells us that Mahfuz intended to portray Zahra as a symbol of Egypt (*Naguib Mahfouz*, 115 n. 48).

28. Some critics have, however, attempted to identify both the actual café on which al-Karnak was modeled and the events and dates framing the conversations taking place in the fictional café.

29. See the interesting treatment of this scene by Trevor Le Gassick, "Mahfouz's al-Karnak: The Quiet Conscience of Nasir's Egypt Revealed," in Le Gassick, ed., *Critical Perspectives on Naguib Mahfouz* (Washington, D.C.: Three Continents Press, 1991), 158.

30. Milson, *Najib Mahfuz*, 144–55. See also el-Enany, *Naguib Mahfouz*, 44.

31. See el-Enany, *Naguib Mahfouz*, 26: "The evident affection is, however, proof of the ambivalence in Mahfuz's attitude towards the rule of Nasser: consistently he has shown himself to be equally aware of both the positive and negative sides of the experiment."

32. Donald Malcolm Reid, review of *Nasser 56*, *MESA Bulletin* 32, no. 1 (summer 1998): 133–34.

# 2

## Demonizing the Other

Israeli Perceptions of Nasser and Nasserism

Elie Podeh

> History in general, and diplomatic history in particular, are the story of human aspirations, achievement, adaptation, and survival. But they are also the tale of human error and fallibility. A common element in many failures is that they did not stem from a dearth of information but rather from incorrect judgment and evaluation of available information.
>
> Yaakov Y. I. Vertzberger, *The World in Their Minds*

## Introduction

This illuminating passage refers to a familiar human phenomenon. Studies show that a possible reason for incorrect judgment and evaluation of information is that the decision-making elite develop subjective perceptions of "the other." Each leader holds a belief system that includes a set of images formed on the basis of individual values, personality, political style, intellect, and past experience.[1] Decisions are made not on the basis of an objective reality but on the basis of a perceived reality that emerges as a result of entrenched images. Relations among nations, therefore, are shaped, inter alia, by the way in which leaders, or elites, view each other.[2]

The term *image* has acquired various definitions in political psychology. Herbert Kelman defined it simply as "organized representation of an object in the individual's cognitive system."[3] Images play an important role in information processing, serving as "screens for the selective reception of new messages" and controlling "the perception of interpretation of those messages that are not completely ignored, rejected, or repressed."[4] In analyzing how people process information, Alexander George posited a series of assumptions that will serve as a basis for this study: (1) Individuals orient themselves to their surroundings by acquiring, storing, appraising, and utilizing information about their physical and social environment. (2) Everyone acquires beliefs and images about the environment, which provide him/her with a relatively coherent way of organizing and making sense of confusing signals. (3) Since information processing is selective, beliefs and images may be biased and stereotyped. (4) Beliefs and images are usually stable, but individuals may change them in light of discrepant information.[5]

In structuring a coherent belief system, decision makers tend to refer to analogies, categories, and labels. According to the schema theory, "because people are limited in what information they can process, they must resort to stored knowledge or cognitive schemas to make sense of the world around them." Moreover, according to Deborah Larson, a person "searches until he has found a schema that summarizes and categorizes one or more similar stimulus configurations in the past."[6] A familiar analogy in world politics is the 1938 Munich script, which stands as a symbol of appeasement and surrender.[7]

Images are particularly associated with the idea of the enemy. Two familiar misconceptions regarding the "enemy" are noteworthy. The first is the tendency of the decision maker to "see other states, particularly adversaries or competitors, as more hostile than they are."[8] The second misconception is "black-and-white" thinking—positing a clear distinction between the good "we" and the bad "they."[9] Such misconceptions may lead to the emergence of diabolism, "the tendency to see another person or group as more diabolical than the facts warrant."[10] These misconceptions were highly relevant to the way the United States and the Soviet Union depicted each other during the Cold War era. The Americans perceived the behavior of the Soviet Union as motivated by aggressive ideological and military considerations reflecting a desire to achieve worldwide hegemony through expansionism. They saw Soviet domestic behavior as dictatorial, exploitive, and delusive.[11] As a result, American leaders adopted a "Cold War terminology," dismissed signals for mutual agreement as propaganda, and considered any search for compromise as appeasement. Predictably, the Soviets felt the same way about the Americans.[12]

Several studies dealing with the effect of American and Soviet images on their respective foreign policies have suggested that the role of images is highly relevant to the Arab-Israeli conflict as well.[13] Surprisingly, however, little research has been devoted to the molding of images and their role in perpetuating this conflict. Moreover, none of the few extant studies are based on the historical method.

In a series of interviews conducted during the 1970s, Daniel Heradstviet found deeply biased Israeli and Arab perceptions of one another.[14] Michael Brecher published a comprehensive study of the link between the psychological environment in general and elite images in particular and its foreign policy decisions in the early 1970s. Based on speeches and interviews, he analyzed the belief system and images of such Israeli leaders as David Ben-Gurion, Moshe Sharett, Golda Meir, Levi Eshkol, Moshe Dayan, and Shimon Peres and their impact on the decision-making process.[15] Brecher argued that Israel's achievements during its first twenty years were not matched in the realm of foreign policy. Arab intransigence and Soviet policy, he wrote, constituted a main obstacle to Israel's supreme goal of peace, but in part "the failure lies in the basic foreign policy decisions, which Israel made in response to her leaders' perceptions of their environment. The qualitative jump in the psychological environment," he concluded, "remains an historic task unfulfilled."[16]

Based on the historical method, this article analyzes images of the enemy held by the Israeli elite during the Nasserite period. More specifically, it explores the way Israeli images of Egyptian president Gamal 'Abd al-Nasser and Nasserism—the movement that represented his ideas and followers—evolved and were sustained, as well as the possible impact of these images on the decision-making process. Inasmuch as the 1950s and the 1960s represented a significant period in the Arab-Israeli conflict, and Nasser was considered Israel's most powerful and vicious enemy, the analysis sheds light on the role of perceived images in the formulation of Israeli foreign policy. The article also supports—though with no attempt to substantiate—Daniel Bar-Tal's assertion that the images and perceptions of the elite reflected widely held attitudes in society.[17] This linkage is particularly plausible because of the existence in Israel of a strong, even charismatic, and to a large extent cohesive leadership that was able to transmit its views effectively through various channels of communication.

The major thesis of this chapter is that the Israeli leadership filtered incoming information regarding the enemy through the lens of Jewish history, life experiences, and current events. Major episodes in the Jewish collective memory were the pogroms in Eastern Europe, the vivid and traumatic memory of the Holocaust, the sense of the few against the many during the 1948 war, and the presence of a siege mentality, especially after 1948.[18] These and other memories—shared or remembered—served as screens, filtering incoming information in a way consistent with the negative image already formed of the enemy. Since the aims of this article are modest, the link made in this article between images and decision making is suggestive rather than conclusive.

## Origins of the Nasserist Image

The results of the 1948 war presented a paradox to the political leadership: on the one hand, a sense of contempt and derision for the Arab states, their corrupt regimes, and the indolent leaders who had led their people to such a crushing defeat at the hands of the Jews in a war of "the few against the many," and on the other hand, the fear of a second round against the Arabs, whose goal would be the annihilation of the Jews and the obliteration of the shame of defeat. An alteration in the first part of the equation could have transformed the Arab threat from an abstraction to reality, for example, had an Arab leader of stature emerged to unite the Arabs politically, advance them economically and socially, and ultimately unify their efforts to destroy the state of Israel. Not surprisingly, as early as January 1949, Ben-Gurion noted this in his diary.[19] Three months later, he reiterated his fear of a unified Arab world that would act against the Jews, using the historic comparison with the Crusaders. He was especially fearful of the emergence of a leader of the same caliber as the Prophet Muhammad; founder of the puritanical Wahhabiyyah movement in the Arabian Peninsula Muhammad 'Abd ibn al-Wahhab; or the secular Turkish leader Mustafa Kemal (Ataturk).[20] It was the last who particularly haunted Ben-Gurion. In his diary, he confessed that the fear of "the possibility of our annihilation" still gnawed at him in view of the "existence of sixty or seventy million Arabs—and it is possible that a Mustafa Kemal will rise up among them."[21] Ben-Gurion admired the leader who was able to introduce such revolutionary changes in Turkey.[22]

Ben-Gurion's profound knowledge of history taught him that the emergence of a charismatic leader is a necessary precondition for attaining unity and spiritual rejuvenation. Bismarck in Germany, Mazzini and Cavour in Italy, and Mustafa Kemal in Turkey were only a few prominent examples. Drawing an analogy to the Arab world from his experience and his erudition, Ben-Gurion viewed Arab unity as a natural process. Indeed, with Nasser's rise to power during the 1950s, it appeared that Ben-Gurion's fears were about to be realized.

The July 1952 Free Officers' Revolution in Egypt, led by Muhammad Nagib and Nasser, was initially welcomed by Israel. The impression was that the group of young officers from the middle and lower middle class would better represent Egypt than the wealthy, illegitimate elite, leading Egypt to a new era of modernization and social justice. Israel also hoped that this regime would be less vulnerable to nationalist rhetoric, which had characterized the old regime, thereby establishing a congenial basis for direct dialogue. Thus, on August 18, 1952, Ben-Gurion, speaking to the Knesset, welcomed the new regime.[23] Moreover, Ben-Gurion and Sharett initiated secret contacts between Israel and Nasser in February 1953; although they did not produce any tangible results, they signaled that Egypt did not desire war.[24]

Once Nagib was removed from power in November 1954, Israeli attention focused on his successor, Nasser. To become acquainted with his worldview, his booklet, *The Philosophy of the Revolution* (written by Muhammad Hasanayn Haykal), was translated by Israeli Military Intelligence in November 1954 and released to the press in December. In this booklet, it was Nasser's conceptualization of Egypt's leadership role in three circles—the Arab, the African, and the Islamic—that became the focus of interest. The simplistic interpretation in Israel (and in the West generally) was that Egypt was bent on attaining hegemony in these spheres. It was believed that the evacuation of British forces from Suez in the wake of the signing of the Anglo-Egyptian Agreement in July 1954 would allow Egypt greater room for maneuver to realize its ambitions. In addition, it was believed that Israel constituted the stumbling block to Egypt's aspirations.

Ben-Gurion read the booklet—he referred to it as a "notebook"—during 1955, as evidenced by his frequent references to it in his diary thereafter. Years later, in an interview after Nasser's death in 1970, Ben-Gurion emphasized that he had read the booklet many times. "In order to better understand the intentions [of Nasser]," he said, "I made sure that I always kept the book with me."[25] Attributing great importance to the written word, Ben-Gurion assumed that *Philosophy* truly reflected Nasser's worldview, constituting an operative political program as well.

A typical reference to *Philosophy* was made by Ben-Gurion at the Knesset in January 1956. He noted that the Egyptian "dictator" published a pamphlet that revealed his ambitions openly: to lead the Arab nation, to become the leader of the Islamic nations, and to be the spokesman of the African continent. During the ensuing discussion, Ben-Gurion quoted the passages in the booklet in which Nasser describes his experience in the 1948 war and the connection of Palestine with the Arab world. Ben-Gurion's conclusion was that "the ambition to destroy Israel is planted deep in Nasser's heart and is a cornerstone of his nationalist viewpoint."[26] A careful reading of *Philosophy* would substantiate that this assertion was derived not from the actual text but from Ben-Gurion's interpretation of it.

Meanwhile, in 1954, secret contacts were held between Israel and Egypt focusing on two points: the release of an Israeli ship, detained by Egypt while trying to pass through the Suez Canal in September 1954, and the prevention of death sentences for a group of Egyptian Jews found guilty of spying for Israel in an incident in July 1954 (an affair known as the "Mishap").

These requests were delivered to Nasser in a secret letter, which was phrased in a highly moderate tone by Prime Minister Sharett.[27] In response, Nasser promised to release the ship's crew and ensure a fair trial for the defendants. With this, the Western mediators who met with Nasser were of the opinion that the Egyptian regime would prevent the handing down of death sentences.[28]

A turning point in the Israeli position toward the Egyptian ruler occurred in the wake of the trial. News was received on January 27, 1955, that two of the defendants had been sentenced to death and others to long prison terms, eliciting shock and disappointment in Israel. Gideon Rafael, the Foreign Ministry official in charge of efforts to save the defendants, believed that Nasser had purposely deceived all the mediators. Sharett's reaction, however, was more restrained.[29] Although Sharett continued his dialogue with Nasser throughout his term as prime minister, in June 1955 he wrote in his diary: "We have lost our faith in him as a result of the hangings."[30]

A further hardening of Israel's stance toward Nasser occurred during the first half of 1955 in the wake of infiltration from the Egyptian border, acts of sabotage and murder. The Israeli assumption was that the Egyptian authorities could prevent such acts if they so desired. Israeli retaliation, and especially the Gaza operation of February 28, 1955, which resulted in the death of thirty-seven Egyptians, was aimed at deterring Egypt from encouraging such infiltration. In practice, Israeli policy caused the deterioration of the military situation and the perpetuation of a vicious circle in which each side in the conflict viewed with suspicion the other side's protestations of peace, conveyed through the secret contacts between the two states until 1954. The Gaza operation appears to have drastically altered Nasser's perception of the possibility of solving the conflict with Israel.[31] Sharett, too, thought, at least retrospectively, that the Gaza operation damaged the possibility of concrete talks with Nasser.[32]

In contrast to Sharett's moderation, Ben-Gurion and Chief of Staff Moshe Dayan were markedly suspicious, advocating an activist policy against the Egyptian ruler. In a debate on the necessity for a retaliatory move, Ben-Gurion pointed to Nasser's "crimes": "He must be taught a lesson again and again—either he does what is imposed on him or he is brought down. He can certainly be toppled and it would be a *mitzva* [good deed] to do so. Who is he, anyhow, this Nasser Shmasser?"[33] Sharett, in contrast, had a different interpretation: He thought that Israel's retaliatory acts damaged the Egyptian self-image, weakened the regime internally, and hurt its attempt to acquire a leadership position in the Arab world. Nasser's moves, in short, were a reaction to the steps taken by Israel rather than aggression against it.[34]

The negative image of Nasser in Israel (and in the West generally) was further reinforced during the first half of 1955 by his neutral stance in the Cold War, which was interpreted as a pro-Soviet position. For example, his vigorous opposition to the pro-West Baghdad Pact was depicted as an anti-Western step, although in actuality it stemmed from inter-Arab rivalries.[35] Two other steps that strengthened Nasser's anti-Western image were his participation in the nonaligned conference in Bandung (April 1955) and Egypt's recognition of the People's Republic of China (May 1955). The fact that Israel was not invited to take part in the Bandung conference, as against Nasser's prominent role in it, constituted further evidence, in Israel's perception, of his true nature.[36]

Yet the event that fixed Nasser's negative image in Israel and in the West was Egypt's Czech arms deal in September 1955. Israel was alarmed by the deal, which totally altered the regional balance of power while also giving the USSR a significant foothold in the Middle East. Gideon Rafael, in an immediate response to Foreign Minister Sharett, wrote: "The Arab world must be taught the lesson that anyone who enters into an alliance with the devil is destined to end up in hell. If this act deters Nasser, well and good; if he is toppled—no matter. Nasser has proven himself as someone who collects advances without producing the promised goods."[37] This message suggests a patronizing attitude toward a rebellious child who violates his master. For Rafael, who had lost faith in Nasser in the wake of the trial in Cairo, the arms deal further reinforced his aggressive and untrustworthy image.

Israel's fear was clearly reflected in the intensive debates carried on in the Knesset, the government, the Knesset Foreign Affairs and Security Committee, and the public generally. Ben-Gurion, Dayan, Mosad head Isser Harel, and many other figures in both the coalition and the opposition began preparing the public for the possibility of a preventive war or a more limited military campaign against Egypt. Some even thought that the elimination of Nasser was necessary.[38] The fear engendered by the arms deal led to the invoking of images and analogies from recent Jewish history. Introducing the new government in the Knesset in November 1955, Ben-Gurion said:

> I cannot pass over in silence the serious and potentially dangerous thing that the Czechoslovakian government calls a "business transaction." ... The rulers of Egypt are buying these arms with one goal only: to uproot the State of Israel and its people.... The head of the ruling military faction in Cairo has announced that its war is aimed not only against Israel but against world Jewry and against Jewish finance which rules the United States. *This kind of talk is known to us from Hitler's day* [my emphasis], and it is highly mystifying that the Czechoslovakian government in particular is ignoring the Nazi dogma that is being sounded anew on the banks of the Nile.... There is a duty to

inform all the aggressors of the world . . . [that] the Jewish people in its land will not be as sheep to the slaughter. . . . Not many nations fight for their freedom and their existence. What Hitler did to six million helpless Jews in Europe will not be done by any enemy of Israel to the free Jews rooted in their homeland.[39]

Similar images and analogies were invoked by spokesmen of various political factions in extensive political debates in the Knesset during the first week of January 1956.[40] Sharett, however, offered a different interpretation. He claimed that the deal aimed to cover up Nasser's military defeats in the Israeli operations, enhance his bargaining position with the Western powers, and stabilize his seniority in the Arab world. Personally, Sharett argued, Nasser could not be called a dictator, as his dictatorship could not be compared to that of Stalin, Hitler, or Mussolini.[41] Although Sharett acknowledged that the deal was a new "trouble," he emphasized that the quest for peace must not be stopped. But Sharett's faith in Nasser, too, was waning.[42]

The worsening of Israeli-Egyptian relations prompted the United States to embark on a secret mediation initiative through envoy Robert Anderson, which lasted from December 1955 to March 1956. In preparation for these talks, Israel's Foreign Ministry drew up several documents about Nasser's personality and the history of Israeli-Egyptian contacts between 1949 and 1955. Gideon Rafael, who was in charge of these contacts, outlined a profile of Nasser, his objectives, and his methods:

> Nasser's character is marked by a strong conspiratorial streak, formed over the long period of his political underground activity. His political stature grew considerably after his first appearance on the international stage at the Bandung conference, where he acquired foreign experience and acquired personal esteem. His success reached a high mark with the Czech arms deal, which raised his prestige in the Arab countries and established him as an international figure to be reckoned with. Nasser's political tactics are intricate and flexible. He switches from moderation to extremism by cool, unemotional calculation. In his struggle with Britain and his fight against Israel, he uses alternately moderation and extremism, violence and appeasement in accordance with the tactical needs of the hour. The amount of force he is ready to use is adjusted to his immediate objective. He tries to avoid tests of strength for which he is not yet prepared. His method is to demand an advance for any action he is asked to undertake, carefully avoiding to commit himself explicitly to defray the payment. He generally formulates his assurances in a noncommittal way: "If you will cease to do so and so and if you grant me this and that, I will be in a better position

to do what you expect from me." He displays an astonishing talent for inventing pretexts when asked to fulfill his undertakings. His system of dodging obligations is remarkably cunning. The right way to deal with Nasser is to put his promises, big or small, to the test of performance.[43]

Rafael's description seems to be tainted by the negative image he had of the Egyptian leader in the wake of the trial in Cairo and the Czech arms deal. This document is important because it provided some background on Nasser for the decision makers.

Ben-Gurion, in talks with Anderson, reiterated his fear that Egypt would initiate a war against Israel as soon as it attained sufficient capability. In such a situation, he claimed, little Israel would face the entire Arab world (40 million), aided by the Soviet Union. During these talks, Ben-Gurion emphasized that "the facts are not consistent with a desire for peace" on Nasser's part. Trying to step into the Egyptian's shoes, Ben-Gurion said, leads him to "doubt Nasser's real desire for peace because he could come to the conclusion that annihilating Israel is possible." The recurring motif in all Ben-Gurion's talks with Anderson about Nasser is mistrust. Sharett, too, did not believe in Nasser's good faith, believing that Egypt was capable of starting a war or staging a provocation that would ultimately result in the outbreak of war.[44] Channels of communication thus closed down, with little chance for information that conflicted with the existing images to filter through. Apparently, Anderson's mission reinforced the negative images that had coalesced beforehand and even blurred the differences between Ben-Gurion and Sharett regarding the Egyptian regime. Sharett's resignation from the government in June 1956, therefore, did not signify the disappearance of an important viewpoint in Israeli policy; that viewpoint simply no longer existed. Golda Meir, whose worldview and images largely resembled Ben-Gurion's, replaced Sharett.[45]

The negative image of Nasser was reflected, too, in somber descriptions of the Egyptian regime. It was presented no longer as progressive or revolutionary but as a corrupt dictatorship. The new ruling elite was often described as a gang (*knufiyya*), and Nasser was labeled a dictator (*rodan*)—a term that became idiomatic for Israeli statesmen and the media in emphasizing the superiority of Israeli democracy over the Egyptian dictatorship. In addition, Nasser's military rank during the revolution—colonel—was used extensively with the aim of deriding his status and emphasizing the illegitimate nature of the regime, which came to power by coup and not by democratic means. A typical depiction of Israel's perception of the Egyptian regime appears in a speech by Ben-Gurion in early 1956:

> A revolt took place in Egypt. . . . Several military figures took control of the regime. Their intent at first might have been perceived as chang-

ing the condition of the Egyptian people. There is no nation in the world where illness and ignorance are so shocking as in Egypt.... Yet this man announced publicly that his intention was that Egypt shall head all the Arab nations, lead the Muslim world, and hold hegemony over the entire African continent. If so, there are two ways to accomplish this: the long and difficult way, by correcting the wretched situation in Egypt ... or a second way, by external conquests and war with those whom the Arab nations hate—a war with Israel. The rulers of Egypt have chosen the second way.[46]

Nasser's decision in July 1956 to nationalize the Suez Canal Company provided the final reinforcement of his negative image in Israel; it served as the ultimate "proof" of his aggressive ambitions. In the Israeli perception (which largely mirrored the Western perception), taking control of the Suez Canal was part of Egypt's broader plan to take control of the oil fields, whose importance was highlighted in *The Philosophy of the Revolution*. Nasser's nationalization move, in this perception, would aid him in achieving hegemony in the Arab and Islamic circles.[47] The press, too, as an unofficial arm of the government, reflected the prevailing opinion of Nasser. The seizure of the canal was interpreted as an attempt to conquer a "living space" stretching from the Persian Gulf to the Atlantic Ocean. If he succeeded, the press warned, he would "continue to weave his expansionist designs toward Jordan, Syria, and Iraq, which will facilitate the encirclement of Israel. And no force will then be able to prevent him from executing the rest of his plan to create the Egyptian Empire."[48]

This description implicitly suggests a comparison to Nazi ideology (living space = lebensraum). This analogy is not surprising in light of the frequent use by statesmen in Israel and the West of analogies to Mussolini and Hitler in describing Nasser's behavior.[49] For Ben-Gurion and other leaders who had experienced the events of World War II, this comparison was immediate and self-evident. The use of these terms engendered a delegitimation and dehumanization of the enemy, thereby laying the groundwork for the use of force against the Egyptian ruler. Israel had long wanted to overthrow and perhaps even eliminate him. The nationalization of the Suez Canal Company simply provided a convenient pretext for Ben-Gurion and his supporters to route him.[50]

While the 1956 Suez War ended with substantial gains for Israel, Nasser's regime survived. His political victory turned him into the recognized leader of the Arab world, with Pan-Arabism becoming the most prominent ideology. These developments symbolized the transition of the Israel-Arab conflict into a more radical phase, at least on the rhetorical level. The conflict had three aspects: a personal rivalry between Nasser and Ben-Gurion,[51] an ideological struggle between Egypt's anti-West and Israel's pro-West perceptions and between Egypt's Pan-Arabism and Israel's fear of remained "besieged" in an Arab "sea," and a political struggle between Egypt's quest for hegemony in the Arab world and Israel's quest for recognition as a player in the Middle Eastern arena. Each side's image of the other in all three aspects played an important role in the exacerbation of the conflict.

The nationalization and the war fixed Nasser's image in Israel. Particularly instructive was the reflection of this image in a document drawn up by Ben-Gurion outlining Israel's propaganda campaign. He emphasized the danger of a Soviet takeover of the Middle East through the Egyptian "dictator" and the Syrian president. If this takeover were not stopped soon by the overthrow of both rulers, Ben-Gurion wrote, "the entire African continent [would] fall into the hands of the Soviets in the near future." The Egyptian regime was described as "a fascist military dictatorship, which oppresses and impoverishes the Egyptian people in order to establish an inflated military force." The regime "inflames Muslim religious and Arab racist instincts in order to carry out expansionist ambitions to control the entire Muslim world," as described in *The Philosophy of the Revolution*. This booklet, Ben-Gurion asserted, "constitutes a kind of *Mein Kampf* of the Egyptian dictator." Inasmuch as the Egyptian regime cooperated with the Soviet Union, "any pretense of friendship toward the West is nothing but a deception." The last point of the document stated that while forces opposed to Nasser exist in the Arab world, "they need active assistance from the free world in order to get rid of these two malignant persons."[52] The document can be viewed as a formal expression of the diabolical and threatening image of Nasser in the eyes of the decision-making elite in Israel, an image that was not to change significantly until the day he died.

### The Heyday of Nasserism

In early 1957 a perception emerged of Nasser as representing a broader phenomenon, dubbed "Nasserism," which constituted a threat to the Western countries and Israel and therefore should be eliminated.[53] The use of the term *Nasserism*, widely adopted in the West, was not surprising, for Nasser's persona played the central role in this movement. So prominent was this persona that events unrelated to him were mistakenly attributed to him. Moreover, Nasserism and communism, from Israel's point of view, complemented one another.

A major event that reinforced the aggressive image of the Egyptian leader was the formation of the United Arab Republic—the unification of Egypt and Syria—on February 1, 1958. The Foreign Ministry viewed the unification as "the beginning of the fulfillment of Nasser's vision of an Arab empire signifying one nation, one government, and one leader—Nasser. . . . We view this as grave . . . due to the reinforcement it gives Nasser militarily and the tension it creates in the region as a consequence of the pressure that will emerge against the pro-Arab governments."[54] Ben-Gurion and Foreign Minister Golda Meir at the Knesset and the Labor Party meeting presented the same approach. Their mistrust of the Soviet Union and of Nasser was so deep that they were convinced that the unification was the product of an Egyptian-Soviet scheme.[55] With the formation of the UAR, the fear that a charismatic leader of the caliber of Bismarck or Ataturk would unify the Arabs appeared to be coming true in the form of Nasser.

The "aggressive" perception of the unification was echoed in the Israeli press and in the Western press translated into Hebrew. The UAR was seen as the realization of Nasser's vision of an Arab empire, as outlined in *The Philosophy of the Revolution,* the parallel version by the Egyptian dictator of Hitler's *Mein Kampf.* The press made frequent use of the term *Anschluss,* identified in the Western collective memory with the annexation of Austria by Hitler, in order to describe Egypt's domination over Syria.[56] Moreover, an editorial in the respected *Ha'aretz* viewed the unification as a first step on the road to the capture of Saudi Arabia, Iraq, Kuwait, and the other major oil states under the leadership of Nasser.[57] This position clearly reflected the thinking of the Foreign Ministry and the decision-making elite.[58]

Five months later, the military coup in Iraq came as a shock to Israeli decision makers; they were convinced that Nasser was behind it. The "fall" of Iraq was perceived as especially menacing because it was regarded as a major bastion of the West. Moreover, the Hashemite dynasty and Prime Minister Nuri al-Sa'id were perceived as natural allies of the West vis-à-vis Nasser's Pan-Arab trend. The fact that a large and strong country like Iraq had ostensibly "fallen" into Nasserist hands must serve as a warning to the weaker Arab states—Jordan and Lebanon. The threat was especially grave in light of the perception of Jordan as an artificial state, unstable and based to a large extent on King Husayn, while Lebanon was caught up, since May, in a civil war that threatened to alter the political structure and its Western orientation.

"At 7 a.m.," wrote Ben-Gurion in his diary, "a thunderbolt struck via the radio: a coup in Iraq." That evening, he summoned the heads of the security establishment in order to discuss the implications for Israel. The head of the military intelligence believed that the speed of the act "proved the existence of a well-organized link with the UAR." In his view, the restoration of the previous regime was impossible, and the coup, therefore, was liable to influence all the Arab countries. He concluded that "the UAR now controls not only the transport of oil but its sources as well. The emirates on the Persian shore will certainly be among the vanquished." A decision was made to take diplomatic steps, clarifying to the United States that "in light of the danger of the conquest of the entire Middle East, including Sudan, Saudi Arabia, and Libya, and the penetration of the Soviets, Persia and Turkey must be activated to suppress the revolutionaries in Iraq." At the same time, supreme efforts would be made to obtain heavy armaments, aircraft, and submarines.[59] At a Knesset committee Ben-Gurion viewed the coup as "the gravest development [in the region] since World War II." His analysis was especially pessimistic and without illusions, for "all the Arab states will be in Nasser's hands soon." Ben-Gurion viewed the developments in the Arab East as a clear parallel to Hitler:

> What happened with Nasser happened with Hitler. . . . No one paid attention that Hitler had already stated what he wanted. It was all in his book, the methods too. Hitler told the truth. No one believed him when he said it. The same is true for Nasser. Nasser put his cards on the table. He clearly stated what he wants in his booklet *The Philosophy of the Revolution*. He wants three things: He wants to be the ruler of the Arab nations, to be the head of Islam, and to be the dictator of the African continent. And he goes about this step by step. All that I have heard about him shows that he is not a fool, he is cunning as a snake. He knows how to speak to each person in his own language. If a pacifist, then Nasser becomes a total pacifist in his discussion with him. If he speaks with someone from the East, he will be a man of the East. If he speaks with a neutralist, he will be a neutralist.[60]

Foreign Minister Meir viewed the coup in Iraq as a scheme carefully and skillfully planned by the Egyptians. Her mistrust of Nasser was total: "In no way do I believe that Nasser is prepared to let us stay alive."[61] Using the same analogies used by Ben-Gurion, Meir emphasized that as Hitler was not satisfied after getting Austria and Czechoslovakia, so Nasser would not be satisfied with Iraq and Lebanon: "Nasser's ambitions are broader, and he won't stop attempting additional conquests until he gets everything he wants."[62]

The American and British decision to dispatch military forces both to Lebanon and Jordan naturally evoked satisfaction in Israel, which tried to extract political and military gains from granting air passage to planes bound for Jordan. Capitalizing on these events, Israel launched a propaganda campaign, which compared Nasserism and Hitler's nationalism. In order to illuminate this link, information was disseminated comparing the aspirations and methods of Nasserism with "Hitlerism."[63] Though this analogy served propaganda purposes, it genuinely reflected a sincere Israeli fear of encirclement. In a closed session of the ruling Mapai Party, Ben-Gurion said:

At this moment, there is a focus for the natural and justified, as well as for the unjustified (expansion and repression) national aspirations [of the Arabs], and that is Nasser. He has already succeeded in unifying two countries.... But not only has he united two states, he has become the hope for the unity in the entire Arab world. And one of its determined goals is the annihilation of Israel. There is no more committed or profound enemy of the existence of Israel in the entire Arab world than Nasser.... What he says is not very different from what Mussolini said and not entirely different even from what Hitler said, at least in relation to Israel and the Jews.... Not only this, but our security situation has become graver.... It is not outside the realm of possibility that Nasser will take control not only of Iraq but also of Jordan, Saudi Arabia, and perhaps Lebanon, so that we are liable to find ourselves surrounded not only by a number of enemies, as we have been all these years... but by a single enemy headed by a military dictatorship whose aim is to establish a large empire that will control the entire Arab world, the entire Muslim world, and the entire African continent, and toward this end—in time—annihilate Israel.[64]

An examination of Ben-Gurion's diary during this period shows that his negative perception of Nasser and the Arabs was ingrained and unshakable, as reflected in three meetings he held with Western diplomats who attempted to mediate between him and the Egyptian president. Their claims that Nasser was a moderate Arab leader, capable of negotiating with Israel, was quickly brushed aside by Ben-Gurion since he thought that Nasser was untrustworthy and unreliable.[65]

The Israeli perception of Nasser and Nasserism was shaped also by *The Philosophy of the Revolution*, which was widely circulated beginning in 1958. Particularly important was the attached postscript written by Benjamin Eliav, reflecting a common Israeli perception of Nasser and Nasserism. Eliav emphasized the role of Egypt in the Arab circle, which he called "a special, Nasser-style imperialism" that stemmed from the high rate of natural increase in Egypt, impelling "migration to the barren expanses of the other Arab countries or a takeover of the sources of oil." In his analysis, Egypt favored attaining its lebensraum through conquest, a product of the "hollow pride of a Levantine-style professional officers' corps, hatred of strangers and unbelievers, unacknowledged feelings of inferiority toward the West and the Christian world, and perhaps also the defeat in Palestine, which called for revenge." Eliav claimed that the idea of lebensraum "was fashioned by the Nazi German advisors who were based in Cairo before the coup and who also sought a release for [their] hatred of the West and hatred for Israel." In any event, he wrote, Nasser's ideological program and propaganda techniques highly resembled Nazi Germany. Nasser's goal was described as the conquest of the three spheres by means of Soviet aid. The UAR was perceived as the nucleus of Arab unity from the Atlantic Ocean to the Arab Gulf, which aimed to erase Lebanon, Israel, and Somalia. According to Eliav's interpretation, Israel was a "geographic wedge that must be eliminated physically as a condition for Egypt's takeover of the oil states and the barren expanses of the Arab states in Asia." In his view, Nasser was trying to play the role that Prussia played in unifying Germany, but he more resembled Perón, for the Arab world, like Latin America, was a conglomerate of varied and separate peoples. In actuality, however, due to geographic and demographic factors, Nasser resembled Hitler most of all. In summary, Eliav wrote, Israeli cooperation with the Arab world was conceivable, yet "not [with] the Nasserist [world], which pursue[d] a vain imperialist dream."[66]

## The Decline of Nasserism

The dismantling of the UAR in September 1961 and Egyptian involvement in Yemen in September 1962 signaled the beginning of the decline of Nasserism. Still, even when the Nasserist threat was ostensibly reduced, the Israeli decision makers continued to evaluate reality in terms of the old images. The reaction to the Tripartite Federation is a case in point. In February 1963, a group of Iraqi army officers who supported the Ba'th Party, under the leadership of 'Abd al-Salam 'Arif, took over the regime. A month later, a similar coup took place in Syria, bringing the Ba'th Party into power in Syria for the first time. The ascendance of two Ba'th regimes, both of which supported Arab unity ideologically and lacked legitimacy, revived the idea of unifying with Egypt. Intensive contacts between the three countries culminated in the Cairo Declaration of April 17, 1963, announcing the intention to establish a tripartite federation at the end of a twenty-month transition period. The contacts between the three, however, soon foundered due to lack of trust between Nasser and the Syrian Ba'th. Israel, however, continued to perceive reality in the context of its old images of Nasser and Nasserism, which were entrenched further during the period of the efforts to form the federation. Israel laid particular emphasis on the explicitly stated intention in the Cairo Declaration of liberating the Arab homeland from the Zionist danger.[67]

In early May, as the federation project seemed deadlocked, Israel's fears remained as potent as ever. Ben-Gurion, in an unusual step, decided to send a series of personal letters to "all the heads of state in the world" maintaining diplomatic relations with Israel so as to alert them to the danger facing the country. The letter emphasized that "this is the first time in our generation that a constitutional document by three states designates the annihilation of Israel as one of the primary, and perhaps the primary goal of the unification of Arab armies." It highlighted that in contrast to Israel's quest for peace, as stated in its Proclamation of Independence, "the aspiration to annihilate Israel has been harbored by the Arab rulers ever since the reestablishment of the State of Israel." Emphasizing the force of the Arab threat, Ben-Gurion made use of the familiar analogy of the Holocaust:

> Forty years ago, the Nazi ruler of Germany, Adolf Hitler, declared that one of the goals of his National-Socialist movement was to wipe out all the Jewish people in the world. The civilized world received this statement with equanimity and indifference perhaps because it was considered a demagogic posture. In World War II, when Hitler temporarily conquered most of Europe, he exterminated 6 million Jews. The rulers of Egypt, Syria, and Iraq perhaps do not know that the [Jewish] people in Israel do not stand in the same desperate and helpless situation that millions of Jews were in [in] the Nazi-occupied lands. The "liberation of Palestine" means, therefore, a horrific bloody war that could spread inestimably.[68]

At the same time, addressing the Knesset on the occasion of Israel's eleventh anniversary on May 6, Ben-Gurion repeated, almost verbatim, all of the arguments appearing in the letter. Moreover, the English version of the speech was sent to all Israeli foreign legations for propaganda (*hasbara*) purposes.[69] A month later, members of the ruling Mapai Party heard from Ben-Gurion a similar exposé. But he was not alone. In the main address delivered by Foreign Minister Meir, she said of Nasser:

> We are [only] one state with a little more than two million people. Against us, and I'm talking only of the Arab world, there are many states and tens of millions of people. . . . In my opinion, one of the most serious problems that we face is the question of how we assess Nasser. . . . He has imperialist ambitions even if this is called "unification." This [the federation] is in fact an attempt to dominate Syria and Iraq. . . . We hear threats against Israel day after day, every hour, and they have become a major theme in what will be the constitution of the Arab federation. . . . It has been said that unification is a necessary revolution, but for what? . . . It is a necessary revolution for a very "sacred" mission called "the liberation of Palestine," that is, throwing Israel into the sea. Seemingly, every friend and any person should be shocked. How can things like this be said in public? There is an element of escapism when we are told: "These are mere words. What do you care? He has said many times before that he wants to destroy you, so why get excited? Even if it is a serious and formal document [the 17 April declaration], you know that it is not important and not serious."

We must not cease explaining the naked truth: Nasser has a dispute not only with Israel.... No Arab state can sleep calmly, and none is free of the shadow of Nasser and his aspirations for domination hovering over it.[70]

On 16 June, Ben-Gurion suddenly decided to resign. Eight days later, Levi Eshkol presented a new government that was essentially a continuation of the previous one. In essence, Eshkol's nomination as prime minister did not bring any noteworthy change in the Israeli image of Nasser and Nasserism. True, Eshkol tended to express a more balanced and moderate position regarding the conflict. But like Ben-Gurion, he viewed the Arabs through the prism of the Second Aliyah: He believed that the Jews would rescue the Arabs from their backwardness; saw the Arabs as a united world; lacked knowledge about their culture; and feared an eventual total destruction at their hands. Eshkol's personal memories of the pogroms in Russia and the Holocaust served as the main screens through which reality was filtered. He viewed the work of German missile scientists in Egypt, the attempts to divert the Jordan River, the Arab summits' anti-Israeli resolutions, and the Palestinian guerilla infiltration as attempts to annihilate Israel. Nasser was seen as a Hitler-type ruler bent on putting the Arab world under Egyptian hegemony. Eshkol interpreted the fact that the years 1964–66 were relatively calm in military terms as justification for a quiet and massive preparation on the part of the Arabs for the final showdown against Israel. Thus, in spite of his known political moderation, no major differences existed between his and Ben-Gurion's images of Nasser.[71] The fact that many figures who surrounded Ben-Gurion remained in Eshkol's government meant that the general negative perception of Nasser and Nasserism hardly changed.[72]

Nasser's image of an untrustworthy leader discouraged Eshkol from responding favorably to the peaceful feelers transmitted to him by a high Egyptian official through Meir Amit, head of the Israeli Mossad, in February 1966. Although Eshkol was not initially averse to the offer, he was persuaded by Isser Harel, the previous head of the Mossad, and other politicians to treat it with skepticism and suspicion because of Nasser's known duplicity.[73]

In late 1966, Nasser's stature declined significantly. Eshkol told party members, "I think it is possible to say that the Nasser of today is not the same Nasser of the previous years in the Arab as well as in the world eyes. ... If we compare between Nasser's statements published in his notebook [*Philosophy*]—to be the leader of the African world, Asia [sic], and the Arabs—and his current position, we will have a true picture of the Egyptian ruler's position today."[74] This thinking, however, did not lead to a change in the Israeli assessment that Nasser and the Arab world were still basically aligned to annihilate Israel.[75] Unsurprisingly, therefore, the May–June crisis in 1967 was interpreted in this context, igniting old images. When, on May 26, Nasser called for "the destruction of Israel," the Foreign Ministry instructed its legations to make use of his speech and to emphasize the following points: "1. His [Nasser's] announcement of his intention to destroy a people constitutes additional testimony to Nasser as a disciple of Hitler; 2. To denounce the Nasser–Soviet Union collusion—the reincarnation of the Hitler-Stalin pact. Like Hitler, Nasser reconfigures socialism. Then, Stalin accused England and France of aggression against Hitler, just as today they sully Israel as aggressive."[76]

With the intensification of the Egyptian threats, the Foreign Ministry continued instructing its representatives to maintain an aggressive line: "Nasser's image [should be portrayed] as the Hitler of the Nile who has always sought hegemony in the Middle East. To fulfill this goal: 1. He was prepared to make use of the experience of Nazis and to be aided by war criminals; 2. He disseminated *Mein Kampf* and the *Protocols of the Elders of Zion* in Arabic translation, as well as varied anti-Jewish literature; 3. He openly announces his intention to annihilate Israel."[77]

Similar ideas appeared in Foreign Ministry guidelines regarding the publishing of articles in the Western press. These instructions included:

> 1. If the United States does not stand behind its word, we will face a new Munich. The only difference between Hitler and Nasser is that the former claimed, after each victory, that he has no further claims, while Nasser says explicitly that his goal is the annihilation of Israel. The events of the past two weeks have proven without a doubt that Nasser's declarations should be treated with the utmost seriousness and must not be dismissed as mere words, as was done at the time regarding Hitler. 2. The attempts to find compromises are nothing but illusions whose outcome is liable to resemble Memel, Danzig, Czechoslovakia, Austria, etc. 3. Israel, it should be strongly emphasized, does not and will not agree to be Czechoslovakia, even if the Western powers lean once again, as they have in the past, toward compromise.[78]

Moreover, a message sent by Eshkol to President Johnson on the first day of the war similarly emphasized the question of the annihilation of Israel and invoked the memory of the Holocaust.[79] All these communications must be viewed as an additional tool in Israel's political warfare against Egypt at a fateful moment, reflecting genuine fears of a besieged society. Yet the use of such terminology and historical analogies attests to the existence of entrenched stereotypical images of the Egyptian leader within the Israeli decision-making elite.

In essence, the war did not alter the image of Nasser in Israel. What did change was Israel's self-image in terms of its ability to face the Nasserist threat. It was now clear that even if his goals did not change, their realization would be postponed indefinitely. With Eshkol's death in March 1969, Golda Meir was elected prime minister. Although she came to Israel in the Third Aliyah (1921), she belonged to the Second Aliyah in terms of her worldview. Like Ben-Gurion and other leaders from the same generation, Meir viewed Nasser as Israel's most dangerous enemy. In her long career as foreign minister, as we have seen above, she frequently expressed negative views of Nasser—a reflection of her overall negative image of the Arabs.[80] Thus, it could hardly be expected that a radical change in her perception of Nasser would be forthcoming during her premiership.

On September 28, 1970, Nasser died of a heart attack. On that occasion, the retired Ben-Gurion told a French correspondent that Nasser was "a very talented person, very alert, . . . the best Arab statesman whom I met or whom I faced." In his opinion, Nasser's greatest fault was that "he did not know the boundary between reality and imagination. If he thought that something was necessary, he did not hesitate to lie. He lied to his people, and that is the gravest thing of all." The interview substantiated that Ben-Gurion's image of Nasser as an Arab Ataturk guided by *The Philosophy of the Revolution* had remained fixed in his mind until the very end of his life.[81]

## Conclusions

Although the Israeli-Arab conflict has been extensively researched, the study of images of the enemy in the decision-making process has largely been neglected. Since images are formed on the basis of a subjective perception of reality, the historian should not only seek facts and interpret them; he should also investigate how these facts are perceived cognitively by the decision makers. Although it is difficult to assess the exact impact of perceptions and images on the decision-making process, it is generally accepted that they are influential. This article concentrates on the analysis of images of the Arab enemy as perceived by the Israeli decision-making elite, focusing on the image of Nasser and Nasserism at the height of the Israeli-Arab conflict (1952–70).

Rethinking Nasserism in the Israeli context shows that beyond the "objective" academic attempts at interpreting this phenomenon, there exist subjective interpretations that are a product of societal perceptions and images. Although the hegemonic Israeli perception of Nasser and Nasserism had emerged in a specific historical context, this perception was based not necessarily on historical facts but on the way these facts were perceived and interpreted by decision makers and bureaucrats and later transmitted to the public through various state socialization agencies. Several conclusions emerge from this study with regard to the way Israelis perceived Nasser and Nasserism.

First, the political elite's image of Nasser was nearly uniform. No significant differences existed between the perceptions of the Right and the Left. Although it may be claimed that the Right consistently presented a more extreme stereotype of Nasser, it did share a common terminology with the labor parties of the Left. Nasser's diabolical image within the Israeli elite (and, as a result, within society at large) remained hegemonic throughout the period under review. Only the radical left—a marginal group in Israeli politics and society—challenged the validity of these perceptions. This group of intellectuals and politicians was organized around the monthly *New Outlook,* but its impact upon the decision makers and the public was negligible.[82]

Within the Israeli political elite, Ben-Gurion contributed decisively to the emergence of Nasser's diabolical image. The rise of Nasser as the spokesman of the Pan-Arab movement at this particular juncture in history (the mid-1950s) coincided with Ben-Gurion's deep-seated fears of the emergence of an Arab Ataturk or Bismarck who would unite the Arabs. In an age in which ideologies transformed societies and states, Ben-Gurion believed that a charismatic leader might resurrect the Arab nation. Although theoretically he could foresee the inevitability of this process, he feared that such a development would have dire consequences for young Israel. With the escalation of the Arab-Israeli conflict in the 1950s, Ben-Gurion's image of Nasser hardened and closed. Eventually, their mutual rivalry also assumed a personal character, tinged by a sense of distrust.

Nasser's negative image in Israel, however, was not acquired at the start of his political career. Foreign Minister Moshe Sharett, and to a certain extent Ben-Gurion, viewed the rise to power of a young generation in Egypt positively, hoping to find the army officers more moderate toward Israel than the previous regime, which faced severe problems of legitimacy. However, the execution of two convicted Jews who were involved in the Mishap and the Czech arms deal (both in 1955) entrenched the negative image of Nasser in the Israeli decision-making elite. Even Sharett's moderation was shaken in the aftermath of these events. Still, with his resignation in the summer of 1956, the only politician capable of challenging this monolithic perception disappeared from the political map.

Prime Minister Levi Eshkol and Foreign Minister Golda Meir were more (Meir) or less (Eshkol) typical representatives of the Ben-Gurion school, which tended to demonize Nasser and Nasserism. Not incidentally, the heads of the army, security, and intelligence apparatuses shared this rather monolithic view of Nasser. Understandably, in a state mentally and physically under Arab siege, the heads of these institutions played an important part in the decision-making process.

Second, the decision-making elite's negative image of Nasser was transferred to the public through various agents of socialization, including the press, radio, and the education system. Conceivably, this process led to the creation of a largely uniform image of Nasser in Jewish society. The elite succeeded in transmitting its worldview as a result of three factors. First, the resemblance in the positions of the Right and the Left, in contrast to most other political issues, delivered an unequivocal message to the public regarding the "correct" stance about Nasser. Second, the media—which felt as a legitimate tool of the elite—transmitted the elites' views. Third, the existence of a deep sense of being isolated and under siege that accompanied the small Jewish society ever since the establishment of the state of Israel magnified the image of the enemy, which was menacing enough due to its vehement rhetoric and its military activities against Israel.[83]

Third, the image of Nasser and Nasserism incorporated the use of several historical analogies: Nasser was generally compared to Hitler, with Mussolini, the Mufti Hajj Amin al-Husayni, and the biblical Amalek constituting other important analogies. Nasser's *Philosophy of the Revolution* was posited as paralleling Hitler's *Mein Kampf,* while the conciliatory policy of the West toward Nasser was compared to the appeasement by Chamberlain before World War II. Wide use was made of "Munich 1938," signifying Western appeasement; the use of this analogy was intended to signal that the adoption of a conciliatory approach to Nasser's aggressive policy would lead to a similar capitulation. In addition, frequent use was made of the memory of the Holocaust. Since Hitler was perceived as the most terrible enemy of all in the history of the Jewish people, and the Holocaust was perceived as the greatest Jewish tragedy, the comparison with the Egyptian ruler was intended to delegitimize and dehumanize him. The purpose of this analogy, which would also be used in the future (e.g., for depicting Yasser 'Arafat in the 1982 Lebanon War and Saddam Husayn during the 1990–91 Gulf War), was twofold: First, it lay the groundwork for the use of force should this become necessary. Second, it entrenched the conviction that the Jews in this conflict—just as in many other conflicts in the past— were the victims of unjustified aggression. The use of these analogies was not surprising because they were cognitively immediate: These episodes took place only a decade or two before Nasser's era, with Israel's decision-making generation having experienced that period personally, whether in the concentration camps themselves or following the events helplessly from outside. Similarly, Arab declarations of their intention to destroy Israel—even if they constituted rhetoric only—were reminiscent of the declarations of the Nazis.

Fourth, this diabolical image of Nasser also affected the way in which his regime was assessed. Within a short time, Nasser's image turned from that of a progressive leader of young officers, bent on revolutionizing his feudal society, to that of a dictator who was busy exploiting his people while his social and economic reforms were serving the elite rather than the masses. Moreover, his Arab policy was seen as part of Egypt's inevitable drive for attaining its "living space" (lebensraum). Even developments taking place on the periphery of the Arab world were often mistakenly related to Nasser.[84]

Finally, this study substantiates the assumption that images do not often change and that the receipt of new, contradictory information does not necessarily alter them. New information received in Israel about Nasser, his personality, and his actions—generally from a third party—did not lead Israeli leaders to change their view of him. Aiming at reducing their cognitive dissonance, they interpreted Nasser's statements and deeds in a way that tended to confirm preexisting beliefs. Messages that could be interpreted differently were often rejected or misinterpreted. In other words, the perception of Nasser by key decision makers was to a large extent "closed." As a result, a largely uniform perception of Nasser emerged within the Israeli political elite: aggressive, expansionist, despotic, and bent on destroying Israel. This static perception of the enemy—termed "cognitive freezing"—placed a barrier between Israel and Egypt that jeopardized chances for a successful dialogue.[85]

It is reasonable to assume that such images influenced the decision-making process, although to what extent is difficult to assess, as many variables affect this process. The historical narrative, however, seems to support the assumption that the decision makers' images of Nasser and Nasserism influenced their perception of reality, which, in turn, influenced how they arrived at their decisions. With this, such a conclusion must be supported by further research, both theoretical and empirical.

The demonization of Nasser by the Israeli decision-making elite was not necessarily a result of deliberate malice or folly. Rather, it stemmed from the leaders' worldview and was strengthened by the harsh reality besetting Israel. In this belligerent climate, which engulfed Israeli society during the Nasserite period, it was hardly conceivable that other interpretations challenging the hegemonic perception would prevail. We may surmise—though this should be substantiated by further academic research—that a similar process of demonization occurred on the Egyptian side of the conflict. Thus, the "war of images" has probably been no less significant and real than the actual "hot" war.

## Notes

1. For a definition of belief system, see Ole R. Holsti, "Cognitive Dynamics and Images of the Enemy," in John C. Farrell and Asa P. Smith, eds., *Image and Reality in World Politics* (New York: Columbia University Press, 1968), 18.

2. For definitions, see Michael Brecher, *The Foreign Policy System of Israel: Setting, Images, Process* (Oxford: Oxford University Press, 1972), 1–12. See esp. his research design on 4, fig. 2. See also Bruce Russett and Harvey Starr, *World Politics: A Menu for Choice*, 5th ed. (New York: W. H. Freeman, 1996), 246, 249; Robert R. Holt and Brett Silverstein, "On the Psychology of Enemy Images: Introduction and Overview," *Journal of Social Issues* 45, no. 2 (1989): 2; Alexander L. George, *Presidential Decisionmaking in Foreign Policy: The Effective Use of Information and Advice* (Boulder: Westview Press, 1980), chap. 3.

3. Herbert C. Kelman, "Social-Psychological Approaches to the Study of International Relations," in Kelman, ed., *International Behavior: A Social-Psychological Analysis* (New York: Holt, Rinehart and Winston, 1965), 24. See also Karl W. Deutsch and Richard L. Merritt, "Effects of Events on National and International Images," in ibid., 133. Their definition is based on Kenneth Boulding's classic study, *The Image* (Ann Arbor: University Press of Michigan, 1956), 5–6.

4. Deutsch and Merritt, "Effects of Events," 134. Michael Brecher used the terms *image* and *perception* interchangeably; see Brecher, *The Foreign Policy System of Israel*, 252.

5. George, *Presidential Decisionmaking*, 56–57. On "closed" and "open" images, see Milton Rokeach, *The Open and Closed Mind: Investigations into the Nature of Belief Systems and Personality Systems* (New York: Basic Books, 1966), chap. 2; Russett and Starr, *World Politics*, 49; Holsti, "Cognitive Dynamics and Images of the Enemy," 21.

6. Deborah Larson, *Origins of Containment: A Psychological Explanation* (Princeton: Princeton University Press, 1985), 51–52. For more on this theory, see Yaakov Y. I. Vertzberger, *The World in Their Minds: Information Processing, Cognition, and Perception in Foreign Policy Decisionmaking* (Stanford: Stanford University Press, 1990), 157; Susan T. Fiske, "Schema-Based versus Piecemeal Politics: A Patchwork Quilt, but Not a Blanket, of Evidence," in Richard R. Lau and David O. Sears, eds., *Political Cognition* (Hillsdale, N.J.: Erlbaum, 1986), 41–65; Susan T. Fiske and P. W. Linville, "What Does the Schema Concept Buy Us?" *Personality and Social Psychology Bulletin* 6 (1980): 543–57; Deborah Larson, "The Role of Belief Systems and Schemas in Foreign Policy Decision-Making," *Political Psychology* 15, no. 1 (1994): 17–33.

7. Larson, *Origins of Containment*, 54. For more on analogies in world politics, see Robert Beck, "Munich's Lessons Reconsidered," *International Security* 14, no. 2 (1989): 161–91; Yuen Foong Khong, *Analogies at War: Korea, Munich, Dien Bien*

*Phu, and the Vietnam Decision of 1965* (Princeton: Princeton University Press, 1992), 33–34.

8. Russett and Starr, *World Politics,* 252. See also Brett Silverstein, "Enemy Images: The Psychology of U.S. Attitudes and Cognitions Regarding the Soviet Union," *American Psychologist* 44, no. 6 (June 1989): 903. For a theory of enemy images, see Brett Silverstein and Catherine Flamenbaum, "Biases in the Perceptions and Cognitions of the Actions of Enemies," *Journal of Social Issues* 45, no. 2 (1989): 53–54.

9. See, e.g., Ralph K. White, "Images in the Context of International Conflict: Soviet Perceptions of the U.S. and the USSR," in Kelman, ed., *International Behavior,* 255.

10. Ralph K. White, *Nobody Wanted War: Misperception in Vietnam and Other Wars* (New York: Doubleday, 1968), 267. Harumi Bafu cited two examples of diabolism: the Western (and Israeli) perception of Nasser as a "megalomaniac" leader of the Arabs with delusions of grandeur, and the Arab perception of Israel's aggressive designs against the Arab world. See his "Demonizing the 'Other,'" in Robert S. Wistrich, ed., *Demonizing the Other: Anti-Semitism, Racism, and Xenophobia* (Amsterdam: Harwood Academic, 1999), 26.

11. See Richard K. Herrmann, "American Perceptions of Soviet Foreign Policy: Reconsidering Three Competing Perspectives," *Political Psychology* 6, no. 3 (1985): 377–81.

12. Frederich C. Barghoorn, *The Soviet Image of the United States: A Study in Distortion* (New York: Harcourt, 1950); Urie Bronfenbrenner, "The Mirror Image in Soviet-American Relations: A Social Psychologist's Report," *Journal of Social Issues* 17, no. 3 (1961): 45–56; Seweryn Bialer, "The Psychology of U.S.–Soviet Relations," *Political Psychology* 6, no. 3 (1985): 263–74; Cheichiro Yatani and Dana Bramel, "Trends and Patterns in Americans' Attitudes toward the Soviet Union," *Journal of Social Issues* 45, no. 2 (1989): 13–32.

13. See, e.g., Silverstein, "Enemy Images," 910; Ralph K. White, *Fearful Warriors: A Psychological Profile of U.S.–Soviet Relations* (New York: Free Press, 1984), 115, 129, 152–53. See esp. Ralph K. White, "Misperception in the Arab-Israeli Conflict," *Journal of Social Issues* 33, no. 1 (1977): 190–221. He attempted to apply certain universal psychological patterns of conflicts to the Arab-Israeli conflict, such as the diabolical-enemy image, the moral self-image, absence of empathy, and non-perception of situational factors influencing the enemy's behavior. Since White's research is limited in scope, some of his generalizations do not rest on solid ground. Moreover, his attempt to judge the validity of Arab and Israeli positions by differentiating between "what seems more true and what seems less true in the perceptions on each side" (213) is bound to raise doubts about his capability as an impartial observer.

14. Daniel Heradstveit, *Arab and Israeli Elite Perceptions* (Oslo: Universitetsforlaget, 1974), 22–23, 51–67, 102–4. See also Heradstveit, *The Arab-Israeli Conflict: Psychological Obstacles to Peace* (Oslo: Universitetsforlaget, 1979), 62.

15. Brecher, *The Foreign Policy System of Israel,* 552.

16. Ibid., 565.

17. Based on the early works of Karl Jung, Gustav Le Bon, and Sigmund Freud,

Bar-Tal argued that individuals who live in groups hold common beliefs that define their reality, not only as individuals but also as group members. Such reality becomes especially important when group members become aware that they share it. See Daniel Bar-Tal, "American Convictions about Conflictive USA–USSR Relations: A Case of Group Beliefs," in Stephen Worchel and Jeffry A. Simpson, eds., *Conflict between People and Groups: Causes, Processes, and Resolutions* (Chicago: Nelson-Hall, 1993), 194. See also Bar-Tal's more comprehensive analysis, *Group Beliefs: A Conception for Analyzing Group Structure, Processes, and Behavior* (New York: Springer, 1990), 36, and chap. 2 on the development of a historical perspective on shared beliefs.

18. For several studies that deal with these ideas, see Daniel Bar-Tal and Dikla Antebi, "Siege Mentality in Israel," *International Journal of Intercultural Relations* 16, no. 3 (1992): 251–76; Daniel Bar-Tal, "The Rocky Road toward Peace: Beliefs on Conflict in Israeli Textbooks," *Journal of Peace Research* 35, no. 6 (1998): 723–42; Raymond Cohen, *Culture and Conflict in Egyptian-Israeli Relations: A Dialogue of the Deaf* (Bloomington: Indiana University Press, 1990), 37–40; Brecher, *The Foreign Policy of Israel*, 549–54; Nurit Gertz, "The Few against the Many," *Jerusalem Quarterly*, no. 30 (1984), 94–104; Herbert C. Kelman, "Israelis and Palestinians: Psychological Prerequisites for Mutual Acceptance," *International Organization* 3 (1978): 172–73. See also Heradstveit, *Arab and Israeli Elite Perceptions*, 66, 107.

19. David Ben-Gurion Diary (BGD), 29 January 1949.

20. Ibid., April 27, 1949.

21. Ibid., October 23, 1950.

22. Zaki Shalom, *David Ben-Gurion, the State of Israel, and the Arab World, 1949–1956* (Sdeh Boker: Center for Ben-Gurion Heritage, 1995), 39 (Hebrew).

23. Quoted by Mordechai Bar-On, *The Gates of Gaza: Israel's Defense and Foreign Policy, 1955–1957* (Tel Aviv: 'Am Oved, 1992), 36 (Hebrew).

24. On these contacts, see Gabriel Sheffer, *Moshe Sharett: Biography of a Political Moderate* (Oxford: Oxford University Press, 1996), 654, 667–68, 758; Michael Oren, "Secret Egypt-Israel Peace Initiatives prior to the Suez Campaign," *Middle Eastern Studies* 26, no. 3 (1990): 353.

25. Interview with *L'Actualite*, reprinted in the Israeli daily *Ha'aretz* (Tel Aviv), October 12, 1970.

26. Quoted from Bar-On, *Gates of Gaza*, 36–37. For the source, see Gamal 'Abd al-Nasser, *The Philosophy of the Revolution* (Tel Aviv: Ma'archot, 1959), 54, 57, 59, 61 (Hebrew).

27. Gideon Rafael, *Destination Peace: Three Decades of Israeli Foreign Policy* (New York: Weidenfeld and Nicolson, 1981), 38. See also Sheffer, *Moshe Sharett*, 760–61.

28. Rafael, *Destination Peace*, 39; Moshe Sharett, *Personal Diary* (Tel Aviv: Ma'ariv, 1978), 689–90 (Hebrew), January 27, 1955; Sheffer, *Moshe Sharett*, 760–62; ISA (Israeli State Archive), FASC (Foreign Affairs and Security Committee), 7564/9, December 28, 1954.

29. Sharett, *Personal Diary*, 690, January 27, 1955. See also Sheffer, *Moshe*

*Sharett*, 776–77. Rafael wrote that "the reply was typical of Nasser's delaying tactics which he perfected over the years into an art." See Rafael, *Destination Peace*, 39.

30. Sharett, *Personal Diary*, 1056, June 13, 1955.

31. Sheffer, *Moshe Sharett*, 789, 811, 816.

32. Sharett, *Personal Diary*, 1518–19, June 28, 1955. See also ISA, FASC, 7564/12, September 6, 1955.

33. Sharett, *Personal Diary*, 1001, May 17, 1955; Sheffer, *Moshe Sharett*, 803.

34. ISA, FASC, 7564/12, September 6, 1955.

35. On the Baghdad Pact, see Elie Podeh, *The Quest for Hegemony in the Arab World: The Struggle over the Baghdad Pact* (Leiden: E. J. Brill, 1995).

36. See, e.g., Bar-On, *Gates of Gaza*, 112–13.

37. ISA, Foreign Ministry files (hereafter FM) 2384/21, Rafael to Sharett, September 29, 1955.

38. Shimon Peres, *The Next Phase* (Tel Aviv: 'Am HaSefer, 1965), 23, 37 (Hebrew); Bar-On, *Gates of Gaza*, 13–27; ISA, FASC, 7564/13, October 5, October 24, 1955. See also Ben-Gurion's view, 7564/13, 9 November 1955; 7564/14, November 30, 1955.

39. *Divrei HaKnesset* (Knesset Record) 19 (1955): 232–33 (Hebrew).

40. Ibid., 686–741. See also the discussions in ISA, FASC, 7564/14, November 30, 1955.

41. ISA, FASC, 7564/13, October 5, 1955; Sheffer, *Moshe Sharett*, 851.

42. *Divrei HaKnesset* 19 (1956): 680–81.

43. Quoted from Rafael, *Destination Peace*, 49. Notably, Rafael chose to highlight only the negative aspects of Nasser. The original document contained this passage as well: "The impression of the great majority of the people with whom Nasser meets is that he is honest, open, peace-loving, and devoted to the good of the people. A strong personality, solid in character. Arab or Asian personalities sometimes cite Nasser's cunning, but the general impression of his interlocutors is that he wins people over by his direct, matter-of-fact, and moderate approach to the problems presented to him. His knowledge of world problems is on the whole lacking and his education is limited." See ISA, FM 2454/2, "Nasser's Arguments and Tactics in Foreign Policy," January 10, 1956.

44. On Anderson's talks, see *Foreign Relations of the United States* (hereafter FRUS), 1955–57, vol. 15 (Washington, D.C.: Government Printing Office, 1989), 12–13, 16–19, 51–56, 58–60, 63–66, 68–70, 72–74, 122–24, 333–36.

45. On Meir's worldview and images, see Brecher, *The Foreign Policy System of Israel*, 302–11.

46. Quoted in Shalom, *David Ben-Gurion*, 23. For another example, see ibid., 22.

47. See, e.g., Golda Meir's comparison of Nasser with Hitler, ISA, FASC, 7565/4, September 11, 1956.

48. *Ma'ariv* (Tel Aviv), August 10, 1956.

49. BGD, July 29, 1956.

50. Bar-On, *Gates of Gaza*, 377; BGD, November 25, 1956.

51. See, e.g., an aside by Sharett in his diary: "I suddenly thought of Ben-Gurion's

urge to compete with Nasser in greatness—apparently it vexes him that he [Nasser] is thought of as great—he [Ben-Gurion] is always indignant about him." See *Personal Diary,* 1326, January 4, 1956.

52. BGD, November 10, 1956. See also Peres, *The Next Phase,* 40.

53. See, e.g., ISA, FM 3112/1, Eliav (Jerusalem) to Washington, March 27, 1957.

54. ISA, FM 3111/44, Foreign Ministry to all legations, January 31, 1958.

55. ISA, FASC, 7566/2, February 4, 1958. See also the session on February 19, 1958. See also Labor Party Archive (hereafter LPA), Mapai Foreign Affairs Committee, February 17, 1958.

56. *New York Times,* February 4, 1958. For this and other Western reports, see ISA, FM 3111/44.

57. *Ha'aretz,* February 2, 1958. See also ibid., February 4, 7, 9; March 14, 1958.

58. ISA, FM 3111/44, briefing by Yosef Nachmias, deputy director of the Ministry, February 18, 1958; 3752/9, a paper by the information department, February 26, 1958.

59. BGD, July 14, 17, 1958. It was later revealed that Ben-Gurion proposed to Dulles the entry of Persian and Turkish troops into Iraq. See ISA, FM 3294/19, Herzog to Harman, February 8, 1961.

60. ISA, FASC, 7566/3, July 16, 1958.

61. Ibid., July 22, 1958.

62. Ibid., August 27, 1958.

63. ISA, FM, 3744/11, Foreign Ministry to all legations, July 21, 1958.

64. Labor Party Archive (LPA), Mapai Foreign and Security Committee, file 2-23-1958-74, September 11, 1958. See also BGD, September 13, 1958.

65. On these meetings, see ibid., September 13, 18, 30, 1958.

66. Binyameen Eliav, "Epilogue," in Nasser, *The Philosophy of the Revolution,* 73–110. Eliav was a former revisionist who had shifted to labor positions in the 1940s, so that to a large extent he represented the center trend in Jewish society. Between 1957 and 1960 he served as a political commentator with "Kol Israel" (The voice of Israel). His broadcasts reflected a similar approach to Nasser as that of his commentary in the book. I am grateful to his daughter, Prof. Miriam Eliav-Faldun, for allowing me to read the transcripts of these broadcasts.

67. The exact wording was "Unification is a revolution because it is closely tied to the question of Palestine and the national obligation to liberate it." See Radio Cairo, BBC/World British Broadcasts/Middle East, no. 1226, April 18, 1963, 7. On this episode, see Elie Podeh, "To Unite or Not to Unite; That Is *Not* the Question: The 1963 Tripartite Unity Talks Reassessed," *Middle Eastern Studies.* 39, no. 1 (2003): 150-85.

68. ISA, FM 4315/5, May 9, 1963; FM 2454/17, 9 May 1963.

69. ISA, FM 2454/17, 6 May 1963.

70. LPA, Central Committee files, 6 June 1963, 2-23-1963-84.

71. Eshkol did not frequently refer to the Arabs in his speeches and interviews. He usually dealt with immigration, settlement, and economic issues. For some of his statements regarding the conflict, see Levi Eshkol, *Bema'aleh Haderekh* (Tel Aviv: Ayanot, 1965), 269–318 (Hebrew). See also Harman to Bitan, January 30, 1965;

April 20, 1965, ISA, FM 4317/9. For a brief analysis of his images, see Brecher, *The Foreign Policy System of Israel,* 291-302.

72. Eshkol himself stated that "the new government is a government of continuity," quoted in Brecher, *The Foreign Policy System of Israel,* 296. For an assessment of Eshkol's governments, see Avi Shlaim, *The Iron Wall: Israel and the Arab World* (New York: W. W. Norton, 2000), 220-25. One exception was Abba Eban, who replaced Golda Meir as foreign minister in November 1965. See ibid., 224.

73. On this episode, see Meir Amit, *Head On* (Tel Aviv: Hed Artzi, 1999), 204-28 (Hebrew); Zaki Shalom, "A Missed Opportunity? The Attempt to Form Direct Contacts between Israel and Egypt prior to the Six Day War," *Hatzionut* 22 (2001): 321-53 (Hebrew).

74. LPA, Central Committee Files, 22 December 1966, 2-23-1966-91.

75. See the discussion at Amit's house with representatives from the Mossad, army intelligence, Foreign Ministry, and academia, 27 November 1967, Shalom, "A Missed Opportunity?" 332-53.

76. ISA, FM 6444/5, Ilan to legations, May 28, 1967.

77. ISA, FM 6444/5, May 31, 1967.

78. ISA, FM 6444/6, June 2, 1967.

79. ISA, FM 4091/23, Eshkol to Johnson, June 5, 1967.

80. Brecher, *The Foreign Policy System of Israel,* 302. For more on her worldview, see 302-11; Golda Meir, *My Life* (London: Steimatzky, 1977), chaps. 10 and 12.

81. Interview with Philippe Ganier-Raymond as it appeared in *L'Actualite,* October 6, 1970. Published in Hebrew in *Ha'aretz,* October 12, 1970.

82. The *New Outlook* was first published in July 1957. Its articles were devoid of any negative or stereotypical images of the enemy in general (and of Nasser in particular), usually portraying current events in a factual manner. For a critical voice on the "objective" nature of the monthly, see Y. Zofeh, "Nasser—Aggressor or Peace-Lover?" *New Outlook* 3, no. 9 (September 1960): 31-34; and the reply, Ze'ev Katz, "Whose Disservice to Peace?" ibid., 35-39.

83. The way in which Nasser and Nasserism were depicted in the media, for example, should be the basis for further systematic study. A cursory reading of the leading Israeli newspapers, *Ha'aretz, Yedi'ot Ahronot,* and *Ma'ariv,* substantiates this argument.

84. See esp. Eliav's epilogue in Nasser, *The Philosophy of the Revolution,* 73-110. This kind of flawed assessment even pervaded academic research. See the references in Joel Beinin, "Knowing Your Enemy, Knowing Your Ally: The Arabists of Hashomer Hatzair (Mapam)," *Social Text* 28 (1991): 100-121.

85. For the use of the term *cognitive freezing,* see Nadim N. Rouhana and Daniel Bar-Tal, "Psychological Dynamics of Intractable Ethonational Conflicts: The Israeli-Palestinian Case," *American Psychologist* 53, no. 7 (1998): 766.

# 3

## History, Politics, and Collective Memory

The Nasserist Legacy in Mubarak's Egypt

Meir Hatina

### Introduction

Under Mubarak, the Nasserist legacy in Egypt has become simply another chapter in its national history. Having enjoyed the status of an official ideology in the mid-twentieth century, Nasserism has been reduced to a dissident ideology, battling for a place of honor in the Egyptian collective memory at the end of the century.[1] For half of Egypt's population (67.9 million by mid-2000)[2]—that is, anyone below the age of twenty—the July 1952 Revolution is a distant episode. Its main spokesman, the Nasserist Party, which joined the legal opposition in 1992, has little influence in national politics.

Nasserism has lost much of its glamour over the years, due not least to Nasser's two successors, Anwar al-Sadat and Husni Mubarak, both of whom turned their backs on the revolutionary legacy. Sadat initiated economic and political openness, reinforced the status of Islam, linked Egypt's future to the West, and signed a peace treaty with Israel.[3] These processes were entrenched by Mubarak, who, in addition, positioned himself as "godfather" in the peace process between Israel and its neighbors.[4] The shift from confrontation to coexistence with Israel meant rechanneling the thrust of the Egyptian polity and constructing a new domestic agenda. Although official and symbolic linkage to the revolution was preserved, state policies in fact reflected a continuous process of de-Nasserization.[5]

Nonetheless, the legacy has survived in the collective memory, which constitutes the pool of the social and cultural experiences and often serves as a political device in promoting competing interpretations and interests.[6] Collective memory, according to the historian John Bodnar, provides perspective and authenticity to views articulated in the present about fundamental issues affecting society.[7] In the Egyptian context, Nasserism offers a historical prism for interpreting the country's present experience. Like any myth appropriated from its archaic time frame, it makes its presence felt in relation to abiding concerns which the political structure was unable to resolve.[8]

Due to its comprehensive character, Nasserism embraces an endless reservoir of heroic episodes side by side with gloomy defeats, and achievements together with failures. This diverse pool of experiences allows all who deal with the revolutionary legacy—whether as opponents or advocates—to construct different narratives in support of their particular political agendas. Most of these writers wear two hats, intellectual and political, as commentators and party members, a symbiosis which blurs the boundaries between analysis and politics. Some belong to the younger generation, who drifted into political channels of dissent in order to express their hopes and desires. In this sense, the Nasserist debate is not over history alone but mainly over the struggle to mold national behavior.[9] This struggle is conducted mainly, but not exclusively, in the print media, in books and articles, as well as in photographs and cartoons. Cartoons constitute a central element of political commentary in the Arab press. Usually humorous in tone, cartoons are a supplementary device to the written text in presenting counterinterpretations of reality.[10] The contested discourse of Nasserism is also waged in television, in plays, and in films. These visual media function as effective transmitters of ideas and symbols to the less educated strata, who form a vital constituency for political mobilization.[11]

The contest over shaping Egyptian national history is typically conducted through polemics and often by mutual mudslinging, generating lively public interest that comes to a head on the annual commemorative day of the revolution, July 23. Public debate at that time becomes intense, demonstrating the diversity and divisions in Egypt's political culture. In examining the public debate on Nasserism and identifying its key players during the 1980s and 1990s, this article reveals the abiding link between history and politics, between past and present.

### The Anti-Nasserist Narrative: Revolution on Trial

The anti-Nasserist narrative was characterized by the delegitimization and demonization of the July Revolution. Its standard-bearers belonged to the liberal wing of Egypt's ideological spectrum,[12] which returned to the public arena during the 1970s after having been divested of its political and cultural influence during the revolution. Many of these spokespersons were prerevolutionary veterans, but others were younger activists whose disdain for

Nasserism was shaped in the era of economic and political openness initiated by Sadat and Mubarak and by interaction with the West.

The main political sponsors of the anti-Nasserist narrative were the Liberal Party (al-Ahrar), established in 1976, and, even more so, the New Wafd Party, established in 1978. The latter saw itself as the successor to the old Wafd and thus as an authentic representative of the quest for parliamentary democracy. The composition of the New Wafd Party consisted of a coalition of professionals and landowners. Lawyers were a prominent group, many of whom were born in the agrarian provinces and successfully transplanted to the urban westernized Cairene environment. Ideological and historical continuity with the old Wafd was provided by veteran party leaders headed by Fu'ad Saraj al-Din, 'Abd al-Fatah Hasan, and Ibrahim Faraj, who had played a major role in national politics in the prerevolutionary period.[13] The identification with the historic Wafd involved protecting its legacy from distortion along with renewing its claim to political leadership. Primary strategies employed included exposing the darker aspects of the revolutionary regime and defaming Mubarak's reign by linking it to the defects of Nasserism.

The anti-Nasserist narrative brimmed with resentment against the revolution, which, it held, had not only eliminated constitutional government and suppressed pluralistic civic culture, but had systematically tarnished the image of the Wafd contribution to Egypt in the collective memory. This derogation, the Nasserist critics claimed, distorted the depiction of all aspects of life in the old regime. The revolution had portrayed Egypt as a poverty-stricken nation afflicted with anarchy and exploitation. Its political parties, interested only in their own survival, were perceived as clearly unable to promote the national struggle for freedom. National resources were controlled by a small group. Parliamentary life was devoid of real content, and none of the elected parliaments completed its constitutional term in office.[14]

The anti-Nasserist writers posited a counterhistory, offering an alternative portrait of the political and social order to the established one. They argued that Egypt on the eve of the revolution was in no way a lifeless entity. It had never surrendered to the tyranny of the Crown and had constantly pursued independence from the British ever since the 1919 Revolt. The period led by the Wafd, Nasserist critics claimed, was one of democracy, freedom of thought, and confidence in the capacity of the Egyptian people for regeneration. These achievements were squandered by the revolution, which revoked the constitution and dismantled the political parties.[15] The revolution indeed gained wide public support, but only in its initial phase. The Egyptians believed that it was designed to solve a problematic situation rather than revoke essential attributes of democracy, such as parliamentary representation and freedom of the press. However, instead of returning to their military camps and devoting themselves to the task of protecting national security, the Free Officers appropriated the people's right to select their own leaders and established a government that appeared to be democratic but was in fact tyrannical.[16]

Nasserist critics blamed most of the defects of Egyptian society on this tyrannical rule, evident until the present day. The defects included discouraging the people from involvement in the political process, growing power of the Islamist opposition, deepening sectarian gulfs, rising crime, and the collapse of social morality.[17] The revolutionary regime's ill-conceived agenda also produced unfortunate results. Its 1952 Agrarian Reform and nationalization laws destroyed any chance for the revival of Egyptian agriculture and industry. It deterred capital investment by the private sector and transformed the public sector into a governmental stronghold controlled by political rather than economic considerations.[18] Pan-Arabism replaced Nile Valley unity with a fictitious Arab unity, which eroded national resources. The illusion of Arab unity began to disintegrate when Syria left the United Arab Republic (UAR) in September 1961, and it collapsed completely in the June 1967 War.[19] Ultimately, the revolution proved to be a deception led by a dictator who sought personal prestige in the national pantheon at the expense of the interests of the Egyptian people.[20] Wafdist journalist Muhmud 'Abd al-Mun'im Murad noted cynically that Nasser's funeral procession in 1970 symbolized the burial of the homeland after suffering under a megalomaniac defeated conqueror.[21] Nagib Mahfuz observed that the course of Egyptian history could have changed for the better if only Nasser and the revolution had joined the Wafd Party instead of suppressing it.[22]

In addition to depicting the July Revolution as tyrannical and impotent, the anti-Nasserist narrative either appropriated or tarnished Nasserist myths. For example, critics of Nasserism displayed the British withdrawal from Egypt, agrarian reform, social justice, assertive nonalignment, and Egypt's relationship with the Soviet Union as achievements of the prerevolutionary Wafd. Other myths were tarnished, specifically Nasser's decision to nationalize the Suez Canal Company in 1956. Both strategies were designed to rehabilitate and enhance the heritage of the Wafd, while downplaying that of Nasserism in modern Egyptian history.

Various writers, including Jamal Badawi, Salah 'Aqqad, Mahmud 'Abd al-Mun'im Murad, and 'Abd al-'Azim Ramadan, challenged the entrenched claim that the revolution was responsible for the end of the British occupation. In their historical version, British involvement in Egyptian affairs had ended a number of years prior to the revolution. Its last manifestation was in the events of February 1942, where a compliant government was put in power under British pressure. After the end of World War II, British influence in the Middle East declined. The role of the British ambassador was no greater than that of any other ambassador in Cairo. Moreover, the British withdrew their troops from the streets of Cairo and other cities in 1947, under the Nuqrashi Wafdist government, having learned their lesson during the rioting that broke out under the Sidqy government in 1946. Renewed rioting in 1951 in the Suez cities after the abolition of the 1936 Anglo-Egyptian treaty also hastened the British withdrawal. In fact, were it not for the revolution, the entire occupation would have ended in 1956, the Nasserist critics argued.[23]

On the subject of the 1952 Agrarian Reform, the anti-Nasserist discourse noted that this plan had been introduced in 1946 at a large economic conference in Cairo with the aim of redistributing landownership and shifting state resources to industrialization. The reform was included in the Wafd's platform in September 1952, two months after the revolution. The depiction of the Wafd as opposed to agrarian reform, therefore, was merely a device to justify the breakup of the party because it constituted a threat to the revolutionary regime.[24]

The anti-Nasserist historiography cultivated by the neo-Wafdists also positioned the Wafd's record in the area of social justice as having preceded that of the revolutionary regime. Ever since its establishment in 1919, according to this account, the Wafd had two primary bases of support: the laborers and the *fellahin*. The establishment of unions and government hospitals in the cities and villages, as well as the promotion of welfare and labor legislation, were prominent components of the Wafd's national agenda during the 1940s. Free and compulsory education was introduced in a two-stage legislative program: elementary education under the government of 1942–44 and high school education under the government of 1951–52.[25] Two additional achievements were attributed to the Wafd in this account: assertive nonalignment, implemented by the last Wafd government during the Korean War, in advance even of India, and relations with the USSR, initiated by Prime Minister Mustafa Nahhas as early as 1943. The Czech-Egyptian arms deal of September 1955 was also portrayed as the product of the Wafd's earlier efforts to obtain arms from the Eastern Bloc.[26]

While this strategy of historical expropriation subverted the revolutionary record by crediting the Wafd with originating positive innovations, it also pointed to the Nasserist regime as primarily responsible for the poor implementation of them. One example is the issue of the Agrarian Reform, whose inflexible and hasty enforcement led to a reduction in land cultivation and the subsequent migration of fellahin to the cities. Another example is the relationship with the USSR, which deteriorated into a one-sided dependency.[27]

Yet another strategy used by Nasserist critics was the tarnishing of existing revolutionary myths, especially the nationalization of the Suez Canal

Company in 1956. This issue rose to the forefront of public discourse in 1996, with the release of the film *Nasser 56,* describing the events leading up to the nationalization of the Suez Canal.[28] As large crowds, including many young people, thronged to the cinemas to see it, the Egyptian public was swept off its feet by nostalgia for a heroic past. The film quickly turned into a vehicle for political dispute and became another element in the struggle over molding Egypt's national history. Pro-Nasserists sought to reinforce the association between the cinematographic account and historic reality, while anti-Nasserists relegated the significance of the film to the domain of art, depicting it as a fictionalized account far removed from truth. An especially vocal exponent of the latter group was the prominent historian and commentator ʿAbd al-ʿAzim Ramadan.[29] In a series of articles published in *Al-Wafd,* subsequently compiled in a book published in 2000, Ramadan criticized the Nasser cult, recommending that the public view its heroes as erring, imperfect human beings, not as saints. The events leading up to the nationalization of the Suez Canal Company, as other events during Nasser's rule, Ramadan wrote, showed Nasser to be far from a rational, responsible leader. He was a dictator who removed his rivals by every means at his disposal and systematically harassed the opposition. His decision to nationalize the Suez Canal was his alone, made without political or military consultation.[30]

Admittedly, nationalization was a goal of supreme significance and was featured in Egypt's declaration of independence, yet the decision was based on misconceptions, Ramadan argued. Nasser ruled out any possibility that the Western powers would use force or declare war in opposition to it. France, he was convinced, would refrain from military action against Egypt because it was preoccupied with Algiers; likewise so with Britain because of its desire to maintain good relations with the Arab world. He also believed that Britain and the United States would restrain Israel from using force. Even after Israel launched its attack against Egypt in the Sinai, and despite warnings by France and Britain to withdraw Egyptian troops from the Canal area, Nasser remained captive to his misconceptions. He realized his mistake only when British and French planes actually appeared in the skies of Sinai and Cairo.[31]

The source of all this evil, Ramadan noted, was Nasser's inclination to solitary decision making—a mode of operation that had faded from world politics during the late nineteenth century, yet was retained in the Arab world. Although Nasser sought justice, he behaved rashly and endangered Egypt's independence by inviting the possible return of the British occupation. Comparing him with a current leader, Saddam Husayn, Ramadan pointed out that even though justice was not one of the Iraqi leader's considerations in invading Kuwait in 1990, the syndrome was similar: solitary decision making whose price was paid by the people in the form of human, military, and economic losses.[32]

Nasser's rash decision in 1956, Ramadan concluded, cost Egypt a military defeat and loss of lives, while providing the small state of Israel with an opportunity to conquer significant areas of the Sinai. In return for Israel's withdrawal of its troops, it was granted permission to traverse the Straits of Tiran, which contributed to its aggrandizement.[33] The quality of a government may be measured by how it learns its lessons, Ramadan observed. However, the revolutionary regime led by the same individual—Nasser—repeated its mistakes when it decided to expel the international peacekeeping force from the Sinai Peninsula and close the Straits of Tiran in 1967. Both decisions led to a state of war with Israel, despite the lack of military preparedness. Consequently, at Nasser's death in September 1970, all of Sinai, the Gaza Strip, the West Bank, and the Golan Heights were in Israeli hands. Nasser's mistakes of 1956 and 1967 reversed the expectation that the era of national independence would bear all the anticipated fruit.[34] Nevertheless, Ramadan acknowledged, the power of the written word in disclosing historic truths is inferior in comparison to that of the cinematographic image. Thus, despite his rash decisions, Nasser would continue to be acclaimed as a hero and a revolutionary.[35]

Two other anti-Nasserists, Anis Mansur and Nagib Mahfuz, both of whom experienced the revolutionary period personally, shared Ramadan's frustration.[36] Both discussed the unbalanced attitude of the Egyptian people toward Nasser as compared with his successor, Sadat. On the one hand, Nasser, who had lost homeland territories to Israel and had offended the honor of Egypt and the Arabs, was still perceived as a hero in Egyptian eyes. On the other hand, Sadat, who had reclaimed lands, honor, and prestige, remained a traitor.[37] Offering a psychological explanation for this uneven perception, Mansur noted that people tend to adulate leaders who are similar to themselves, both in their strengths and weaknesses. Nasser's failures evoke compassion and empathy, whereas Sadat is judged more harshly precisely because of his numerous successes. The cult of Nasser, clearly reflected in the public response to *Nasser 56*, may thus be evidence of a flawed willingness among the Egyptian people to follow their leaders blindly.[38]

Another possible explanation for the cult of Nasser, not mentioned by these writers, may have to do with the dreary reality of Egyptian society and its unresolved socioeconomic problems. Nasserism, as a myth of national liberation and social justice, bruised as it may be, did manage to evoke pride and confidence. Conceivably, this myth might have accounted for the lip service paid to the revolutionary legacy by the Sadat and Mubarak governments, despite their adoption of other policies in practice.

While Ramadan, Mansur, and Mahfuz expressed reservations about sev-

"Indeed, sir, the pictures are life-size!" (*Al-Ahrar*, July 17, 1994). The intent is to protest the diminishment of Sadat's importance. He is shown as almost nothing next to Nasser.

Cover illustration of Anis Mansur's book *'Abd al-Nasir* (4th ed., Cairo: al-Maktab al-Misri al-Hadith, 1994). The cartoon illustrates the Nasser worship in Egypt despite his repressive policies.

eral of Sadat's and Mubarak's policies—such as their muted response to the granting of political freedom and their ambivalence regarding the Islamic phenomenon—these writers carefully refrained from identifying the two regimes with the ills of the revolution.[39] In this they represented a minority position in the anti-Nasserist narrative. The leaders of this camp, including such Wafdist writers as Lam'i al-Muti'i, Muhammad 'Asfur, and 'Izzat Saqir, emphasized the continuity between Nasser and his successors in an effort to undermine Sadat's and Mubarak's political credibility. Extrapolating events from the past, these writers tailored their analysis of historic events to current political ends. The extremists among them claimed that the existing political order was "the same forum in a different garb," its essentially authoritarian nature unchanged.[40]

Less critical writers acknowledged that Mubarak had ended the single-party system and abolished constraints on freedom of speech, yet stressed that authentic democracy was still a distant goal. They pointed to the need to conduct free and honest elections, to ensure equality in resource allocation and state funding of parties, and to revoke the constitutional provision, retained from the Nasserist era, of assigning half the parliamentary seats to laborers and fellahin. Progress on the road to democracy would dissociate Mubarak's government from the Nasserist legacy of failures; a diversion from this path would only tarnish Mubarak's rule by the inevitability of conspiracies, torture, and corruption.[41] This sharp criticism of Mubarak's rule ever since his advent to power in October 1981 has further demonstrated the relatively high quality of public discourse in Egypt, especially as compared with other Arab states. While freedom of political action was restricted, freedom of expression was extensive, providing a safe device for venting popular dissatisfaction. The display of tolerance toward opposition critics in a more pluralistic and cosmopolitan society thus became an essential component of the legitimacy of the regime.

Mubarak's policy, which turned its back on the Nasserist legacy in almost every area, served to facilitate the anti-Nasserist cause. Mubarak introduced structural economic reforms, privatized public corporations, and legislated incentives for local and foreign capital investments.[42] Even the grand ethos of the July Revolution—the September 1952 Agrarian Reform—was set aside in a new Land Act (Act 96, 1992), which canceled the stringent supervision over land-lease fees that Nasser had set up. The act allowed landowners to determine leasing fees according to market prices. Although the government conceived this law as a breakthrough to stimulate economic development, fellahin associations and left-wing parties perceived it as a means to dislodge the fellahin from their land in the interests of wealthy landowners.[43] Overall, the government's economic policy was described by Nasserist adversaries as an admission by the state of the defects of the revolution,⁴⁴ and as such provided added stimulus to the efforts of the anti-Nasserists to promote their own political agenda.

## The Nasserist Narrative: A Political Culture on the Defensive

The focused anti-Nasserist campaign and Mubarak's de facto dissociation from the revolutionary heritage put Nasserism's adherents on the defensive. Most were identified with the Arab Democratic Nasserist Party or with the National Progressive Unionist Grouping (NPUG), both of which were in the parliamentary opposition. The Nasserist Party emerged unofficially in early 1987 and was legalized by court rule in 1992. Its members were drawn from the Nasserists' second rank, led by Farid 'Abd al-Karim and later by Diya' al-Din Da'ud. The NPUG, legalized in 1986, drew its membership from the middle-class intelligentsia, which included Nasserist elements, leftist students, and workers. The party leader was Khalid Muhi al-Din, one of the original Free Officers who held Marxist views.⁴⁵

The neo-Nasserists used every medium open to the opposition in the Mubarak era to promote their political philosophy, most notably their weekly organs, *Al-'Arabi* and *Al-Ahali*.⁴⁶ Still, they found themselves in an inferior position in the struggle over the Egyptian collective memory. A review of their major arguments reveals a deep ideological conviction in the revolution side by side with a considerable apologetic element. Their strategy was a mirror image of that of their rivals: They delegitimized the prerevolutionary period, attacked the wholesale dismissal of Nasserism, and praised its achievements as an antithesis to the existing order. Their proudest banner was the revolution's achievements in the realm of social justice; their Achilles' heel was its suppression of democracy.

The most outstanding exponent of the Nasserist narrative was Muhammad Hasanayn Haykal, who also embodied the revolutionary heritage personally as Nasser's closest aid and the editor in chief of the state-sponsored dailies *Al-Akhbar* and *Al-Ahram*.⁴⁷ Haykal branded as a priori false any attempt to identify the Nasserist era with exploitation and corruption. He contended that such efforts weakened the foundations of every succeeding government. In his view, sweeping condemnations leave no one free of blame, especially in light of the steps taken by Nasser's successors, Sadat and Mubarak, to modify, clarify, and supplement the revolutionary experiment without canceling its essence. Any attempt to represent the post-Nasser era as a new or separate revolution appropriates Sadat and Mubarak's greatest assets: agrarian reform, the struggle against imperialism, the advancement of industrialization, the completion of the Aswan High Dam, and the promotion of Arab unity.⁴⁸ By emphasizing historic continuity, Haykal cautioned, those who renounce the revolution deny a fundamental element of their own legitimacy. Haykal acknowledged that Nasser had erred in various fields, noting that he had admitted, for example, his responsibility for the military defeat in the June 1967 War. However, on balance, Haykal held, despite the internal strife and international conspiracies, the good achieved in the Nasserist era outweighed the bad.[49]

In his published work, Haykal laid out the parameters of the defense of the Nasserist narrative, which were followed by other writers, such as Jalal 'Arif, 'Abd al-Halim Qandil, Muhammad Shuman, Lutfi Wakid, and Muhammad Sayyid Ahmad. They emphasized that the revolution continued to nurture the hopes of millions of Egyptians for freedom, justice, and honor. Although the path was arduous, painful, and paved with war and defeat, this was a direct consequence of the elevated goals that the revolution set for itself, including the struggle for national independence, social equality, and Arab unity. However, the achievements of the revolution in these areas, Nasserist advocates asserted, were eroded after Nasser's death and disappeared completely under Mubarak.[50] During Mubarak's tenure, Egypt had fallen hostage to international financial institutions and had retreated in the face of American and Israeli dictates. This resulted in the neglect of society's deprived strata, a rise in unemployment, and the sale of Egypt's public sector to foreign corporations, thereby further widening socioeconomic gaps. Arab unity, too, had been reduced to a phrase devoid of content due to the disputes and divisions that reached a climax in the Gulf crisis of 1990–91.[51]

Although the Nasserists acknowledged Mubarak's achievements in promoting national projects, they held that he lacked a defined and decisive policy that would lead the country from one stage of progress to the next. This, they said, was the main difference between Nasser's revolutionary strategy and Mubarak's quest for stability. Revolution aims to reshape society and achieve the impossible; stability cools national fervor and promotes social stagnation.[52]

In harnessing the revolutionary legacy to condemn the existing order, the Nasserists focused on economic and social issues, namely, the welfare and quality of life of the people, rather than political issues, specifically democracy. Their appeal for democratic governance, which had been suppressed by the revolution, lacked conviction, and their defense of the revolution on this issue was apologetic in nature. Nasser, they said, believed in political freedom, yet made it contingent on the attainment of social equity. He held that the establishment of social justice and the removal of divisions between rich and poor were essential before popular democracy could be achieved. Agrarian reform, nationalization, public education, and equal opportunity in employment were crucial to the creation of a new social fabric that would act as a catalyst in bringing about political freedom.[53]

However, the Nasserists had difficulty in explaining the fact that even

"Your revolution happened a long time ago. Now it is our revolution!" (*Al-Ahali*, July 22, 1992). The speaker represents the corrupt business class that emerged in the wake of the economic openness introduced by Sadat and Mubarak.

Two ordinary Egyptians put up headstones for the public sector and for agrarian reform at Nasser's burial plot, symbolizing the nullification of these two main policies of the revolution (*Al-Ahali*, July 26, 1995).

though these steps had been implemented early in the revolution, the centralistic government remained in place for two decades. This played into the hands of liberal critics who unequivocally opposed a separation between social and political liberties. The collapse of the communist experiment in Eastern Europe in the mid-1980s, they argued, proved that the one could not be achieved at the expense of the other.[54] Despite these differences in perspective, liberals and Nasserists were united in their defiance of the existing order and in their commitment to democratization. Beyond these goals, however, they were in direct confrontation. For the anti-Nasserists, the consequences of the revolution proved to be a mirage. For the Nasserists, it remained the ultimate vision of a brighter future.

Some writers, by contrast, presented a less dichotomous and more balanced account of Nasserism. They included Salah 'Isa, Hasanayn Kurum, Yunan Labib Rizq, and Abu al-'Ala Madi, who represented a broad spectrum of ideologues, from liberals and leftists to Nasserists and Islamists. Their less contentious approach lent their claims a more authentic and constructive dimension. Averse to degrading the symbols of Egypt's history, they rejected both the Wafd's perception of the revolution as a black episode that should be blotted out from memory and the Nasserists' idealization of the revolution as the factor that liberated Egypt from imperialism and corruption.

These moderate commentators viewed the mutual invalidation of both narratives as bordering on an obliteration of Egypt's national memory and engendering cultural disorientation.[55] Rather, tolerance was necessary, based on acknowledged historic truths that cannot be denied. The Nasserists were called upon to recognize that the prerevolutionary Wafd was not responsible for all the upheavals in the 1930s and 1940s, given that most of the time it was not at the helm. Moreover, the Wafd had attained social and political achievements and its leaders were popularly elected.

The Nasserists were also required to face up to the considerable injustice done to the Muslim Brothers, many of whom had been harassed and tortured without justification. The Brothers, for their part, were called upon to cease attributing the 1954 assassination attempt on Nasser's life to a scheme fomented by Nasser himself and to stop depicting the trials of Islamists in 1965 as fictitious show trials. The Muslim Brothers needed to admit that some in their ranks sought to undermine Nasser's government. As for the Wafdists, they were called upon to acknowledge Nasser's achievements as following up on the Wafd initiatives of the prerevolutionary period and as putting its ideals into practice.[56]

Two writers in this vein were Salah 'Isa, a prominent member of the NPUG, and Hasanayn Kurum of the Liberal Party. They posited the revolution as a link in the history of Egypt's nationalist struggle, which began as far back as the popular opposition to the French occupation (1798–1801). In their opinion, the nationalist leadership had always been divided between moderates and hawks (the latter included Nasser), yet the common goal of all was the attainment of independence and progress for Egypt.[57] By advocating historic continuity, 'Isa and Kurum attempted to broaden the legitimacy of the revolution and to incorporate it more integrally into Egypt's national heritage. In this endeavor, they gained the support of another writer, Faraj Fuda, a former member of the New Wafd Party, who stated that "the revolutionary regime is no more than a single chapter in a long history, neither its beginning nor its end." Fuda noted that the adverse aspects of Nasserism, such as repressive rule and the undermining of Nile Valley unity by recognizing Sudan's right to independence, must not obscure its positive aspects, which included social justice and the separation of religion and state. An objective assessment of the revolution, he pointed out, would also provide direction and hope for the younger generation.[58]

Fuda was known as an avid supporter of the separation of religion and politics and a sharp critic of the Islamist groups, whom he viewed as enemies of progress and democracy. He praised the civil character of the revolutionary regime and the strong-arm campaigns it conducted against its Islamist rivals.[59] In the same vein, Yunan Labib Rizq and Milad Hanna, left-wing Copts, lauded the revolution's egalitarian attitude toward religious minorities, which put an end to the practice of mobilizing religion for political purposes, as carried out by the Wafd and the king. They credited Nasser with molding a state determined to treat its citizens with justice and equality. The Arab unity he promoted was largely secular and was directed primarily to the countries of the Fertile Crescent, where minorities were protected and respected.[60] In emphasizing the revolution's civic political culture and its staunch resistance to the Islamist challenge, Fuda, Rizq, and Hanna were translating history into current terms. Their aim was to warn Mubarak that the politicization of religion and a stance of moderation toward the Islamist opposition would only erode the authority of the state and reinforce sectarian divisions.[61]

This relatively balanced account of Nasserism made use of history to spur the present government to take action on problematic existential issues in Egypt: the Islamist threat, the status of the Copts, and democracy. Such moderate thinking was rejected by supporters of both established narratives—the Nasserist and the anti-Nasserist—who questioned the government's fundamental legitimacy. The anti-Nasserists claimed that Mubarak was an heir to Nasser, while the Nasserists insisted that Mubarak had turned his back on Nasser's legacy. The ongoing aggressive dispute between the advocates of these two narratives over their role in the national memory relegated the appeal for constructive criticism and unprejudiced judgment to the realm of intellectual exercise. Tariq Hijji, a prominent young writer, pointed to the reflection of this regrettable outcome in the deterioration of dialogue and the surge in contentious writing. In his view, the principle of acceptance of the "other," deriving from the diverse and complex nature of society, was the only way to initiate an era of progress. Without it, he warned, Egypt and the Arab world would remain in the backyard of the community of enlightened nations.[62]

### The Official Narrative: Between Myth and Reality

Mubarak's administration was the object of criticism by both proponents and opponents of Nasserism. It found itself caught between a mythologized heritage and the constraints of the present; between the desire to nurture historical continuity and the impulse to highlight the unique aspects of Mubarak's contribution. The government's overall strategy was to pay lip service to the revolution without imbuing this allegiance with content. This approach was reflected in official accounts of Nasserism, especially in the state media on the anniversary of the revolution and in the defined parameters of Mubarak's speeches. Mubarak carefully avoided taking an active part in the public debate over Nasserism, although he allowed himself to direct barbs at the revolution's antagonists and its blind followers, both of whom were also his own political rivals.

Mubarak praised the revolution for liberating Egypt from political anarchy, ending the social exploitation, and disseminating liberty, yet he also stressed the dynamic orientation of history toward progress and renewal. No human experience takes place in a vacuum; rather, it interacts with its circumstances. Likewise, the quality of any revolution is contingent upon its adaptive capacity, based on practical experience and lessons drawn from outcomes. Mubarak called for the reassessment of certain revolutionary achievements, including centralization of the economy and nationalization, which had generated a cumbersome public sector and stifled the private initiative so essential to economic development. The vision of Arab unity, he pointed out, had also been promoted with undue haste, and sometimes with excessive forcefulness, disregarding the complexity of Arab reality that was better suited to long-term, gradual preparation involving coordination. The revolution, Mubarak concluded, heralded neither the beginning nor the end of history. Its dynamic nature enabled the adaptation of its platform to the spirit of the times.[63] These emphases, which demonstrated continuity through a new reading of the past, defined the official parameters of the debate.

Expressing loyalty to the Nasserist heritage, the official narrative stressed the economic and social changes brought about by the revolution in a country whose national resources had been controlled by 0.5 percent of the population.[64] The narrative linked this historical argument to present politics, charging that those who cherish the prerevolutionary reality, that is, the Wafdists, lack any real political or moral justification for their stand.[65] In contrast to other revolutions in the history of mankind, the official account claimed, the July Revolution proved that important changes could be effected in the lives of nations without bloodshed. The revolution thus came to symbolize the protection of liberty, justice, and national honor.[66]

However, like other revolutions, the July Revolution had also deviated and erred, most importantly in failing to institute democracy. This led to an exaggeration of the role of the leader and his confidants, and an underestimation of the collective structure, without which a government lacks genuine public legitimacy. In this Nasser had repeated the mistake made a century earlier by Muhammad 'Ali, who denied his primary source of power—the diverse streams of the popular national movement—and established a one-man rule. Sometimes, Mubarak's supporters noted, extenuating circumstances justify the absence of democracy in a revolutionary era, for example, the imperative to restructure the balance of power in society or overcome external challenges. However, this cannot change the fact that the establishment of a democratic government was relegated to the bottom of the Free Officers' agenda.[67]

The emphasis in this account on the revolution's failure in the area of democracy sought to highlight the democratic character of Mubarak's regime and deflect criticism by the political opposition. Mubarak was represented as the harbinger of the third phase of the revolution. Its two earlier phases, under Nasser and Sadat, had witnessed shocks and radical changes. Under Mubarak, the revolution achieved stability and returned to its proper track. This was accomplished despite the difficult circumstances of the collapse of the political and security structures following Sadat's assassination, a deteriorating economic situation, and regional isolation in the wake of the peace treaty with Israel. The official narrative identified Mubarak as the figure responsible for completing the final transformation from revolution to democracy.

The shift from revolutionary to constitutional legitimacy was marked by the encouragement of political participation through the establishment of new parties and a free press, as well as the reinforcement of the legislative and judicial authorities.[68] One writer noted in *Al-Akhbar* that by so doing, Mubarak stood as an antithesis to the destruction wrought by both his predecessors, especially Nasser, and as such was worthy of the title "Egypt's rebuilder."[69] In differentiating Mubarak from his predecessors, the official narrative provided a platform for prominent writers, such as Nagib Mahfuz, who was critical of Nasserism and praised Mubarak's achievements.[70]

Besides criticizing Nasserist authoritative rule, the official narrative also attempted to obscure the link between the revolution and Nasser personally. The revolution was represented as that of the Egyptian people, with the army serving to implement the people's will and to end an era of corruption and tyranny.[71] Although Nasser was depicted as an important leader, he was portrayed as one of several leaders who had raised the banner of national struggle, including 'Umar Makram, Mustafa Kamel, Muhammad Farid, Sa'd Zaghlul, Mustafa Nahhas, and Muhammad Nagib.[72] The official discourse thereby aimed to remove Mubarak from the shadow of Nasser's charismatic leadership—a standard that was difficult for any successor to meet. Mubarak, who lacked the pretension to be a hero, projected more of an image of a technocrat.

The official diminution of Nasser's personality was also accompanied by an emphasis on the relativity of his era, that is, a chapter in history that had come to an end. By relegating Nasserism to a specific time frame, the official narrative aimed at achieving two goals: first, divesting the Nasserist ideology of its hallowed and timeless nature and, second, dispelling public anxiety over radical change so as to reinforce the existing social order and institutions. According to Mubarak's adherents, the circumstances under which Nasser operated differed from those of the present, and any appeal for reconstructing the past contradicted historical logic and the forward thrust of life itself. Moreover, the revolutionary regime had lacked a coherent ideology and a clear-cut platform. Although the revolution left behind principles worthy of further development, including national liberation and social justice, new thinking and a new strategy were required.[73] In practical terms, the official expression of loyalty to the spirit of the revolution negated Nasserism as a normative code for contemporary governmental behavior.

While the official narrative, in contrast to the oppositionist ones, was state-sponsored, its hegemonic status in the Egyptian public was doubtful. Clearly, the laborers and the fellahin, the two primary, yet poorest, sectors in society, had difficulty in accepting the privatization of public corporations, the downsizing of the public sector, and the partial reclamation of landowners' rights, which had been revoked by the revolution. While this open-door policy did not return Egypt to the days of the pashas, as leftists charged, it certainly engendered public grievances.[74] In this sense, the ethos of social justice nurtured by Nasserism cast a threatening shadow over Mubarak's regime. It became the litmus test for the government's commitment to bridging social gaps and promoting a more equitable distribution of wealth. It also prevented the government from straying too far into the pasture of economic liberalization.

## Conclusions

The historiographic discourse over the Nasserist heritage in Egypt constitutes an essential component of the struggle to shape Egyptian collective memory. The issue is closely related to the political debate over the national agenda of Mubarak's government. The ideological and party affiliations of the interlocutors—the Wafd, the Muslim Brothers, the Nasserist Party, and the Left—largely dictate their attitude toward the revolution. These political groups, most of which are in the opposition, bitterly disagree over the country's revolutionary heritage, yet find themselves on the same front in calling for greater political freedom under Mubarak. Legacies of the past, alongside frustration with the existing political order due to the inability of the opposition to block, let alone replace, governmental policies, have been absorbed into the judgmental assessment of the revolution. In reality, the emotional confrontation with the past has turned into a political contest in the present, providing contemporary actors with a sense of group identity, solidarity, and representation in the ideological marketplace.[75]

A minority of writers less preoccupied with current political rivalries have also made their voices heard. Their discourse about the Nasserist past has been more constructive, aimed at encouraging the government to take more decisive steps to handle the grave challenges facing Egyptian society. They perceive in Nasserism the sense of civic and secular community that they seek to reestablish in the face of the Islamist threat and the sectarian strife between Muslims and Copts.

Mubarak's regime has not been indifferent to the turbulent debate over Nasserism. In fact, it plays an active role in this debate, viewing it as one of the arenas for the government's contest with its political rivals over the proper image of the Egyptian polity. The official memory criticizes the wholesale denigration of the revolution, yet also opposes its excessive idealization. It seeks to mold a dynamic revolutionary heritage, responsive to the constraints of the times. This two-edged strategy aims to emphasize historical continuity with the revolution so as to reinforce the legitimacy of the current regime and to justify deviations from the revolutionary path at the same time. For Mubarak, who essentially grew up in the military establishment and was politically unaffiliated during the 1950s and 1960s, Nasserism is a burden of the past rather than a political asset for the present. The anniversary of the revolution, firmly anchored in the national calendar, is marked by ceremonial speeches by the president, but it is marginalized in public life during the rest of the year.[76]

The political and ideological pluralism initiated by Sadat and reinforced by Mubarak has nurtured numerous narratives competing for hegemony, both politically and culturally. The diverse nature of the Nasserist experience provided an almost endless repertoire of concepts and events that could be used by various protagonists to support their cause. Wafdists blamed the revolution for Egypt's economic evils and incomplete democracy. The Nasserists depicted it as a lever for promoting social justice, progress, and Arab unity. The Muslim Brothers condemned the revolution's secular policy, attributing rising religious extremism to it. Many leftists, in contrast, perceived the revolution as an exemplary model for the separation of religion and state.[77]

Almost all of the opposition groups praised Nasser's stand against Israel, despite his military defeats, thereby defying the bilateral peace treaty made a decade after his death. The government, for its part, viewed the revolution as one of various stages in the history of the Arab-Israeli conflict. The official account emphasized that the peace strategies adopted by Sadat and Mubarak were responsible for the return of the lands lost in the June 1967 War,[78] an argument reinforced by the official celebration of Sinai Liberation Day (April 23).

In this context of multiple narratives, which reveals the multifaceted nature of Egypt's political culture, Nasserist historiography finds itself in a position of dissent, in contrast to its dominant position in the revolutionary era. The marginalization of this narrative helps to explain its harsh rejection of postrevolutionary policy.

Ultimately, Nasserism during Sadat's rule, and even more so during Mubarak's tenure, evolved into a bruised yet compelling myth, lacking a genuine hold on the national agenda but still casting a shadow on the Egyptian scene. Its survival is the result of the continued contention with the unsolved problems of the Egyptian polity and the longing for their resolution by a sweeping and decisive leadership. The pragmatic and cautious policies adopted by Mubarak are perceived in public discourse as an effective means for stability and continued improvement, rather than as a catalyst for profound structural change, especially in the economic and social realms. These areas constitute the government's Achilles' heel, guaranteeing that Nasserism will not be marginalized as merely an episode in the distant past. Social justice, national honor, Arab unity, and a firm stand against Israel and the West were the cornerstones of the revolution. Although their potency was eroded toward the end of Nasser's reign, they continued to represent high ideals that were not to be easily obliterated.[79] They evolved into cultural myths laden with historic significance and emotional conviction, thereby preserving the place of Nasserism in the Egyptian national pantheon.[80]

## Notes

1. See, e.g., Joel Gordon, "Secular and Religious Memory in Egypt: Recalling Nasserist Civics," *Muslim World* 87, no. 2 (April 1997): 97–98, 102–3.

2. United Nations, Department of Economic and Social Affairs, *World Population Prospects: The 2000 Revision* (New York: United Nations, 2001), 24, table 1. (http://www.un.org/esa/population/wpp2000at.pdf).

3. On the Sadat era, see, e.g., Shimon Shamir, *Egypt under Sadat: The Search for a New Orientation* (Tel Aviv: Dvir, 1978, Hebrew); Raymond A. Hinnebusch, *Egyptian Politics under Sadat*, 2d ed. (Boulder: Lynne Rienner, 1988); Michael Winter, "Islam in the State: Pragmatism and Growing Commitment," in Shimon Shamir, ed., *Egypt from Monarchy to Republic* (Boulder: Westview Press, 1995), 50–53.

4. On Mubarak's regime, policies, and challenges, see Gudrun Krämer, *Ägypten unter Mubarak* (Baden-Baden: Nomos, 1986); Robert Springborg, *Mubarak's Egypt* (Boulder: Westview Press, 1989); Charles Tripp and Roger Owen, eds., *Egypt under Mubarak* (London: Routledge, 1989); Moheb Zaki, *Civil Society and Democratization in Egypt, 1981–1994* (Cairo: Ibn Khaldun Center, 1995); Meir Hatina, *Islam in Modern Egypt* (Tel Aviv: Hakibbutz Hameuchad, 2000), 36–45 (Hebrew); Paul Rivlin, *Economic Policy and Performance in the Arab World* (Boulder: Lynne Rienner, 2001), 101–12.

5. Sadat, upon acceding to power in 1970, turned against the Nasserist elite as a preliminary step to establishing his "corrective revolution" (*thawrat al-tashih*). Mubarak, recognizing the managerial skills of the Nasserists and eager to counteract the bourgeoisie and growing Islamist activism that emerged as powerful forces under Sadat, recruited Nasserists into his service but took care to curtail any broad-based Nasserist upsurge. See Shamir, *Egypt under Sadat*, 24–30, 140–60; Hinnebusch, *Egyptian Politics under Sadat*, 40–69; Springborg, *Mubarak's Egypt*, 20–21, 37–38.

6. Samuel N. Eisenstadt, *Tradition, Change, and Modernity* (New York: John Wiley, 1973), 119–21. See also Edward Shils, *The Intellectuals and the Powers and Other Essays* (Chicago: University of Chicago Press, 1972), 35–36; John Bodnar, *Remaking America* (Princeton: Princeton University Press, 1991), 13–15; Gordon, "Secular and Religious Memory in Egypt," 106–7.

7. Bodnar, *Remaking America*, 14–15. See also Maurice Halbwachs, *On Collective Memory* (Chicago: University of Chicago Press, 1992), 25–26.

8. See, e.g., Edward H. Carr, *What Is History?* (Harmondsworth: Penguin Books, 1961), 20–30; Eric Hobsbawm, "Introduction: Inventing Traditions," in Eric Hobsbawm and Terence Ranger, eds., *The Invention of Tradition* (Cambridge: Cambridge University Press, 1983), 1–11. On myths and their political and social functions, see Mircea Eliade, *Myth and Reality* (New York: Harper and Row, 1963), 5–7; Emmanuel Sivan, *Arab Political Myths*, 2d ed. (Tel Aviv: 'Am Oved, 1997), 9–12 (Hebrew); Haggay Ram, *Myth and Mobilization in Revolutionary Iran* (Washington, D.C.: American University Press, 1994), 6–10.

9. A similar interplay between politics and history can be found in the 'Urabi Revolt episode. See Thomas Mayer, *The Changing Past: Egyptian Historiography of the Urabi Revolt, 1882–1983* (Gainesville: University of Florida Press, 1988).

10. See, e.g., Fatma Müge Göçek, "Political Cartoons as a Site of Representation and Resistance in the Middle East," *Princeton Papers* 6 (spring 1997): 2–3.

11. See, e.g., Sivan, *Arab Political Myths*, 11. See also Susan Ossman, *Picturing Casablanca: Portraits of Power in a Modern City* (Berkeley: University of California Press, 1994), 19, 183–84.

12. An additional element in the tarnishing of the Nasserist legacy was the Islamist trend, embodied mainly in the Muslim Brothers, which was violently suppressed by the revolution and continued to be marginalized by the existing order. The Islamist narrative is beyond the scope of this article, inter alia, because its spokesmen nullified not only the Nasserist historical record but also the perceived Western political culture that had developed in Egypt from the early nineteenth century onward. Instead, the Islamists posited a counterculture based on the call to establish an Islamic order as the sole solution to societal ills. On the Muslim Brothers' stance regarding the revolution and its political implications for the present, see, e.g., *Liwa' al-Islam* (July/August 1986), 30–32; (June 1987), 12–19; (July 1988), 7–8; Muhammad Muru, *Al-Haraka al-Islamiyya fi Misr* (Nicosia: al-Dar al-Misriyya, 1994); Hasanayn Tawfiq Ibrahim, *Al-Nizam al-Siyasi wal-Ikhwan al-Muslimun fi Misr* (Beirut: Dar al-Tali'a, 1998).

13. On the social composition and political platform of the Liberal Party and the New Wafd, see Springborg, *Mubarak's Egypt*, 202–7; Hinnebusch, *Egyptian Politics under Sadat*, 208–20; Krämer, *Ägypten unter Mubarak*, 77–90.

14. Jamal Badawi in *Al-Wafd*, July 28, 1994; July 24, 1995.

15. *Al-Wafd*, July 22, 1995; Sharif Kamil in *Al-Ahrar*, July 13, 1992; Muhammad Isma'il 'Ali in *Al-Wafd*, July 23, 1992; 'Abd al-'Azim Ramadan in *Al-Wafd*, July 29, August 14, 1996; 'Abd al-'Azim Ramadan, *Awraq min Ta'rikh Misr* (Cairo: al-Hay'a al-Misriyya al-'Amma lil-Kitab, 1995), 295–96. See also Najib Mahfuz, *Hawla al-Taharrur wal-Taqaddum* (Cairo: al-Dar al-Misriyya al-Lubnaniyya, 1996), 97–98; Raja' al-Naqqash, *Najib Mahfuz Safahat min Mudhakkiratihi* (Cairo: Markaz al-Ahram lil-Tarjama wal-Nashr, 1998), 191–95.

16. Wahid Ghazi in *Al-Ahrar*, July 30, 1990; Lam'i al-Muti'i in *Al-Wafd*, July 15, 1990; Salah al-Aswani in *Al-Wafd*, July 26, 1993; Badawi in *Al-Wafd*, July 24, 1994; Ramadan in *Al-Wafd*, August 20, 1996.

17. Ghazi in *Al-Ahrar*, July 29, 1991; Badawi in *Al-Wafd*, July 24, 1994.

18. Salah 'Aqqad in *Al-Wafd*, July 16, 1992; Muhammad 'Awda in *Al-Wafd*, July 22, 1992; 'Izzat Saqir in *Al-Wafd*, July 24, 1994; 'Abbas al-Tarabili in *Al-Wafd*, August 24, 1996.

19. *Al-Wafd*, July 22, 1992; Mahmud 'Abd al-Mun'im Murad in *Al-Wafd*, July 23, 1993; Anis Mansur, *'Abd al-Nasir al-Muftara 'Alyhi wal-Muftari 'Alayna*, 4th ed. (Cairo: al-Maktab al-Misri al-Hadith, 1994), 172–73.

20. Murad in *Al-Wafd*, July 23, 1993; Mahfuz, *Hawla al-Taharrur wal-Taqaddum*, 21–22, 25–26, 31–32.

21. Murad in *Al-Wafd*, July 23, 1993.

22. Al-Naqqash, *Najib Mahfuz*, 194.

23. Badawi in *Al-Wafd*, July 24, 1994; Ramadan in *Al-Wafd*, July 29, 1996.

24. Ramadan in *Al-Wafd*, July 29, 1996; Ramadan, *Awraq min Ta'rikh Misr*, 296–301.

25. 'Aqqad in *Al-Wafd*, July 23, 1992; Badawi in *Al-Wafd*, July 24, 1995.

26. Ramadan in *Al-Wafd*, July 29, 1996.

27. Mustafa 'Abd al-Raziq in *Al-Wafd*, July 15, 1992; Saqir in *Al-Wafd*, July 24, 1994; Sa'id 'Ukasha in *Al-Wafd*, July 27, 1994; Ramadan in *Al-Wafd*, July 29, 1996.

28. See chapter 13 of this volume, "The Nightingale and the Ra'is," by Joel Gordon.

29. On Ramadan's biography, see David Sagiv, *Fundamentalism and Intellectuals in Egypt, 1973–1993* (London: Frank Cass, 1995), 79–80.

30. 'Abd al-'Azim Ramadan, *Al-Haqiqa al-Ta'rikhiyya Hawla Ta'mim Sharikat Qanat al-Suways* (Cairo: al-Hay'a al-Misriyya al-'Amma lil-Kitab, 2000), 21–25.

31. Ibid., 21–25, 27–31.

32. Ibid., 29–31, 51, 81–85.

33. Ibid., 99–104, 107, 125–35. See also al-Naqqash, *Najib Mahfuz*, 195–96.

34. Ramadan, *Al-Haqiqa al-Ta'rikhiyya*, 51–63, 72–73, 125–35; Ramadan in *Al-Wafd*, July 18, 25, 1994; Ramadan, *Awraq min Ta'rikh Misr*, 212–13.

35. Ramadan, *Al-Haqiqa al-Ta'rikhiyya*, 43.

36. Mansur was dismissed from his post in *Al-Ahram* during the revolution on Nasser's orders after publishing a critical article, while Mahfuz was exposed to various types of harassment due to critical essays that angered several prominent officials. Mahfuz, however, stated in his memoirs that Nasser was convinced of the sincerity of his writings, which were aimed at the country's welfare and not at incitement. See Mansur, *'Abd al-Nasir*, 6; Sagiv, *Fundamentalism and Intellectuals in Egypt*, 78; al-Naqqash, *Najib Mahfuz*, 127–36.

37. Najib Mahfuz in *Al-Ahram*, July 23, 1992; Najib Mahfuz, *Amam al-'Arsh* (Cairo: Maktabat Misr, 1983); Mansur, *'Abd al-Nasir*, 6–8, 179–83, 189–93, 215, 291–93. See also al-Naqqash, *Najib Mahfuz*, 224–25; Rif'at al-Sa'id, *Ta'mmalat fi al-Nasiriyya*, 3d ed. (Cairo: al-Mada, 2000), 8–11; Tariq Hijji, *Naqd al-'Aql al-'Arabi* (Cairo: Dar al-Ma'arif, 1998), 155–59.

38. Mansur, *'Abd al-Nasir*, 189–93, 313–14.

39. Ibid., 179–83; Mahfuz in *Al-Ahram*, July 23, 1992; al-Naqqash, *Najib Mahfuz*, 228, 231–33; Ramadan, *Al-Haqiqa al-Ta'rikhiyya*, 8–10.

40. See, e.g., al-Muti'i in *Al-Wafd*, July 15, 1990; Muhammad 'Asfur in *Al-Wafd*, July 26, 1990; Saqir in *Al-Wafd*, July 21, 1991.

41. 'Aqqad in *Al-Wafd*, July 16, 1992; Midhat al-Harmil in *Al-Wafd*, August 19, 1996.

42. On Egypt's economic reforms, see Sa'id al-Najjar, *Tajdid al-Nizam al-Iqtisadi wal-Siyasi fi Misr* (Cairo: Dar al-Shuruq, 1997); Economist Intelligence Unit, *Country Profile, Egypt 1997–98* (London: EIU, 1998), 13–24; Robert Springborg, *Political Structural Adjustment in Egypt: A Precondition for Rapid Economic Growth?* (San Domenico: European University Institute, June 1999), 22–26; Rivlin, *Economic Policy and Performance in the Arab World*, 101–12: Ahmad Sayyid al-Najjar, ed., *Al-Itijahat al-Iqtisadiyya al-Istratijiyya-2000* (Cairo: al-Ahram Center for Political and Strategic Studies, January 2001), 225–54.

43. The new Land Act of 1992 was implemented in 1997 at the close of a five-year grace period. See Hatina, "Egypt," *MECS* 21 (1997): 321–22.

44. See, e.g., 'Ukasha in *Al-Wafd,* July 27, 1994.

45. Springborg, *Mubarak's Egypt,* 37–38, 198–99, 208–9; Krämer, *Ägypten unter Mubarak,* 62–68; Ami Ayalon, "Egypt," *MECS* 16 (1992): 375–76.

46. Another Nasserist weekly, *Sawt al-'Arab,* began publication in August 1986, but was closed two years later because of an article defaming the Saudi royal family, which was described by the authorities as damaging to Egypt's vital interests. The paper resumed publication in London in 1989. See *Al-Shira'* (Beirut), August 21, 1989.

47. On Haykal and the revolution, see Munir K. Nasser, *Press, Politics, and Power: Egypt's Heikal and al-Ahram* (Ames: Iowa State University Press, 1979); Sonia Dabous, "Nasser and the Egyptian Press," in Charles Tripp, ed., *Contemporary Egypt* (London: Routledge, 1993), 110–19. See also Sagiv, *Fundamentalism and Intellectuals in Egypt,* 74. Haykal's close identification with the revolution earned him the Nasser Prize, awarded by the Lebanese Institute for Arab Unity Studies in July 1999. The institute has initiated several projects to perpetuate the Nasser legacy, including publishing his speeches and interviews, granting student scholarships, and financing the construction of lecture halls in several campuses throughout the Arab world. *Al-Mustaqbal al-'Arabi,* September 1999, 72–79.

48. Muhammad Hasanayn Haykal, *Li-Misr la li-'Abd al-Nasir* (Cairo: Markaz al-Ahram lil-Tarjama wal-Nashr, 1987), 20–21, 41–45. See also *Al-Mustaqbal al-'Arabi* (September 1999), 82–84, 93.

49. Haykal, *Li-Misr la li-'Abd al-Nasir,* 46–47, 53.

50. Sa'd al-Din Ibrahim in *Al-Ahali,* August 1, 1990; Jalal 'Arif in *Al-'Arabi,* July 25, 1994; 'Abd al-Halim Qandil and Muhammad Shuman in *Al-'Arabi,* July 25, 1994; Qasim 'Abduh Qasim in *Al-'Arabi,* August 26, 1996. See also Amin Huwaydi in *Al-Mustaqbal al-'Arabi* (December 2000), 83–89.

51. Lutfi Waqid in *Al-Ahali,* July 24, 1991; Muhammad Sayyid Ahmad in *Al-Ahali,* July 22, 1992; Shuman in *Al-'Arabi,* July 25, 1994; Diya' al-Din Da'ud in *Al-'Arabi,* July 18, 1994.

52. Mahmud al-Jiyar in *Al-Ahali,* July 25, 1990; Mahmud al-Maraghi in *Al-'Arabi,* July 24, 31, 1995.

53. Haykal, *Li-Misr la li-'Abd al-Nasir,* 61, 85; Khalil Hasan Khalil in *Al-Ahali,* July 25, 1990; July 20, 1994; Sami Sharaf in *Al-'Arabi,* July 25, 1994; al-Maraghi in *Al-'Arabi,* July 31, 1995.

54. Muhammad 'Asfur, quoted in *Al-Wafd,* July 22, 1992; Najib Mahfuz, *Hawla al-Din wal-Dimuqratiyya* (Cairo: al-Dar al-Misriyya al-Lubnaniyya, 1990), 125–26; Najib Mahfuz, *Hawla al-Taharrur wal-Taqaddum,* 31–32.

55. Yunan Labib Rizq in *Al-Musawwar,* June 26, 1992; *Al-Ahali,* July 21, 1993; Salah 'Isa in *Al-'Arabi,* August 3, 1998; Abu al-'Ala Madi in *Al-Hayat,* May 19, 1999. See also Rif'at Sayyid Ahmad, *Thawrat al-Jinaral* (Cairo: Dar al-Huda, 1993).

56. Hasanayn Kurum in *Al-Ahrar,* July 23, 27, 1994; Salah 'Isa in *Al-'Arabi,* August 3, 1998; Abu al-'Ala Madi in *Al-Hayat,* May 19, 1999. Madi was the founder of the Wasat (Center) Party, established in 1996 as a splinter of the Muslim

Brothers. The party claimed to represent a different sort of Islam moderate, with no monopoly on the truth and supportive of a pluralistic political system. Its platform included respect for the constitution, defense of freedom of belief, condemnation of terror, and an appeal for constructive dialogue between the state and the Islamists. Such declarations, however, did not help the Wasat Party to obtain a legal license from the government, which suspected that the party was a branch of the Muslim Brothers formed to promote their revolutionary ideas under the guise of democracy. On the Wasat Party, see Ami Ayalon, "Egypt," *MECS* 20 (1996): 266–67; Hatina, "Egypt," *MECS* 21 (1997): 309–11. See also Tal'at Rahim, *Al-Wasat wal-Ikhwan* (Cairo: Markaz Yafa lil-Dirasat wal-Abhath, 1997).

57. 'Isa in *Al-'Arabi*, August 3, 1998; Kurum in *Al-Ahrar*, July 28, 1994.

58. Faraj Fuda, *Al-Wafd wal-Mustaqbal* (Cairo: n.p., 1983), 63. On Fuda's political biography, see Hatina, *Islam in Modern Egypt*, 48–71.

59. Meir Hatina, "On the Margins of Consensus: The Call to Separate Religion and State in Modern Egypt," *Middle Eastern Studies* 36, no. 1 (2000): 55–60; Fuda in *Al-Ahrar*, May 13, 1991, and *Mayu*, August 12, 1991. See also his *Al-Nadhir* (Cairo: Dar Misr al-Jadida, 1989), 31–34. Fuda's amity toward political Islam and his renouncement of the Shari'a's relevance to modern times resulted in his murder by Islamist radicals in 1992.

60. Yunan Labib Rizq and Abu Sayf Yusuf, *Al-Ahali*, July 22, 1992; Milad Hanna, *Qubul al-Akhar* (Cairo: Dar al-Shuruq, 1998), 153–56. Other writers put forward different accounts of Nasser's policy toward Islam. Amin al-Mahdi, for example, argued that the revolution gave rise to the emergence of the religious trend. In clashing with the Muslim Brothers, Nasser reinforced the status of al-Azhar as a source of legitimization for his regime. As a result, al-Azhar gained state facilities and a free hand in prosecuting advocates of civil and secular liberties. In al-Mahdi's phrase, "al-Azhar became an Islamic Vatican." Some of its members also established militant groups after the revolution. Amin al-Mahdi, *Al-Sira' al-'Arabi al-Isra'ili: Azmat al-Dimuqratiyya wal-Salam* (Cairo: Dar al-Ma'arif, 1999), 89–118. Other writers claimed that the militaristic character of Nasser's rule, in which the norm was blind obedience and an immutable conviction in the ultimate truth of the regime's policies, inspired the thinking of radical Muslims. Fu'ad Zakariya, *Al-Haqiqa wal-Waham fi al-Haraka al-Islamiyya al-Mu'asira*, 3d ed. (Cairo: Dar al-Fikr, 1988), 111–12. See also Sayyid al-Qimani, *Al-Fashiyun wal-Watan* (Cairo: al-Markaz al-Misri li-Buhuth al-Hadara, 1999), 59–64. A more equivocal evaluation was presented by Hasan Hanafi in *Al-Ahrar*, July 24, 1995; *Al-Ahali*, July 26, 1995.

61. On government-Islamist opposition relations, see Barry Rubin, *Islamic Fundamentalism in Egyptian Politics* (London: Macmillan, 1990), 19–27, 150–55; Springborg, *Mubarak's Egypt*, 215–31, 240–45; Hatina, *Islam in Modern Egypt*, 32–45. See also Ami Ayalon, *Egypt's Quest for Cultural Orientation* (Tel Aviv: Moshe Dayan Center, 1999), 19–26, 30–40; Fouad Ajami, *The Dream Palace of the Arabs* (New York: Vintage Books, 1999), 203–21. On Muslim-Copt relations, see Ami Ayalon, "Egypt's Coptic Pandora's Box," in Ofra Bangio and Gabriel Ben-Dor, eds., *Minorities and the State in the Arab World* (Boulder: Lynne Rienner, 1999), 53–71.

62. Tariq Hijji, *Al-Thaqafa Awalan wa-Akhiran* (Cairo: Dar al-Ma'arif, 2000), 31–32, 54–57.

63. See, e.g., Mubarak, quoted in *Al-Ahram,* July 23, 1995; *Al-Akhbar,* July 24, 1997.

64. On this, see also the introduction to this volume.

65. 'Ali al-Dali in *Mayu,* September 5, 1983.

66. Rajab al-Banna, *Al-Ahram,* July 28, 1991; Salah al-Din Hafiz in *Al-Ahram,* July 31, 1991, July 23, 1993; Mursi 'Atallah in *Al-Ahram,* July 20, 1995; Ihsan Bakr in *Al-Ahram,* July 22, 1995.

67. Ahmad Faris 'Abd al-Mun'im, *Al-Ahram,* July 30, 1992; July 23, 1993; 'Atif al-Ghamri in *Al-Ahram,* July 27, 1994.

68. Hafiz in *Al-Ahram,* July 24, 1991; 'Abd al-Mun'im in *Al-Ahram,* July 30, 1992.

69. Jalal Dawaydar in *Al-Akhbar,* July 23, 1996.

70. See, e.g., Najib Mafuz in *Al-Ahram,* July 23, 1992.

71. Bakr and Jamal Hammad in *Al-Ahram,* July 22, 1995.

72. Bakr in *Al-Ahram,* July 23, 1993; July 22, 1995.

73. al-Banna in *Al-Ahram,* July 26, 1992; Munna Hilmi in *Al-Ahram,* July 26, 1994; 'Atallah in *Al-Ahram,* July 20, 1995.

74. See, e.g., Kurum in *Al-Ahrar,* July 27, 1995; Muhammad 'Abd al-Quddus in *Al-Sha'b,* October 21, 1996. See also Hatina, "Egypt," *MECS* 21 (1997): 321–22; *Al-Ahram Weekly,* May 3, 2001.

75. See also Clifford Geertz, *The Interpretation of Cultures* (New York: Basic Books, 1973), 204–5.

76. The official celebration of another anniversary day that originated in the revolutionary era, Evacuation Day (Yawm al-Jala') of the British troops from Egypt, was abolished by Mubarak on the grounds that taking a day off would interrupt vital national productivity. Other anniversary days, such as Police Day (January 25) and Workers' Day (May 1), were retained because of their political significance. See *Al-Wafd,* July 23, 1991; Sivan, *Arabic Political Myths,* 135–36.

77. Within the leftist camp, only the Socialist Labor Party (SLP), an offspring of the prerevolutionary Young Egypt movement, displayed a positive attitude toward reinforcing the status of Islam in the state. This was mainly the result of the alliance between the SLP and the Muslim Brothers established during the 1987 elections. The alliance, however, provoked opposition within the SLP and exposed it to frequent harassment by the government. See Springborg, *Mubarak's Egypt,* 201–2; Krämer, *Ägypten unter Mubarak,* 68–73.

78. Shuman in *Al-'Arabi,* July 25, 1994; 'Isam 'Amir in *Al-Ahrar,* July 25, 1994; 'Adil Husayn in *Al-Sha'b,* July 25, 1997; 'Atallah in *Al-Ahram,* July 20, 1995. See also Mubarak, quoted in *Al-Ahram,* July 24, 1997.

79. See also Gordon, "Secular and Religious Memory in Egypt," 104–5.

80. Geertz, *The Interpretation of Cultures,* 210–11.

# II.

# Political and Social Aspects of Nasserism

# 4

## Nasserism's Legal Legacy

Accessibility, Accountability, and Authoritarianism

Nathan J. Brown

### Introduction

Liberal ideas of the rule of law have moved to the center of Arab political discourse. To be sure, the Arab world continues to be known for autocratic and arbitrary government. Nevertheless, rulers increasingly cite the rule of law as a basis of governance and legitimacy, and their opponents increasingly attempt to hold them to the liberal standards that the rulers themselves articulate.

Different political ideas have dominated Arab political debates. In the 1950s and 1960s, nationalist issues were paramount, and those regimes suspicious of rising nationalist sentiments found themselves very much on the defensive. In the 1960s, socialism joined nationalism as the prevailing ideology in many Arab countries. Only a few regimes (chiefly the monarchies in the Arabian peninsula) eschewed the socialist label altogether. These ideas have since receded, though they have not disappeared altogether. In recent years, a new stress on legality and accountability, in its more liberal forms, has emerged. Arab regimes increasingly justify their own existence in terms of such ideas, and opposition political parties cast their critique of the prevailing order by seeking to show that these regimes do not meet the standards that they themselves set.

There is a considerable range in the ideological elevation of the rule of law, with several Islamic and liberal variants. Yet it is still striking how most Arab societies have recently turned to the rule of law in their debates over the proper political order. For instance, immediately after taking the throne, the new kings of Morocco and Jordan both spoke of the necessity to uphold the rule of law. The Palestinian political leaders elected in 1996 took office with an oath, which they themselves approved, to uphold a constitution that had not yet been written. Several Arab governments have accepted offers from international donors—including the European Union, the United States Agency for International Development, and the World Bank—to provide financial and technical support for building the rule of law. Many who rejected liberal principles in the past, often on the Marxist and non-Marxist Left, have created human rights and other organizations based on liberal legal principles.[1] Even the Islamist opposition increasingly refers to liberal legal principles and adopts the "rule of law" as a slogan.[2]

The ideological reign of the rule of law may be short of hegemonic, but it never fails in coloring recollections of the past. In other words, many Arab leaders and intellectuals use such ideas not only to understand the present but also to interpret the past. And the past (especially the 1950s and 1960s) does not appear in a positive light from this new perspective. Arab socialism stands out particularly poorly as an ideology that subverted the strength, integrity, and autonomy of legal processes and institutions in service of authoritarian goals. It must be emphasized that there is some truth in this understanding of the past but some distortion as well.

The liberal and legal critique of Arab socialism can be quite devastating in its analysis of what was actually accomplished during the period, but it is often misleading in presenting what Arab socialism promised. It is true that liberal legal institutions were undermined, but only by way of attempting to increase accountability. That is, Arab socialism did not simply repudiate liberalism; rather, it often promised to meet liberal goals more effectively. As such, an accurate portrayal of what Nasser's government promised and what it delivered may help us to understand why some of the changes made in the name of Arab socialism have been far more difficult to repudiate than others.

In this chapter, I will argue that prevailing liberal ideas have led to the inaccurate image of Nasserism as an ill-advised social contract between the ruler and the ruled. I will further argue that Nasserism presented itself at the time as offering no such bargain. Indeed, far from undermining mechanisms of accountability, Nasserism was to devise more effective ones. Thus, prevailing interpretations of Nasserism in the Arab world (and in current scholarship) misstate the Nasserist project.

The first section of this chapter will focus on current interpretations of Nasserism. The second part will correct these interpretations by analyzing Nasserism as it presented itself at the time. This more accurate understanding of the ideology will help to explain the institutional changes that actually took place and those that have since remained. In the third section, I will thus move beyond the level of ideology to examine actual institutional changes, focusing on ways in which Nasserism changed the prevailing legal culture. In the final section, I will seek to show which elements of the Nasserist legal program have survived and why, as well as how Nasserism offered a different sort of accountability and legality. The Nasserist vision was not fully realized (nor even fully pursued), but it has left important institutional traces that have inhibited some efforts to move to a fully liberal vision of the rule of law.

### The Nasserist Bargain Remembered

The Nasserist era is currently remembered—both inside and outside Egypt—primarily for its authoritarianism and socialism. Both aspects of Nasserism have left a heavy burden on Egyptians today. Authoritarianism may have diminished in its extent, but most of the political forms introduced in the Nasserist period continue, including unchecked presidential authority, abusive security services, limitations on political organization, and stultifying bureaucracy. Similarly, socialism may no longer prevail as the official ideology, but few political or economic analyses of Egypt are written without reference to the bloated public sector, inefficient industry, unsustainable welfare commitments, and limitations on private initiative and foreign investment.

The two aspects of Nasserist governance are now generally seen as closely related, insofar as authoritarianism and socialism are both aspects of unaccountable state authority. Indeed, the relationship between authoritarianism and socialism is seen to go still deeper, with prevailing views now casting Nasserism as an implicit bargain between the ruler and the ruled. Egyptians are held to have traded (or been compelled to trade) their political rights for welfare gains during the Nasserist period, with talk of a "social contract" widespread in many circles. Egyptians were guaranteed jobs, cheap food, free education and medical care, and low rents (both in urban housing and rural farming), for which they forfeited their political voice.

The portrait of Nasserist politics as an exchange of freedom for bread underlines much of the recent social science scholarship on the period. The idea of the "allocation state" or the "no representation without taxation" argument, for instance, is based on the assumption of an inverse relationship between democratic governance and the provision of welfare services (or the absence of material demands by the state).[3] Social scientists have claimed that when a state demands little materially from its citizens, or when it becomes a primary source of welfare benefits, the sorts of links between state and society necessary for liberal and democratic politics atrophy or fail to develop. In other words, when the state taxes little but distributes a lot, citizens look to their government not for a voice but only for material benefits. An innovative twist on this view casts material consumption itself as a form of political participation: In a Nasserist (and post-Nasserist) environment, accepting state benefits becomes the principal form of political participation.[4]

It should be noted that it was not social scientists who coined the term *social contract* to refer to the supposed Nasserist bargain. Instead, it was Egyptian intellectuals who sought to force their rulers to concede a measure of political liberalization to accompany the economic liberalization that began in the 1970s. By the 1980s, calls for a revised social contract were a staple of Egyptian intellectual life.[5] The Egyptian regime, in seeking to jettison some of its welfare commitments from the Nasserist period, was portrayed as seeking to repudiate, or at least revise, the social contract. In return for concessions on subsidies, employment, and housing, Egyptians would be given a real voice in the country's governance.

Egyptian intellectuals argued that the regime, which no longer provided the sorts of services that citizens had come to expect, would have to offer something else in return. If Egypt's leaders were forced to raise commodity prices, unfreeze rents, and decrease welfare benefits, the only way that citizens could accept such changes was to be brought into the decision-making process. Thus, political reform was a necessary price that leaders would have to pay if they wished to pursue economic reform.

By casting Nasserism in this way, Egyptian intellectuals were setting up an argument for political liberalization and even democratization. Thus, since the mid-1970s, when Egypt embarked, albeit uncertainly, on economic liberalization (*al-infitah al-iqtisadi*), some intellectuals have insisted that such measures be taken only if the citizenry could become more involved in the process of governance. Only then would the short-term economic sacrifices associated with liberalization be tolerable. Calls for a new social contract were met with a limited official response: Political freedoms increased but were kept circumscribed, and mechanisms of democratic accountability remained embryonic at best. But the calls were not unheard. After being reelected to a fourth term in 1999, President Husni Mubarak picked up the vocabulary, speaking extensively (though vaguely) of a new social contract in Egypt. Therefore, the understanding of the Nasserist "social contract" has a strong contemporary as well as historical focus.

Did the Nasserist social contract actually exist? At a minimum, it contains a degree of exaggeration, and its extreme identification with Nasser is overdrawn. Many of the welfare commitments of the Nasserist period can easily be traced back before 1952, generally to the period during and immediately after World War II. Rent and price controls were imposed during the war. Education was expanded throughout the twentieth century, and higher education began to expand and become accessible to the middle class under postwar governments. Social reform was a frequent theme of intellectual writings beginning in the mid-1930s. Nationalist economic policies were not an invention of the Free Officers; rather, they were made possible by Egypt's legal independence. In the 1937 Montreux conference, Egypt's prerevolutionary regime secured the abolition of the capitulations, which had barred the country's government from jurisdiction over non-Egyptian citizens and thus made it very difficult to implement any laws related to the economy. In the fifteen years between the Montreux conference and the July 1952 coup, Egyptian governments took advantage of the new freedom to enact some restrictions on foreign investment and landownership.

Even the authoritarian aspects of the Nasserist period—though quite real—generally worked by modifying pre–July 1952 political structures rather than repudiating them. There were some exceptions: The monarchy and the pluralist party system were abolished outright. But many other institutional changes—especially in the legal arena—involved less revolutionary changes, as will be seen. Most legal and judicial structures continued to operate, though there were periodic efforts to bring them under greater executive domination. Most Egyptian institutions and structures were bent to serve new ends.

The image of Nasserism as a bargain of welfare gains in exchange for political silence is thus perhaps less than accurate. Prerevolutionary governments laid the groundwork for the new welfare policies and some of the authoritarian tools later developed more fully under Nasser. But the real objection to the idea of the Nasserist social contract is more fundamental, namely, that there simply was no such bargain, either explicit or implicit in the Nasserist program. Rather than promising an end to accountability, Nasserism promised a new and far more effective set of mechanisms to make those who wielded authority accountable to the population.

## Nasserism's True Promise

Nasserism repudiated liberal structures and ideologies. Yet it did so not by repudiating liberal goals of accessibility and accountability but by promising to meet those goals more effectively. The political and economic leadership of the country was supposed to be made more responsive to popular interests and desires. Egypt was to become not a classless society but rather a society in which no class could dominate another. Rather than losing their voice, the people of Egypt were gaining new ways by which to express and effect their desires.

Socialism certainly meant an increase in state power, but this was presented as a means and not as an end. Arab socialism was not an ideology that claimed to enhance the authority of the rulers; instead, it was purported to enhance the responsiveness of institutions to the people. Existing Egyptian institutions and practices were portrayed as serving the elite or foreign interests. Parliamentary democracy was denounced not because of what it stood for—popular accountability—but because it failed to provide that accountability in any meaningful way. The prerevolutionary order was denounced because it forced lower-class Egyptians into positions of subservience. The reorientation of Egyptian society promised by the July 1952 Revolution was not simply institutional in nature; indeed, cultural changes went far deeper. As other contributions in this volume demonstrate, Egyptian cultural life became increasingly populist.

A radical shift in the officially propagated images of peasants and workers illustrates this most dramatically. Throughout the first half of the twentieth century, the most common word used to describe Egyptian peasants was *ignorant*.[6] Urban workers generally fared little better. The root of official and intellectual disdain for lower-class Egyptians was a strong cultural estrangement. In the 1930s and 1940s, the prevailing language began to change: Peasants were still deemed victims of ignorance, but this provoked reform efforts, albeit limited and often paternalistic, rather than contempt.

In the 1950s, and especially in the 1960s, Egypt enthusiastically adopted a nationalist "myth of the peasant"—a more radical version of the populist glorification of the peasantry current in late nineteenth- and early twentieth-century European nationalist movements. Peasants were transformed from the embodiment of ignorance to a symbol of authenticity. And peasants were not alone in acquiring new symbolic power. Urban workers joined in the nationalist favor, too. The Egyptian revolution was now a social revolution that enabled the downtrodden—workers and peasants alike—to stand with pride rather than subservience alongside their erstwhile social superiors. The abolition of titles was a first symbolic step in this direction, but by the 1960s the new populism was far more widespread. Nationalist art adopted the *gallabiyya*-clad peasant as the symbol of the nation, celebrated as well in songs and films.

The new populism extended beyond symbolism to state institutions, though this reorientation took more time. Despite the Free Officers' first fateful decision to ruthlessly crush a strike in Kafr al-Dawwar, by the end of the 1950s the regime had shifted to co-optation, and labor unions had become a pillar of the regime.[7] The 1952 Land Reform was the first concrete step taken by the regime to demonstrate its commitment to Egypt's rural majority. While the land redistribution was the most prominent act, the revolutionary government accompanied this measure by other far-reaching steps, such as rent control and the formation of agricultural cooperatives. By the time the Arab Socialist Union (ASU) was formed in the next decade, the regime had moved beyond claiming to act for workers and peasants. It now promised to represent them in a more active sense. Half of the seats in parliament were reserved for workers and peasants, who formed two of the most critical "working forces of the nation."

Thus, even as the old structures of the parliamentary monarchy were being dismantled or brought to a standstill, new structures and practices were emerging that promised to represent and serve all the people of Egypt. Egypt's multiparty system and its monarchy had proved incapable of working for the people's interests, according to the new regime. It was claimed that Egypt's leaders before July 1952 had represented only themselves or petty and partisan interests. The central creed of the revolution, then, was not simply that it would act in the people's interest but that it would speak with their voice. Socially and politically dominant elites could no longer rule for their own benefit; they had to account for their actions to the people.

The Nasserist promise of accountability clashed most severely with liberal conceptions in the area of law. For the Nasserist regime, the law was to hold authorities accountable not so much by constitutional mechanisms as by anticipating and serving popular needs. This can be seen most clearly in the attempt to bring about a new Nasserist vision of law in the form of a new socialist legality. Although this vision was never fully implemented, it was much discussed.[8]

Prior to July 1952, Egypt's legal elite had been largely liberal and nationalist in outlook. The bar association was a bastion of nationalist sentiments. Its struggle for national independence had concentrated on securing the abolition of the capitulations. Many members of the country's pre–July 1952 political elite had legal training as well. With a few exceptions, most of these made the transition to the post–July 1952 regime fairly easily. While there were some clashes between the legal elite and the regime during the 1950s, the conflict was generally muted. The first few years of the regime saw the construction of a series of special courts and show trials to move against adversaries and old-regime political leaders. The legal community withheld public criticism of these measures. In 1954 and 1955, Nasser silenced the country's previously bold administrative court structure and again encountered little opposition. In 1956, the regime finally issued a new constitution that concentrated authority in the hands of the president. Despite such measures, however, the bulk of Egypt's legal system remained unchanged. Not until later did the regime begin to articulate an alternative legal vision.

Beginning in the mid-1960s, a group of leading political and legal figures called for a transformation of Egypt's legal culture. Some limited their appeals to the area of legislative change, specifically for laws supportive of socialist transformation.⁹ Others pushed even further for an entirely new socialist legal orientation, arguing that fundamental changes were needed as part of the effort to build a socialist society.

On an ideological level, the new socialist legality was to repudiate liberal ideas about law. The separation of powers was denounced as a capitalist ruse. Much of Egyptian legislation was condemned because it was written before July 1952, making Egypt's laws the alleged products of imperialism, feudalism, and capitalism. Of course, new laws could be written, but that process would take time. In the meantime, judges were urged to value socialist principles over the letter of the prerevolutionary law. This new orientation was advocated by those who claimed that it would serve the people and their interests far more faithfully than a literal emphasis on the law. Law was held to be the tool of the people and, as such, should advance rather than inhibit the realization of their desires. Furthermore, judges should not attempt to insulate themselves from popular pressures; instead, they should seek to serve the people. The old emphasis on judicial independence was criticized as merely creating a judicial ruling class that was isolated from the people. In short, this new socialist legality was to make the legal system much more accountable to the people than the old liberal, elitist order.

The fullest articulation of the call for a new socialist jurisprudence and legal structure appeared in a series of editorials by ʿAli Sabri in *Al-Jumhuriyya* in March 1967. The institutionalization of the new socialist legality entailed a series of structural changes, according to ʿAli Sabri and other fellow advocates. ʿAli Sabri himself focused on the inclusion of the judiciary in the ASU, and this topic drew the most attention in public discussions (and probably in private deliberations of the political leadership of the country). Yet, while attention was devoted to the idea, proposals remained fairly vague. Other proposals were made, such as unifying Egypt's judiciary under a single supreme court that would be responsible for striking down inappropriate, prerevolutionary laws and recommending changes in legislation. Popular participation in the judiciary was discussed, sometimes with the idea of electing judges or appointing prominent public personalities to serve on the bench; most frequently, some sort of jury system was advocated.

It is quite easy to be cynical about these ideas in hindsight. Indeed, in view of the authoritarian measures taken in the name of the socialist legality, as well as the broader failures of Nasserism, it is difficult to avoid harsh judgments of the regime. Yet, before moving to survey what the regime did, it is necessary to understand what it promised (and quite probably sought) to do. Egypt's leaders did not ask residents to accept authoritarianism; on the contrary, it offered them more meaningful participation.¹⁰

## Nasserism's Legality in Practice: Delivery on the Promise?

As harshly as Nasserism is remembered by its critics, and as hard-pressed as its apologists are to defend its record in the legal arena, the situation was far different during the Nasserist heyday of the 1960s. Then it was the liberals who struggled to justify their resistance to the new socialist legality without repudiating it totally. Rather than the liberals, the harshest contemporary critics of the Nasserist legal record were those who claimed that it did not go far enough. Most direct criticism while Nasser was still alive focused not on rejecting the Nasserist offer of greater accountability but rather on claiming that more radical action was necessary to meet it.

The ambitious proposals floated in the 1960s, at the height of Nasserist ideologies, were never fully implemented. Indeed, the period saw institutional changes that, though significant, constituted far less than the legal revolution called for by the Nasserists. Only at the end of Nasser's presidency did the regime move wholeheartedly in the direction of the new socialist legality, and then only for a limited time. For most of the 1950s, and even for much of the 1960s, the regime successfully avoided the legal system by constructing a series of exceptional courts and removing issues deemed critical from the purview of the courts.

Throughout the Nasserist period, concrete changes in the legal system itself were largely limited to two areas: first, there was a marked decrease in the independence of the judiciary, justified in terms of popular needs and desires; and second, the courts were made more accessible.

### Judicial Independence

Despite the regime's reputation for contempt of the judiciary, there were only two periods during which an effort was made to subjugate the judiciary. The first was an outcome of the March 1954 crisis involving a confrontation between the supporters and opponents of a return to constitutional life. The Free Officers—led by Nasser himself—who opposed the return to the barracks saw 'Abd al-Razzaq al-Sanhuri (the country's leading jurist) and the State Council he headed as a clear obstacle.[11] While the State Council had provided a key legal rationale for the Free Officers when they deposed the king and later abolished the monarchy, it was becoming less helpful over time. Al-Sanhuri had helped draft a post–July 1952 constitution, which the regime regarded as premature and far too liberal and democratic. The State Council clearly would have had no choice but to support an application of the existing legal order for which the Free Officers had little respect. Consequently, the regime sponsored a violent demonstration at al-Sanhuri's office, which degenerated into a physical assault on one of the most influential legal figures of Arab history.

Shortly thereafter, al-Sanhuri was dismissed on the pretext that he had served as a minister before the July 1952 coup and was thus tainted by the old order. The following year, a new law reorganizing the State Council was decreed, and all existing members of the body were dismissed. While most were immediately reappointed, about twenty were retired or assigned to nonjudicial positions. Dismissing al-Sanhuri allowed the regime to scuttle his draft constitution as well—or at least to introduce substantial changes. Al-Sanhuri's committee had envisaged the replacement of Egypt's monarchical regime with a parliamentary one. The regime opted instead for a presidential system. The resulting document, promulgated in 1956 and followed by a series of revisions, allowed in practice for almost unlimited presidential power; it made Nasser a far more dominant figure than the kings who had preceded him.

In 1969, a more systematic effort was undertaken to subjugate the rest of the judicial system. Oddly, the move came more than two years after the series of editorials by 'Ali Sabri referred to above. The judiciary itself constituted an obstacle. The Judges' Club—hitherto a social rather than a political body—sensed the possibility of change and issued a call in 1968 for the regime to engage in some liberalizing reforms. Weakened after the June 1967 War and facing rising domestic opposition, Egypt's rulers did not immediately respond. When action was finally taken in the summer of 1969, only some of the steps advocated by the socialist critics of the legal system were adopted.

The most notorious measure—the "massacre of the judiciary"—resembled the 1955 move against the State Council. In the name of judicial reorganization, all existing judicial personnel were dismissed, subject to reappointment. Most were reappointed, but the more politically troublesome judges were retired or given other assignments. This time, however, the regime did not stop with a change in personnel. An effort was made to build a new institutional structure for the judiciary. The measures were explicitly justified in terms borrowed from the call for a new socialist legality. A new Supreme Court was created to stand above the entire judicial apparatus, ruling not simply on the basis of legislated texts but also according to the needs and desires of the people. The explanatory memorandum to the decree-law establishing the court argued as follows:

> While the state has dealt with many of the most apparent inadequacies of legislation, the task of the judiciary in interpreting and applying is what sets into motion stagnant texts. The legislator depends on, or is hindered by, his task according to what is handed down in the way of interpretation of texts, especially because legislation is not always able to follow the changes that occur in a society with the necessary speed.

This makes the task of the judge in the stage of transition to socialism of the utmost importance and ensures his vanguard role and his responsibility to preserve the values of the society and its principles as an element completing his independence. The independence of the judge is not a characteristic the society bestows on him; rather, it is established in the interests of justice and the people.[12]

In addition to the Supreme Court, a new organization for judicial appointment and promotion—the Supreme Council of Judicial Organizations —replaced the older Supreme Judicial Council. The cumbersome change in name obscured a fundamental political shift. The older body allowed for a considerable amount of judicial independence by placing most matters relating to the judiciary in the hands of a body composed only of judges. The new body not only had a longer name; it also was placed under the chairmanship of the president of the republic (and effectively under the watchful eye of his minister of justice). This was designed to ensure that the judiciary would no longer stand aloof from the people but would now be held accountable to popular will.

While the measures of 1969 were far-reaching, they did not resolve all the matters raised by the socialist critics of the legal order. First, the reforms were issued by presidential decree, giving them a fairly precarious legal basis. Any permanent changes would eventually require changes in legislation and even the constitutional text. The new structures did represent a far stronger measure of executive control of the judiciary, but there was no guarantee that the result would be a positive move toward developing socialist jurisprudence. Judges were not brought into the ASU, as many had proposed, and the ideological bent of the new structures, such as the Supreme Court, would depend on presidential appointment. Adoption of some of the other measures suggested, such as popular participation in the judiciary, was postponed.

Only in 1971 were the changes of 1969 given a constitutional basis and, to some extent, even furthered. Egypt's "permanent constitution" of 1971 gave the new socialist legality a stronger basis by enshrining the new institutions—the Supreme Court and the Supreme Council of Judicial Organizations—in its text. Indeed, the 1971 constitution went even further by mandating some popular role in the judicial process, though it fell short of specifying what this would mean in practice. Moreover, an entirely new office was created: the Socialist Public Prosecutor, responsible for "taking procedures to secure the rights of the people, the safety of the society and its political system, and commitment to socialist behavior."[13] The post was to be filled by presidential appointment and was to assume responsibility, along with a new Court of Sequestration (Mahkamat al-Hirasa), for impounding the assets of political and economic adversaries of the prevailing order.

## Accessibility

The second effect of Nasserism was to make courts far more accessible to most Egyptians. This was accomplished through three sorts of measures, two of them intentional. First, legislative changes of the Nasserist period gave workers and tenants greater rights than they had previously enjoyed, with evictions, confiscations, and dismissals becoming more subject to review by the courts. In a sense, the effect of Nasserist reforms was to reconfigure property rights in some fundamental ways. This was often done by converting previous emergency measures (such as rent control on urban housing) to permanent status. Sometimes, as with land reform, Nasserism exceeded similar previous measures. The result was to render ownership of farmland or urban real estate restricted to only two privileges. First, the landlord was entitled to collect rent only in accordance with the amount fixed by the state. Second, the landlord could reclaim a property only if all members of the tenant's family had vacated it. However, even these limited rights were difficult to enforce because the courts were clogged by a tremendous amount of litigation involving just such matters. A landlord wishing to evict a tenant had few legal rights and even fewer tools to use.[14]

Indeed, this was the second measure adopted in the Nasserist period: Specific steps were taken, or not taken, as the case may be, to make it easier for Egyptians to go to court. Workers filing labor cases were forgiven court fees; other court fees (fixed by law in the 1930s) were never adjusted to keep face with inflation, which effectively reduced them greatly. In some ways, courts were more accessible to working-class litigants than to their wealthier counterparts. In some commercial cases, where fees are determined by the value of the case, a significant commercial dispute can carry with it very high litigation costs.

Third, the Nasserist period saw law schools open to enormous numbers of students and thus lose considerable prestige. Many Egyptian legal figures, very proud of the country's strong legal traditions, regarded this phenomenon with horror. Having the unintentional effect of flooding the country with lawyers, the move did not allow most graduates to enter full-time legal practice. However, the result was to bring legal counsel within the financial capacities of large numbers of Egyptians.

Whereas in many countries the complaint is often heard that justice goes to the wealthy, in Nasser's Egypt justice went to the patient. Litigation often did not cost much money, but it absorbed tremendous amounts of time. Like the universities, the courts changed. Now filled with lower- and middle-class Egyptians seeking justice, the courtrooms were no longer austere, distant, and forbidding; instead, they had become places where the country's elite felt increasingly uncomfortable.

Older Egyptians often speak of the changes wrought by Nasserism in Egypt's urban geography. Before the revolution, poorer Egyptians were not welcome in certain sections of Cairo. Garden City, parts of the Nile bank, and Qasr al-Nil Street were for pashas and professionals. Those wearing *gallabiyyas* were welcome only as servants, doormen, and laborers. This is often held to have changed after the revolution. Members of the old elite decry the resulting deterioration, as formerly quiet and fashionable areas have become crowded, noisy, and dilapidated. Other Egyptians wax nostalgic not for prerevolutionary Cairo but for the revolutionary period that brought the collapse of the elitist era.

In a sense, the courts are no different. Nasserism is held responsible—for good or ill—for opening Egyptian courts to all comers. The charge is largely accurate. The imposing structure built to house the Mixed Courts (which had jurisdiction over cases involving foreign interests until they were abolished in 1949) was transformed into the seat of the Court of Cassation (the supreme appellate court for the regular judiciary) and other high judicial bodies; it now stands as an overcrowded, decaying monument to Nasserist legal reform.

## Lingering Nasserist Legacy

In the 1970s, Nasserist ideology was gradually abandoned. The transformation initially took the form of correction rather than open repudiation. The regime promised not to draw up a new social contract but to meet the Nasserist promise of accountability and welfare more effectively. The initiatives of the late 1960s, especially in the legal realm, were criticized for not meeting these goals. Rather than make the political and economic authorities more accountable, they had built up unaccountable "centers of power." Welfare commitments were either maintained or expanded for most of the 1970s.

The first area of "correction" centered on various legal institutions. The judges dismissed in Nasser's 1969 "massacre of the judiciary" were reinstated, and Anwar al-Sadat apologized to them. The position of socialist public prosecutor was maintained, but with a greatly reduced role that was completely removed from socialism. The legal changes of the late 1960s and early 1970s gave the regime many tools for remolding the judiciary. Sadat used few of these tools and gradually discarded most of them totally. The Supreme Court was changed to a Supreme Constitutional Court in 1979; now given an unprecedented degree of independence, the court turned from its former mission of promoting socialism to a new mission of enforcing the liberal freedoms vaguely promised by the 1971 constitution.[15] The Supreme Council of Judicial Organizations, while maintained, had most of its authority taken away, and the older, exclusively judicial organs (including the Supreme Judicial Council) were revived. The State Council regained its autonomy.[16] By the early 1980s, the effects of the Nasserist legal revolution on the judiciary had been completely erased.

Yet the post-Nasserist regime had far more difficulty jettisoning its commitment to increased accessibility. The changes of the Nasserist era in this regard were approached gingerly if at all. Legislative changes in favor of workers, urban renters, and rural tenants were left alone for two decades, and only in the 1990s were some legislative changes made. Thus, the law continued to give significant protection to large numbers of Egyptians, who turned to the courts in increasing numbers. Furthermore, post-Nasserist governments have made no move to change the various procedural ways in which courts have become user-friendly to poorer litigants (such as low court fees). Instead, the emphasis has been on finding ways to cope with the large number of cases rather than on decreasing the burden. For instance, the government has moved to create a system in which judicial personnel are assigned to prepare a civil case in order to ensure that it is actually ready for trial. Egyptian courtrooms remain noisy, crowded, and inefficient places. Like other public services opened up to the middle class and sometimes the working class during the Nasserist period (such as public transportation), the effect has been to emphasize quantity rather than quality.

Indeed, it is notable in this regard that Egypt's rulers have maintained significant trappings of Nasserist socialism to this day. The 1971 constitution, written as Nasserism was only just beginning to recede, contains strong welfare commitments, extensive references to socialism, a requirement for the representation of workers and peasants in parliament, and a recognition of the leading role of the public sector. Over the three decades since its adoption, the regime moved to modify this language only once (in 1979), and then only in the most limited way. Some of the constitution's provisions have been gutted (so that a peasant has become virtually anyone who works in, or has studied, agriculture). Other elements of the constitution (such as those related to the public sector) have met with little enforcement. But the regime remains unwilling to consider constitutional reform, as often as the idea comes up. It is not merely increased liberalization that is feared; it is also public repudiation of the Nasserist legacy and commitments.

In short, Egypt's rulers have had a far easier time in increasing the independence of the judiciary than they have had in diminishing the accessibility of the courts. Nasserism continues to color Egyptian law—not by making it answer immediately to rulers but by making it accessible to the people. Precisely for that reason, however, the lingering effects of the Nasserist promise harm economic liberalization. The problem is that the courts are seen not as overly politicized but as inefficient and overburdened with petty problems of estranged wives, tenacious tenants, and dismissed workers.

Liberally minded economists and business leaders regard the Egyptian legal system with horror. Cases take years to decide, petty cases clog the courts, and judges are expected to rule in hundreds of cases without being given the necessary administrative support to make rulings, much less implement them. Rather than reform the system, business leaders seek to opt out of it by developing their own arbitration mechanisms. In 1994, a new arbitration law greatly expanded the legal support for arbitration in Egypt. Egyptians who can afford to avoid the legal system generally seek to do so; many have abandoned Egypt's courts in the same way that they have deserted some of the older wealthy neighborhoods.

## Conclusion

In 1991, one of the most prominent judges in Egypt told me: "Give us two more years and we will destroy everything Nasser did to this country." His prediction was inaccurate; an entire decade since then has yet to erase Nasserism's effects. Some elements of the Nasserist legal revolution have been extremely difficult to remove. Indeed, the lingering effects of the Nasserist legality actually extend far beyond the country's borders. After all, Nasserism not only represented a specific kind of socialism; it also contained a strong commitment to pan-Arabism. And Egyptian legal influence in the Arab world probably reached its height during the Nasserist period. Legal officials in the Arabian Gulf still talk of "Egyptian imperialism."

Arab countries gaining their independence have generally turned to Egypt for assistance in drafting their constitutions and law codes, staffing their law schools, and serving as judges and even as lawyers. While the Nasserist regime was suspicious of the country's old legal elite, it generally greeted this turn to the Egyptian model quite warmly. While Nasser did prevent his nemesis al-Sanhuri from traveling abroad to help some countries write their law codes and constitutions, hundreds of other Egyptians managed to go (and al-Sanhuri contributed as well, though he was forced to do so by mail). The Kuwaiti constitution was drafted by one of al-Sanhuri's students; the Iraqi law code was drafted by al-Sanhuri himself.

The export of Egyptian law has not ceased. Egyptian judges and law professors continue to travel to give legal advice, adjudicate disputes, and teach students. Egyptian lawyers continue to dominate law faculties in the Gulf. Egyptian law books are studied in law schools throughout the Arab world, and Egyptian court decisions are studied not simply by students but by judges as well.[17] The most recent effort in the Arab world at legal construction—the Palestinian Authority—has already turned heavily to Egyptian models, texts, and expertise.

Thus, wherever one goes in the Arab world, one encounters Egyptian laws, constitutional provisions, judges, and textbooks. And one hears that the courts are clogged and inefficient. To be sure, some of these flaws stem not from Nasserism but from the much earlier Egyptian adaptation of a civil law system. Nevertheless, with housing and labor law in the Arab world often dominated by Egyptian language and written by Egyptian-trained lawyers, it is difficult to deny that Nasserist Egypt exported not only its texts and personnel but also its problems.

The Nasserist promise amounted to greater accountability and accessibility through Arab socialism. In reality, this promise was only partially fulfilled. On the one hand, Nasserism delivered authoritarianism rather than accountability. On the other hand, increased accessibility was given and even appears to be permanent, at least in part. In Egypt today, the regime eschews vague socialism for vague liberalism. The rule of law has replaced the rule of the people. Once again, accountability is promised while authoritarianism is delivered—though generally in a less heavy-handed manner than existed under Nasser. Yet, despite the abandonment of socialism, the increased accessibility to legal institutions promised by Nasser is a burden that the current regime cannot find a way to repudiate.

## Notes

1. For an example of an Egyptian Marxist adopting a liberal, rule-of-law critique of the Egyptian revolution, see Salah 'Isa, "Huquq al-Insan fi Dasatir al-Batrirkiyya al-Thawriyya bayna al-Jumhuriyya al-Ri'asiyya wal-Jumhuriyya al-Barlamaniyya" (Human rights in the constitutions of revolutionary patriarchalism between presidential republicanism and parliamentary republicanism), *Al-Yasar* (January 2000): 15–30.

2. See, e.g., the statements of various Hamas leaders in "Role of the Opposition: Dialogue," *Shu'un Tanmawiyya* 7 (autumn 1998): 18–28. I have argued elsewhere that Islamist conceptions of the rule of law show evidence of growing—though still not unlimited—hospitality to liberal conceptions. See *Constitutions in a Nonconstitutional World: Arab Basic Laws and the Prospects for Accountable Government* (Albany: State University of New York Press, 2001), chap. 6.

3. See, e.g., Giacomo Luciani, ed., *The Arab State* (Berkeley: University of California Press, 1990); Lisa Anderson, "Absolutism and the Resilience of Monarchy in the Middle East," *Political Science Quarterly* 106, no. 1 (1991): 1.

4. Diane Singerman, *Avenues of Participation: Family, Politics, and Networks in Urban Quarters of Cairo* (Princeton: Princeton University Press, 1995).

5. The leading journal, *Al-Ahram al-Iqtisadi,* carried regular articles on the "new social contract."

6. I have written of the "ignorance" of Egyptian peasants elsewhere; see *Peasant Politics in Modern Egypt: The Struggle against the State* (New Haven: Yale University Press, 1990), chap. 3.

7. See Joel Beinin and Zachary Lockman, *Workers on the Nile: Nationalism, Communism, Islam, and the Egyptian Working Class, 1882–1954* (Princeton: Princeton University Press, 1987).

8. The discussion of socialist legality in the next several paragraphs draws on my earlier work, *The Rule of Law in the Arab World: Courts in Egypt and the Gulf* (Cambridge: Cambridge University Press, 1997). Readers wishing a more detailed treatment of the proposed socialist legality should consult chapter 4 of that book.

9. See, e.g., "Changing of the Laws," *Al-Akhbar,* August 28, 1966; the editorial, "The Legal Revolution," *Al-Jumhuriyya,* August 28, 1966; Jamal al-'Utayfi, "On the Road to Socialist Legality," *Al-Ahram,* October 20, 1967.

10. It is interesting in this regard that while Sadat moved uncertainly in a more liberal direction, he could present himself as far more explicitly authoritarian in his paternalistic self-portrait as the head of the Egyptian family. In the 1950s and 1960s, such rhetoric was eschewed; the president was portrayed as being one with the people, not their father.

11. The State Council served both as an advisory body to the executive on legal matters and as the country's administrative court structure, adjudicating in disputes wherein a state organ was a party.

12. The text is printed in 'Abdallah Imam, *Madhbahat al-Qada* (Cairo: Maktabat Madbuli, 1976), 136–37.

13. Article 179, Permanent Constitution of the Arab Republic of Egypt.

14. In doing research on litigation in Egypt in the early 1990s—when the Nasserist legal changes still prevailed in housing matters—I came across far more cases of landlords using indirect measures (such as allowing housing to fall into disrepair or keeping a small herd of water buffalo on the roof) than going to the courts. Even in the rare instance in which the landlord had the law on his side, tenants could use a variety of methods to drag litigation out over several years.

15. See Nathan J. Brown, "Judicial Review in the Arab World," *Journal of Democracy* 9 (October 1998): 85–99.

16. James H. Rosberg, "Roads to the Rule of Law: The Emergence of an Independent Judiciary in Contemporary Egypt," Ph.D. thesis, Department of Political Science, Massachusetts Institute of Technology, 1995.

17. In giving lectures to audiences in several Arab countries, I have generally found that Egyptian legal authorities and structures (and even important court decisions) need little explanation because they are already familiar.

# 5

## Sports, Society, and Revolution

Egypt in the Early Nasserite Period

Yoav Di-Capua

> Sports create a collective spirit ... and we are in need of such a spirit, since individualism ruined the basis of our power.
>
> Muhammad Nagib, *Al-Ahram,* July 27, 1953

> The history of societies is more widely reflected in the way they spend their leisure than in their work or politics
>
> Herold Perkin, sports historian, quoted in Neil Tranter, *Sport, Economy, and Society in Britain, 1750–1914,* 94

### Introduction

In the aftermath of World War II, Egyptian public life was turbulent and characterized by a deep sense of dissatisfaction. The apparent failure of Egypt's liberal experiment worried the bourgeoisie and the aristocracy. Likewise, the failure to transform Egypt's agrarian structure into a more egalitarian one weighed heavily on the shoulders of Egypt's rural inhabitants. A profound stasis in economic life concerned both workers and the middle class. And ultimately, Egypt's failure to free itself from the yoke of British imperialism affected Egyptian society as a whole. Students, intellectuals, urban workers, peasants, and the petit-bourgeoisie were all disillusioned by the failure to secure Egypt's independence. It was a pessimistic and disillusioned period.

Trying to deal with this gloomy atmosphere, the Free Officers strove to reshape all aspects of Egypt's public life. Political institutions were abolished, the king was deported, economic life took a new direction, and social and agrarian reforms were launched. These transformations were by no means limited to the political and social arenas. A cultural revolution was silently taking place as well. Honorific titles (pasha) were abolished; a new dress code was introduced to include the "safari suit" and the abolition of the *tarbush*. In addition, the regime introduced new experimental revolutionary art, new symbolic language, revisionist historiography, and inspiring revolutionary myths.[1] Changes in public architecture and public iconography were compatible with this trend. In short, a new revolutionary culture was gradually taking shape.

This is the departure point for our inquiry. The aim of this chapter is to discuss and analyze the role and importance of sports in Egypt's revolutionary regime. In particular, I will focus on a specific trend, namely, the "sports revival" movement launched by President Muhammad Nagib, which dominated Egyptian sports until the mid-1950s. In the late 1950s, this movement seemed to disintegrate, with Nasser directing sports in a slightly different way, one which remained dominant well into the 1970s. This second stage in the evolution of sports under the revolution will be briefly discussed here as well.

A close look at the history of Egyptian sports before and after the July 1952 Revolution reveals a break in the way in which sports were conceived, practiced, and organized. Of course, in some long-term respects (especially those related to the famous football clubs) there was also continuity, but in the years under discussion the overall picture is one of swift change. This change requires an explanation that views sports in the wider context of Egypt's political community, morals, common values, aspirations, and social bonds. In other words, sports can offer a sensitive and insightful way of looking at the changing identities and political preferences of peoples and regimes.

In the following pages, I will depict the change that occurred in the field of sports. I will argue that the way in which sports were perceived and practiced reveals a great deal about the challenges and goals that faced the new regime, as well as about its populist style. In particular, sports revealed the need of the regime to modernize Egypt. Thus the main suppositions of modernization, such as a binary perception of center and periphery, were accepted and reflected through sports. In order to understand the realities that the revolution aspired to change and the patterns by which its continuity was sustained, we now turn to discuss the role of sports in the first half of the twentieth century.

## Sports under the Monarchy

At the risk of oversimplification, it is possible to say that in the period preceding the revolution, sports were evident in two major and conflicting forms: the colonial, elite sports clubs and the Egyptian indigenous sports unions. These frameworks rendered services to different communities (both of which were marginal in terms of population percentages) and therefore belonged to different social, national, and cultural environments. However, they were not unknown to each other. The Egyptian sports unions were a later development of the colonial clubs and can be read as a nationalist response to them.

Generally speaking, modern sports were introduced to Egyptian society by the British colonizer.[2] The first sports clubs that were established, or appropriated, by the British favored the Indian model. This implies that sports clubs combined sports with sociocultural activity.[3] The members of the urban sports clubs (mainly in Cairo and Alexandria) belonged to the upper class. Magda Baraka, a social historian of Egypt, attempts to characterize this group in social and economic terms, and suggests identifying it by three sociocultural parameters: wealth, descent and kinship, and education and behavior.[4] By adopting these parameters, she highlights the cultural criterion of lifestyle, crucial for an understanding of sports clubs within their social milieu.

Notwithstanding the difficulty of definition, a word is in order regarding the formulation of clubs in terms of the members' national and ethnic identity. The Gazira club in central Cairo serves as an example for member profiles in the colonial clubs. Up to 80 percent of members were either British officials and their families or Anglo-Egyptians (i.e., British citizens who resided permanently in Egypt).[5] Whether they were administrators, teachers, businessmen, or army officers, they were all functionaries in the colonial apparatus.[6] The rest were "foreigners."[7] Unlike the British, who for the most part had arrived in Egypt as a result of the 1882 occupation, the "foreigners" had lived in Egypt for a longer period. By far the smallest and most insignificant class of members was that of the aristocratic Egyptian families. Originally from the countryside, these families left the village and immigrated to the city in order to create a dual economic and political power base. This pattern set in motion a modernization process (modern education, vocational training, involvement in politics, etc.), which included sports activities as well.[8] In a wider context, all three classes constituted only a small portion of the population as a whole. Most Egyptians living in rural areas had a different lifestyle altogether and hence did not practice modern sports activities or any other form of modern leisure.[9]

Jean-Marc Ran Oppenheim's work on the Alexandria club demonstrates the kind of cultural atmosphere that prevailed in the sports clubs.[10] The mentality of the British elite and upper class was dominant. The lingua franca in the clubs was either English or French. The use of Arabic was not looked upon with favor among these classes.[11] Moreover, since the cultural background of the members was mainly European, Egyptian customs hardly infiltrated the clubs. This widespread acceptance of European lifestyle was also reflected by the members' preferences in food and dress.

A brief look at the types of sports activities practiced in the clubs reveals an elitist taste as well. Golf, polo, horse riding, shooting, archery, hunting, yacht sailing, and swimming were integral parts of British upper-class culture. Needless to say, this culture was inaccessible and alien to the average Egyptian citizen. Popular sports, such as football, boxing, wrestling, and weightlifting, which were practiced by the British working classes, were slowly introduced to the urban Egyptian middle class. The limited types of sports activities that required cooperation and teamwork suggests that colonial sports in Egypt stressed individualism and distinctiveness as favored values. These types of sports were compatible with the image of the aristocratic sportsman. The genuine aristocrat was presented as someone who was socialized from a very early stage in life to appreciate various sports. As opposed to the nouveau riche, who concentrated on the consumption of goods, the aristocrat made it clear that it was not so much about luxury as it was about hierarchy and differentiation.

Sports clubs were planned in advance in order to serve as social clubs, accessible only to those familiar with the British and colonial cultural codes.[12] It was in these places that the well-to-do families could intermingle and socialize. Intermarriage and business relations among club members were common. One should also bear in mind that in the absence of sophisticated forms of organization (municipalities, town councils, and civil organizations), the clubs served as a place in which decisions were informally made regarding communal matters.[13]

It follows that the sociocultural reality in the Egyptian clubs was derived from the way in which sports functioned and were perceived in Britain itself. British sports historian Neil Tranter has argued that "for most of the social elite sport was an opportunity for differentiation not conciliation. And was used to restrict rather than expand contact with social inferiors."[14] This tendency was appropriated by the British colonizer and put into practice in India as well as in Egypt.

Recent criticism of colonial rule suggests that colonial systems, while propagating the colonizer's culture under the guise of accessibility and equality, denied the indigenous people true participation in practice. As put forward by one of the most prominent critics of colonialism, "[T]he premise of its power was a rule of colonial difference, namely, the preservation of the alienation of the ruling group."[15] Current postcolonial debate defines colonial sports as either "cultural imperialism" or "cultural hegemony."[16] Both definitions, although different from each other, seem to suit the Egyptian reality.

The fact that for the colonizers the clubs meant structured leisure in a controlled and protected environment, while for the colonized they meant humiliation and ostracism, caused some Egyptians to consider an organized response. This response was intimately connected with the advance of nationalist sentiment among Egyptians, resulting in the rise of the pre-1919 Ahali (indigenous) spirit. Ahali activities involved mostly private enterprises, such as magazines, private salons, social clubs, and even political parties.[17] In 1907, a group of Egyptians who were excluded from the British clubs decided to establish their own club: al-Ahali.[18] Although al-Ahali was modeled on the British precedent and, ironically enough, its first president was British (1907–8), it sought to provide the urban upper and upper middle classes with the benefits of participation in sports from within their own familiar environment. In 1908, Ahmad Zaghlul became its president, and the club was turned into the stronghold of the growing secular and liberal indigenous elite. In 1947, the monarchic millionaire Ahmad 'Abbud Pasha became its third president, serving until he was deposed by Nasser in late 1961.[19]

A second influential club was Qasr al-Nil bil-Jazira. Established in 1910, it followed a similar pattern of organization. A short time after its inauguration, its name was changed to al-Mukhtalat club (so named because its members belonged to many ethnic and national groups). Like the al-Ahali club, it came to be identified with "*bashawat,* politicians, and businessman."[20]

Following the 1919 revolution against British occupation, sports were put forward as a means for national revival. In 1921, the first football union was formed, soon to be joined by the establishment of other unions.[21] These developments marked the transference of sports from a limited and local practice to a national, and even an international, arena. As opposed to the pre-1919 period, now the state and the monarch found much interest in the organization of sports. This interest culminated in King Fu'ad's decision to establish the Civil Committee for Physical Education in 1924. The aim of the committee was to propose ways to organize sports, modeled on the European example.[22] As part of the new interest of the monarchy in sports, al-Mukhtalat football club changed its name for the third time, to the Faruq club.[23]

'Abbas Ibrahim Halim, a prince and a combat pilot who spent most of his adult life in Europe, is an example of rather futile efforts to promote sports among the masses. For more than a decade, Halim had been involved with the organization of the workers, believing that these two efforts were compatible. However, most of Halim's efforts in the field of sports were limited to the already existing aristocratic forms of sports and, therefore, in the end had little to do with the masses.[24]

After World War II, organizational developments, as well as growing awareness on the side of the nationalists, brought to the surface an urgent need to "Egyptianize Sports" (Tamsir al-Riyada). British sports clubs were now understood not only as elitist but also as antinationalist institutions in need of reform. This tendency was intensified after the revolution. As in other places in which nationalist revival occurred, sports were perceived as an important tool for the organization and conscription of citizens behind the national movement.[25] Writing in 1940, Faraj al-Sayyid, an ardent sports advocate, claimed that a physically healthy individual was a precondition for national revival and progress.[26] This idea, though originally European, marks an important trend that was later to be appropriated and put to work by the revolutionary regime.[27]

Of similar importance was the conception of sports as a means to disseminate values. As it was put by one of the members of the monarchy: "Sports could teach the Falah obedience, love of order, and tolerance."[28] Although this notion was not successfully implemented, it reveals a deep awareness and understanding of what needed to be done in order to educate the masses and transform them into disciplined and modern citizens. However, while the importance of physical education for the young generation was indeed acknowledged, it failed to acquire the dimensions of a popular cultural movement. The existing forms of sports remained primarily "elitist" and required expensive infrastructure and services.[29] Nationalist clubs and unions were limited in number and were in constant need of financial support. Some of this support came from the indigenous monarchic elite, identified with certain clubs, such as al-Ahali and Faruq, even as late as the 1960s. However, since the commercialization of sports did not occur, sports organizations were left dependent on the limited financial resources of the state. Thus, the significance of this period in relation to sports lies in the introduction of ideas and ideals rather than in their successful implementation.

## Sports and Revolution

As already mentioned, sports in the postrevolutionary era came to be closely associated with the political and ideological structure of the state. It is widely recognized that "the state plays a very different role in general, and in relation to culture and sport specifically, in liberal-democratic, capitalist societies, in fascist dictatorships, and in state socialist societies."[30] As such, a word is in order about the nature of the Egyptian revolutionary regime, which was distinctly populist. The characteristics of this populism may be summarized as follows: urban in nature and origin, a multiclass orientation, extravagant exhibitionism, and a constant need for public demonstration of achievements, charismatic authority, and militaristic appearance.[31] All of these characteristics were evident in the regime's involvement in sports.

The history of sports under the revolution can be roughly divided into two periods. The popular movement of the "sports revival," of which Nagib was an ardent supporter, characterized the first period. Enhancing the grip of the regime over some of the private clubs, as well as backing off from mass participation in sports, marked the second period. Nasser, 'Abd al-Hakim 'Amr, and their protégés were the main figures behind this trend. The differences between the two stages are subtle, and in general there is a great deal of continuity within the revolutionary period. Although my concern here is mainly with the first period, answers to the following questions will not differ greatly if they are to be asked regarding the later period as well:

1. Who controlled the way sports were organized?
2. How were sports represented and interpreted?
3. Who participated and in what form?

In less than two years, the revolutionary regime managed to gain control over all aspects of public life associated with sports. This effort was not directed in particular toward sports but was part of a larger effort to create a new state-culture through the bureaucratization and reorganization of public life.[32] In a relatively short time, the state apparatus established special committees to organize and institutionalize sports and leisure. Since in 1952 sports were still not part of a wide popular movement, equipped with its own infrastructure (i.e., teams, self-supporting financial systems, fan clubs, etc.), the task of the regime to penetrate and manipulate sports activities was relatively easy. Thus the private Faruq club was forced to change its name, now for the fourth time, to al-Zamaleq. Along with the al-Ahali club, al-Zamaleq was to popularize football to an unprecedented degree.

At the same time, under the supervision of Ahmad al-Tuwani, a veteran sports activist, hundreds of state sports clubs were established all over the country, and sports became a fundamental component of school and university curricula.[33] The organization of nationwide competitions and sports festivals followed these developments. This cultural change was soon to be dubbed "the revival of sports" (*al-nahda al-riyadiyya*), a trend covered by the newly published sports magazines.[34]

This "revival of sports" had three origins: the conviction that society at large should be modernized, the advent of a nationalist mode of thinking, and a pressing political need to create firm bonds with the populace at large. As already mentioned, nationalists targeted colonial sports clubs as being outposts of imperialism. Under the revolution, this tendency turned into a state policy. At the beginning, only unfavorable articles appeared in the press, depicting the colonial clubs, in contrast to the revolutionary sports clubs, as rich, snobbish, and aristocratic frameworks financed by public funds.[35] In a later stage, the colonial clubs were nationalized and, ironically, turned into the fortresses of the new revolutionary elite.[36]

As part of the introduction of revolutionary state culture, the very meaning of sports was altered. Before the revolution sports were regarded as a physical activity performed by individuals or groups mainly for their own benefit; now every form of mass participation for the benefit of the collective was defined as sports. Hence, sports became an affair of the "state apparatus" to an unprecedented degree. As part of the Free Officers' gambit to reorganize public life, by the mid-1950s the state had become the main sponsor and promoter of most cultural activities.[37] Sports, under the new inclusive definition, were to play an important role in the new cultural agenda. As early as January 1953, the organization of leisure in the public sector had already been accomplished, primarily in the form of state sports clubs.[38] This process in Egypt's public sector was encouraged not only to create a "community spirit" but also to improve production.[39] Mass organization of sports was intended to teach workers that, with relatively little effort, they could improve their physical condition, build up their resistance to diseases, and thus improve their productivity. This pattern of organization resembles the Italian model of *Dopolavoro* (after-work) compulsory culture, in which sports accounted for an important component.[40]

The attempt to organize mass leisure had several goals. First, it served as a means to control the urban Egyptian middle class. Second, it was aimed at disseminating values, such as unity, equality, cooperation, and discipline, which were important to the regime and reflected its belief in modernization. These beliefs and other intellectual components that fueled the "revival of sports" are evident in a letter sent by Nagib to the editor of the new sports magazine *Al-Abtal*: "I hope that the magazine will fulfill its task by creating a physically strong and healthy generation vigorous in its beliefs, mentality, and spirit for the purpose of creating a strong internal united and organized front. A front that is capable of coping with all aspects of life in times of peace and war."[41]

Following this same line, the editor claimed that sports are the basis for a sound and correct nationalism. Both views highlight the notion that sports should prepare Egyptians for national struggle.[42]

The importance of sports, for the fitness of the individual as well as for the monopoly of the nation over its human resources, was already a well-known concept. Added to a blend of other intellectual traditions, such as "social Darwinism," the result was a firm belief in the right of the nation and its revolutionary representatives to train its citizens. The underlying assumption was that, as was the case for individuals, the nation's ability to survive depended on its physical potency and strength.[43] Hence the nation was in constant need of strong, healthy individuals. Under the revolution, the fragments of already existing ideas came into focus and were formulated into official state policy. These notions were represented as desired values and idealized national goals, by far the most important of which were the "unitary national state" and "national unity."

The setting in which sports was implemented as a means for the dissemination of values was that of the "revolutionary festival." In 1953–54, the regime organized several festivals in which Egyptian citizens participated.[44] Since most of the festivals took place in the city, transportation was organized for the countryside peasants. Festivals have a unique psychological importance as a meeting point between the individual and the collective. Using the term *effervescence,* the French sociologist Émile Durkheim captured the nature of this individual-collective atmosphere. An atmosphere of effervescence causes individuals to perceive themselves as an integral part of a greater collectivity. In such situations, "men see more and differently than in normal times. Changes are not merely of shades and degrees; men become different."[45] It follows that the experience of the festival breaks down the mental, moral, and physical barriers between the individual and the collective. It is an activity in which one feels rather than thinks. Under the influence of these forces, individuals might be more flexible to reconsider, and perhaps even to change, their social, political, and moral beliefs.

Another aspect of effervescence has to do with the immediate physical and temporal environment of the festival. Mona Ozouf, who worked on French revolutionary festivals, argues that the festival serves as a powerful tool for the dissemination of values by changing the dimensions of time and space. The festival creates a new agenda, which is different from the normal routine of the individual. Most Egyptian festivals lasted four or five days, which were consecrated for sports and mass rallies and were therefore declared holidays from work. The activities were scheduled around the clock in such a way that one could spend the whole week in the streets.[46] In the words of Ozouf, "Separated from daily rhythms, men relinquish the serious use of their time, and their ties with ordinary moral and social values become undone. The festival gives bounds to an autonomous activity: there is, then, between the festival and men's daily life an insurmountable antagonism."[47]

In addition, sports festivals were characterized by their simultaneity. The open space created a simultaneous experience of peoples and minds. Collective physical activities, some of them repetitive in nature (such as marches), only intensified the collective atmosphere and the sense of togetherness. Social, political, and other differences were abolished, and the common denominator shared by all was highlighted. This was one of the methods by which the concept of unity and social harmony was practically experienced and internalized.

The state-sponsored conveyance of rural peasants to major cities in order to participate in sports competitions was adopted in order to narrow the gaps between "center and periphery." This created a common meeting ground and enabled an active interaction between people who formerly had only rare opportunities to socialize. For the first time, numerous amateur popular sports teams, all organized by the regime, competed on an equal basis.[48] These games provided not only a unique setting for citizens to meet their peers but also an opportunity for the army to compete against civilians. This was encouraged in order to reinforce the idea of the "people's army."[49] For a country which had historically suffered under the yoke of distant kings or elitist colonizers, the competition between civilians and army officers as equals, subject to the same rules of the game, was indeed revolutionary.

Since the biggest football clubs, al-Ahali and al-Zamaleq, were still in the hands of the old monarchic elite, the Free Officers could not spare any effort to push their initiative forward. Members of the Revolutionary Command Council (RCC), including the president himself, were often present at sports festivals and other national sports events, even if these took place in a remote province. For provincials who paid taxes for years without ever seeing their kings and sultans, this too was a revolutionary development. It was perhaps the first time in modern Egyptian history that millions of inhabitants could feel that they were "seen" by the regime, although few actively participated in sports competitions.[50]

Popular competitions between youth took place in the public squares of Cairo, which were specifically redesigned for such occasions. Other parts of the city were rebuilt as well in order to create enough space for mass festivals.[51] As a whole, it seems that most of the new revolutionary urban projects were "mass oriented," reflecting the unique way in which changes in public architecture and space go hand in hand with sports as a political agenda.

Standing as a symbol for all of this, and in particular advocating the concept of "national unity," was the torch race. The opening ceremony of the July 1954 Four Days Festival was held at night. A runner bearing a torch made his way from the provinces to Republic Square (Maydan al-Jumhuriyya) in the capital, thus symbolizing by his physical trajectory the political bond between center and periphery. The effect was dramatic as the runner approached the main stage and set fire to twenty-four torches, each symbolizing a province.[52] At about the same time, similar ceremonies were held in all major towns around the country. These symbolic events marked the commitment of the regime to equality and the consolidation of the country as one homogeneous national unit. This represented a revolutionary change from the historical approach whereby the provinces were regarded by the regime as merely a place for the conscription of soldiers, employment of laborers, and collection of taxes.

In 1954, as part of the "sports revival," live radio broadcasts of popular sports events increased. In addition, special radio magazines, exclusively dealing with sports, were initiated.[53] These measures were of great importance, since radio was one of the means used to unite the population. Concurrently, sports news no longer appeared in the back pages of the daily newspapers but, rather, on front pages. Sports events could now reach almost every citizen in the country. As students of nationalism have demonstrated, the rationale behind such steps is here as elsewhere, that if one cannot participate physically, one can at least imagine oneself to be part of a greater collective.

As part of the attempt to introduce sports to more traditional sectors, sports bureaucrats and national leaders stressed the bond between Islam and sports. Accordingly, the daily prayer was portrayed as a healthy sports exercise. The late Eighth Caliph Harun al-Rashid was noted to be a superb polo player who favored physical training. And Nagib himself touted the advice of the Prophet Muhammad to practice sports, such as swimming and archery.[54]

The concept of "national unity" was also closely associated with "upward social mobility" and equal opportunity for all. To prove that these were not mere slogans but social realities, the mass media accentuated the extraordinary achievements of amateur sportsmen, who became popular heroes almost overnight. Unlike the aristocratic hero who was educated in a fancy sports club, the revolutionary heroes were outstanding athletes of humble origin. They usually had no professional training, and no one knew them or their families. Precisely because they were just another face in the crowd, common people could identify with them and feel as if they themselves could be the subject of such praise and glory. When their pictures were published in the newspapers, showing them receiving awards from the president or another high-ranking officer, everyone could identify with them.[55] As was the case in Argentina under Perón, the message of the regime was clear: In the revolutionary era, talent, rather than social position, determined one's standing. Equal opportunities were open to all.[56]

Two institutes for professional sports training were established in Cairo and Alexandria, offering intensive professional training to a limited number of young, talented sportsmen. Those who were accepted were glorified, praised, and perceived as leaders of a new revolutionary generation. Other professional sportsmen were offered easy admission to institutions of higher education.[57] Like other nations, Egypt was in need of real professional sportsmen to demonstrate its national potency in the international arena, as well as in the Pan-Arab games.[58]

The veneration of young sportsmen was part of a larger phenomenon of a cult of youth. Anticipation of a nationalist and revolutionary young generation, which would fulfill Egypt's national aspirations, was not a novelty in Egypt's public life.[59] Egypt's new revolutionary regime not only acknowledged the importance of the young generation but, with characteristic enthusiasm, did everything at its disposal to actively conscript youth for its cause. The measures taken by the regime revealed two interesting points. The first was the unprecedented equal treatment of young men and women, and the second was the adoption of a very broad interpretation of sports to include all kinds of organized youth movements. Such an interpretation prepared the ground for the conscription of youth to paramilitary organizations. From that point onwards, sports, as a fun activity, and militarism, as a national imperative, were perceived as identical forms of commitment.

In order to integrate all of these factors, the regime established a special apparatus for the organization of youth. Under the management of 'Adl Tahir, a retired army officer, the Higher Committee for the Patronage of Youth (HCPY, al-Majlis al-A'la li-Ri'ayat al-Shabab) sought to propagate physical education in organized forms.[60] Since they carried a clear moral message, the tasks of the HCPY were far from being merely recreation: "The purpose is to create a sound, mentally, physically, and morally capable Arab citizen. One who believes in God and the nation, and who is willing to sacrifice for the sake of the society."[61]

The projects carried on by the HCPY varied. The regime sought to include citizens from all classes throughout Egypt. The main organizational project was the establishment of special Youth Clubs throughout the country, with much attention directed toward the countryside. The clubs provided the youth with sports facilities as well as social activities. The social environment in the clubs offered "unguarded" interaction of men and women, which went against traditional gender divisions.[62]

A large variety of activities, among them "youth holidays," "labor brigades," sports festivals, and summer camps, created exceptional opportunities for young men and women to meet and cooperate in a well organized environment. Although this kind of interaction was more prevalent in the big cities, in peripheral areas it was indeed regarded as an innovation. These activities brought Egyptian youth together to physically experience "unity." On these occasions, special workshops for the clarification of national tasks were held. Thus, from a very early stage in life, youth were expected to be truly committed to a "national" cause. The workshops stressed the importance of youth leadership for the future of the nation. In fact, one of the declared missions of the HCPY was to "manufacture" such leaders for the benefit of society.[63]

The gender historian Allen Warren stressed the appeal that military-style activities held for some young men, particularly in regard to work brigades.[64] The Egyptian work brigades had a silent militaristic and masculine nature. The fact that until the early months of 1957 British forces had occupied Egyptian territory is significant in this respect. As long as the active national struggle for independence continued, youth were regarded as potential soldiers. The conscription of youth (men and women) was more than a symbolic matter of uniforms and marching, since it resulted in the actual use of firearms.[65] When the British occupation ceased, youth were conscripted as "soldiers in the army of modernization and progress."

In contrast to other institutions of sports that changed or disappeared altogether in the late 1950s, youth organizations were taken very seriously by Nasser, who regarded them as outposts of immediate support for his politics. Indeed, when Anwar al-Sadat started his own political project in May 1971, one of the first things he did was to arrest the heads of the youth organizations that supported the Nasserist line.[66]

Having dealt with the "sports revival," as it was manifested until the late 1950s, a word is in order regarding trends in sports organization in the subsequent period. Politically, two events assisted in the rise of Nasser to a position of undisputed leader: the 1956 Suez War and the unification of Egypt with Syria (the United Arab Republic) in February 1958. After this period, one can discern a different policy toward sports, one with a clear Nasserist imprint. Since by 1958 the state had already managed to infiltrate the popular arena, it only remained to establish its authority over the football clubs, still governed by supporters of the old monarchy.

In 1958, Nasser appointed his chief of staff, 'Abd al-Hakim 'Amer, to head Egypt's Football Association. Two years later, in the wake of a large "nationalization" enterprise, which broke the financial power of football sponsors, such as 'Abbud Pasha, 'Amr managed to secure the appointment of his brother Hassan as president of al-Zamaleq. In 1965, 'Amer persuaded Nasser to appoint 'Abd al-Muhsin, the former commander of the Egyptian troops stationed in Yemen, to head al-Ahali.[67] These developments complemented the need felt by Nasser himself to establish a popular football club that would be exclusively identified with the revolution. For that purpose, he appointed his bureau chief, Sami Sharaf, to head the newly established al-Shams club, which was to be the largest of its kind in the Middle East. Admission was denied to "collaborators," "feudalists," and supporters of capitalism.

After 1958, and in particular after the "socialist turn," Nasser seemed to be personally involved in planning and implementing a national sports policy.[68] By this time, popular interest in football is estimated to have engaged an unprecedented 70 percent of the population. In an interview he gave in 1997, Sami Sharaf contended that the philosophy of the revolution in regard to sports was to create leisure and proper education in a social, economic, and revolutionary context and to accentuate the role of youth in it.[69] Although most of the thousands of rural sports clubs established in the previous period were on the brink of collapse, Sharaf's words suggest continuity from the philosophy of earlier days.

However, the difference between the two periods is still evident. While until 1958 there was a state effort to ensure mass participation in sports events, in the second period Nasser directed sports activities on a more representational level. Thus, the masses were no longer expected to practice sports on an individual basis, and Nasser seems to have developed more efficient mechanisms to unite citizens and mobilize them in the achievement of collective goals.

In sum, sports under the revolution were subjected to an energetic state apparatus, which promised that the regime's message would be seen, heard, sensed, memorized, and physically practiced daily.[70] The intensity of the message was such that its internalization was inevitable. In short, the "sports revival" sought to create and mobilize a new brand of political public. Indeed, the success of the Egyptian government motivated the Sudanese government to employ exactly the same methods and rhetoric.[71]

## Conclusions

Apart from what has been said thus far regarding sports under the revolution, the way in which sports were defined, practiced, and discussed reveals the regime's fascination with the idea of modernization. Almost all of the assumptions and premises of modernization were to be found in sports: secularism, equality, bureaucratization, specialization, rationalization, and the obsession with records.[72] Through sports, the regime strove to narrow the gaps between center and periphery; improve productivity; promote self-control, order, and discipline; and improve health and hygiene. Passive fatalism, a passive role for women, and other traditional characteristics were categorically rejected. The new revolutionary man or woman was expected to embody these virtues and encourage others to do so as well. The history of sports in the period under discussion clearly reveals the desired goals of the Free Officers and some of the means with which they could be achieved.

However coercive was the introduction of the modernist vision, it was effective and, at least initially, attracted citizens to participate. The first years were indeed characterized by a great enthusiasm, but that enthusiasm gradually waned. Václav Havel's critique of a similar state culture in his country seems to capture the atmosphere which brought the "sports revival" to an end:

> Instead of events, we are offered nonevents; we live from anniversary to anniversary, from celebration to celebration, from parade to parade, from a unanimous congress to unanimous elections and back again; from a Press Day to an Artillery Day, and vice versa. It is no coincidence that, thanks to the substitution for history, we are able to review everything that is happening in society past and future, by simply glancing at the calendar. And the notoriously familiar character of the recurrent rituals makes such information quite as adequate as if we had been present at the events themselves.[73]

The history of sports under the revolution uncovers the scope of the "revolutionary imagination" and its ill-fated dream of powerful and inclusive revolutionary culture. Hence, this chapter tells us more about the prevailing temper, actions, pathos, experiments, visions, hopes, and revolutionary dreams than about sports per se.

### Notes

I would like to thank Russell Hopley and Stephennie Mulder for their time, effort, and good advice.

1. Joel Gordon, *Nasser's Blessed Movement: Egypt's Free Officers and the Revolution* (New York: Oxford University Press, 1992), 3–39. See also *Al-Ahram*, January 23, 1953; Lilian Karnouk, *Contemporary Egyptian Art* (Cairo: American University in Cairo Press, 1995), 5–31.

2. Some sports clubs, such as that of Alexandria, were established by the foreign European community before the British occupation of 1882. Gradually, they all became British in essence.

3. Ibrahim M. Hilmi and Askar F. Nahed, "Ideology, Politics, and Sports in Egypt," *Leisure Studies* 3, no. 1 (1984): 97–99.

4. Magda Baraka, *The Egyptian Upper Class between Two Revolutions, 1919–1952* (Reading: Ithaca Press, 1998), 45.

5. *Al-Abtal*, February 1953, 26.

6. Jean-Marc Ran Oppenheim, "Twilight of a Colonial Ethos: The Alexandria Sporting Club, 1890–1956," Ph.D. diss., Columbia University, 1991, 113–60.

7. In order to differentiate this class from the "real Egyptians," Egyptian nationalists used the term *foreigners* to call attention to their European origins.

8. *Al-Abtal*, February 1953, 26. Baraka, who had access to the Jazira club files and records, claims that only in 1950 did the club become legally accessible to native

upper-class Egyptians, since until then it had been primarily a British enclave. See Baraka, *The Egyptian Upper Class*, 192–93.

9. In fact, the concept of leisure itself is an urban and modern one. Hilmi and Nahed, "Ideology, Politics, and Sports in Egypt," 97–99.

10. It is, however, less beneficial for understanding sports in a larger context, since Oppenheim's research does not use Arabic sources. Oppenheim, *Twilight of a Colonial Ethos*, 1–13.

11. Most of the members hardly knew Arabic at all.

12. The Ma'adi sports club in Cairo is a good example, since it served the diplomatic community, and most of its members were European in culture. See Samir W. Raafat, *Ma'adi, 1904–1962: Society and History in a Cairo Suburb* (Cairo: Palm Press, 1995), 33–46, 67–73.

13. Oppenheim, *Twilight of a Colonial Ethos*, 140–60.

14. Neil Tranter, *Sport, Economy, and Society in Britain, 1750–1914* (Cambridge: Cambridge University Press, 1998), 41.

15. Partha Chatterjee, *The Nation and Its Fragments: Colonial and Post Colonial Histories* (Princeton: Princeton University Press, 1993), 10, 14–34.

16. Allen Guttmann, *Games and Empires: Modern Sport and Cultural Imperialism* (New York: Columbia University Press, 1994), 171–88.

17. Baraka, *The Egyptian Upper Class*, 67.

18. Faraj al-Sayyid, *Al-Riyada fi Biladina* (Cairo: Mtba'at al-Ma'arif, 1940), 50–51.

19. Abu al-Ma'ati Zaki, *Lu'abat al-Riyada wal-Siyasa* (Cairo: al-I'lamiyya, 1997), 41–44.

20. Ibid., 63–64.

21. Al-Sayyid, *Al-Riyada fi Biladina*, 16–17.

22. Egypt was one of the first countries in the world to join the world Olympic games. Since 1912, Egypt has participated in all Olympic games. See Faraj al-Sayyid, *Ruwad al-Riyada fi Misr* (Cairo: Markaz al-Aharam lil-Tarjama wal-Nashr, 1988), 12–16.

23. Zaki, *Lu'abat al-Riyada wal-Siyasa*, 63.

24. Halim was among the founders of the Royal Automobile Club. Joel Beinin and Zachary Lockman, *Workers on the Nile: Nationalism, Communism, Islam, and the Egyptian Working Class, 1882–1954* (Princeton: Princeton University Press, 1987), 195–99.

25. Inspired by Egypt, the Arabs of Palestine witnessed the same national development with respect to sports as a means for national revival. Tamir Sorek, "Leumiyut Palastinit beMedina haMandatorit: Mador Hasport Kesokhen Zehut" (Palestinian nationalism in the mandatory state: The sports column as an agent of identity), *Zmanim* 18 (spring 2000): 15–25 (Hebrew).

26. Al-Sayyid, *Al-Riyada fi Biladina*, 11–12.

27. In late-nineteenth-century Europe, active participation in sports was widely regarded as a requirement for the high standard of physical, mental, and moral well-being. Tranter, *Sport, Economy, and Society in Britain*, 57.

28. Ibid., 39.

29. Members of the monarchy and the Egyptian elite were engaged in "British" types of sports as well. King Faruq himself established a hunting club. Ibid., 52–54.

30. John Hargreaves, "Sport, Culture, and Ideology," in Jennifer Hargreaves, ed., *Sport, Culture, and Ideology* (London: Routledge, 1982), 46.

31. Michael Conniff, "Introduction: Towards a Comparative Definition of Populism," in Conniff, ed., *Latin American Populism in Comparative Perspectives* (Albuquerque: University of New Mexico Press, 1982), 13–27.

32. See Revolutionary Command Council resolutions regarding public life after six months in power: *Al-Ahram*, January 23, 1953.

33. Ahmad al-Tuwani, *The Egyptian Revolution in Three Years* (Cairo: Information Administration, 1955), 103–8.

34. *Al-Ahram*, July 23, 1953; *Al-Jumhuriyya*, July 23, 28, 30, 1954; *Al-Thawra wal-Riyada* (Cairo: al-Dar Nashar al-Thaqafa, 1966); *Al-Abtal*, February 1953, 44. Two new sports magazines appeared in the early 1950s: *Al-Abtal* (Heroes) and *Al-Riyada wa-Awqat al-Faragh* (Sports and leisure). The first was published by the RCC and appeared for the first time in January 1953, whereas the second was a private journal that was first published in May 1954.

35. *Al-Thawra* (Damascus), August 5, 1954; *Al-Abtal*, February 1953, 26.

36. Oppenheim, *Twilight of a Colonial Ethos*, 198–99.

37. Writing about a similar phenomenon in fascist Italy, Victoria De Grazia defined the attempts at organization and the creation of "state apparatus" culture as the "culture of consent." De Grazia, *The Culture of Consent: Mass Organization of Leisure in Fascist Italy* (Cambridge: Cambridge University Press, 1981), 1–24.

38. Other enterprises included the establishment of "popular theaters," which performed in workplaces and in urban public spaces free of charge. See the theater's schedule for January 1953 in the center of Cairo: *Al-Ahram*, January 22, 1953.

39. *Al-Abtal*, January 1953, 26; *Al-Ahram*, January 23, 1953; Hasan 'Imad, *Al-Riyada wal-Shabab fi 'Ashr Sanawat* (Cairo: Kutub Qawmiyya, 1962), 29–32.

40. I was not able to verify to what degree workers were forced to participate. The overall impression is that workers and other state employees felt obliged to participate as a result of an "atmosphere" or a vague commitment to the "system."

41. *Al-Abtal*, January 1953, 1.

42. Ibid., 2. A similar perception of sports also prevailed under Perón in Argentina, where it focused on the potential of sports for inspiring fraternity, cooperation, social solidarity, national identity, discipline, and loyalty. See Raanan Rein, "El Primer Despotista": The Political Use and Abuse of Sport in Perónist Argentina," *International Journal of History of the Sport* 15, no. 2 (1998): 58.

43. For the origins of these perceptions, see R. Holt, "Contrasting Nationalisms: Sport, Militarism, and Unitary State in Britain and France before 1914," *History of Sport* 12 (1995): 39–54.

44. In 1953 alone, festivals took place in January, March, April, and July. *Al-Ahram*, January 23, July 23, 1953; *Al-Abtal*, February 1953, 28.

45. Émile Durkheim, *The Elementary Forms of Religious Life* (New York: Mac-

millan, 1965), 240–41. Although Durkheim dealt with religious ceremonies, he argued that such an atmosphere is also evident in revolutionary situations.

46. See the schedules of some sports festivals, as published by the daily press: *Al-Ahram,* January 21, 22, 24, 1953; *Al-Balagh,* January 20, 22, 1953.

47. Mona Ozouf, "Space and Time in the Festivals of the French Revolution," *Comparative Studies in Society and History* 17, no. 3 (1975): 372.

48. *Al-Abtal,* January 1953, 26; April 1953, 22–23; *Al-Ahram,* January 23, 25, 1951.

49. *Al-Ahram,* January 22, 1953. The army, which was responsible for the revolution, claimed that it was acting on behalf of the people. Hence it called itself the "people's army." Gordon, *Nasser's Blessed Movement,* 39–57.

50. Sports were not the only means by which the regime directed its attention to the periphery. Such efforts were also evidenced by the ceremonies in which RCC members distributed confiscated land to poor peasants. *Al-Akhbar* (Cairo), July 17, 1954. See also Nasser's speech from May 2, 1954, in which the values of unity and equality were stressed. See Ahmad Yusuf Ahmad, ed., *Al-Majmu'a al-Kamila li-Khitab wa-Ahadith wa-Tasrihat Gamal 'Abd al-Nasir* (Beirut: Markaz al-Dirasat al-Wahda al-'Arabiyya, 1995), 193.

51. *Al-Abtal,* April 1953, 22–23. The most famous reorganized square was the Isma'iliyya Square. During the January 1953 festival, the square's name was changed to Liberation Square. Other changes in public space resulted in the construction of Cairo's stadium. See plan in *Riyada wa-Awqat al-Faragh* (May 1954): 59–61.

52. *Al-Ahram,* July 23, 1954; *Al-Jumhuriyya,* July 23, 1954.

53. Farhad Ammar, "Al-Idha'a wa-Risalatuha al-Riyadiyya," in *Al-Thawra wal-Riyada,* 29–36.

54. *Al-Abtal,* February 1952, 5; May 1953, 22. Nagib's speech: *Al-Ahram,* July 27, 1953.

55. See, e.g., *Al-Abtal,* January 1953, 14–15; March 1953 21; *Al-Jumhuriyya,* July 30, 1954.

56. Rein, "El Primer Despotista," 56.

57. 'Imad, *Al-Riyada wal-Shabab fi 'Ashr Sanawat,* 13, 57–60.

58. The first Pan-Arab games took place in Alexandria in July 1953. See al-Sayyid, *Ruwad al-Riyada fi Misr,* 24.

59. For the history of students, youth, and politics in Egypt, see Haggai Erlich, *Students and University in Twentieth-Century Egyptian Politics* (London: Frank Cass, 1989), 95–132.

60. *Al-Riyada wa-Awqat al-Faragh,* November 1954, 41; 'Imad, *Al-Riyada wal-Shabab fi 'Ashr Sanawat,* 10–12.

61. 'Imad, *Al-Riyada wal-Shabab fi 'Ashr Sanawat,* 21.

62. Ibid., 10–21, 57–60.

63. Ibid., 57.

64. Allen Warren, "Sports, Youth, and Gender in Britain, 1880–1940," in Clyde Binfield and John Stevenson, eds., *Sport, Culture, and Politics* (Sheffield: Sheffield Academic Press, 1993), 61.

65. *Al-Abtal,* April 1953, 10.

66. Zaki, *Lu'abat al-Riyada wal-Siyasa,* 8–9; *Al-Hayat al-Ahaliyya li-Ri'ayat al-Shabab wal-Riyada* (Cairo: al-Haya al-'Amma, 1976).

67. Zaki, *Lu'abat al-Riyada wal-Siyasa,* 49–50, 78–85.

68. He had an office in the al-Shams club, although apparently he rarely used it. Ibid., 115.

69. Ibid., 85, 97–118.

70. See a speech by Nagib accentuating the proper values manifested through sports: *Al-Ahram,* July 27, 1953; *Al-Abtal,* March 1953, 46; *Al-Balagh,* January 25, 1953; 'Imad, *Al-Riyada wal-Shabab fi 'Ashr Sanawat,* 21.

71. Hasan 'Umar, *Al-Riyada fi 'Ahd al-Thawra* (Khartoum: State Press, 1963).

72. Guttmann, *Games and Empires,* 2–3.

73. Václav Havel, *Open Letters: Selected Prose, 1965-1990* (London: Faber and Faber, 1991), 74. See an open letter of complaints about the status of sports in Egyptian society during that period: *Al-Riyada wa-Awqat al-Faghar,* November 1962, 3–21. For a more contemporary view, see Hasan al-Mustakawi, "Al-Ahali wa-al-Zamaliq," *Wujhat Nazar* 5 (July 2003): 52–57.

# 6

# Nasserist and Post-Nasserist Elites in an Official Biographical Lexicon

Uri M. Kupferschmidt

## Introduction

This chapter presents a review of the *Mawsu'a al-Qawmiyya lil-Shakhsiyyat al-Misriyya al-Bariza,* a two-volume biographical dictionary listing over 4,300 Egyptians. The *Mawsu'a* was published in 1992 by the State Information Service, which, as an official agency, is a typical formation of the Nasserist regime and era.[1] The dictionary is meant as a "historic national project" aiming to build a progressive Egypt. Hence the term *qawmiyya,* an ideological label typical of the period following the revolution, figuring in the title of the work. The introduction to this biographical lexicon declares that it includes the "highest and noblest" achievements of the elite (for which the terms *safwa* or *nukhba* are used). Typically, the semimilitary or semisocialist term *kadir* (cadre) is also used.

We speak here about the second edition, which replaced a heavily criticized first edition published in 1989. Although 14,000 Egyptians were originally supposed to be included, the first edition contained only 1,525 names, and many prominent people were offended by not being listed. Names and data were collected in a heavy-handed way, it seems, from the various employers—state ministries and agencies, higher councils, universities, and public sector companies—rather than from the personalities themselves.

At first sight, this is a type of biographical lexicon of the format commonly called *Who's Who,* the first of which was published in the United States in 1899 and which has been widely emulated elsewhere as well.[2] Not a few of these have been published for such diverse countries and continents as Japan, China, Russia, and Latin America, albeit often in the West and for Western reference purposes. For the Arab world, we have at our disposal several types of serialized *Who's Who,* which are only partly helpful as to Egypt.[3] This *Mawsu'a* undoubtedly intends to fill a gap and has its merits as such, but one has to be aware that its approach is closer to a *nomenclatura* list than to a more subjective selection on the basis of meritocratic criteria. One could therefore argue that the *Mawsu'a*'s contents represent the "state" more than "society," even though, for practical purposes, the two can hardly ever be fully separated.[4] In any case, this source reflects the social changes, both planned and spontaneous, which came with the Nasserist revolution.

The Nasserist era, indeed, saw important social changes. Not only were the exponents of the ancien régime ousted from power but the result was a process of restratification (the depth or permanence of which is arguable). The former landowning elites (and foreign residents) were politically and economically neutralized, or they left Egypt altogether, and new opportunities were created for army officers. The lower strata of society gained easier access to secondary and higher education (with many new high schools and universities being founded); *fellahin* and workers, at least in theory, received more rights and benefits; and a few women saw professional careers opening up. A so-called new middle class was emerging at the time, alongside reform projects, such as the Agrarian Reform and family planning. Many of these changes appear to be ambiguous or debatable when analyzed in retrospect today, but in a compendium published by a state agency they are quite conspicuous.

Although conceived as a reference work, this type of primary source in general also tends to hold a certain attraction for the historian who is interested in society and social change, in particular because it facilitates systematic quantitative or prosopographic research. Yet the historian must be painfully aware that collective biographies of all sorts, however tempting, also tend to have serious pitfalls, as Lawrence Stone has shown.[5]

One built-in bias of this type of source, relevant here, is that it can hardly claim to be comprehensive, as it inevitably tilts toward the higher echelons of government and society. Such compendia may contain information on the lower social strata (fellahin, artisans, workers, etc.) only insofar as the latter achieve unequivocal upward meritocratic mobility. Biographees are generally chosen for their positions of responsibility, their noteworthy activities, or—more problematically from the point of view of "objectivity"—their creative achievements. Hence large majorities, in particular the lower and middle strata of society, remain invisible.

Moreover, the systematic study of political or social elites and, all the more so, mere samples taken from among these elites, let alone their public images, often raise more questions than they yield answers or conclusions. As far as the Middle East is concerned, this field focusing on (various, but especially power) elites may—for the time being—have passed its academic heyday in the 1970s.[6] Thus, although we are inclined to question the *Mawsu'a*'s value as a source for a comprehensive, broad, or objective study of contemporary Egyptian elites (political, military, and economic as well as cultural elites coexisting but not necessarily interacting), it is nevertheless worthwhile to draw a few less ambitious conclusions.

Indeed, in addition to the mass of invaluable biographical information supplied, which cannot easily be ignored, the *Mawsu'a* symbolizes a landmark in the changing political culture of Egypt. In the first place, it clearly breaks with the cosmopolitan elite under the monarchy, moving on from the era of the revolution to its aftermath under Anwar al-Sadat and Husni Mubarak. To the best of my knowledge, this is the first comprehensive postrevolution *Who's Who*. The appearance of such a compendium was long overdue. It was possibly delayed by the still ongoing crystallization of a new postrevolutionary elite itself or otherwise held up by ideological or practical hesitations. Some prominent Egyptians whom I questioned about the reasons for this lack of useful reference works generally felt that the time had not been ripe. Whatever the case, the decision to compile the *Mawsu'a* occurred in the fall of 1985, well after Mubarak's ascendancy.

In the monarchical period, there had been a French-cum-English annual, called *Le Mondain Egyptien* or *Who's Who*, the last of which had appeared in 1956. As a private publishing venture, it catered mainly to the upper class and thus still applied to a starkly different—a very mixed, elitist, and cosmopolitan—Egypt. One may interpret a cryptic remark in the *Mawsu'a*'s introduction to the effect that this work is "made in Egypt" as an allusion to the predecessors mentioned. There have been several subsequent efforts to publish biographical dictionaries, but these generally—probably deliberately —were of a historical nature and could not substitute for contemporary reference works.[7] Even so, in contemporary Egypt, elementary information —readily available in democracies—remains, or remained until recently, difficult to come by. This refers to the lack of even telephone directories until the 1990s and the need for a governmental or parliamentary almanac, systematically summing up their members' *full* biographical, professional, and educational backgrounds.[8]

In many respects, one is inclined to designate the *Mawsu'a* as a Nasserist document, a Nasserist *lieu de mémoire*. This, of course, does not mean that biographees fit into one ideological mold or that there is one agreed-upon definition of Nasserism.[9] Rather, the work reflects the practice of a certain political culture. Moreover, all those mentioned in it were born before 1950.

This means that the upstarts who received their higher education and career opportunities after the Nasserist period are still limited in this compendium.

Published under Mubarak (the *Mawsu'a* opens with extensive biographies of the president and his wife), it may be said to be reminiscent of Nasserist discourse while representing a post-Nasserist tendency toward a relatively greater openness and transparency of government. One may question whether such a compendium would have been released to the larger public before the present era. This is the regime's Hall of Fame, a "Légion d'Honneur," one could say, a visiting card of the regime, but for that reason all the more interesting (in addition to being useful). The *Mawsu'a* embraces much more than the usual "power elite" studied, even including "cultural icons" (famous writers, singers, movie stars, athletes, etc.).

We cannot make any definite statement as to the ratio between quantity and quality or between inclusion and exclusion. Not all those persons described are linked to the Nasserist regime or owe their careers in an immediate sense to a certain ideological conviction; on the contrary, the lexicon also contains known figures of the opposition (e.g., Ma'mun al-Hudaybi and other figures of the Muslim Brothers). However, one can say that most of their careers were influenced by the new opportunities and social changes of the Nasserist era.

## Methodological Problems

The material is arranged according to the classical alphabetical Arabic system of first names rather than family names (thus we have 827 Muhammads, 176 Mahmuds, and 89 Mustafas). True, this may be the easier way of listing them in a society without stabilized "modern" family names yet. For the researcher—certainly for this historian—it is a more awkward system. Even where we imagine that some of the family names are related to politicians or other notables prominent before the July 1952 coup, we are unable to say so with certainty.

Nearly all biographical entries contain information on dates and places of birth, marital status and children, education, professions, membership in professional associations in Egypt and abroad, awards, decorations, honors, etc. The mention of any books and articles written, however scantily, turns this *Mawsu'a* into an invaluable instrument. A typical aspect relates to membership in the important specialized advisory High Councils of State, which in themselves are a Nasserist phenomenon. Lacking, on the other hand, are private addresses. In accordance with official practice in Egypt, the compendium does not mention religion, but Copts and other Christians may sometimes be identified by their names.

A number of keys or indices, such as those relating to official posts, occupations, expertise, or honors, open up the possibility of systematic research. The breakdown according to occupations, on which this chapter is based, may raise reservations. Like the *Mawsu'a* itself, it may not be a high point of accuracy, but it must be accepted as the basic conceptual division of its makers.[10]

### Occupational Structure

In the modern technocratically oriented society that Egypt has aspired to build since the July 1952 Revolution, it should not come as a surprise that engineers form the largest professional group (513 names), followed by scientists (489), physicians (432), and agronomists (364). It should not come as a surprise that law studies lost their preeminence to engineering, medicine, and other scientific fields. Professional rather than political ambitions began to determine the careers of the youth.[11] There are 34 such professional rubrics, some more arbitrary or less systematic than others, closing with small professional groups such as nurses (12, a female professional preserve), philosophers (19), geographers (22), dentists (32), pharmacists (78), and even historians (66). In addition, 102 of "our experts abroad" are described.

### Educational Background

Undeniably, the *Mawsu'a* proves the gradual spread of free higher education institutions over Egypt—in other words, the proportional loss of dominance in the position held by Cairo University. Still, this venerable institution, founded in 1908 as the Egyptian University and then evolving into Fuad I University, served as the alma mater of 48 percent of the engineers and 44 percent of the journalists. In regard to other groups, it retains its formative predominance as well, at least among this generation of prominent persons. The University of Alexandria, founded in 1942, turned out only 13 percent of the engineers and 6 percent of the journalists. 'Ayn Shams, which opened its gates in 1950, trained 9 percent and 6 percent of these professionals, respectively. These proportions have no doubt increased over the past decades. On the other hand, the Azhar's impact appears here to be marginal, even after its nationalization and expansion as a full-fledged university in the 1960s, except with respect to religious offices, and the American University in Cairo cannot be considered a central factor.

Worth noting is the growing impact of the later universities, such as Hilwan University (founded in 1955) and the universities of Asyut (1957), Mansura (1957), Suez Canal (1961), Minuf (1965), and Zaqaziq (1978).

Their impact on the elites may not yet be impressive from a numerical point of view or in terms of a national professional contribution, such as that of Cairo University; however, these newer institutions are quite visible in the *Mawsu'a,* especially when it comes to the staffing of new faculties. One can often see how they have trained their own personnel or even sent them abroad for that purpose.[12] The way in which basic information for the biographies was gathered probably also explains the relative prominence of at least two prestigious research institutes, the National Research Center and the Nuclear Research Center.

## Some Profiles of Professional Groups

Let us say a few words about select professional groups that interest us more than others against the background of some assumed changes since the beginning of the Nasserist era.

1. *Armed forces:* Under the heading "Armed Forces," we found 184 entries, of which 18 are Free Officers or others who were explicitly involved in the July 1952 coup d'état. Often, the biographies specifically mention participation in past wars, from 1948 in Palestine to Yemen (1962–67), as well as from October 1973 to the Gulf War of 1991. Some are not only military men proper but also medical specialists with high positions at army hospitals—Ma'adi, for example—or even the personal physicians of 'Abd al-Nasser, Anwar al-Sadat, and Husni Mubarak.

Most of these individuals graduated from military academies or specialized university programs. Not unexpectedly, approximately 20 percent of them underwent training in the Soviet Union or in Czechoslovakia (3 percent). Although one sees a few cases of training in Britain or in the United States, they hardly assume statistical importance. Of the professional groups surveyed here, those in the military appear to be slightly older than the rest, none of them being born after 1941—an aspect probably related to the inclusion of their army ranks. What is fascinating in this group is the possibility to follow up on how careers develop with the gradual embourgeoisement of the regime.[13] We find here those army officers who went on to become managers of military industries and—not unlike the case of Israel—those who moved on to civilian posts, such as governorships, ambassadorships, public companies, and even some in sports organizations, a few having become members of the Majlis or the Shura.

2. *Engineers and agronomists:* Obviously, we meet here only a very select top of 512 engineers (including 9 women) of an estimated total of 180,000 engineers in Egypt in the 1980s. As has been argued, most of the engineers in the country fall into the ranks of the lower technocrats and bureaucrats,

which puts them in a different status bracket, excluded here, from this *Mawsu'a* population.[14] The bias here may already be clear from the fact that 58 percent of this superior bracket enjoyed (partial) higher academic training abroad, many supposedly with government endorsement. Most received their training in Britain, the United States, West Germany, Canada, and the like, but also—still in the 1950s and 1960s—some in the USSR or Czechoslovakia, though maybe less than expected. Thus their training was spread around to quite a few countries, with France and Switzerland representing the more frequent cases of smaller engineering powers.

This top group of engineers is found to be primarily employed by the public sector, with very rare cases of employment by private or foreign companies. As such, the activities of this group highlight Egypt's prestige projects of the Nasserist era, for example, the Aswan High Dam, the takeover of the Suez Canal in 1956, massive electrification projects, and expansion of the petroleum industry and other heavy industries.[15] In a few sporadic cases, engineers entered huge contracting firms, such as the Muqawilun al-'Arab, or worked temporarily elsewhere in the Arab world.

One would expect the large group of 364 agronomists to have rural rather than urban roots, with all the surrounding social implications. Indeed, it turns out that a higher percentage of the agronomists, as compared to the engineers, were born in the countryside and also tend to have a higher than average number of children (see below).

3. *Mass media:* Journalists constitute an equally interesting group, with 18 of the 196 entries belonging to women.[16] Furthermore, although one expects to see the statistical impact of the formidable expansion of radio services and the emergence of television broadcasting, which had received much of the state's attention under the Nasserist regime, this does not appear to be the case. Strangely enough, only nine biographees are included in this field, whose number equals more or less that of the engineers with employment connected to the electronic media. Indeed, the emphasis here falls on the written press, a veteran professional field in Egypt, but one virtually nationalized in the 1950s. It is fascinating to follow the apparently uncomplicated rotation of journalists between the various big newspapers, both old and new—from *Al-Akhbar, Akhbar al-Yawm,* and *Ruz al-Yusuf* to *Al-Ahram* and *Al-Jumhuriyya*—which seems to be a result of this homogenization. Later opposition newspapers are mentioned as well. Clearly, *Al-Ahram,* as a sort of media empire, with its Center for Strategic Studies, emerges as the coveted apex of a journalistic career, with the other large publishing organizations, such as *Dar al-Hilal* and *Dar al-Ma'arif,* carrying only slightly less prestige.

Another interesting aspect of this group is its academic formation: 35

journalists studied law, 33 studied literature (a career choice clearly preferred by women), and 22 studied journalism proper (although regular courses in journalism at Cairo (Fuad I) University and the American University in Cairo had already started in the 1930s). The juridical training of relatively many journalists is intriguing, though its exact meaning or consequence—even if we seem to be aware of frequent legal battles over the profession—remains moot. The legal profession itself has been in decline, to some extent owing to the discreditation of many ancien régime notables who had studied law; we may speculate that journalism offered an honorable alternative. There is an additional aspect that deserves our attention: Only a minority of 289—and generally not those in the print media—received academic training abroad (with France as the leading destination, followed by the United States and Britain). The journalistic profession therefore remained very much within the fold of the Arabic language and culture.

4. *Religious establishment:* A final example consists of the 113 personalities mentioned in the index under the simple heading *al-din,* namely, religion. Their al-Azhar formation stands out, and possibly this was the main criterion to include them here. Most of them apparently remain there teaching after graduation, but others become muftis or waqf managers. There are a few interesting cases of Muslim clergy who have been sent abroad to serve as emissaries at various Islamic centers. Altogether, the impression here—even more so than in other professional categories—is that the material has been thoroughly screened and limited.[17] On the other hand, this is the only category in the *Mawsu'a*—apart from the mere incidence of Coptic private or family names—where Copts (and a few members of other denominations) are specifically mentioned as such (21). These are mainly higher clergy, in some cases with an academic theological background, but in a few conspicuous cases also with secular university training in, for example, medicine.

## Rural and Urban Descent

It seems that of the 4,300 personalities in the encyclopedia, an overwhelming majority of those in essentially urban occupations were born in rural localities—in the Delta provinces rather than in (more sparsely populated) Upper Egypt. This confirms that basic patterns of migration have essentially not changed since the end of the nineteenth century. The term *rural,* however, offers a challenge because such localities as Tanta, Mansura, Damanhur, and many others that are less known, have gradually evolved from villages into towns. Due to the Egyptian registration system, only the "governorate" of Cairo can unequivocally be considered "urban," while even Alexandria is, properly speaking, a "district" (and not a few of those born there may therefore, in theory, be of village origin).

One may argue whether there is a big difference in professional aspirations and outlook between an Egyptian professional with an urban background and one with a rural background. There are many possible gradations and variations, but most people will change their habits and desiderata when moving to an urban environment. What is interesting here is the difference between the various careers: 45 percent of the engineers were born in Cairo or in the district of Alexandria, as against only 38 percent of the armed forces and 35 percent of the journalists. It turns out that 86 of the 364 agronomists (24 percent) were born in Cairo or Giza, with another 6 (probably) born in Alexandria proper; this somewhat surprising urban background thus amounts to no less than a quarter. The biggest divide, however, is formed by the dismal percentage of those in the religious establishments born in Cairo or Alexandria (0.7 percent), which confirms the persistence of patterns known from previous centuries.[18]

## Number of Children

In compiling the data on the average number of children of parents in the above professional careers, a number of thought-provoking points emerge. First, although most personalities are listed as "married," some appear without their family composition, or with the mere addition "with children" (*lahu abna'*—rather than *lahu awlad*), or with the designation *wa-ya'ul* (meaning "supports a family," *'a'ila*).

We cannot know whether such omissions deliberately conceal a bias toward larger families, but one gets the distinct impression that the number of children among the elites included in the *Mawsu'a* is smaller than the average for the Egyptian population at large (fertility differentials for urban and rural locations in the 1970s ranged between 6.32 and 5.87, while a decade later they were 4.40 and 6.44, respectively).[19] According to the present data, 49 percent of the engineers, 48 percent of the military personnel, 45 percent of the journalists, and 42 percent of the agronomists have no more than two children. The percentages for those having three children in these professional categories are, respectively, 27, 28, 27, and 37 percent, while larger families are conspicuously less frequent. Again, among the religious establishment as a whole, and in particular among the Muslims, families with three, four, and more children are much more common.

These data thus tend to prove that family planning was an established fact among these elites for decades before it spread to the lower strata in the late

1960s. Historically, one factor which for a long time may have substantially slowed down the effect of the government's efforts to lower the birth rates was a big social and psychological gap between the upper and lower strata. The populations surveyed here, however, most probably developed an earlier awareness of the need to plan their families.[20] It is of interest to mention the frequent use of the designation *wa-lahu ibn wa-binta,* one son and one daughter (all professional groups surveyed here fall into the range of 21–29 percent, with engineers, interestingly, holding the record for this "one plus one" formula). While this pattern conforms to more Western, or perhaps more generally modern, ideals and patterns, it can also be associated with the slogans and posters of the Egyptian family planning campaigns (always depicting two children, an older boy and a younger girl).[21]

## Women

The *Mawsu'a* altogether contains the names of 371 women (about 8 percent of the total). This may not be an impressive proportion in Western terms, but it is remarkable in Egypt. Although the tendency toward women's emancipation has been unmistakably present for decades, the editors may have made a special effort in this respect in conformity with the spirit and achievements starting in the Nasserist period. Indeed, this is a major difference from all earlier biographical compendia for Egypt.

A partial compilation of data on this group enables us to add something to the available studies on women in the more restricted spheres of political and public life. Indeed, here too we find ten women as members of the *majlis,* and four of the *shura.* However, the scope of female activities in the *Mawsu'a* is much wider. First, 49 percent of them were born in the two big cities, representing a much higher percentage than the proportion for males. This shows that an urban environment can serve as a tremendous asset for women embarking on a professional career—not discarding, of course, the other half of the women, who did come from a variety of rural places! Second, the percentage of women having only two children is also significantly higher than for the overall professional groups surveyed above: 70 percent of the women have one or two children, and 25 percent have three, while the remaining 5 percent have four or more.

The most popular choice of academic training is in languages and literature, but medicine comes in as a strong second (and jointly with dentistry and pharmacy, it even overtakes the first). Then follow pure science and agriculture, as well as a host of other academic topics. Separate mention can be made of the nursing profession (the only one in the *Mawsu'a* that is a female preserve), as well as careers in music (17 cases) and physical education (10 cases). Female professional careers appear to evolve somewhat differently from their male counterparts: The predominant employment of the women in the *Mawsu'a* is as university staff (106), many with the rank of professor, with a few in the existing separate girls' colleges (of al-Azhar, for example). With an additional 36 women working at higher research institutes, this amounts to more than a third. Of course, this figure reflects another bias of the source for the present data.[22] There are, naturally, also prominent women in the cinema industry and in the theater, as well as in the relatively popular career of journalism, as already mentioned.

## Conclusions

The *Mawsu'a* was published under Mubarak, but its conception still reflects the Nasserist era.

The appearance of the *Mawsu'a* may be considered a landmark in the political culture of Egypt. Of course, even a more rigorous perusal of such a compendium cannot substitute for a full-fledged inquiry into social changes. This chapter has tried to follow up how the Nasserist regime and its successors accorded new priorities and emphases to their own society and the transformations therein. A cross-tabulation of all data in the *Mawsu'a* (such as using date of birth, first enrollment at university, or date of first employment) was beyond the purpose intended here. Rather, the present approach was to remain on a simpler statistical level, sometimes even an impressionist level. If such a project were to be undertaken, its results would perhaps enable us to see more clearly at what point in time (or political era) there were new departures in the careers of the various professional groups.

Career options are known to change due to the opening up of new political or economic opportunities in society or due to shifts in ideological orientations, such as (re)autocratization or (de)liberalization. Biographical lexicons, especially official ones, may change accordingly, in particular in the selection of the elites from which they draw their biographees. We are already curious to see the next edition of this official *Mawsu'a*—a post-Infitah one.[23]

## Notes

1. Originally founded in 1954 as the Information Department, it has borne its present name since 1967. See http://www.uk.sis.gov.eg/about/htlml/aboutsis.htm.

2. See *Who's Who in America*, 54th ed. (Chicago: Marquis, 2000). While its present edition contains 120,000 names, the first edition mentioned 8,602 persons (one for every 10,000 Americans at the time, see vi). Thus the present *Mawsu'a* still

falls short even of that proportion (4,300 biographies for a population of about 60 million, which is approximately 1 for 14,000).

3. *Who's Who in the Arab World, 1999–2000* (Munich and New Providence: K. G. Saur and Publitec, 1998), with 6,000 biographies in nineteen countries, the first edition of which was published in Beirut in 1966. Cf. the same editor's *Who's Who in Lebanon, 1999–2000* (Beirut, 1999). See also *The International Who's Who in the Arab World*, 2d ed. (London, 1984). In addition, there are some locally produced biographical lexicons, e.g., Hani Hurani et al., *Who's Who in the Jordanian Parliament* (Amman: al-Urdun al-Jadid Research Center, 1997), and others in Arabic.

4. Several of the persons listed have died since the date of publication; on the other hand, many have been included in a small appendix in later additions. For our discussion of the different professional categories, both have been disregarded.

5. Lawrence Stone, *The Past and the Present Revisited* (London: Routledge and Kegan Paul, 1987), 45–73.

6. Typical elite studies of the 1970s, focusing on recruitment, circulation, networks, modernization, etc., with contributions on Egypt are found in George Lenczowsky, ed., *Political Elites in the Middle East* (Washington: American Enterprise Institute, 1975); Frank Tachau, ed., *Political Elites and Political Development in the Middle East* (Cambridge, Mass: Shenkman, 1975); and I. William Zartman, ed., *The Study of Elites in the Middle East* (New York: Praeger, 1980). Focusing on the ministerial level is Maysa al-Jamal, *Al-Nukhba al-Siyasiyya fi Misr, Dirasat Hala lil-Nuhkba al-Wizariyya* (Beirut: Markaz Dirasat al-Wahda al-'Arabiyya, 1993). To this one may add, among others, Nazih Ayubi, *Bureaucracy and Politics in Contemporary Egypt* (London: Ithaca Press, 1980), and parts from Raymond W. Baker, *Egypt's Uncertain Revolution under Nasser and Sadat* (Cambridge: Harvard University Press, 1978); Mark N. Cooper, *The Transformation of Egypt* (London: Croom Helm, 1982); R. Hrair Dekmejian, *Egypt under Nasir: A Study in Political Dynamics* (Albany: State University of New York Press, 1971); Raymond A. Hinnebusch, *Egyptian Politics under Sadat* (Cambridge: Cambridge University Press, 1985); Robert Springborg, *Family, Power, and Politics in Egypt* (Philadelphia: University of Philadelphia Press, 1982); and Robert Springborg, *Mubarak's Egypt: Fragmentation of the Political Order* (Boulder: Westview Press, 1989).

7. Muhyi al-Din al-Ta'ami, *Mu'jam Bashawat Misr* (Cairo: Madbuli, [1992?]), which is a mere reprint from prerevolutionary directories. Slightly more useful is *Lam'i al-Mati'i, Mawsu'at Hadhihi al-Rijal min Misr* (Cairo: Dar al-Shuruq, 1997), which contains some ninety-five names of personalities, most of whom are deceased. A most welcome addition of Western origin is Arthur Goldschmidt, *Biographical Dictionary of Modern Egypt* (Boulder: Lynne Rienner, 1999), which also contains useful bibliographical notes.

8. Even the Internet site of the Majlis al-Sha'b (http://www. parliament.gov.eg/cgi-win/apapo.exe/exe/1) states little more than names, tickets of election, and status in parliament (with thanks to Eran Arighi for drawing my attention to this site).

9. On the various definitions of "Nasserism," see the introduction to this volume.

10. See the irregular count of engineers.

11. Donald M. Reid, "Educational and Career Choices of Egyptian Students, 1882–1922," *IJMES* 8 (1977): 349–78; cf. Hadi Abu Akeel and Clement H. Moore, "The Class Origins of Egyptian Engineer-Technocrats," in C. A. O. van Nieuwenhuyze, ed., *Commoners, Climbers, and Notables* (Leiden: E. J. Brill, 1977), 279–92.

12. Being sent abroad on a government scholarship is an interesting aspect itself.

13. For comparison, see Mark N. Cooper, "The Demilitarization of the Egyptian Cabinet," *IJMES* 14 (1982): 203–25.

14. Clement H. Moore, *Images of Development: Egyptian Engineers in Search of Industry*, 2d ed. (Cairo: American University in Cairo Press, 1994), esp. 109–30.

15. There is also a businessmen section in the *Mawsu'a*, but it lists a majority of managers in the public sector. Of the forty-four mentioned under this heading, only a very few were or are in the service of private companies. Of course, their number may be on the increase, but the process is still without momentum in this *Mawsu'a*. See Eric Gobe, "Les Hommes d'Affaires et l'État dans le Capitalisme de l'Infitah (1974–1994), *Monde Arabe, Maghreb-Machrek* 156 (1997): 49–59.

16. Preceded by engineers, scientists, physicians, and agronomists.

17. Consider also membership of the Higher Islamic Council and the (Coptic) *majlis milli*.

18. For comparison, see A. Chris Eccel, *Egypt, Islam, and Social Change* (Berlin: Klaus Schwarz, 1984), 290–94.

19. Gad G. Gilbar, *Population Dilemmas in the Middle East* (Portland: Frank Cass, 1997), 115; Janet Abu-Lughod estimated "a typical Cairene family" at 4.7 persons in *Cairo: 1001 Years of the City Victorious* (Princeton: Princeton University Press, 1971).

20. See John Waterbury, *Burdens of the Past, Options for the Future* (Bloomington: Indiana University Press, 1978), 49–66, for elite perceptions during the relevant period.

21. Posters and billboards propagating family planning represented at least three versions of dress and milieu, depicting an urban, a *fallahi*, and a Nubian family of parents with two children. On demographic trends and the rate of increase, which indeed is recently declining, see the different interpretations by Ami Ayalon, "Demography, Politics, and Tradition in Mubarak's Egypt," in Ami Ayalon and Gad G. Gilbar, eds., *Demography and Politics in the Arab States* (Tel Aviv: Hakibutz Hameuhad, 1995), 49 (Hebrew); Saad Eddin Ibrahim, "State, Women, and Civil Society: An Evaluation of Egypt's Population Policy," in Makhlouf Obermeyer, ed., *Family, Gender, and Population in the Middle East: Policies in Context* (Cairo: American University in Cairo Press, 1995), 57–79; and Philippe Fargues, "State Policies and the Birth Rate in Egypt: From Socialism to Liberalism," *Population and Development Review* 23, no. 1 (1997): 115–38. On Egypt's family planning policy since the Nasser era, see chapter 12 of this volume.

22. This does not preclude the mention of many in women's organizations (Huda al-Sha'rawi), children's councils, family planning boards, the Red Crescent, etc.

23. On the post-Infitah period, see Samiya Sa'id Imam, *Man Yamlik Misr?!*

*Dirasa Tahliliyya lil-Usul al-Ijtima'iyya li-Nukhbat al-Infitah al-Iqtisadi fi al-Mujtama' al-Misri* (Cairo: Dar al-Mustaqbal al-'Arabi, 1986); Ahmad Anwar, *Al-Infitah wa-Taghayyur al-Qiyam fi Misr* (Cairo: Misr al-'Arabiyya lil-Nashr wal-Tawzi', 1993). However, we also see signs of deliberalization. See Eberhard Kienle, *A Grand Delusion: Democracy and Economic Reform in Egypt* (London: Tauris, 2001).

# III.

# Nasser's Foreign Policy

# 7

# 'Abd al-Nasser's Regional Politics

## A Reassessment

Avraham Sela

## Introduction

Thirty years after Gamal 'Abd al-Nasser's death, his legacy seems to have been rejuvenated among both Egyptians and non-Egyptians, a phenomenon which might tell us more about the perceptions and state of mind among Arab nationalists at the close of the century than the "real" impact of Nasser's achievements and failures.[1]

Indeed, Nasser scored a striking success in shaking the political order both in and among Arab states, especially in the Fertile Crescent, by releasing powerful social forces that had been in a process of revolutionary transition. In hindsight, however, while he may have helped boost those forces, it is doubtful whether his own aims had been served by the popular upsurge. He became a hero of the masses, but had he ever possessed control of those masses? Even when Nasser succeeded in "exporting the revolution," to what extent did it serve his declared pan-Arab goals, be it Arab solidarity, unity, or conformed foreign policy? And to what extent were those revolutionized regimes willing to back Egypt?

Nasser's fateful mistakes and failures in conducting his Arab and regional policies are not entirely ignored, even by his ideological followers, though they are glossed over rather than keenly discussed. The legacy of Nasser in an Arab national perspective assumes an unmistakably apologetic and defensive tone marked by empathy and longing. Nasser is portrayed as an authentic and faithful delegate of his generation: irrevocably committed to his imperative mission but defeated by strong hostile powers—including Arabs—who conspired against him. In retrospect, the preciousness of the Nasserist legacy looms larger and clears him of overall responsibility for the disasters that his decisions and policies brought to Egypt and the Arab world as a whole. Hence, staunch Nasserists lament the abandonment of the values and principles that underlay Nasser's daring leadership and reiterate the need to revive and carry on his legacy. In their view, this legacy is especially valid and necessary in view of the continued erosion of the Arab nation's free will since Nasser, caused primarily by a systematic attack by historically hostile external forces.[2]

The post-Sadat years, and especially the 1990s, saw a renewed longing for Nasserism. Even some of his current critics and political adversaries, among them Egyptian Marxists, kept celebrating Nasser's birthday, with only the Muslim Brothers and their offshoots maintaining their bitter enmity to Nasser's practical and ideological legacy.[3] It is noteworthy that recent academic and military studies have been fairly critical of his pre-1967 legacy, especially in regard to the military's condition and unrealistic regional politics.[4]

The Arab retrospective discussion of Nasser's regional policies shows no substantive self-searching or earnest effort to critically review Nasser's specific decision making and policies, nor does it explain the consequences of his charismatic appeal to the masses. What is more salient is the lack of any attempt to question or review basic assumptions and beliefs that underpinned Nasser's messianic brand of pan-Arabism. Indeed, this live image of Nasser among Arab nationalists might serve as a convenient point of departure for a critical review of his legacy. However, this chapter by no means aims to counter that image or affect the views of committed Arab nationalist readers on that legacy.

Students of Nasser's legacy have been puzzled by his inconsistent political behavior and insufficiently explained political aims and major decisions.[5] Indeed, was Nasser's focus on the regional Arab arena a reflection of his "captivity" by the excited—at times, even ecstatic—response of the Arab masses, especially in the Fertile Crescent countries?[6] Or was it a result of Nasser's own intentions and needs? These questions are of primary importance particularly because of Nasser's immense charismatic appeal among the masses throughout the Arab world, which he fully utilized by approaching and inciting them directly above the heads of, and often against, their rulers.

From a Nasserist viewpoint, Nasser's championship of pan-Arabism and the Palestine issue has been explained in quite different ways. Nasser himself kept explaining that his pan-Arab vision and commitment to the eradication of colonialism were a defensive response to Israeli and imperialist aggression toward Egypt, as epitomized by the 1956 Suez War.[7] On the other hand, 'Ali Sabri, a former prime minister and central member of the Free Officers, explained the foreign policies of the regime in terms of establishing an international stature and influence. According to Sabri, such stature was a prerequisite for making Egypt attractive for the United States and the USSR to provide with military as well as economic aid so necessary for its social and economic development.[8]

Edward Carr observed that relations between the individual and society also apply to the leader who is a product and reflection of his own social environment.[9] His critique of the "great-man theory in history" is of particular relevance to Nasser, whose remarkable ability to forge myths and employ them for mass mobilization was evident in his self-made image of the hero-savior of the Arab nation at large. Already in his *Philosophy of the Revolution,* published in 1954, Nasser spoke of the "role in search of a hero," which, in the course of the years, he interpreted as his own unchallenged all-Arab chieftainship and played to the end in conjunction with dramatic foreign policy actions.[10]

In a historical perspective, the Nasserist revolution had no sound sociopolitical organization or ideology, hence the development of its domestic and foreign policies took a course determined by "trial and error" and "strategies of survival,"[11] in accordance with fluctuating circumstances, opportunities, and constraints. Nonetheless, by the mid-1950s the Free Officers' regime had become increasingly identified with unequivocal opposition to foreign domination and a strong quest for rallying all Arab states behind this approach, namely, behind Egypt's regional leadership. The initial success of this policy obviously encouraged the regime's growing adoption of, and commitment to, ideas of pan-Arab nationalism, which were much more prevalent in the Fertile Crescent than in Egypt itself.

Notwithstanding the debate on the origins and development of Nasser's revolutionary "philosophy" before he attained power,[12] his regime was strongly driven by a quest for radical social and political changes in both domestic and regional contexts. Indeed, much of Nasser's international conduct, particularly at the regional level, can be explained in terms of the system of values, symbols, and interpretation of history which this regime adopted to shape Egypt's post-1952 identity and role.[13] It is in this context that Nasser's Arab policies, best expressed in his capricious, self-interest interpretation of Arab unity, can be explained. His ultimate aim was to establish his unchallenged championship of the Arab world, which he apparently perceived as vital for Egypt's national security and which in fact represented continuity rather than change in the regional policies conducted by the preceding monarchic regime.[14]

The components of Nasser's role conception were reflected in his ideology and policies:[15]

  a. An uncompromising struggle for national liberation from Western domination—of which Israel was perceived as an indivisible part—

and humiliation as well as from those social groups identified politically and economically with the foreigners, hence the definition of an imagined triangular enemy—Imperialism, Israel (and Zionism), and the (Arab) Reaction—which became instrumental in defining the Nasser regime's own identity and duties.

b. Building an independent state with strong army and advanced economy, modernizing the society, giving it a new birth, and preparing it to play a new international role.

c. Promoting Arab national unity as a historical imperative and existential necessity to all the Arabs vis-à-vis the unity of imperialism and its regional allies. This goal, so it was alleged, was not only attainable but most reasonable in view of the immense gains from unifying all the Arab human and material resources: a prerequisite for the restoration of Arab self-respect and dignity (*'izza wa-karama*).

d. Attaining worldwide stature as a leading force of decolonization and support for national liberation movements, turning Cairo into a Mecca for Third World liberation movements.

In this context, the presentation of Nasser's goals as a continuum along which he moved in search of—or rather, in defining—his objectives, ranging from a minimum of Arab solidarity to a maximum of Arab unity,[16] is hardly consistent with Nasser's behavior. Indeed, he manifested adaptability to the changing conditions, but only partly. If anything, the changes were in tactics and style as well as in the means used to secure his objective, which was nothing but a recognized regional hegemony, whether attained through "solidarity," "unity," fear, or subversion. His adoption of a conciliatory policy—the "summitry" —toward regional Arab rivals in early 1964 was an attempt to rescue his plunging posture at a cost he could not sustain for long. Adversely, his aggressive policies toward his Arab rivals (in 1962–63 and again in 1966–67), in response to major failures and battered prestige, indicate anything but adaptability.

Whatever policies were conducted to attain the above aims, however, the boundaries between vision and immediate to medium-term goals were often vague or nonexistent, representing the absence of clear priorities. When such boundaries were finally drawn, it was under intolerable conditions and at a staggering cost. This was clearly represented by the definition of the political community in the name of which Nasser's political message was propagated and socialized. Nasser's vacillation between Egyptian and pan-Arab identities represented an unmistakable dialectic between the two roles, performed on both political and ideological levels. At times, this dialectic resembled a "zero sum game," in which the rise of one brought the other down. However, there were also intervals of balance and coexistence between the two roles. A reflection of the regime's perceived needs and alternative options, the movement between Egyptian and pan-Arab nationalisms received clear political and ideological expression, primarily in Nasser's own speeches and the officially constructed public discourse.[17]

The following discussion aims to focus on the roles undertaken by Nasser as a key explanation for his performance, particularly in the sphere of regional politics. More specifically, I wish to underline the overburdened and incongruent nature of the roles of an authoritative ruler of Egypt and a symbol of pan-Arab nationalism. These two roles not only had to address different political entities—the state of Egypt and the Arab nation at large (*al-umma al-'arabiyya*), respectively—but necessitated different types of rationale, discourse, and practice: *raison d'état* vs. *raison de la nation*. While the first was to be strictly based on Egypt's definite capabilities and calculated costs, the other was inevitably visionary, saturated with symbolism and romanticism, addressing "the masses," a notion of no clear boundaries. Above all, the pan-Arab trajectory entailed inescapable confrontation with regional actors, and not only Israel, as well as with their international allies. Embodied in one system of power, this duality of roles and conceptions entangled him in a disastrous contradiction, which sentenced Egypt to long years of futile and costly collisions with regional and international powers that exhausted its resources and culminated in the grand fiasco of June 1967.

## Nasser's Regional Politics: Continuity or Change?

As convincingly shown by P. J. Vatikiotis, Nasser's political thought and praxis, like many others of his generation, had their origins in Egypt's political reality of the 1930s. This trend was dominated primarily by the struggle for national liberation, the crisis of identity, and the unbridgeable socioeconomic and value cleavage between the elite and the rest of society. At that time, the Society of Muslim Brothers and the Young Egypt Party—especially from the early 1940s—strongly advocated Egyptian involvement in regional Arab-Muslim affairs, primarily the Palestine conflict. While the latter propagated its vision of Egypt's regional Arab and Muslim leadership, it was the Muslim Brothers who played a key role in linking Egypt to the Arab Fertile Crescent through their growing involvement in the Palestine conflict. In 1948, they formed the largest force of volunteers in the Palestine War, including some army officers who would later be involved in the July 1952 Revolution.[18]

Nasser's pan-Arabism may well be reminiscent of his pre–July 1952 political upbringing. Yet his adoption of this idea as an official policy represented continuity—a fact most studies on Nasserism tend to ignore. In fact, the search for regional Arab leadership had been a central theme of Egyptian foreign policy since the late 1930s. Nor was the idea of Egypt as an indivisible part of the Arab world new to leading Egyptian figures and institutions closely linked to the court, personified by the Arab League secretary-general 'Abd al-Rahman 'Azzam.[19] It was the growing agitation of radical popular movements for the sake of Palestine that led to the increasing attraction of King Faruq and political movements to the idea of pan-Arabism, culminating in the military invasion of Palestine, together with other Arab states. Like Faruq, Nasser employed the Palestine card to promote his pan-Arab leadership.

What enabled Nasser to inject new life and unprecedented magnitude into the idea of pan-Arabism was a combination of power, historical opportunity, and the marketing capabilities of militant and populist anti-imperialist speech. There is little disagreement that Nasser's initial breakthrough into the political consciousness of the Arab masses in the Fertile Crescent countries took place during the course of 1955. That year provided Nasser with a series of opportunities, which he masterfully seized and exploited. Such face lifting was essential after the ill-received agreement he had signed with Britain in October 1954,[20] the attempt on his life by a member of the Muslim Brothers, and his all-out clamping down on the movement.

The advent of Nasserism in the mid-1950s, as a movement of protest and defiance of Western influence, revived the traditional Egyptian-Iraqi competition for regional hegemony, now assuming an unprecedented ideological fervor. Although both regimes sought to protect their narrow individual state interests, the confrontation over the Baghdad Pact was also a struggle between two generations, represented by Nuri al-Sa'id and Nasser, over reshaping the region's political orientation in the postcolonial era.[21] Indeed, for "Nuri's political school," Nasser's Arab neutralism was a revolutionary concept.[22]

Beginning with Nasser's aggressive campaign against the Baghdad Pact and his participation at the historic meeting at Bandung, through the Czech arms deal, the nationalization of the Suez Canal Company, and the end of the Anglo-French-Israeli joint offensive from which Nasser came out as a hero-victor, all signaled defiance of the foreigner—whether Western imperialism, Zionism, or Israel—rather than embracement of the pan-Arab idea. That the regime accompanied its new foreign policy with an effort to reconstruct Egypt's identity as an indivisible part of the Arab nation left the regime on shaky ground, relying primarily on Nasser's charisma.[23]

Nasser's success in mobilizing the Arab masses, however, needed more than the invention or creation of myths. In 1955, when the Free Officers' regime shifted its focus to regional foreign policy, it had succeeded in stabilizing the domestic arena and securing its grip on the reins of power. Henceforth, Nasser could launch his foreign affairs from a position of relative strength and security, which none of the ruling elites in the Fertile Crescent could claim. By adopting the Baʻthi idea of pan-Arabism (*qawmiyya*) and turning it into Egypt's official message, Nasser struck an irresistible chord with an emotionally saturated and effectively delivered myth. This, combined with his political and bureaucratic resources, as well as his own charismatic personality and his antagonistic incitement against the Western powers and Arab rulers alike, proved extremely effective in penetrating the Arab masses and mobilizing them to action. The success scored by Nasser in this respect, however, also reflected the weak and shaky Arab regimes that he was targeting. So successful was this formula that it became Nasser's major source of legitimacy and influence across the Arab world. Yet this approach exposed him to critical risks as a result of external setbacks.[24]

Most studies on Nasser's Arab policy tend to focus on his image, personality, and political action, while ignoring the social and political realities in the targeted Arab states. In fact, many of the underlying social and political causes that gave rise to the Free Officers' coup—and later, revolution—also prevailed in the Fertile Crescent countries and may help to explain the meteoric rise of Nasser to the position of idol of the masses. Nasser's seizure of the pan-Arab myth was met with tremendous acceptance there mainly because these societies had also been in the midst of social and political turbulence due to long-standing processes of structural changes from below. Moreover, unlike Egypt, which had just begun its involvement in the Palestine conflict, by the late 1930s the doctrine of Arab nationalism had become the dominant public discourse in the Fertile Crescent countries, especially for the urban middle class.

The advent of the Free Officers' Revolution was preceded by years of growing domestic turmoil and decline of the constitutional, parliamentary, and relatively liberal ancient regimes in Egypt and the Fertile Crescent states. In a way, they represented a Middle Eastern version of the Weimar Republic. Indeed, the late 1940s and early 1950s brought unprecedented challenges, both domestic and regional, to bear on the ruling elites, unmasking their institutional weakness, questionable legitimacy, and overall inefficacy, especially in mobilizing their respective societies' loyalties and resources. These traditional ruling elites, consisting primarily of landowners, were accused of failing to provide a proper ideological prescription, let alone cure, for the society's illnesses and growing needs. Their class-based rigidity and incompetence, underlying a continuous state of social and political immobilism throughout the interwar years, resulted in growing criticism and alienation among the burgeoning middle class. This domestic instability was a reflection of potent new social and political forces on the verge of revolution. Rapid population growth, urbanization, the spread of education, and the growing working class—all became increasingly evident in the interwar years, though without corresponding political and institutional reforms.[25]

Soon enough, groups of the newly emerging urban professionals, merchants, clerks, teachers, and students came to fill the intellectual and organizational vacuum left by the historic national movements that remained exclusively interested in the struggle for independence.[26] This new urban middle class led the politicization and nationalization of the masses, disseminating chauvinist, nationalist, and Islamic discourses against foreign domination. At the same time, they also represented an outcry for social, economic, and political reforms whose frustration led to a growing alienation from and hostility toward the ruling upper class, which was identified both culturally and economically with the hated foreign power.[27]

The shift toward full independence in the Fertile Crescent countries in the late 1940s further aggravated the socioeconomic and political difficulties of the "new states." Moreover, they were increasingly burdened by competing loyalties: to primordial, ethnic, and religious communities, on the one hand, and to suprastate abstract entities—regional as well as Arab nationalisms and Islam—on the other. Interstate mutual agitation and rivalries over the leadership of regional Arab unity constituted another source of regime instability, which forced the ruling elites to adopt the pan-Arab nationalist discourse on both domestic and regional levels as a means to achieve legitimacy and political survival.

Even more significant, Arab rulers were compelled to adopt policies against their best judgments and perceived state interests, which culminated in their military intervention in the 1948 Palestine War. Indeed, nowhere was this pattern of pressure "from below" on decision makers more salient than in the case of the Arab growing involvement in the Question of Palestine. The long struggle for national liberation and the humiliating defeat in the Palestine War further eroded the legitimacy of the traditional elites and heralded their imminent collapse. The Arab League, which had sponsored the Arab collective action on Palestine, was held responsible for the shameful defeat and turned out to be a broken promise of Arab unity.

The immediate post-1948 years were thus saturated with a salient and hardly separable drive for social and political revisionism on both domestic and regional Arab levels. As much as these years demonstrated the old regimes' ineptitude, corruption, and distance from their own societies' needs and expectations, they also deepened the traditional hostility toward the West. Already before Nasser came to the political scene, radical Arab movements spanning the entire political spectrum had been constantly fomenting this hostility and increasingly employing it against the direct or indirect presence of imperialism on any Arab land. Indeed, if there was a single most significant meaning to Arab nationalism in Arab societies before or after Nasser's advent, it was this deep hostility toward any manifestation of foreign presence in the region. Clearly, this trend gathered tremendous momentum in the aftermath of the Palestine War, closely linked to the growing popular pressure for a "second round" against Israel.[28]

Nasser's Arab politics assumed diverse forms, strategies, aims, and ideological definitions over time. Any attempt to analyze one of them in separation from the others might miss a spectrum of subtle nuances and approaches that Nasser adopted in conjunction with the fluctuation of circumstances and his perception of reality at any given time. For the sake of clarity and avoidance of a dichotomy between the two basic roles ascribed to Nasser, the following discussion is divided thematically and chronologically. While each of them refers to a specific "role" and approach, the discussion in each of them critically examines a range of motives, as well as the immediate and long-term results of those roles.

### Nasser's Pan-Arabism: A Self-Defeating Vision

The prevalence and magnitude of Arab nationalism in the political life of the Fertile Crescent societies from the interwar period through the early 1960s reflected a profound longing for the lost regional unity under a hegemonic political center, which traditionally combined Islamic religion and state (*din wa-dawla*). The shaping of the previously Ottoman Arab territories in the form of new states and the discrepancies in power and resources among them denied any single actor sufficient capabilities to attain regional hegemony or to seriously endanger the regional status quo.[29] From the late 1930s onward, Egypt's primacy in the region had been increasingly recognized by public circles in the Fertile Crescent countries, due to its political, economic, and cultural weight as a center of Islamic and secular higher education, huge human resources, strong statehood, and geostrategic significance.[30] This primacy officially materialized in the leading role that Egypt came to assume with the establishment of the Arab League in 1945.

Egypt's role, however, was to balance inter-Arab relations rather than dominate them and to keep at bay the revisionist schemes for regional unification woven by the Hashemite Iraqi and Jordanian monarchs. Indeed, Nasser's deviation from this role, in his attempts to promote Egypt's regional status to hegemony, proved capable of thoroughly destabilizing the inter-Arab status quo and paralyzing the Arab League, its primary institutional expression, by challenging its rules and norms. Yet, even at the apex of Nasser's regional impact, Egypt lacked sufficient means and capabilities to coerce other Arab actors or to assume effective regional hegemony.[31]

Whether or not Nasser genuinely sought to attain Arab unity, in hindsight it seems more relevant to ask how did he interpret—or rather, employ—this idea, under changing circumstances and needs, within the context of his regime's overall foreign relations and political goals. Clearly, in the union with Syria, Nasser exhaustively manipulated the idea of Arab unity by continually reinterpreting it in accordance with his own interests. Moreover, hidden in Nasser's political conduct and messianic discourse toward the Arab world was a core claim on monopolizing the interpretation of common Arab national values and visions. Nowhere was this claim more visible than in Nasser's erratic shifts of slogans and definitions of Arab unity, which indeed reflected his own changing needs and aims.

In campaigning against the Baghdad Pact, Nasser claimed unequivocal conformity of all Arab states with Egypt's opposition to the Western schemes of defense alliances in the Arab region. During the United Arab Republic (UAR) episode, the leading slogan was "Unity of Rank" (*wahdat al-saff*), denoting inter-Arab coexistence regardless of ideological differences. Following its breakup, Nasser shifted to his most militant slogan of social revolution ever, "Unity of Purpose" (*wahdat al-hadaf*). Within a year, however, this policy bankrupted, forcing him to adopt a slogan with a rather egalitarian hue—"Unity of Action" (*wahdat al-'amal*)—which, for about two years, underpinned the atmosphere of relative inter-Arab cooperation epitomized by the summit conferences.

In the spring of 1966, Nasser revived the "Unity of Purpose" battle cry, which expressed his frustrated expectations from the conciliatory policy that he had conducted in the Arab arena, as well as the continued deterioration of his relations with the United States. Implicit in the new guiding principle was Nasser's true purpose: to besiege his Arab adversaries by inciting their peoples against them, bringing internal pressures to bear on them.[32] This return to a militant regional policy was sustained until the beginning of the May 1967 Arab-Israeli crisis and was apparently a major underlying cause of Nasser's conscious slide into war.

Except for short intervals, Nasser himself was halfhearted in his self-aggrandizement. With hindsight, Nasser's years in power were marked by a constant drive for pan-Arab hegemony—especially in the Palestine-centered "core" area—rather than for a merger with other Arab states. Pan-Arab ideology was a useful myth, rather than an operative agenda, in Nasser's striving for unchallenged Arab leadership. Apparently, pan-Arabism remained more appealing to the masses in the Fertile Crescent than in Egypt itself, despite the efforts invested by the Nasserist regime to socialize this doctrine to his own constituency.

What remains unexplained is the repeated manifestation of vulnerability and insecurity, often about images rather than realities, implied in Nasser's impulsive political conduct in the Arab arena. Paradoxically, Nasser was willing to cooperate with monarchist and Western-oriented Arab regimes, which were less of an ideological challenge to him, against revolutionaries when it suited him.[33] Iraq's revolutionary regime in particular posed a serious challenge to Nasser's unionist concept and aspirations for regional hegemony because it employed a similar "revolutionary" discourse, turning against the West and becoming a recipient of Soviet arms. No wonder Egypt's worst conflict was with Iraq. In March 1959, Nasser severed diplomatic relations with Iraq, which remained in force until Qassem's demise four years later. Conversely, Nasser's inter-Arab policy became marked by revolutionary pan-Arabism when Egypt's stature in the region or his own regime's security had been challenged. Indeed, the fluctuations in Nasser's inter-Arab policy can best be explained by the ups and downs in his domestic and regional stature. Hence Fouad Ajami's description of Nasser's pan-Arabism as a "fusion of idea and policy" is an impressionist observation rather than a reality supported by historic evidence.[34]

The unification with Syria was the exception. Nasser was initially reluctant to enter into this venture, and when he finally succumbed to the Syrians' pressure, he flatly dictated his own draconian terms. Syria's secession from the UAR, much as a result of his ruling of Syria as a subjugated province rather than as an equal partner, was the first critical crisis in his regional Arab politics. Nothing attested more to the gap between Egypt's limited capabilities and Nasser's far-reaching ambitions than his avoidance of military intervention in Syria to quell the secessionist rebellion, primarily because of the lack of territorial contiguity. Paradoxically, what made the union possible was the lack of territorial contiguity between Egypt and Syria. Hence, the merger with Egypt could not wipe out Syria's boundaries or stop Syria from seceding.[35] The union's breakdown was to consolidate still further the political forces within Arab states determined to preserve their independence.[36]

Nasser's response to the breakup—represented by the slogan "unity of purpose"—was clearly meant to recover his battered prestige and tighten his grip on power in Egypt by adopting more radical social and economic reforms. The new policy ostensibly set a higher, more demanding standard as the minimal prerequisite for Arab unity. In practice, however, it was tantamount to a declaration of indiscriminate war against his Arab rivals, "reactionaries" and "revolutionaries" alike. The new slogan was synonymous with social revolution in the name of which Nasser now claimed the right to interfere with domestic Arab affairs. As such, it reflected his wounded pride and threatened regional leadership but could hardly contribute to the advancement of inter-Arab solidarity or cooperation.[37]

Even after the establishment of the UAR, Nasser's adherence to Arab unity was a matter of pragmatism rather than ideological commitment. This was demonstrated by his support for the emergence of new Arab entities, which went against the very rationale of melting those entities into one Arab unit. In the summer of 1961, a few months before Syria's secession from the UAR, Nasser recognized Kuwait's independence and led a collective peacekeeping Arab effort to protect the new Arab state from possible Iraqi invasion, followed by supporting its acceptance as an Arab League member. Obviously, Nasser's motivation was to contain Iraq's irredentist claim on Kuwait, for which he needed the support of Saudi Arabia and Jordan. Yet this policy facilitated the creation of another Arab state by British imperialism, which Nasser frequently blamed for the fragmentation of the Arab world.[38] Similarly, Nasser did not object to the resumption of secessionist Syria's membership in the Arab League, though he symbolically preserved the UAR as Egypt's name. Above all, Nasser advanced an all-Arab recognition of an institutionalized "Palestinian entity" in the form of the Palestine Liberation Organization (PLO), which, in principle, contradicted the aim of Arab unity.[39]

Not only was Nasser at best ambivalent toward putting Arab unity into practice but his antagonistic approach to other Arab regimes in fact made them all the more sustainable in defiance of his pressures. The shift of interest to regional Arab politics in early 1955 introduced Egypt as an intrusive power in interstate relations in the Fertile Crescent, with a magnitude that superseded its previous balancing role of the Arab system. Ambitious states saw Egypt as a competitor, while weaker ones feared the threat it constituted to their political independence.

More significantly, Egypt became increasingly involved in the domestic affairs of the Mashriq states, confusing the relations between ruler and ruled. The advent of this policy heralded the collapse of the Westphalian order struck by the foundation of the Arab League in 1945, whose most important principle was the commitment of the members to mutually respect each other's sovereignty. Whereas the Arab League was essentially meant to preserve the regional status quo and prevent any one member from attaining hegemony, Nasser's Arab policies injected frenzy and instability into inter-Arab relations, blurring the separating lines between state, people, and nation.

Nasser's practice of directly calling upon the Arab masses' allegiance and mobilization for action constituted a threat to the sovereign rulers of these states. Its most conspicuous manifestation was the rise of "Nasserist" groups in several Arab states, which served as Egypt's political agents. Cairo's "Voice of the Arabs" was one of various means of subversion used by the Nasserist regime to interfere with other Arab states' domestic affairs. These tactics demonstrated the shaky nature of these Arab regimes, the permeability of their national boundaries, and their exposure to competing external authority. These and other Arab regimes were thus obliged to follow Nasser's line because they lacked the power to repress the opposition forces in their own societies. The success of this policy was most evident in Jordan, thanks to a large and embittered Palestinian population whose politicians were first to embrace Nasser as their hero and redeemer of Palestine.[40]

Under Nasserist pressure, Jordan—as well as Syria—were forced to refrain from joining the Baghdad Pact. Jordan was also forced to get rid of the British command of the Arab Legion; to join the Egypt/Saudi Arabia/Syria Pact; and to replace the British annual subsidy with an Arab one. In retrospect, however, Nasser's pressures kept Arab regimes alert and instigated constant tightening of their control over society by restricting political freedoms and eliminating or containing opposition and nonstate actors, such as the Nasserist groups. Arab rulers were thus temporarily forced to comply with domestic demands affected by Egyptian agitation. This, however, proved to be a far cry from successful coercion by Egypt, as these rulers never lost their ability to reverse such actions at the first opportunity.[41] Moreover, the Nasserist threat drove Arab regimes to call upon Western allies to interfere on their behalf, demonstrated by the landing of British and American troops in Jordan and Lebanon, respectively, in summer 1958.

The charismatic authority exercised by Nasser represented a temporary alliance with popular Arab nationalist movements—Ba'thists, Nasserists, or Arab Nationalists—in the Fertile Crescent countries. It was a convergence of interests in which the latter expected to benefit from Nasser's material resources and legitimacy, as well as from his methods of interference in internal affairs of their respective countries. It was this cross-national alignment that blurred state boundaries and exposed the permeability and vulnerability of the targeted Arab states. Yet, even as Nasser was an invaluable asset to those movements, their willingness to accept his patronage was bound to end once they seized power, such as in the case of the Ba'th rise to power in both Syria and Iraq. Even the Arab Nationalists, the most ardent supporters of Nasserism, had defected from his orbit by the mid-1960s and had joined his critics on ideological grounds.[42]

Nasser's regional policy attested to the intolerable burden of being a champion and living symbol of pan-Arabism and, at the same time, a head of state who was unable to realize his vision by coercion, despite his regional centrality. He had to brandish the sword against Israel and yet preach restraint; to collaborate with the Arab monarchs while still threatening them with resumption of his revolutionary policy. This ambivalence enabled Syria to hoist the banner of war against Israel and to question Nasser's legitimacy and claim for pan-Arab leadership, which eventually forced him to adopt this as his own regional policy. Nasser's failure to maintain strict control of the joint Arab plan through inter-Arab financial and political trade-offs resulted from the turbulent nature of domestic and inter-Arab politics in the Mashriq's countries.

The entrenchment in a revolutionary brand of pan-Arabism after the breakup of the UAR deepened Nasser's isolation in the Arab arena and rendered compromise with his rivals inconceivable. The repercussions of this policy turned out to be disastrous to the fragile improvement scored in U.S.–Egypt relations thanks to Kennedy's efforts, the main result of which were significant American food aid shipments to Egypt. Yet, just as the Cairo-Washington rapprochement had culminated in an agreement on three years of food aid to Egypt in October 1962, Nasser's intervention in Yemen that month and his later entanglement in hostilities against Saudi Arabia undermined the relations between Washington and Cairo.[43] In the latter case, Nasser continued to conduct his regional-based interests even at the high risk of provoking American concerns for their oil interests in Saudi Arabia—a scenario that Nasser could hardly overlook.[44] Likewise, the Yemen Civil War overburdened Egypt's economy and foreign relations with the United States. Moreover, it posed his continued inaction against Israel in sharp contrast to his massive military involvement in Yemen and provided his Arab critics with an effective weapon in their efforts to divert his policy to their own ends.

### Nasser and the Palestine Conflict

The inconsistencies between Nasser's roles as a ruler of Egypt, on the one hand, and a champion of the Arab nation at large, on the other, were clearly reflected in his views and actions regarding the conflict with Israel. Since the 1930s, the Question of Palestine had been closely and inseparably interwoven in the doctrine of Arab nationalism and turned into its most powerful "core issue." This meant that whoever adopted the pan-Arab discourse or sought to mobilize external Arab recognition and support had to place the cause of Palestine at the top of his agenda. Nonetheless, the first decade of Nasser's regional policy represented continuity of the prerevolutionary regime, which can be defined as "short of war hostility." This included political and economic boycott, strategic maritime blockade, and sporadic guerrilla raids by Palestinians. In 1954–55, Nasser conducted a secret diplomatic exchange with Israeli prime minister Moshe Sharet, which ended at an impasse.[45] Nasser's preference for Arab-oriented foreign policy in early 1955 was bound to lead him to confrontation, rather than coexistence, with Israel. This trajectory was also underlined by Israeli military actions, including attacks on Egyptian targets along their mutual border, in retaliation for violent attacks launched mostly from the Gaza Strip. As of 1955, Nasser embarked on massive arms procurement, mounted guerrilla activities against Israel, and closed the Straits of Tiran, all of which accounted for Israel's participation in the tripartite Sinai operation.

The post-Sinai security provisions along the Israel-Egypt border and the Straits of Tiran forced Nasser to avoid taking action against Israel from his own border. His soaring prestige following the withdrawal of British, French, and Israeli troops from Egyptian territory helped him to shape a new Arab agenda that would benefit his quest for pan-Arab hegemony without immediately committing himself to war with Israel. The new agenda set Arab unity as the primary aim, the attainment of which was portrayed as a prerequisite to the liberation of Palestine. Indeed, until 1964, Arab strategy in the conflict with Israel was marked by uncertainty, lack of a defined political or military plan, and a vast discrepancy between vision and reality.

With Israel considered an illegitimate entity, the Arab objective in the conflict could only be defined in terms of elimination of the state of Israel, entirely precluding diplomacy and peaceful resolution. However, no clear Arab program of action—whether political or military—had been worked out to accomplish this objective. Arab strategic and political thought focused on justifying the objective and explaining its feasibility regardless of practical constraints, postulating that the disappearance of Israel was historically inevitable. Indeed, the Arab objective in the conflict with Israel was a utopian goal that fitted into the messianic doctrine of Arab nationalism.[46]

The absence of a specific program of action reflected Nasser's awareness of the impracticability of the Arabs' objective in the conflict—vague and undefined as it was—in view of their limited military capabilities, their political weakness and internal divisions, and the wide international support for Israel's legitimate existence. Thus, until 1964, the Arab policy on the Palestinian conflict remained confined to diplomatic activity in the UN and repetition of resolutions reiterating the right of the Palestinian refugees to return to their homes. The Palestinian problem was not a priority in Nasser's political agenda, as evidenced by the 1962 National Charter, which made no reference to Palestine.

Under Nasser's leadership, the absence of a clear Arab strategy in the conflict with Israel was thus officially admitted and legitimized. Yet as the realization of the goal was presented as more distant, Nasser's hostile attitude toward Israel became more absolute and decisively expressed, reiterating his commitment to the objective of elimination. However, until May 1967, Nasser repeatedly argued that the option of war against Israel should not be taken, giving priority to the establishment of regional hegemony in the name of Arab unity. He advocated an indefinite postponement of war against Israel to give the Arabs time to prepare for the decisive, all-out showdown, which he portrayed as a comprehensive Arab effort—military, economic, and industrial—to build an immense Arab capability, not only to fight Israel but also to deter "those behind Israel." Clearly, the total war envisioned by Nasser was little more than an instrument to enhance and legitimize his regional policies.[47]

This indefinite and evasive strategy and continued procrastination of the war against Israel turned Nasser's antagonistic speech and subversive policies toward Arab rivals into a self-made trap. The discrepancy between vision and praxis exposed him to embarrassing charges that questioned his commitment to the issue of Palestine and, indirectly, the legitimacy of his claim for pan-Arab leadership. In the late 1950s and early 1960s, it was mainly Qassem of Iraq whose criticism of Nasser's military inaction against Israel brought the latter to advocate the establishment of a "Palestinian Entity." Clearly, Nasser wished to demonstrate his political action for this cause and to lessen the pressures on him to lead an all-out war against Israel. The ascendancy of the Ba'th Party to power in Syria in March 1963 further aggravated Nasser's predicament. Deriving from the guerrilla experience of current national liberation movements, the new Syrian regime confronted Nasser with a contradictory strategy, strongly supported by the emerging Movement for National Liberation of Palestine (Fatah) to wage a popular war for the liberation of Palestine as a necessary step toward Arab unity.

Late 1963 demonstrated the deadlock that Nasser's efforts in the Arab arena had reached. The cumulative effect of consecutive failures—the breakup of the UAR, the entanglement in the Yemen quagmire, and hostile relations with monarchist and revolutionary regimes alike—had eroded Nasser's posture in the Arab world. Most important, Israel's imminent operation of its National Water Carrier Project lent power to the Syrian pressures to launch an immediate war against Israel, for which he had been neither prepared nor willing to sustain a serious blow to his pan-Arab leadership. Nasser responded by calling his Arab colleagues to a summit under the banner of Palestine, the ultimate source of legitimacy and most powerful rallying force in Middle East politics.

Nasser's initiative for a summit was a major—though not irreversible, as it turned out by 1966—shift in the form and substance of inter-Arab politics from that starting in the mid-1950s. Nasser's new slogan of "Unity of Action" (for the sake of Palestine, or against Israel) can be defined as "preventing war by controlled escalation," reflecting his narrowing options for securing regional stature. The joint Arab action consisted of a three-pronged agenda pertaining to the issue of Palestine—diversion of the Jordan River's tributaries; promoting Arab preparation for war against Israel under a joint Arab command; and developing the newly established PLO. The new rallying theme was meant to preserve Nasser's regional leadership and legitimacy, while preventing an untimely war with Israel.

Shifting the Arab-Israeli conflict to a national liberation war indeed constituted a radical change in the Arab concept of war against Israel. Yet, until 1967, Nasser's policy concerning the "Palestinian Entity" clearly manifested an intention to confine the struggle for Palestinian national liberation to the political sphere, thereby limiting Egypt's active role in the liberation of Palestine. Nasser's new concept drew on the rapid process of decolonization in Asia and Africa; Moscow's official endorsement of national liberation movements in early 1961; and Nasser's efforts to establish himself as a primary leader in the Third World.[48]

## Nasser and the Shaping of Regional Order

Although Nasser's intrusive Arab policy was a major cause for regional instability, it was, above all, geared to secure regional Arab conformity under Egyptian hegemony, not to radically alter the regional order itself. Thus, in late 1963, when his aggressive inter-Arab policy reached a deadlock, with Syria threatening to entangle Egypt in an undesirable war against Israel, Nasser opted to return to the "Westphalian" Arab regional order envisioned by the Arab League's founders.[49] To support the shift, apart from bringing the Arab League back in, Nasser reinvented the forum of all Arab heads of state as an overall authority entrusted with supervising the new Arab regional order. Yet a shift from imposed conformity to state sovereignty necessitated a parallel process of "normalization" of the conflict with Israel, which had become subject to collective Arab strategy on the Palestinian issue. That Egypt led this trend is explained by both the impasse reached by Nasser's Arab policies and the high stakes of a military confrontation with Israel at a time when significant Egyptian forces had been bogged down in the Yemen Civil War. That Nasser could abruptly account for such a shift and receive an all-Arab approval reflected recognition not only of Egypt's regional primacy and Nasser's personal prestige but also a quest for relaxation and stabilization of inter-Arab relations.

Beginning in January 1964, Arab summitry heralded a new era in regional Arab politics. A growing inter-Arab dialogue conducted on a state-to-state level replaced Nasser's intrusion in the name of revolutionary pan-Arabism. The shifting nature of inter-Arab relations from politics of symbols and absolute truths to "negotiated order" reflected a recognition of the detrimental gulf between revisionist visions and political realities, and the need to control this contradiction. The transformation—albeit fragile and reversible at its start—was determined by the state system's obligation to face its limited resources and capabilities.

The prestigious forum of all heads of Arab states inherited the Arab League's primary role as an institutional expression of the regional states' system in which every member was equal regardless of its capabilities or political philosophy. The single most important factor that led to the institutionalization of summitry after 1964 was the steady pressure from the core Arab states—primarily Egypt—to support their policies in the conflict with Israel. The impact of the new Arab regional order had been apparent in Arab intellectuals' interpretation of pan-Arab nationalism in terms of solidarity and cooperation rather than of political unity.[50]

The summit conference served as a mechanism of collective moral authority assigned to bridge the contradictions between pan-Arab nationalism and realpolitik through reinterpretation of *raison de la nation* and adjustment to *raison d'état*. In the absence of an overall Arab authority, policy making on all-Arab core issues deviating from Islamic and pan-Arab national commitments needed legitimization by a supranational forum representing the entire Arab national community, that is, all Arab states. Arab summits indeed followed the Arab League's rule that only unanimous decisions committed the member states.[51]

By virtue of representing the collective Arab will, the summit became a useful instrument for legitimizing deviation from hitherto established core Arab norms and values, such as officially shelving war against Israel to an indefinite future. No less important, the advent of the Arab summit provided a normative mechanism that narrowed the options for individual regimes or nonstate actors to take on contradictory policies or call for an alternative all-Arab conformity. Indeed, this forum was repeatedly called to legitimize the post-1967 efforts of the confrontation states to retrieve their occupied territories through diplomatic means. Arab summits thus played an essential role in the process of state building by legitimizing the gradual departure of individual Arab regimes from suprastate commitments. That the Arab summit conducted this process in its handling of the Palestine conflict—the core issue of Arab-Muslim collectivism—lent it credibility and moral legitimacy.

## Epilogue: Post-1967 Primacy of Egypt

The devastating results of the June 1967 War forced Nasser to revise his overall regional strategy in the context of both inter-Arab relations and the conflict with Israel. Egypt's interests and constraints shaped the terms of the change, and Nasser, his shaken regime notwithstanding, remained pivotal to collective Arab action, which was reconstructed in the Khartoum summit in September 1967.

In addition to the mass destruction of arms and combat units, the loss of the main sources of revenues in foreign currency—the Suez Canal, Sinai oil, and tourism—was particularly devastating for Egypt's economy, which would hardly grow until the October 1973 War.[52] Militarily defeated and besieged by domestic challenges to his regime, Nasser had little choice but to secure his position at home and gain time for full military recovery, keeping all options open to reclaim the lost territories. The concept he adopted thus combined the acceptance of international diplomatic efforts and a decision to maintain the military option, which, given his limited capabilities, could only assume the form of a limited war. Nasser's new political realism was accompanied by strong determination to rebuild his regime as well as his regional stature.

This strategy, however, had to be consistent with Arab national premises and goals from which Nasser could not have easily departed and without which he would have lost further legitimacy and Arab material support. Already in his resignation speech following the defeat in the June 1967 War, Nasser stated that "what was taken by force will be returned by force," calling for a unified Arab effort and the use of Arab oil to realize this goal. Indeed, a political settlement *with* Israel was entirely precluded by Nasser, who insisted on unconditional Israeli withdrawal to the prewar borders, along the perimeters of the latter's 1957 withdrawal from Sinai. Thus he rejected Israel's official proposals, submitted less than two weeks after the war ended, for direct talks on permanent peace in return for its full withdrawal to the international border—save modifications needed for security.[53]

Nasser perceived war as a prominent and necessary means to recover Sinai from Israel, hence the priority he gave to rebuilding the Egyptian armed forces. It reflected a realistic conclusion that no matter what the prospects of recovering the lost territories by diplomatic means, the minimum requirements would oblige a restoration of Egypt's military capability and unabated armed pressure on Israel. Resumption of the military option would also strengthen his bargaining position toward Israel and promote his legitimacy on both domestic and regional levels. To realize this end,

Nasser was willing to turn fully toward the Soviets, offering Moscow military and naval facilities even at the expense of eroding the hitherto sacrosanct value of absolute Egyptian sovereignty.

Recovering the lost territories was given priority over the Palestine issue, although without spelling this out explicitly. This was defined by Nasser's phrase "elimination of the traces of aggression and restoration of the rights of the Palestinian people." This ambiguous formula was meant to demonstrate pragmatism to the international community by stressing the quest for Israeli withdrawal to the 1967 borders. At the same time, it was necessary to reassure the Arab militants—represented by the PLO, Syria, and Algeria—that Egypt was still committed to the liberation of Palestine. In effect, it was this priority which determined Egypt's strategic war goal, as defined by the Egyptian General Command and approved by the government in November 1967 "on the basis of the Khartoum summit resolutions." It was phrased as the "liberation of the occupied land of Sinai . . . until the Egypt-Palestine border, and *political use* [emphasis added] of the success for restoration of the Palestinian people's rights."[54]

Notwithstanding its infamous three no's on possible change of attitude toward Israel, a careful reading into the Khartoum resolutions and behind-the-scene debates reveals the beginning of a shift of Arab perception of the conflict with Israel from one revolving around Israel's legitimacy to one focusing on territories and boundaries.[55] Clearly, Nasser was the main actor behind this shift. This was underlined by his immediate acceptance of UN Security Council resolution 242 (November 22, 1967), which was to become the cornerstone for future peacemaking efforts in the Arab-Israeli conflict. The summit was also the first step in legitimizing diplomacy as a major means in the conflict with Israel. The opposition that this underlying premise triggered was to become the main fault line of inter-Arab relations in the years to come.

Ironically, Nasser—with King Husayn—triggered a renewed debate around the concept of phased struggle based on realism and persistence, originally brought up by Bourguiba in 1965.[56] Their antagonists reasonably argued that the combination of limited war and diplomacy would compromise the Arab strategic goal of eliminating Israel, hence they demanded continued military struggle. Nasser's own approach was apparently still marked by intrinsic inconsistency between the incremental process and the absoluteness of the objective.[57]

The Khartoum summit also signaled a turning point in inter-Arab relations. Nasser's abandonment of his revolutionary slogans and assertive inter-Arab policies and his acceptance of a "political action" in the conflict with Israel soured relations with Syria and seriously weakened the revolutionary camp. The distinction between "revolutionary" and "conservative" regimes became essentially outmoded, especially in view of Nasser's need for urgent financial aid, which could only be met by the oil producers. The new inter-Arab alignment underpinned Egypt's total withdrawal from Yemen, indicating the end of its interventionist policy out of its national borders.

Nasser's death in September 1970, symbolically coinciding with the crush of the Palestinian guerrilla organizations by the Jordanian army (Black September), signaled the end of the revolutionary era in Arab politics. The departure from revolution was reinforced when, two months later, Hafiz al-Asad seized power in Syria. Thus the ascendancy of new regimes in two central Arab states paved the way for an era of pragmatic inter-Arab alignment away from Nasser's overshadowing image. It was this alignment which enabled full adoption of the strategy of phases in the conflict with Israel, which Nasser had apparently endorsed but only halfheartedly followed.

## Conclusions

Nasser's inter-Arab policy was marked by a deep sense of national insecurity and righteous grandeur. Its frustration resulted primarily from Egypt's insufficient resources and capabilities and other limits put on it by regional and nonregional actors alike who contested Nasser's quest for regional hegemony. Personifying Egypt's quest for regional hegemony, Nasser played the role of the rebuking prophet, a standard-bearer whose choices and interpretations were beyond debate. His claim for legitimate interference in other Arab states' domestic affairs in the name of pan-Arabism was bound to collide with the sovereign state's prerogatives and praxis.

It is here where Nasser's failure was most conspicuous. Once and again he let his imagined role—nurtured by his immense popularity among the masses—take priority over and defeat rational calculations, especially in terms of Egypt's military and economic capabilities. Yet it is doubtful whether Nasser himself would have accepted such a dichotomy between his regional pan-Arab role and that of the ruler of Egypt, which he apparently perceived as inseparable. Had he been able to distinguish between these "roles," he could have otherwise tackled the hasty unification with Syria, the disastrous military intervention in Yemen, and most of all, the drift to war with Israel in May and June 1967—to mention only the most salient and costly decisions he made.

Whatever rhetoric or action was deployed by the Nasserist regime in the sphere of inter-Arab relations or the conflict with Israel, its mainstay was the consolidation of its own capabilities, power, and sovereignty. The thrust of Nasser for regional hegemony in the name of pan-Arabism forced others to develop counteralliances, sometimes with nonregional powers, as a means to deter regional Arab threats and enhance national security. It is indeed ironic that Nasserism, often conceived as the epitome of pan-Arabism, was in effect a powerful catalyst in the process of state formation and self-defeating in its perceived efforts to melt the Arab states' differences into one political unit or even a collective action. On the whole, the fierce inter-Arab struggle for power—although by far more violent than Malcolm Kerr's term "Arab Cold War" denotes—was crucial to state formation and definition of state sovereignty and boundaries versus an abstract supranational Arab entity.

Until 1967, Nasser's conduct of his relations with other Arab states was marked by self-convicted unilateral dictation, with no willingness whatsoever to negotiate or accept compromises. Even in the 1964–65 summitry period, when he ostensibly proved capable of coming to terms with his Arab rivals, in fact he was only playing for time. Adamant not to surrender any of his regional assets or aims, he opted for a dangerous strategy that was intended to rescue his image and prevent war with Israel, but was bound to actually escalate the chances of war. That Egypt could achieve much more in terms of regional leadership and cooperation with other Arab states by avoiding aggressive policies became evident only under Sadat.

Following the June 1967 defeat, Nasser himself showed realism and more flexibility in his search for the recovery of the occupied territories from Israel by adopting a combined strategy of power and diplomacy. His acceptance of resolution 242 was meant to win him time for domestic and military recovery as prerequisites for the liberation of Sinai by force rather than by keenly relying on the international efforts to bring about an Israeli withdrawal from the territories occupied in June 1967. Yet the shift toward Egypt's particular needs and departure from the previous antagonistic approach toward other Arab regimes could hardly wipe out Nasser's threatening image from the latter's memory. The result was a measured Arab financial aid to Egypt and little willingness on the part of the confrontation states to share with Egypt the burden of the war of attrition against Israel.

## Notes

1. "Thalathuna 'Aama 'ala Wafat Jamal 'Abd al-Nasir" (a panel), *Al-Mustaqbal al-'Arabi* 23 (December 2000): 79–111; Basim al-Jisr, "'Abd al-Nasir wal-Haraka al-Qawmiyya al-'Arabiyya," ibid., 94.

2. See Muhammad Hasanayn Haykal's presentation, "Ja'izat Jamal 'Abd al-Nasir," *Al-Mustaqbal al-'Arabi* 22 (September 1999): esp. 82–92; 'Abdallah Imam, *'Ali Sabri Yatadhakkar: Bi-Saraha 'an al-Sadat* (Cairo: Dar al-Khayal, 1997), 98–101; Husam 'Issa, "Misr . . . Ila Ayn?" *Al-Mustaqbal al-'Arabi* 21 (November 1998): 34–35.

3. Joel Gordon, *Nasser's Blessed Movement: Egypt's Free Officers and the July Revolution* (New York: Oxford University Press, 1992), 198; Emanuel Sivan, *Radical Islam: Medieval Theology and Modern Politics* (New Haven: Yale University Press, 1985).

4. See, e.g., 'Abd al-Mun'im Sa'id, "Al-Taghayyur fi al-Siyasa al-Kharijiyya ba'd al-Hazima," in Lutfi al-Khuli, ed., *Harb Yunyu 1967 Ba'da 30 Sana* (Cairo: Markaz al-Ahram, 1997), 161, 171–73. See also Taha al-Majdoub, "Al-Jaish al-Misri Ba'da Yunyu 67," ibid., 118–20.

5. P. J. Vatikiotis, *Nasser and His Generation* (London: Croom Helm, 1978), 17.

6. See, e.g., al-Jisr, "'Abd al-Nasir," 91–92; Peter Woodward, *Nasser: Profiles in Power* (London: Longman, 1992), 81.

7. Salwa al-'Amad, "Al-'Uruba wa-Filastin fi Siyasat 'Abd al-Nasir wa-Dawruhuma fi Sun' Jadhibiyyatih al-Siyasiyya," *Shu'un Filastiniyya*, no. 244–45 (August 1993): 39–43.

8. Imam, *'Ali Sabri*, 98–99.

9. Edward H. Carr, *What Is History?* (Harmondsworth: Penguin Books, 1964), 44–55.

10. Ibid., 53; Gamal Abdel Nasser, *The Philosophy of the Revolution* (Buffalo: Smith, Keynes and Marshall, 1959), 59–62; John S. Badeau, "The Role in Search of a Hero: A Brief Study of the Egyptian Revolution," *Middle East Journal* 9, no. 1 (fall 1955): 373–84.

11. Imam, *'Ali Sabri*, 100–101. For a leftist Ba'thi perspective of Nasser's developing revolution, see Muhammad 'Umran, *Tajribati fi al-Thawra* (Damascus: n.p., 1970), 114–15.

12. R. Hrair Dekmejian, *Egypt under Nasir: A Study in Political Dynamics* (Albany: State University of New York Press, 1971), 50–51; Gordon, *Nasser's Blessed Movement*, 3–6; Israel Gershoni, "An Intellectual Source for the Revolution: Tawfiq al-Hakim's Influence on Nasser and His Generation," in Shimon Shamir, ed., *Egypt from Monarchy to Republic: A Reassessment of Revolution and Change* (Boulder: Westview Press, 1995), 213–19; Vatikiotis, *Nasser and His Generation*, 15–16 and more thoroughly in chaps. 1–4, tracing the pre-1952 roots of Nasser's political perceptions.

13. On the Nasserist images and values, see Adeed I. Dawisha, *Egypt in the Arab World: The Elements of Foreign Policy* (New York: John Wiley, 1976), 123–39.

14. For an explanation of Egypt's quest for regional leadership and its boundaries of national security, see Imam, *'Ali Sabri*, 97–100; Sa'id, "Al-Taghayyur," 162–64. See also Dawisha, *Egypt*, 5; Yehoshua Porath, *In Search of Arab Unity* (London: Frank Cass, 1980); Ali E. H. Dessouki, "Egypt and the Peace Process," *International Journal* 4, no. 3 (1990): 57–58.

15. On the concept of role, see Kalevi J. Holsti, *International Politics: A Framework for Analysis* (Englewood Cliffs, N.J.: Prentice-Hall, 1977), chap. 5; Lisbeth Aggestam, "Role Conceptions and the Politics of Identity in Foreign Policy," *ARENA*, Working Papers Series, 1999; Michael Barnett, "Institutions, Roles, and Disorder," *International Studies Quarterly* 37 (1993): 271–96. For a discussion of this aspect in the case of Nasser, see Dawisha, *Egypt*, 123–25.

16. Dawisha, *Egypt*, 140–53.

17. Gad Gilbar, "Between Arabism and Egyptianism," in Shimon Shmair, ed., *The Decline of Nasserism, 1965–1970: The Waning of a Messianic Movement* (Tel Aviv: Mif'alim Universitayim, 1978), 208–17 (Hebrew).

18. Vatikiotis, *Nasser and His Generation*, esp. chaps. 1–4.; James P. Jankowski, "Egyptian Responses to the Palestine Problem in the Interwar Period," *IJMES* 12 (1980): 1–38; Vatikiotis, *Nasser and His Generation*, 72–78, 85–97. It is noteworthy that some 150 volunteers of "Young Egypt" also took part in the war.

19. 'Awatif 'Abd al-Rahman, *Misr wa-Filastin* (Kuwait: al-Majlis al-Watani lil-Thaqafa wal-Funun wal-Adab, 1980), 85ff.; James P. Jankowski, "The Government of Egypt and the Palestine Question, 1936–1939," *Middle Eastern Studies* 17 (1981): 427–53; Thomas Mayer, *Egypt and the Palestine Question, 1936–1945* (Berlin: K. Schwarz, 1983); P. J. Vatikiotis, *The Modern History of Egypt* (London: Weidenfeld and Nicolson, 1969), 343–45, 352–53. See also Ralph M. Coury, *The Making of an Egyptian Arab Nationalist: The Early Years of Azzam Pasha, 1893–1936* (Reading: Ithaca Press, 1998); Elie Podeh, "The Emergence of the Arab State System Reconsidered," *Diplomacy and Statecraft* 9, no. 3 (1998): 68–71.

20. Bashir Da'ouk, *Nidal al-Ba'th fi Sabil al-Wahda wal-Huriyya wal-Ishtirakiyya*, vol. 3 (Beirut: Dar al-Tali'a, 1964), 9, 22–23; Naji 'Allush, *Al-Thawra wal-Jamahir* (Beirut: Dar al-Tali'a, 1973), 175–76; Walid Kazziha, *Revolutionary Transformation in the Arab World* (London: Croom Helm, 1975), 58.

21. Leonard Binder, *The Ideological Revolution of the Middle East* (New York: John Wiley, 1964), 198–229; Shimon Shamir, "The Decline of the Nasserist Messianic," in Shamir, ed., *Decline of Nasserism*, 1–38 (Hebrew); Elie Podeh, *The Quest for Hegemony in the Arab World: The Struggle over the Baghdad Pact* (Leiden: E. J. Brill, 1995), 2–3.

22. William R. Louis, *The British Empire in the Middle East, 1945–1951* (Oxford: Oxford University Press, 1984), 244–53, 331–44; Mahmud Riyad, *Mudhakkirat Mahmud Riyad, 1948–1978* (Beirut: al-Mu'assassa al-'Arabiyya lil-Dirasat wal-Nashr, 1985), 63–73; Mohamed H. Heikal, *Cutting the Lion's Tail: Suez through Egyptian Eyes* (New York: Arbor House, 1987), 52–59.

23. Dekmejian, *Egypt under Nasir*, 54.

24. Ibid., 50–53.

25. On this regard, see the introduction to this volume.

26. Dekmejian, *Egypt under Nasir*, 18–20; Kazziha, *Revolutionary Transformation*, 1–16.

27. Michael Eppel, "The Elite, the Effendiyya, and the Growth of Nationalism and Pan-Arabism in Hashemite Iraq, 1921–1958," *IJMES* 30, no. 2 (May 1998): 227–50.

28. Kazziha, *Revolutionary Transformation*, 21–31.

29. Paul Noble, "The Arab System," in Bahgat Korany and Ali E. H. Dessouki, eds., *The Foreign Policies of Arab States* (Boulder: Westview Press, 1984), 48; Muhammad Hasanayn Haykal, *Kharif al-Ghadab* (Beirut: Sharikat al-Matbu'at, 1983), 148.

30. Yehoshua Porath, *In Search of Arab Unity, 1930–1945* (London: Frank Cass, 1986); Podeh, *Quest for Hegemony in the Arab World*, chap. 1.

31. Jamil Matar and A. D. Hilal [Dessouki], *Al-Nizam al-Iqlimi al-'Arabi* (Beirut: Markaz al-Dirasat al-Wahda al-'Arabiyya, 1983), 113; Malcolm Kerr, *Regional Arab Politics and the Conflict with Israel* (Santa Monica: Rand, 1969), 11; Fouad Ajami, "Geopolitical Illusions," in Steven L. Spiegel, ed., *The Middle East and the Western Alliance* (London: Allen and Unwin, 1982), 155–58.

32. Avraham Sela, *The Decline of the Arab-Israeli Conflict: Middle East Politics and the Quest for a Regional Order* (Albany: State University of New York Press, 1998), chaps. 3–5.

33. Hasan Abu Talib, "Mu'tamarat al-Qimma wa-Tahaddiyat al-'Amal al-Mushtarak," *Al-Siyasa al-Dawliyya*, no. 80 (April 1985): 9–13; Malcolm Kerr, *The Arab Cold War: Gamal 'Abd al-Nasir and His Rivals, 1958–1970* (Oxford: Oxford University Press, 1971), 14.

34. Fouad Ajami, *The Arab Predicament: Arab Political Thought and Practice since 1967* (Cambridge: Cambridge University Press, 1981), 128. On Nasser's fluctuating inter-Arab policy, see Anouar Abdel-Malek, *Egypt: Military Society, the Army Regime, the Left, and Social Change under Nasser* (New York: Vintage Books, 1968), 125–29, 157–66; Raymond A. Hinnebusch, *Egyptian Politics under Sadat: The Post-Populist Development of an Authoritarian-Modernizing State* (Cambridge: Cambridge University Press, 1985), 21–29; John Waterbury, *The Egypt of Nasser and Sadat: The Political Economy of Two Regimes* (Princeton: Princeton University Press, 1983), 94–100; Kerr, *Arab Cold War*, 28–30.

35. Patrick Seale, *The Struggle for Syria: A Study of Post-War Arab Politics, 1945–1958* (Oxford: Oxford University Press, 1965), 308–26; Kerr, *Arab Cold War*, 7–16; Patrick Seale, *Regional Arab Politics*, 19–20; Muhammad Hasanayn Haykal, *Sanawat al-Ghalayan* (Cairo: Markaz al-Ahram, 1988), 271–81; Dawisha, *Egypt in the Arab World*, 29–31. For a recent study of the UAR, see Elie Podeh, *The Decline of Arab Unity: The Rise and Fall of the United Arab Republic* (Brighton: Sussex Academic Press 1999).

36. Haykal, *Sanawat al-Ghalayan*, 275–76; Cecil Hourani, "In Search of a Valid Myth," *Middle East Forum* 47 (1971): 40.

37. Kerr, *Arab Cold War*, 28–30; Dawisha, *Egypt in the Arab World*, 34–35; *Al-Ahram*, February 23, December 22, 1962; *Al-Mithaq al-Watani* (Cairo, August 1964).

38. Indeed, the Arab Nationalist Movement (Harakat al-Qawmiyyin al-'Arab), supported an Iraqi-Kuwaiti union, but later changed its view in accordance with its support of Nasser. See Kazziha, *Revolutionary Transformation*, 34–35.

39. 'Abd al-Hamid Muwafi, *Misr fi Jami'at al-Duwal al-'Arabiyya* (Cairo: al-Hay'a al-Misriyya al-'Amma lil-Kitab, 1983), 202; Abdel-Malek, *Egypt*, 256, 260.

40. Podeh, *Quest for Hegemony in the Arab World*, 149–95.

41. This, for example, was evident in King Husayn's clamping down on the opposition from 1957 to the mid-1960s. See Avraham Sela, *The Palestinian Ba'th* (Jerusalem: Magnes Press, 1982), chaps. 2 and 3 (Hebrew).

42. The Nasserist regime maintained its financial support to the Arab Nationalist Movement until 1967. Kazziha, *Revolutionary Transformation*, 79.

43. William J. Burns, *Economic Aid and American Policy toward Egypt, 1955–1981* (Albany: State University of New York Press, 1985), 126.

44. Muhammad Hafiz Isma'il, *Amn Misr al-Qawmi fi 'Asr al-Tahaddiyat* (Cairo: Markaz al-Ahram, 1987), 97; Muhammad Fawzi, *Harb al-Thalath Sanawat, 1967–1970* (Cairo: Dar al-Mustaqbal al-'Arabi, 1986), 22–26; Haykal, *Sanawat al-Ghalayan*, 626–28; Muhammad Hasanayn Haykal, *Al-Infijar 1967* (Cairo: Markaz al-Ahram, 1990), 63, 222.

45. Michael B. Oren, *The Origins of the Second Arab-Israeli War* (London: Frank Cass, 1992), 95–128.

46. Yehoshafat Harkabi, *Arab Attitude to Israel* (Jerusalem: Israel Universities Press, 1971), 1–49; Yehoshafat Harkabi, *Arab Strategies and Israel's Response* (New York: Free Press, 1979), 3–16; Kerr, *Regional Arab Politics*, 33–40; Fawzi, *Harb al-Thalath Sanawat*, 49.

47. Labib Shuqair, ed., *Hadith al-Batal al-Za'im Jamal 'Abd al-Nasir Ila al-Umma* 4 (Cairo: Dar al-Tahrir, 1965): 314, 338; *Al-Ahram*, February 23, 1964; Haykal, *Al-Infijar 1967*, 208; Harkabi, *Arab Strategies and Israel's Response*, 8–12.

48. Yehoshafat Harkabi, *Palestinians and Israel* (Jerusalem: Keter, 1974), 35 (Hebrew).

49. On the principles of the Westphalian system and its dynamics, see Lynn Miller, *Global Order: Values and Power in International Politics* (Boulder: Westview Press, 1990), 20–29. On the Arab League's principles, see Sela, *Decline of the Arab-Israeli Conflict*, 38.

50. Hassan Nafaa, "Arab Nationalism: A Response to Ajami's Thesis on the "End of Pan-Arabism," *Journal of Arab Affairs* 2, no. 2 (1983): 181–82.

51. With one exception (Cairo, 1990), and two summit breakdowns (Rabat, 1969; Fez, 1981), all Arab summits closed with statements emphasizing united position. Sela, *Decline of the Arab-Israeli Conflict*, 21.

52. Eliezer Sheffer, "The Egyptian Economy between the Two Wars," in Itamar Rabinovich and Haim Shaked, eds., *From June to October: The Middle East between 1967 and 1973* (New Brunswick, N.J.: Transaction, 1978), 140–42.

53. East Jerusalem and the Gaza Strip were not included in the proposal.

54. Quoted by Fawzi, *Harb al-Thalath Sanawat*, 193–96, 199; Dawisha, *Egypt in the Arab World*, 51.

55. Yoram Meital, "The Khartoum Conference and Egyptian Policy after the 1967 War: A Reexamination," *Middle East Journal* 54, no. 1 (winter 2000): 64–82.

56. Bourguiba defied the common Arab attitude toward the Palestine issue by suggesting recognition of Israel in its 1947 UN Partition Plan borders. This was meant to be the first step, if accepted, in cutting Israel down to size, to be followed by further steps to defeat the Jewish state. In case Israel refused to accept the Arab offer, it would weaken its international legitimacy. Sela, *Decline of the Arab-Israeli Conflict*, 80–81.

57. Harkabi, *Arab Strategies*, 22; Fawzi, *Harb al-Thalath Sanawat*, 188.

# 8

# 'Abd al-Nasser and the United States

Enemy or Friend?

David W. Lesch

The relationship between the United States and Gamal 'Abd al-Nasser's Egypt fluctuated, it seemed, from American administration to administration. Washington could never quite figure out whether Nasser was an asset or a detriment to U.S. interests in the Middle East. From initial optimism that he was the leader of a new type of regime in Egypt that could be the centerpiece of American Cold War strategic designs and economic modernization theories in the region, he was soon thereafter seen as a willing and unwilling Soviet puppet through whom the Kremlin would advance its own interests in the Middle East. In the late 1950s and early 1960s, particularly during the Kennedy administration, Nasser (or more to the point, Nasserism) was again seen from the White House as possibly a valuable strategic partner in the Cold War struggle with the Soviet Union, only to be relegated again to a position characterized as obstreperous, obfuscating, and obstructionist—someone who was beyond the pale of reasonable diplomacy, who sanctioned Soviet encroachment, and who was too deeply embedded in the Arab-Israeli dispute. To the end, Nasser was something of an enigma to Washington.

There were consistent splits in the policy-making apparatus, ever since the July 1952 Revolution, between those who felt Nasser could be a friend of the United States and those who believed he was the enemy. These distinct positions were reflected in the roller-coaster policy formulations emanating from various administrations, which ran the gamut from cooperation to confrontation and seemed to be inversely proportional to Nasser's relationship with the USSR. It also reflected a typically reactionary U.S. foreign policy that bounced up against Nasser's own policy swings, which were ultimately based upon the need to stay in power and the pursuit of nationalist and regionalist interests.

## Friend to Foe

### Act I

In the new Cold War environment following World War II, the United States, as articulated through the Truman administration, began to develop interests and thus policies toward the Middle East.[1] Its main concern was that instability in the area would only create opportunities for the USSR, enabling it to establish a foothold in the Middle East by means of an association with the growing leftist movements that had been identifying themselves with an anti-Zionist and anti-West platform. This approach fell in line with the administration's overall global policy approach of containment of communism, as articulated in National Security Council (NSC) resolution 68 of April 1950. From Washington's point of view, of course, this stability in the Middle East was defined in terms of a regime aligning itself with the West and not with the Soviet bloc. It also meant a willingness on the part of various Arab regimes and Israel to settle their differences, which would prevent the festering Arab-Israeli dispute from becoming a disruptive factor that could impede safe access to and easy transport of Middle East oil and open up areas of ingress for the USSR.

Truman's Point Four technical assistance program and the Mutual Security Program were designed to foster a more stable and pro-West political environment through the carrots of military and economic aid. Ultimately, however, with the exigencies of the Cold War bearing down on policy makers and the perception that there was insufficient time to develop a stable politico-economic environment conducive to liberal democratic capitalism in any sort of evolutionary fashion, simply having someone or some junta in power who looked to the West and not to the East came to be the best recipe for securing stable, pro-West regimes—whether indigenously or artificially fomented.[2]

In this regard, the July 1952 Revolution brought the Revolutionary Command Council (RCC) to power. Ostensibly led by the popular General Muhammad Nagib but secretly orchestrated by Nasser, the RCC seemed to fit the bill on several fronts. This was a group of mostly junior officers who had entered the military academy in the 1930s following the lifting of certain restrictions on entry. Until then, the academy had closed off a military career to all but the rich and landed; this created a military that was anything but professional. These junior officers were pragmatic military men, not ideologues, who would understand such things as the need for arms, the construction of military alliances, and the reality of the Soviet and communist threat. The Free Officers railed against corruption, which had so characterized King Faruq's monarchy and the feudalist-controlled party structure embodied by the Wafd Party.

The new Egyptian leaders were intent on implementing the type of reform that the United States felt was necessary in order to redirect capital away from landed interests and toward more productive utilization in the industrial and commercial sectors, thereby engendering market-oriented economic growth and stability. Washington believed that the dilapidated nature of the King Faruq regime, especially after the humiliating loss to the nascent state of Israel in 1948, was more of a threat to Egyptian stability (and thus regional stability) in the long run. Better to consign this inept regime to history now than to wait for further internal implosion and possible regional conflagration that could be taken advantage of by both internal and external communist forces. In this sense, the United States was not at all displeased with the events of July 1952, and depending upon which source one might consult, Washington may have played a role in at least encouraging, if not sanctioning, the Free Officers' putsch.[3]

The change of regime, it was thought, might also allow for a fresh start in Anglo-Egyptian negotiations, which under Faruq had drawn to a standstill. In any event, for the sake of regional stability, the United States was more than willing to put up with a military dictatorship, or what has been called a transitional authoritarian regime, until conditions evolved whereby the installation of democratic institutions could be attempted. Indeed, this was the rationalization of the Free Officers themselves for not immediately reinstituting a parliamentary system—Egypt simply was not ready for it, and any premature return could jeopardize the revolution itself.[4]

With political and economic stability, long-term objectives could be achieved: removing the British from Egyptian soil, reducing the power of and/or eliminating detrimental foreign interests and *mutamasriyyun* elements, and attaining sufficient regional stature. To help the transitional authoritarian regime in this regard, the Central Intelligence Agency (CIA) assisted in establishing Egyptian intelligence (the GIA) so that the RCC could ward off any oppositional, particularly communist, movements. A working relationship with the new regime, especially with Nasser, seemed to have been established.[5] In November 1954, the U.S. ambassador to Cairo, Jefferson Caffery, concluded that the new regime "had done more for Egypt in two years than all their predecessors put together before them."[6]

An additional carrot for American interests regarding the socioeconomic constitution of the revolutionaries was the fact that they were not of the *effendi* class, which had become so dependent upon the British. In this way, the Free Officers were not only avowed anticommunists, apparently willing to work with the United States in the development of its Cold War strategic designs for the region; they were also not beholden to London. Therefore, Washington, despite overall cooperation with the British regarding containment of the USSR, could again nudge their European ally aside and fill another emerging vacuum of power, as had already happened in Iran in 1946, in Israel in 1948, and, in the case of the Truman Doctrine, in Greece and Turkey in 1947.

The British were quite disturbed about discussions in 1952 in policy circles in Washington, particularly in the State Department and among the Joint Chiefs of Staff, advocating military assistance to the RCC that would, although in modest amounts at first, help the new Egyptian regime stabilize itself as well as possibly draw it closer to participation in Western defense plans for the region.[7] Not only was London suspicious of American intentions in Egypt at British expense; it also feared that these arms might find their way into the hands of anti-British guerilla organizations, who would use them against British soldiers and facilities in the Suez Canal base.

Regardless, President Truman nixed any formal military aid to Egypt, succumbing to growing pro-Israeli domestic pressures and to those who feared the onset of an arms race in the region by shattering the 1950 Tripartite Declaration. Although Truman granted Egypt a $10 million subsidy for the purchase of wheat surpluses, Nasser was certainly disillusioned and disappointed by Truman's refusal to sanction military assistance.[8] It would be a harbinger of things to come and a consistent dilemma faced by succeeding administrations regarding military aid to Arab states still at war with Israel.

Egypt's strategic value to the West had been amply displayed during World War II as the headquarters for Allied Forces in North Africa and as the location for the immensely important Middle East Supply Center. With the emergence of the Cold War, Egypt's position was no less important, especially as the Berlin blockade, Soviet activities in Eastern Europe, and the onset of the Korean War in 1950 made it imperative to the United States and Great Britain that the West maintain base rights in Egypt along the Suez Canal. Toward this end, Egypt became a linchpin in various attempts by Washington and London to organize a pro-West regional defense system designed to contain communist expansion by linking up NATO with SEATO, thereby filling the gap in the West's strategic plan to encircle the communist behemoths, the USSR and the People's Republic of China. The details and complexities of the negotiations and attempts by British, American, and Egyptian officials to create a pan-Arab defense scheme, centered around Cairo and linked to the West (the so-called Middle East Command

and Middle East Defense Organization), have been amply examined elsewhere.[9] Suffice it to say that the nationalist aspirations of Egypt did not correspond with the British and American objective of maintaining strategic access in Egypt by weaving such an agreement into Egyptian participation in a pro-West regional defense scheme.

When the Eisenhower administration came to power in January 1953, there existed much optimism in the Arab world that American policies might become more favorably disposed toward the Arabs. This was based on the known disposition of Eisenhower and his secretary of state, John Foster Dulles, to direct foreign policy in the Middle East on a more evenhanded basis.[10] The new administration recognized the increasing importance of the Middle East oil reserves and oil transport routes and the region's strategic position on the southeast flank of NATO bordering the south-central regions of the USSR. And with the exigencies of the New Look foreign policy guiding the American approach, the need for the construction of a regional defense system in the Middle East gained immediate urgency.[11]

In order to better assess the complex Middle East situation and, in particular, the feasibility of a regional defense pact, Eisenhower sent Dulles on what was essentially a fact-finding tour of Middle East and South Asian capitals in May 1953.[12] From his trip Dulles concluded that Arab inclusion, particularly Egypt's, in a pro-West regional defense pact was not a feasible objective at the time.[13] Not only was there tremendous domestic opposition in the Arab world to adherence to any type of organization that included Great Britain and/or France, but there was also the complicating factor of the Arab-Israeli conflict, which compelled the United States to detach its defense schemes as much as possible from a dispute that raised the ire and opposition of pro-Israeli groups at home and made it impossible to straddle both sides of the fence in the region. This simply could not be done before an Anglo-Egyptian agreement as well as an Arab-Israeli settlement. With this in mind, Eisenhower and Dulles concentrated on forming a regional pact based on the non-Arab northern tier countries of the Middle East, focusing on Turkey, Iran, and Pakistan, and thus remaining aloof from the Arab-Israeli dispute and inter-Arab rivalries. A series of bilateral agreements in 1954 produced the foundation of what came to be known as the Baghdad Pact, signed in February 1955.[14]

The United States did not formally join the Baghdad Pact, preferring an observer status.[15] Although there are differing views on the extent of American knowledge of the announcement and signing of the Baghdad Pact, it seems to me that the Eisenhower administration ultimately acquiesced to it, believing that this could be the beginning of launching Iraq into the role that Washington had hoped Nasser's Egypt would play: a prominent Arab state as the centerpiece of an anticommunist regional defense pact, possibly leading other Arab states into joining it and, in doing so, creating a more favorable environment for an Arab-Israeli settlement.[16] Indeed, this would be the beginning of an "if not Egypt then Iraq" approach by the United States in its seemingly never-ending search for a regional ally that would help protect Washington's strategic interests while leading a moderate Arab consensus into peace with Israel. This policy would continue long after Nasser had left the scene.

The shift in the focus of the Western defense schemes from an Arab-led pact to that of the northern tier actually worried the Egyptians to a certain degree, insofar as they were fearful that they had lost any leverage, particularly American pressure, that might force the British to make the necessary concessions regarding withdrawal from the Suez Canal base. Attempted rapprochement with Turkey, futile arms requests to the United States, as well as inter-Arab political machinations were all utilized by Nasser in order to prevent Egypt's isolation in the region, which would, from his point of view, result in either coerced concessions to Western demands or possibly his own overthrow by distraught elements in the country (or even within his own regime).

In actuality, the switch to the northern tier approach reduced Egypt's strategic importance as a partner in Western defense schemes and thus opened the door for an agreement with London, which finally came to fruition in October 1954. The agreement arranged for the evacuation of British troops from the Suez Canal base, but it also included clauses allowing for a British return under certain war-induced conditions, something for which Nasser was heavily criticized by elements of Egyptian opposition groups, particularly the Muslim Brothers.

All of these various strands came together in the first few months of 1955. The Israelis, full of trepidation over the formation of the Baghdad Pact and continued Fidayyun raids, lashed out at Egypt in February 1955 (only a few days after the announcement of the Baghdad Pact) in its infamous Gaza raid, killing scores of Egyptian soldiers in the process. Nasser was absolutely humiliated and embarrassed, for his regime had come to power in large part based on the premise that the corruption of the previous regime, which had so hampered the Arab war effort in the 1947–49 Arab-Israeli War, had ended. These were purported to be professional military men in power, who would, at the very least, reorganize the military into an efficient fighting force. With the Gaza raid, it seemed on the surface that very little, if any, progress had been made. Egypt was still a whipping boy to the Israelis—and no less suspicious of American complicity.

The sequence of events that followed the Gaza raid and the formation of the Baghdad Pact is well known. During this panoply of events between 1954 and 1956, Nasser had, in the eyes of Washington, gone from a potential friend to an outright foe of the West. Despite the Eisenhower administration's pressure on the tripartite invaders in 1956, which, in effect, saved Egypt and allowed Nasser to survive much more than intact, the Egyptian president's anti-Baghdad Pact, anti-Israeli, and neutralist position had soured the relationship with the United States. Ultimately, the strategic interests of the United States vis-à-vis the Cold War could not be reconciled with Egyptian nationalist interests and Nasser's own regional objectives.

An Anglo-Egyptian accord was delayed until after the regional defense plan had already shifted its focus away from Egypt, and U.S. attempts (Johnston and Alpha plans) to broker negotiations between Cairo and Jerusalem, to settle the Palestinian refugee problem, and to clear the way for Egyptian participation in a regional defense pact with an overall Arab-Israeli peace had failed due to both Egyptian and Israeli intransigence.[17] With the USSR's termination of diplomatic relations with Israel in February 1953 and American efforts in the UN Security Council in early 1954 to ensure free passage through the Straits of Tiran (which the Soviets vetoed and which drew intense Egyptian criticism), the Cold War lines were beginning to be drawn in the Middle East. Nasser had become the strong, stable leader that many in Washington had hoped for, but, unfortunately for American interests, he had the gall to pursue his own interests.[18]

The fruition of the transformation from friend to foe was the Eisenhower Doctrine, announced by the president in January 1957. Ostensibly, the doctrine offered military and economic aid to any state in the Middle East that requested it in order to fend off the advances of "international communism." The stated objective was to fill the vacuum of power created by the British and French humiliation at Suez before the Soviets could exploit the situation to their own advantage. The doctrine's regional interpretation was to "rollback" Nasserism, this growing anti-Western force which was seen at the time as a willing dupe of the Kremlin, and attempts were made by the White House to build up other leaders in the Arab world who might possibly rival the Egyptian president and become the long sought-after strategic partner of the United States.[19] The United States began realizing what the British had long feared: that Nasser's policies, whether generated by regional objectives or not, were at least indirectly aimed at undermining Western interests in the area to the benefit of the Soviets. Washington thus felt compelled to assume the role of the British and the French in fending off this threat. Since Nasser had shown that he was a skilled strategic diplomatic player and that he embodied a vibrant anti-Western ideologically based movement, he was a dangerous enemy—but he would not stay so for very long.

## Act II

Perhaps the first overt realization by the Eisenhower administration that the Middle East was not simply a passive recipient of East-West ingress occurred during the latter stages of the American-Syrian crisis of 1957.[20] This event also marked a change in Washington's attitude and approach toward Nasser as it began to see him (or maybe more appropriately, Nasserism) as a possible ally in its efforts to contain the USSR in the Middle East. After all, the United States was now dealing with an entire movement rather than an individual leader.[21]

The crisis itself began in August 1957 when Syrian authorities uncovered a covert plot, sponsored by the United States, to overthrow what Washington thought was a regime that was becoming too closely tied to the USSR. Rather than act as if it were caught red-handed, the Eisenhower administration saw this development as further proof of Syria's leap toward the USSR. From Washington's point of view, the crisis created an opportunity to rally pro-West Arab allies to precipitate action against the leftist regime in Damascus. The problem was that Washington's Arab friends were not particularly interested in aggressive action against their Arab brethren. So soon after Suez and with Nasser at the height of his popularity, such pro-West countries as Iraq, Jordan, and Saudi Arabia could only instigate virtually worthless diplomatic initiatives, lest they be accused of kowtowing to the United States. Nasser had long set the tone of pan-Arab nationalism, and any regime perceived to be doing the bidding of the West would indeed be on shaky ground domestically.

Bereft of its Arab allies, Washington looked to its fellow NATO member on Syria's northern border, Turkey, which had been nervously eyeing events in Damascus. With the USSR bordering it to the north, Ankara was all too eager to exert pressure on Syria in order to prevent it from becoming a Soviet satellite in the heart of the Middle East. When Turkey started mobilizing its troops on the Syrian border, the USSR directly entered the game by threatening Ankara if the latter engaged in military action against Syria. Suddenly, what had been confined to a regional crisis was turning into an international one, with the Soviets and Americans facing off against each other in the Cold War battleground of the Third World.

Nasser, however, took advantage of the superpower standoff to match words with deeds by sending what was really only a symbolic number of troops to Syria to ostensibly help his Arab brethren fight off the Turks. In short order, Nasser had won the day by fending off any Arab pretenders to his mantle of leadership, and he had "saved" the Syrian regime from subservience to Moscow. Nasser had worked long and hard to keep Syria from joining the Baghdad Pact and building up pro-Nasserist assets within the country, and he was not about to lose this level of influence to the Soviets or Syrian communists.

Taking stock of these developments was the Eisenhower administration, which had essentially failed at the domestic, regional, and international levels to correct the situation in Syria. Therefore, why not entrust the job to Nasser, the only man who could prevent the Soviets from gobbling up Syria? He had kept the Soviets at arm's length in Egypt, despite his reliance on Moscow for military arms, and he had repressed communist movements within his own country. Maybe he could do the same in Syria. It certainly was seen in Washington as the lesser evil of all the alternatives. Indeed, there had been budding cooperation between U.S. and Egyptian officials, recognizing the shared interests vis-à-vis Syria, at the United Nations in October and November 1957 during the latter stages of the crisis. Washington's knowledge of and acquiescence to Cairo's actions in Syria, and ultimately even the merger of Syria and Egypt into the United Arab Republic (UAR) in February 1958, reduced the danger of misinterpreting events that could spin out of control and coated the crisis with a more sanguine veneer.

To wit, a close confidant of Nasser, Muhammad Hasanayn Haykal, informed American officials on December 11, 1957, that the Egyptian president

> had investigated recent information we [United States] had given him relative to the communist connections of [Syrian military chief of staff 'Afif al-] Bizri and is now convinced Bizri [is] a communist and that something must be done about it. . . . He [Nasser] asks of us only that we keep hands off Syria for a maximum period of three months and particularly that we do not do nothing [sic] which could have unintentional effect of making heroes out of Bizri, [communist parliamentary deputy Khalid] Bakdash, and [wealthy and influential pro-Soviet official] Khalid al-'Azm.[22]

In this same telegram, Haykal suggested that there were "several ways of attacking the Syrian problem" but that the "only country with the capability [to] succeed, and which can do so with minimal repercussions is Egypt. Of [the] countries primarily concerned with [the] Syrian situation, the United States and Egypt have the greatest interest in ensuring that country [has] a stable, anti-communist government."[23] Nasser only needed two months, as the UAR was formed in February. The regional solution Eisenhower and Dulles had so desperately wanted had emerged, albeit from an unexpected source.

In fact, the Eisenhower administration had come full circle. At the beginning of the year, with the introduction of the Eisenhower Doctrine, Nasser was the enemy. By the end of the year, the administration was tacitly working with Nasser in a budding relationship that helped pave the way for the formation of the UAR.[24] In other words, considering the failures of U.S. policy to contain Soviet influence in the Middle East to date, it finally dawned on pertinent policy makers that maybe Arab nationalism in the form of Nasserism could be something of an ally in the area against Soviet expansionism. This new line of thinking would be formalized in 1958 and carried out in earnest under the Kennedy administration, but its seeds were already sown at the end of the American-Syrian crisis.

NSC resolution 5820 of October 1958 (signed by Eisenhower on November 4, 1958), while adhering to the same objectives that had been delineated in previous policy dictates, outlined the new approach to Arab nationalism.[25] Of course, it was the Iraqi Revolution in July 1958 that helped to nudge things in this direction. The new regime in Baghdad seemed to welcome, and even embrace, communists into the government—a development that, not unlike the situation in Syria in late 1957, brought about a convergence of interests between Cairo and Washington. The NSC planning board now believed that working with Nasserist pan-Arabism was an "essential element in the prevention of the extension of Soviet influence in the area."[26] Although there was some disagreement within the administration over how close the United States should associate itself with Nasser, it was clear that Washington would improve relations with him in at least the short term. As such, the United States would try to work with, rather than against, nonaligned nations. This new policy emphasized the economic aspects of the relationship much more than in the recent past, which heretofore had generally relied more on strategic and political relations relative to the Cold War.[27]

Nasser also desired a better working relationship with the United States. Iraq, ironically, was as much, or even more, of a threat to his stature in the region now than it had been before the revolution. As the Iraqi president, 'Abd al-Karim Qassem, drew closer to the communists within his country, and as Moscow subsequently grew closer to Baghdad, clearly relieved to find someone in the Arab world who wholeheartedly welcomed communist participation in government, Nasser began to distance Egypt from the USSR. In terms of the Cold War, this move, which became clearly noticeable by December 1958, automatically triggered an improvement in relations with the other superpower. Thus, the stage was now set for a dramatic reversal in relations between Egypt and the United States, since Arab nationalism was coming to be seen in Washington as capable of "mustering ideological weapons far more powerful than anything the United States or its allies could bring to bear."[28]

In order to safeguard oil supplies, which really meant protecting Saudi

Arabia, and to curtail Soviet influence, Washington would work with Nasser. It was hoped that this might relieve some of the pressure of the Arab radical states on the conservative oil-rich monarchy in Riyadh while taking advantage of the apparent split between communists and nationalists in the Arab world. However, with Dulles's death in May 1959, a lame-duck presidency, and the sobering experience of the Middle East in recent years, the Eisenhower administration adopted a low-key approach toward the region for the remainder of its tenure in office. Since there seemed to be no pressing issues, and since the Arab states were content to bicker amongst themselves, the White House was all too happy to remain on the sidelines.

While other issues (Berlin, Cuba, and Vietnam, for instance) were certainly higher on the foreign policy priority list during the abbreviated Kennedy administration, the Middle East did receive some serious attention. Kennedy brought a whole new ideological conception of the Third World to the White House. Especially coming on the heels of Khrushchev's speech in January 1961, promoting wars of liberation in the Third World, Kennedy also saw these areas as opportunities to combat the USSR and expand U.S. influence. Popular nationalists were not to be feared but embraced, and in the Middle East this meant only one person: Nasser. As such, Kennedy viewed Nasser in the same league as great leaders of the nonaligned movement, such as Sukarno, Nkrumah, and Ben-Bella. In addition, after the Syrian secession from the UAR in September 1961, Nasser was seen in Washington to be in a weakened position, and therefore less able to stir up trouble in the region, while being more amenable to American demarches.[29] Of course, an alternative point of view might say that free of constraints, Nasser could use this honeymoon with Washington to build up his position in the region, which would inevitably pit him against the United States and the interests of its pro-West allies in the region—again!

Even before coming to office, Kennedy had given some indication that he would be evenhanded toward Arabs and Israelis, despite the sense of his being beholden to the Jewish vote for helping him to win his razor-thin presidential victory in 1960. While a member of Congress, he had criticized the Eisenhower administration for supporting France in its attempt to suppress the Algerian rebels. During his presidential campaign, he expressed strong support for Israel. But some Jewish leaders noted that while his running mate, Lyndon Johnson, had shown his support through action over the years, Kennedy had really only paid lip service thus far.

In addition, soon after taking office (and foreshadowing a later policy initiative), Kennedy circulated a letter to five Arab leaders promising his support for the UN Conciliation Commission to resolve the Palestinian refugee problem on the basis of repatriation and compensation for lost property.[30] The United States had also voted against Israel in the UN regarding a resolution condemning Jerusalem for a retaliatory raid against Syria. Finally, as a clear indication of Kennedy's desire to improve relations with Nasser, he appointed John Badeau as the new U.S. ambassador to Egypt. Badeau was a known and respected Arabist and former president of the American University of Cairo.

Recognizing the shifting winds in Washington, Nasser also sent out positive signals. After his visit to Cairo, Chester Bowles, Kennedy's ambassador-at-large to the Third World (itself an indication of the new policy direction), commented that "the leaders of the UAR are pragmatists searching for techniques that will enable them to expand their economy rapidly and to maintain their political grip. . . . If Nasser can gradually be led to forsake the microphone for the bulldozer, he may assume a key role in bringing the Middle East peacefully into our modern world."[31] The Kennedy team was made up of policy makers convinced that state-to-state relations could be scientifically managed (even though Kennedy's actual relationship with Nasser was carried out through the highly personal diplomacy of letters exchanged between them). They believed that the relatively quiescent state of the Middle East could be used to their advantage to sway Egypt, and possibly others, onto the path of socioeconomic development and modernization. After all, had they not turned Iran's potential "red" revolution into a "white" one?

As such, the Arab-Israeli conflict could indeed be, as the Egyptians put it, placed in the "icebox" in order to allow time for the new relationship (and policy) to develop. Under these favorable regional conditions, uncomplicated by a multitude of forces as they had been in the 1950s (and would even be more so in the not-too-distant future), it was believed that an Arab-Israeli peace might be possible, without its conclusion having to first await a crisis situation. As a result, Kennedy approved increased grain shipments to Egypt under the already existing PL-480 program. A total of $432 million in PL-480 assistance was allocated to Egypt in October 1961 over a three-year span, which would ultimately constitute over 30 percent of Egypt's supply of wheat during this period.[32] Indeed, Nasser adeptly played the superpowers off against one another, extracting huge amounts of aid from each side that contributed significantly to Egypt's impressive economic growth in the early 1960s.[33]

The policy seemed to work and, on the whole, was able to withstand small bumps in the road. Nasser appreciated Washington's cautiousness following the embarrassing and politically damaging breakup of the UAR (after initial accusations that the CIA had a prominent role in causing it). It weathered Nasser's severe criticism of the United States for its policies in such areas as the Congo and Cuba. It also withstood Egypt's military intervention in Kuwait in the summer of 1961 upon the latter's formal independence from Great Britain, in order to protect the Shaykhdom from an irredentist Iraq. This development, which Washington actually welcomed, placed Nasser in the same camp as the U.S. conservative friends in the region, Jordan and Saudi Arabia.

Despite sporadic clashes between Israeli troops and Palestinian guerrillas in late 1961 and skirmishes on the Israeli-Syrian border in early 1962, the Middle East seemed to be free of an impending major crisis for the time being. Seeing that this relative calm was an opportune moment to begin building bridges between Israel and Arab states on substantive issues, Kennedy pushed forward a new plan in mid-1962, making good on an earlier promise to Arab leaders to deal directly with the Palestinian refugee problem. During this process, it was hoped that a new dialogue could be established between Israel and Egypt that might possibly lead to a settlement of the Arab-Israeli conflict. So much for keeping the Palestinian issue in the "icebox"! It was called the Johnson Plan, named after Dr. Joseph Johnson, who was head of the Carnegie Endowment. Essentially, the plan allowed Palestinian refugees the choice of returning to Israel or resettling in neighboring Arab states, with compensation for lost properties and relocation costs. While Johnson was convinced that only a small portion of the refugees (fewer than 10 percent of the 1.2 million) would actually choose to return to Israeli territory, the Israeli leadership determined that even 10 percent would, in their view, amount to an unacceptable fifth column inside the country. The most Israel would be willing to accept was 20,000 refugees, a number that was likewise unacceptable to many Arab leaders.

Seeing the reluctance of the Israeli government for the plan, the Kennedy administration began to link military aid as an additional enticement to sweeten the pot. Particularly in demand by the Israelis were the Hawk surface-to-air missiles, for which the sale was approved in September 1962. Kennedy administration officials also saw the military aid as a way to influence Israeli policy and to curtail the development of any Israeli nuclear option. Little did Kennedy officials know that they were setting up a paradigm for peace negotiations between Israel and Egypt that would be carried out more rigorously in the 1970s, namely, military and economic aid to relieve mutual anxieties along with American involvement as a guarantor of any agreements.

Administration officials believed that both sides indicated a willingness to make concessions, and they engaged in relatively intense diplomatic negotiations during the summer of 1962. Israeli opposition to the Johnson Plan was more real than Washington realized, however, and along with an increasingly negative stance from domestic Jewish groups, Kennedy's advisors began to recommend his disengagement from the plan as quickly as possible.[34] Also dismembering the plan was the fact that news of the impending sale of Hawks to Israel had begun to leak out to the Arabs, who were not at all pleased.[35] Kennedy had obviously misjudged his position, whereby he thought that he could play both sides of the fence. Apparently, all this did was raise the ire of each (especially Israel) to a point that was counterproductive.

Whatever hope the plan had was finally dashed in September 1962, when a republican coup d'état in Yemen overthrew the monarchy of Imam Muhammad al-Badr. The event divided the Arab world in such a way that placed the United States in a very difficult position between Egypt and the conservative Arab Gulf monarchies. While Nasser felt compelled to assist the "progressive" forces on the republican side, in part to rebuild the status that had been so diminished with the Syrian secession from the UAR, the Saudi and Jordanian regimes were obliged to support countercoup attempts by the royalist forces regrouping along the Saudi-Yemeni border. The situation created a dilemma for Kennedy. On the one hand, he had to support Riyadh in order to maintain the important U.S.–Saudi relationship, especially when Egypt launched aerial forays into Saudi territory in an attempt to strike at royalist forces. On the other hand, in doing so he risked alienating Nasser, someone with whom the president had established a level of confidence and trust.[36]

The Saudis even claimed that Washington's new relationship with Nasser actually had the effect of encouraging him to intervene in Yemen and to raise the volume of pressure against the conservative regimes. In order not to alienate Nasser, and as something of a fait accompli based on the conclusion that the Yemeni people would be better off without the inept monarchy anyway, the United States recognized the new Yemen Arab Republic in December 1962. By way of explaining this action, Kennedy stated that "we must keep our ties to Nasser and the other neutralists even if we do not like many things they do, because if we lose them the balance of power could swing against us."[37]

The depth of the dilemma for Kennedy had become apparent by early 1963, when the Saudis stepped up their support for the royalist forces amid rampant rumors of pro-Nasserist coup attempts in Riyadh. Kennedy, wanting to stem the downward slide in U.S.–Saudi relations, and responding to pleas by oil lobbyists, authorized a token level of American military forces to the Kingdom (Operation Hard Surface). Although purely symbolic and intended as a way to shore up relations with Riyadh, the move angered Nasser and pushed Egypt and the United States farther apart. It was a no-win situation, and the longer the conflict continued the deeper the wedge that was driven between Washington and Cairo.

By the end of Kennedy's time in office, the policy focus relative to the Middle East surrounded the question of a security guarantee and increased military aid to Israel. Washington was no longer interested in the Johnson Plan or the fate of the Palestinian refugees. If the Yemen Civil War had been resolved in a relatively short time, then Kennedy's Middle East balancing act might have been preserved. But the conflagration continued on into the June 1967 War, costing Egypt about $1 million per day, and persistently weakening Nasser's position from another angle, which eventually influenced his fateful decisions leading up to the war.

In any event, the situation would soon be overtaken with the assassination of Kennedy in November 1963, as well as the heightening of tensions in the inter-Arab and Arab-Israeli arenas due to the planned completion by Israel of its diversion of the Jordan River headwaters. The Kennedy balancing act was destined to fail. Lyndon Johnson's support for Israel and antipathy toward Nasser were well known, and increasing pressure was being exerted on Nasser to respond to Israeli actions.[38] Similar to the U.S.–Saudi relationship in early 1957, when the Eisenhower administration attempted to befriend and build up King Sa'ud as a strategic partner, events outside of the relationship ultimately forced Sa'ud, and now Nasser, to adopt positions inimical to American interests.

Johnson's foreign policy lacked the subtle distinctions between communists and nationalists that Kennedy had made. His policy toward the Middle East seemed to be something of a throwback to the early Eisenhower years. It was a globalist foreign policy, one that saw the USSR lurking behind every trouble spot, seeking to enhance its power and influence with nationalist leaders who were either willing or unwilling dupes to Kremlin designs. Yet, whereas Eisenhower and Dulles tended to see Israel as something of an obstacle to their objectives in the region, Johnson was sympathetic and even empathetic toward the Jewish state. Egypt's continuing presence in Yemen, its backing of the Congo rebels, the warming of relations with the USSR, the entrenchment of socialist policies, the burning of the USIA library in Cairo in November 1964, and the shooting down of an American plane owned by one of Johnson's friends—all tended to confirm for Johnson that Kennedy's wooing of Nasser had been ill-conceived.

The Johnson administration increased U.S. support for the conservative Arab regimes threatened by radical Nasserism and built upon Kennedy's military aid commitments to Israel.[39] As such, food aid to Egypt ended in 1965, and although there was a brief renewal later in the year, this was revoked in June 1966, probably not uncoincidentally when Zakariyya Muhi al-Din, one of Nasser's pro-American confidants, was removed as prime minister.[40] It seemed as though the Johnson administration was taking careful measure of Egyptian actions and would punish Egypt in an almost Pavlovian fashion when, in the eyes of Washington, it stepped out of line.[41] Reflecting the change in approach of the Johnson administration, Nasser's view is summed up well by Kirk Beattie:

> Egyptians saw this turn of events in the context of U.S. efforts to unseat prosocialist Third World leaders: Patrice Lumumba's assassination in the Congo in 1961; intervention in Vietnam in 1963; the overthrow of Joao Goulart's regime in Brazil in 1964; the successful coup against Kwame Nkrumah in 1965; and the overthrow of Sukarno [in Indonesia] in 1966. Nasser thought he was next in line. Egypt's leaders suspected the Saudis and the CIA were behind the reactivation of domestic opponents (the Muslim Brothers and Wafdists) and had a hand in the 1965 Brotherhood conspiracy. All told, they were convinced that Johnson had declared a silent war on Egypt.[42]

But the Middle East under Johnson, at least until the June 1967 War, took a backseat to his Great Society programs and the deepening involvement in Vietnam. If the Kennedy administration took advantage of the relative calm in the Middle East as an opportunity to take steps toward a settlement of the Arab-Israeli conflict, the Johnson administration savored it as one less distraction to deal with so that it could concentrate its energies elsewhere. A clear indication of this was the revolving door filling the position of the assistant secretary of state for Near Eastern affairs at the State Department; in early 1967 of all times, the position was actually left vacant for several months. Likewise, in late 1966 through early 1967, the State Department Policy Planning Council did not have anyone assigned to the Middle East. To the extent that there was any attention paid to the Middle East prior to the June 1967 War, it consisted of trying to persuade Nasser to limit his arms acquisitions from Moscow, provide military aid to the conservative Arab states threatened by Nasserism, and increase military assistance to Israel in order to allay its fears of Nasser's military buildup and the arms headed for the Arab monarchies.[43]

The first objective seemed to be inconsistent with the latter two; indeed, they appeared to be inversely proportional. As Steven Spiegal states, "Once the United States sought to balance the mounting Russian arms aid to Cairo, Damascus, and Baghdad by supplying arms to the conservative Arabs, increased military assistance to Israel was inevitable despite official hesitations." By 1968, arms aid to Israel had risen to $995.3 million from $44.2 million at the end of the Kennedy administration. The "special relationship" had indeed become quite special, and Nasser was increasingly viewed as an obstacle to U.S. interests in the region. He had again become a foe of the United States.[44]

It is not the purpose of this chapter to analyze American policy as it directly related to the seminal June 1967 War—this has been accomplished elsewhere. Suffice it to say that the Johnson administration, focused on events in Southeast Asia, did not see the looming crisis developing in late 1966 through much of the first half of 1967 until it was actually overtaken by the well-known events in May and June that precipitated the Israeli pre-emptive strike. The Israeli unorthodox military response resulted in the defeat of its Arab combatants and the acquisition of the Sinai Peninsula and Gaza Strip from Egypt, the West Bank (including East Jerusalem) from Jordan, and the Golan Heights from Syria. It *is* the purpose of this chapter, however, to examine the repercussions of the war in terms of U.S. policy toward Egypt.

The June 1967 War changed the modern face of the Middle East in several important ways:

(a) With the occupied territories, a new situation was created.
(b) The land-for-peace framework was established with NSC resolution 242 (passed in November 1967) as a direct result of the war; that is, a bargaining situation was formulated, albeit an asymmetrical one because Israel held all the land acquired in the war.
(c) The war sounded the death knell to Nasserism and, in effect, Arab nationalism.
(d) In the latter's wake, Islamism was resuscitated as an effective alternative to secular pan-Arabism.
(e) Divisions in Israel began to manifest themselves over the question of how much, if any, land to return to the Arabs in exchange for peace and recognition.
(f) The war perforce caused the superpowers to become more intimately involved in the Arab-Israeli conflict, with all the associated dangers of a possible direct superpower confrontation or possibilities of peace brought about by superpower cooperation in the mutual interest of avoiding direct confrontation.

In order to avoid the possibility of events in the region leading to a superpower confrontation, the Johnson administration (and the Kremlin to a certain degree as well) initially engaged in steps that might defuse the crisis and create parameters for a peaceful resolution to the conflict. Arab-Israeli hostilities were still acute, and Johnson did not want a second barrier erected to the "woman he really loved," namely, the Great Society programs. In general, there was a great deal of resentment in the Arab world toward the United States for aiding and abetting Israel's overwhelming victory.[45] While this viewpoint confused intent with the Johnson administration's relative passivity during the June crisis and aloofness before the war, it would still be a difficult obstacle to overcome for Washington to establish itself as an evenhanded broker. The problem now, however, was that the war, if anything, greatly complicated the Arab-Israeli situation. Johnson himself doubted Israel's willingness to return the occupied lands for peace, and the Arab states, as indicated from the Arab League Summit Conference, held at Khartoum in August 1967, were in no mood to negotiate from such a clear position of weakness.[46]

In contrast with the antipathy with which the Arabs viewed the United States, Israel's popularity in the country soared to new heights after its spectacular victory, making it that much harder for Johnson, even if he were predisposed to do so, to pressure Israel into making concessions. After the Egyptian sinking of the Israeli destroyer *Elath* in October 1967, along with the Israeli response against Egyptian refineries in Suez City, it became clear to administration officials that, in fact, hostilities had not been satisfactorily put to rest. An international forum, the UN, should take the lead in addressing the issue. (It is a matter of debate whether this was a case of passing the buck or recognizing that international attention to the problem might bring pressure to bear on all parties to make the necessary concessions.) However, one thing is definite: By involving the USSR in the process and collecting its vote for a peaceful resolution on record in the Security Council, the Johnson administration believed that it had again insulated the conflict from direct superpower confrontation, which simplified the issue of pursuing détente with Moscow in direct relation to the U.S. position in Vietnam. The result was the ambiguous UN Security Council resolution 242, which established the land-for-peace framework but did not specifically delineate how much land Israel would exchange for peace and for secure and recognized borders.

The United States was not willing and possibly not even able to insert itself in the mix, and the actors in the region were not, at least on the surface, predisposed to negotiate a settlement. Israel felt invincible, and the Arab states, particularly Nasser, wanted to improve their bargaining positions before entering into any negotiations; ultimately this was the rationale for the War of Attrition in 1969–70. However, despite outward pretensions, both sides had shown a measure of flexibility and willingness to discuss the issues in the months after the war, though the Johnson administration lost much of its interest in the region, especially after passage of UN resolution 242.[47]

Rather than seeing the UN resolution as an initial salvo toward a settlement, it seemed to be satisfied that it had put the Arab-Israeli issue back in the "icebox." Following the war, the Middle East did migrate to the front burner for a short time, but only in relation to attempts to place it back as much as possible into an insulated condition. In any event, with the Tet offensive in Vietnam in early 1968 and the subsequent decision by Johnson not to run for reelection, the Middle East lost its brief moment of salience. Without sustained interest from the United States, there would be no progress toward a negotiated settlement. There would be no more concerted efforts from a lame-duck administration primarily interested in leaving as soon as it could with as little damage as possible. Nasser, perforce, retrenched following the war, patching up his relations with the Arab monarchies in order to obtain much-needed financial aid, finally getting out of the Yemeni quagmire, and generally speaking, toning down his "revolutionary" rhetoric and "radical" policies. A stalemate thus ensued, which had to await a War of Attrition and an all-out war from his successor, Anwar al-Sadat, to reactivate the diplomatic process.

David Ben-Gurion reportedly stated on one occasion that there were three Nassers: First, there was the moderate who came to power in 1952, with whom both the Americans and Israelis had positive intimations for two years or so; then there was the antagonist to Israel, who lasted from about 1954 until after the June 1967 War; finally, there was the one who, having been chastened by the June 1967 War, tacked back in a moderate direction and was possibly ready to make a deal.[48] If this was in fact the case, and it seems logical, Nasser's relationship with the United States may have been an unfinished play. The questions remains, however, whether or not Act III would have been similar to the first two acts, or whether Nasser would have continued on the road toward alignment with the United States a la Sadat.

## Conclusion

When asked shortly after the July Revolution whether he was a "leftist" or a "rightist," Nasser reportedly responded, "I'm a conspirator."[49] Nasser was also reportedly quoted with the following statement, again in the early years of the Free Officers' regime: "I'll tell you what's inside me and then I'll shut up. I have an idea which has overtaken me and I don't know if it's wrong or right; however, I want during the next two to three years to arrive at the point where I can push a button and the country moves like I want it to—I push a button again and it stops."[50]

Nasser was clearly committed to his version of Arab nationalism, antiimperialism (particularly removing the British from Egypt), and establishing social justice. But he was a pragmatist in doing so, and, ultimately, staying in power was the primary objective in what became a Bonapartist regime. As it happens to many authoritarian leaders, Nasser soon believed that *only* his staying in power could save the country from social, economic, and political ruin. Accordingly, Nasser's relations with the United States were based on a pragmatism that dictated shifting foreign policies when necessary in order to maintain and build up his position in Egypt, as well as in the Arab world. He saw himself in the same vein as Tito, an independent force in the nonaligned movement with enough maneuvering room to go back and forth between the superpowers; indeed, it is probably not a coincidence that he met with Tito more than with any other leader (twenty-two times between 1955 and 1970).[51]

Although the thrust of this chapter deals with the question of whether the United States considered Nasser a friend or an enemy, the title could very well refer to whether Nasser regarded Washington as friend or foe. Ultimately, Nasser did not entirely fit into a Manichaean mold—he was neither a friend nor an enemy of the United States. He simply led a strategically important country in a strategically important region that happened to fall within Washington's Cold War defense schemata. To Nasser, the United States was simply one great power to be played off against other great powers, and his methodology reflected that which he employed at the domestic level in order to secure and enhance his internal power position. The United States was a country to be allied with when necessary and to be criticized and opposed when circumstances dictated it—and certainly shifting priorities and stylistic changes from U.S. administration to administration during Nasser's tenure in power were not conducive to any sort of consistent and stable relationship.

American policy toward Egypt, as it typically has been elsewhere, was reactionary, especially since the Middle East as a whole was never at or near the top of the foreign policy priority list for any significant length of time during the Nasserist period. The combination of these fluid elements on both sides of the equation destined the relationship to run the gamut from cooperation to confrontation. The predisposition of succeeding American administrations to react to events in the region seemed to portray Nasser as the protagonist in the Middle East drama, when he was more often than not pursuing policies at the domestic and regional levels that had little direct relevance to the relationship between the United States and Egypt.

In the end, American Cold War objectives vis-à-vis the USSR and the protection of oil resources, as well as its special relationship with Israel, could never be entirely reconciled with Nasser's agenda. The United States had portrayed Nasser at various times as a military dictator or as a Third World socialist revolutionary, but after all was said and done, he was, as he himself stated in 1952, simply a "conspirator." Often in U.S. foreign policy, particularly with the expansion of media coverage since World War II, foreign leaders are personalized, and sometimes demonized, in order to garner public support for this or that policy. Therefore, the subjective sobriquets of "friend" or "enemy" and the like are often invoked to describe someone like Nasser, when, in fact, he was neither one nor the other.

## Notes

1. Policy statement, June 26, 1950, 611.83/6–2650, Record Group (hereafter RG) 59, National Archives (hereafter NA), Washington, D.C.

2. Kermit Roosevelt, *Arabs, Oil, and History* (New York: Harper, 1949), 92. And as Kirk Beattie points out, articles written by the noted commentator Joseph Alsop in February and March 1952, calling for the removal of the corrupt Faruq regime and replacement by a benevolent military dictatorship, could not help but be noticed by the Free Officers. Kirk J. Beattie, *Egypt during the Nasser Years: Ideology, Politics, and Civil Society* (Boulder: Westview Press, 1994), 58.

3. On this question of the extent of U.S. prior knowledge of the coup, see Miles Copeland, *The Game of Nations: The Amorality of Power Politics* (New York: Simon and Schuster, 1969); Wilbur Crane Eveland, *Ropes of Sand: America's Failure in the Middle East* (New York: W. W. Norton, 1980). Both Copeland and Eveland were CIA officers in the Middle East during this period and had intimate knowledge of a number of American-sponsored covert activities, although they disagree on the extent of U.S. knowledge of or involvement in the 1952 Free Officers' coup. It seems logical, however, as Copeland argues, that at the very least, elements of Nasser's cabal were in touch with American embassy officials in Cairo to gauge the U.S. response and to help make sure that the British, who had 80,000 troops at the Suez Canal base, did not intervene militarily to restore the monarchy. The failure of the 'Urabi revolt in the 1880s at the hands of British intervention weighed heavily on the minds of the Free Officers. In fact, the Soviets believed that the coup was orchestrated by the United States and initially adopted a very negative view toward the new regime. See chapter 9 in this volume.

4. Beattie, *Egypt during the Nasser Years*, 70, 79.

5. In fact, in Nasser's internal power struggle with the front man of the RCC, Nagib, apparently the United States supported Nasser against him and, according to some, even encouraged Nasser to remove Nagib.

6. Quoted in Beattie, *Egypt during the Nasser Years*, 102.

7. Peter Hahn, *The United States, Great Britain, and Egypt, 1945–1956* (Chapel Hill: University of North Carolina Press, 1991), 149–51.

8. Ibid., 152.

9. See ibid. and John C. Campbell, *Defense of the Middle East: Problems of American Policy* (New York: Praeger, 1960); William Roger Louis, *The British Empire in the Middle East, 1945–1951: Arab Nationalism, the United States, and Postwar Imperialism* (Oxford: Clarendon Press, 1984); Elie Podeh, *The Quest for*

*Hegemony in the Arab World: The Struggle over the Baghdad Pact* (Leiden: E. J. Brill, 1995), chap. 2.

10. On the Eisenhower administration's policy toward the Middle East, see David W. Lesch, *Syria and the United States: Eisenhower's Cold War in the Middle East* (Boulder: Westview Press, 1992).

11. This revolved around the concept of massive retaliation, which required "the availability of advantageously located bases from which to launch an attack on the centers of Soviet power, as well as an increased dependence on local forces to deal with local aggression on the Communist periphery and to protect these bases." See "The Problem of Regional Security," State Department post files, Cairo embassy, May 8, 1954, RG 54, NA, and Records Administration (RA), Suitland, Md.

12. "Conclusions on Trip," n.d., John Foster Dulles Papers, box 73, John Foster Dulles Collection, Seeley G. Mudd Library, Princeton University. U.S. aid to Israel between 1945 and 1953 amounted to approximately $250 million, while U.S. aid to all the Arab and African countries during the same period amounted to about $108 million. Harry Byrode, "The Development of United States Policy in the Near East, South Asia, and Africa during 1953," *Department of State Bulletin* 30 (March 8, 1954): 367. Dulles's findings were essentially crystallized into policy in NSC resolution 155/1, approved by the president on July 11, 1953.

13. Haykal reported that Dulles told Nasser, "The question of selling arms to Egypt would be easier if Egypt could come to an agreement with Britain, especially if this agreement was within a system of collective defense of the Middle East." Muhammad Hasanayn Haykal, *Nahnu wa-Amrika* (Cairo: Dar al-'Asr al-Hadith, 1965), 77.

14. On the Baghdad Pact, see Podeh, *The Quest for Hegemony in the Arab World*.

15. On American policy toward the Baghdad Pact, see Elie Podeh, "The Perils of Ambiguity: The United States and the Baghdad Pact," in *The Middle East and the United States: A Historical and Political Reassessment*, 3d ed., ed. David Lesch (Boulder, Colo.: Westview Press, 2003), 100–120.

16. See Lesch, *Syria and the United States*, 50–53. A typical comment along these lines was outlined in a State Department report in May 1954: "For if Iraq takes the plunge, it seems likely that with some encouragement from the United States, Lebanon and Syria would shortly follow. The pressure on Egypt to come to terms on the Suez would mount steadily. Recalcitrance would seem a less attractive policy to the Saudis. In short, the prospects would seem good for moving a major part of the Near East into overt alignment with the free world, thereby delivering a telling blow to Asian-African neutralism, and effecting a really significant shift in the global balance of power. In such a context, even the Arab-Israeli problem might not prove so utterly intractable as it has been these several years." See "The Problem of Regional Security," State Department post files, Cairo embassy, May 8, 1954, RG 84, NA, and RA.

17. For more on the Johnston and Alpha plans, see Hahn, *The United States, Great Britain, and Egypt*, 94–109, 132–39.

18. Nasser's growing exasperation with the United States at this time is evident in the following statement of April 1954: "The American insistence on creating a pact in the Middle East is going to wreck the Arab world and stand in the way of its unity.

There is duplicity in American policies in this area. They say one thing and do another.... It seems clear that the United States is walking with the wheel of imperialism so far. The United States should hasten in welcoming the Arab hand of friendship which has long been extended toward her; otherwise, she will miss the boat. We began our relations with the United States full of hope for just solutions of the problems in the area, but this hope has now vanished or is on the verge of vanishing." Al-Ahram, April 16, 1954, quoted in Gail E. Meyer, *Egypt and the United States: The Formative Years* (Rutherford, N.J.: Fairleigh Dickinson University Press, 1980), 112–13.

19. The Eisenhower administration attempted to build up the inept King Saʻud of Saudi Arabia as this potential rival to Nasser, an ill-conceived plan that, for the most part, backfired by the summer of 1957. See David W. Lesch, "The Role of Saudi Arabia in the 1957 American-Syrian Crisis," *Middle East Policy* 1, no. 3 (1992): 33–48.

20. On the American-Syrian crisis of 1957, see Lesch, *Syria and the United States*, 138–209.

21. On Nasser's role in the American-Syrian crisis, see David W. Lesch, "Gamal ʻAbd al-Nasser and an Example of Diplomatic Acumen," *Middle Eastern Studies* 31, no. 2 (1995): 362–74.

22. Telegram from the Cairo embassy to the State Department, December 11, 1957, *Foreign Relations of the United States* (hereafter *FRUS*) 8:744–46.

23. For more information on the contacts between the United States and Nasser regarding Syria, see Elie Podeh, *The Decline of Arab Unity: The Rise and Fall of the United Arab Republic* (Brighton: Sussex Academic Press, 1999), 39–42.

24. On the formation of the UAR in February 1958, see ibid., 25–48.

25. There was not a direct evolutionary line, however, between the American-Egyptian rapprochement during the American-Syrian crisis and this new approach indicated in the NSC report. For instance, an NSC report in January 1958 generally viewed the Middle East in very much the same manner that had been prevalent during most of the Eisenhower years, i.e., preoccupation with the USSR, which acted in concert with Arab nationalist movements (NSC 5801/1, January 1958). It seems as though bureaucratic inertia had not caught up with the subtle shift in attitude toward Nasser evident during the American-Syrian crisis.

26. Operations Coordinating Board, U.S. Policy toward the Near East, NSC 5820, *FRUS, 1958–1960*, vol. 11, October 30, 1958, 3.

27. Fawaz A. Gerges, *The Superpowers and the Middle East: Regional and International Politics, 1955–1967* (Boulder: Westview Press, 1994), 130.

28. Operations Coordinating Board, Report on the Near East, NSC 5820/1, *FRUS, 1958–1960*, vol. 11, February 3, 1960, 5–6.

29. The traditional U.S. concern about the Hashimite monarchies in Jordan and Iraq gaining the upper hand and pressuring the Saudis was no longer much of a concern after the Iraqi Revolution. Keeping Nasser close to the United States was seen as an efficient way to protect Saudi Arabia, which would otherwise have been a natural target for Nasser's progressive Arab nationalism (as it had been in the past and as it would be in the near future).

30. Burton I. Kaufman, *The Arab Middle East and the United States: Inter-Arab Rivalry and Superpower Diplomacy* (New York: Twayne, 1996), 32.

31. Quoted in Douglas Little, "From Even-Handed to Empty-Handed: Seeking Order in the Middle East," in Thomas G. Paterson, ed., *Kennedy's Quest for Victory: American Foreign Policy, 1961–1963* (New York: Oxford University Press, 1989), 162.

32. Kaufman, *The Arab Middle East and the United States*, 32.

33. The United States contributed $1.124 billion ($949 million in food aid) between 1959 and 1966, and the USSR contributed $842 million during the same period, with the Eastern bloc countries adding another $273 million. Beattie, *Egypt during the Nasser Years*, 193.

34. Little, "From Even-Handed to Empty-Handed," 166.

35. Nasser was notified of the Hawk sale ahead of time by U.S. officials, and he reportedly appreciated being so informed, but once news spread across the Arab world, Nasser was compelled to at least adopt a prima facie negative posture.

36. The relationship between Washington and Riyadh had cooled noticeably since early 1961, when Crown Prince Faisal refused to renew the U.S. lease on the airbase at Dhahran, possibly, in part, due to Kennedy's new approach to Nasser, which had always been viewed by the Saudi regime with derision. Countering the Kennedy view, which contended that improving the relationship with Nasser actually helped to protect Saudi Arabia, the Saudis believed that such an approach only gave Nasser the wherewithal and perceived flexibility to cause more problems in the area.

37. Quoted in Little, "From Even-Handed to Empty-Handed," 170.

38. The pro-Nasser Ba'thist coups in both Syria and Iraq in early 1963, along with the subsequent negotiations for union with Egypt, added to the pressure on Nasser to engage in anti-Israeli actions and rhetoric that damaged his relationship with the United States. It has also been suggested that the coups lessened the enthusiasm in Washington for Nasser, even during the last months of the Kennedy administration, by bringing Arab nationalists to power who, at least in Iraq, cracked down on communists. The new regimes in Damascus and Baghdad, true to the precepts of NSC 5820, were ideal vehicles through which U.S. interests could be advanced, and they would probably be less troublesome than Cairo. See Malik Mufti, "The United States and Nasserist Pan-Arabism," in *The Middle East and the United States: A Historical and Political Reassessment*, 2d ed., ed. David W. Lesch (Boulder: Westview Press, 1999), 168–87.

39. Kennedy's policy implied a link between military aid and concessions on the refugee resettlement plan, whereas Johnson's military assistance was based more on affinity and domestic politics than on any overall strategic design.

40. Beattie, *Egypt during the Nasser Years*, 196–97.

41. Reacting to this paternal U.S. approach, Nasser publicly stated on December 23, 1964, that "the American ambassador says that our behavior is not acceptable. Well, let us tell them that those who do not accept our behavior can go and drink from the sea. . . . We will cut the tongues of anybody who talks badly about us."

Quoted in William J. Burns, *Economic Aid and American Policy toward Egypt, 1955–1981* (Albany: State University of New York Press, 1985), 159.

42. Beattie, *Egypt during the Nasser Years*, 197. See also Muhammad Hasanayn Haykal, *The Cairo Documents: The Inside Story of Nasser and His Relationship with World Leaders, Rebels, and Statesmen* (New York: Doubleday, 1973), 205–49.

43. Steven L. Spiegel, *The Other Arab-Israeli Conflict: Making America's Middle East Policy from Truman to Reagan* (Chicago: University of Chicago Press, 1985), 120, 130–31.

44. Ibid., 134, 135.

45. Egypt, Syria, Iraq, Yemen, Algeria, and Sudan all broke diplomatic relations with the United States shortly after the war, while traditionally pro–U.S. Arab states maintained their distance from Washington.

46. As Johnson stated at an NSC meeting on June 7, 1967, "By the time we get through with all the festering problems, we are going to wish the war had not happened." Quoted in Kaufman, *The Arab Middle East and the United States*, 60.

47. Moshe Maʻoz, "From Conflict to Peace? Israel's Relations with Syria and the Palestinians," *Middle East Journal* 53, no. 2 (summer 1999): 399.

48. Statement by a member of the audience who reportedly knew David Ben-Gurion, at the conference "Nasserism in Historical Perspective," held in December 1999 at the Hebrew University of Jerusalem and the University of Haifa. Whether or not the statement is true, I believe the thrust of it to be so.

49. Quoted in Beattie, *Egypt during the Nasser Years*, 68.

50. Quoted in ibid., 83.

51. Ibid., 119.

# 9

## Nasser and the Soviets

A Reassessment

Rami Ginat

### Introduction

Soviet-Egyptian relations under 'Abd al-Nasser have been the subject of many studies. Some have dealt with it comprehensively, and some peripherally. Broadly speaking, the evolution of the research that deals with the Soviet Union and the Middle East can be characterized by three phases of works.

The first group, the so-called contemporary research, consists of works that were written from the 1950s until the late 1980s. These works were mainly based on Soviet and Arabic press, memoirs of Arab and Soviet leaders, official statements and publications, and interviews with incumbent and former leaders. The studies were largely written to reflect precise historical occurrences and lacked deep historical perspective.[1]

The second group includes works written in the 1980s and early 1990s, with a focus on the 1940s, 1950s, and early 1960s.[2] Here the researchers extensively used the above sources, but they also utilized British, American, and Israeli archives, as well as other sources, that were not available to the first group. These works, which examine Soviet policy in the Middle East, were written from a deeper historical perspective and led to a breakthrough in our understanding of the process that led to the Soviet involvement in Middle Eastern affairs. Nevertheless, there are some problems with these works. Most of them give us a clear picture of the political processes as implemented by and seen through the eyes of higher-level policy makers, yet do not always provide us with the small details that reveal policy making at its lower level. Moreover, these works did not use Soviet archives due to the fact that they were not accessible at the time. Both the advantages and disadvantages of British and American archives lay in the respective interests of the two countries in the Middle East at the time, which were inextricably bound to the Cold War context. Their fear of Soviet penetration into the Middle East made the task of their diplomats in the area—to get information, both official and clandestine, concerning the Soviet moves in the region—all the more complex. Most of this information is now available in Western archives and should be consulted very carefully.

The third group refers to pioneering works written in the late 1990s, mainly articles and more comprehensive works that have not yet been completed.[3] The short scholarly experiment of using Soviet archives (including personal experience) teaches us that access to the Soviet documents is very selective.[4] The researcher has to inform the archivist of the topic of research in advance, and the latter decides what sort of documents will be made available to the researcher. It often happens that one scholar, for unknown reasons, is allowed to consult certain documents that others are prevented from seeing. The real fear, under the current circumstances, is that scholars will base their accounts totally on selective Soviet source material drawn from various Soviet archives, without consulting Western archives and other sources, both new and old, under the misguided belief that they have now managed to produce the ultimate historical work. In other words, we need both Soviet and Western archives; otherwise, the historical picture may be distorted entirely. The use of these archives will contribute significantly to the quality of our research; however, we also need to utilize Arab state archives. Unfortunately, since these are not accessible at the present time, one can only look forward to the day when Arab states will open their archives to scholars and the public.

This article can be placed in the aforementioned second group. It is noteworthy that much of the Soviet source material concerning this subject is not yet available from the former Soviet archives.

## Soviet-Egyptian Relations in the Pre-Nasserite Era

Until recently, the prevailing belief in both Soviet and Middle Eastern research maintained that Soviet interest and political activity in the Middle East under Stalin were marginal. It was also suggested that a full-fledged Middle Eastern policy crystallized only after Stalin's death in 1953, with the change attributed to Khrushchev's ascendancy.[5] In contrast to the above belief, I maintain that the nature and quality of Soviet-Egyptian relations were not necessarily influenced by structural changes within the Soviet ruling elite but were mainly determined by political, social, and ideological developments in Egypt. That is, Egyptian governments decided whether or not to tighten relations with the Soviets, basing their decisions purely on beneficiary considerations and utilitarian purposes. Such an example can be found while examining the establishment of diplomatic relations between Egypt (led by the Wafd of Mustafa al-Nahhas, 1942–44) and the USSR (led by Stalin), which was then emerging as one of the two superpowers.[6] The Soviets, to a large extent, responded positively to these initiatives. Since the dismissal in October 1944 of the Nahhas government by King Faruq, who objected to diplomatic relations with the Soviets, relations between the two countries had been practically at a standstill until 1947–48, when Mahmud Fahmi al-Nuqrashi, a former Wafdist, took power.

In August 1947, the new prime minister managed to persuade the Soviets to support Egypt's demand in the UN Security Council, calling for the immediate withdrawal of British troops from Egyptian land. This Soviet move led Nuqrashi to declare that Egypt "would consider the possibility of neutrality in the international arena and that Egypt would seek the support of other powers in its struggle against Britain."[7] In February 1948, he sent a military mission to purchase arms in Prague, and in March his government concluded a great commercial barter agreement with the Soviets.[8] Egyptian Foreign Minister Ahmad Muhammad Khashaba explained why his government did so, saying that Britain and the United States were conducting an anti-Arab policy. The two powers, he declared, "made many mistakes, and continually alienated the Arabs, mainly by the American attitude to the Palestine question and the British policy regarding Egypt and Iraq."[9]

However, the turning point in relations between the two countries took place a couple of years later, when a Wafdist government led by Nahhas took power in January 1950. Egypt's policy of neutralism under that government was shaped and implemented by Muhammad Salah al-Din, the foreign minister.[10] He resolutely rejected Western proposals for establishing a Middle East Command, and he was the motivating force behind his government's decision in October 1951 to abrogate the 1936 Anglo-Egyptian Treaty. Just a short while before this decision was made, Egypt and the USSR were negotiating the conclusion of a nonaggression pact. During these talks, the Soviets made it obvious that a prerequisite to positive conclusion was the termination of the Anglo-Egyptian treaty.[11]

As a result of Egypt's policy of neutralism, its relations with the Soviets significantly improved. The Soviets were prepared to furnish arms to Egypt by way of new barter agreements, and many commercial agreements between the two countries were concluded. Moreover, a high level of mutual understanding and cooperation found expression in the UN. In order to eliminate the influence of the Western powers in Egypt, the Soviets were willing to cooperate with every group that acted against Western domination. That is, the Soviets and Egyptians had a common interest: the termination of Western hegemony in the Middle East. This was the formula that brought the two countries closer together soon after the July 1952 Revolution, and one might say that the roots of the later Soviet-Egyptian honeymoon originated in this period (1950–52).[12]

The downfall of the Wafd in January 1952 inaugurated a period of mutual suspicion and distrust in Soviet-Egyptian relations. The July Revolution was understood by the Soviets to be another attempt by the West to bring to power in Egypt a government that would serve Western interests. This development, they concluded, had been facilitated by "the interests of foreign imperialists," as well as by the rivalry between the Americans and the British for domination in the Middle East. They believed that there was a link between the United States and the Free Officers—a matter which would strengthen American influence and thus would increase the prospect of Egypt's inclusion in a Western military alliance.[13]

### The Reestablishment of Soviet-Egyptian Relations, 1953–1958

The negative Soviet approach toward Egypt's military regime arose from understandable considerations. It seems that the Soviets knew of the close relations between the American embassy and the Free Officers, both before and after the coup. Indeed, soon after the coup, American influence in Egypt increased significantly.[14] The new Egyptian leaders did not hide their sympathy toward the United States.[15] In fact, as they were opposed to communism, and both distrusted and disliked the British, the United States became their favored alternative. Soon after the coup, they declared publicly their intentions to be affiliated with the West, albeit on certain conditions. On September 18, 1952, Muhammad Nagib delivered a message to Jefferson Caffery, the American ambassador to Cairo, conveying the new regime's complete support for the United States and unalterable opposition to communism. On September 19, Secretary of State Dean Acheson reported to President Truman that Caffery had developed considerable influence and might be able to get Egypt into the Middle East Defense Organization (MEDO). He assumed that the creation of a vacuum in Egypt following the complete collapse of British influence could be filled by the United States. The military officers wished to create favorable conditions for "selling the United States to the Egyptian public," but this development could only come about if the United States would supply arms and support Egypt financially.[16]

However, the American-Egyptian honeymoon was ephemeral. The Free

Officers' efforts to persuade the United States to prove its good intentions by supplying Egypt with military and economic aid did not meet with success. Truman explained his refusal, saying that selling military equipment to Egypt would create pressure from Israel and other Arab countries for similar assistance. At the same time, Britain's refusal to evacuate its troops and to buy Egyptian cotton led Egypt's rulers to seek other sources of supply and export.[17]

Late in 1953, owing to the Free Officers' inability to implement their political credo—that is, the liberation of Egypt—it would appear that Nasser adopted Salah al-Din's policy of neutralism in order to manipulate both American and Soviet interests, which he would then use to his own advantage in furthering Egypt's foreign policy. This policy was translated into practice in December 1953, when Nasser sent Deputy War Minister Hasan Rajab on a tentative tour of the Soviet bloc countries, in order to bring the West to heel. The tour had two goals: first, to widen economic relations with the Eastern bloc and, second, to seek alternative sources of arms. Nasser calculated that the dialogue with the Soviets would expedite British evacuation, enabling broader ties with the West, which Nasser declared was his preferred partner in trade, aid, and arms supplies. However, Nasser's Janus-faced policy was too subtle for U.S. Secretary of State John Foster Dulles to appreciate, especially in light of his covert flirtation with the Soviets in the winter of 1953–54, which paved the way for arms deals with the Soviet bloc.[18]

Despite the American-Egyptian row over the Baghdad Pact of February 1955, Nasser contacted Dulles in April 1955, once more with the intention of concluding a major arms deal.[19] Yet Nasser had contracted to purchase Czech arms only two months earlier, in February 1955, and discussion was also well under way for a major arms deal with the Soviets. This deal, which was concluded in July and announced on September 20, 1955, upset the entire Middle East military balance.[20] One month earlier, in August 1955, Dulles had approved the Egyptian request, only to be rebuffed by Nasser. His negotiations with the Soviets, which had begun as a tactical ploy, had netted him a much better deal, based on an easy repayment package, a large quantity and high quality of weapons, and a "no-strings" concession or compulsory membership in a military alliance—terms that the West was unwilling to offer. Dulles, reacting in a letter to Nasser, seemed more nonplussed than angered: "We have placed full confidence in your repeated assurances regarding Egypt's identification with the West. . . . [O]ur economic assistance programs, . . . approval of arms purchases, and my statement on August 26 on the Arab-Israel situation are all based on that same general thought."[21] Clearly, Nasser did not allow his early Western orientation to influence his military or economic considerations, an example of the irrelevance of ideology to the regime in its first years.

The plan to construct the Aswan High Dam was another example of Nasser's policy of playing the United States off against the USSR and vice versa. In their efforts to fill the economic void created in Egypt's relations with the West, the Soviets had already made an attractive offer to the Rajab delegation, while visiting Moscow in the winter of 1953–54, to assist in constructing the dam.[22] The Soviets made another tempting offer in June 1955, this time offering to supply equipment for the project together with financial assistance and engineering services. They offered a thirty-year loan of an unspecified amount at 2 percent interest, repayable in Egyptian cotton and rice.[23] But nothing came of the Soviet offers of 1955. In December, the United States offered to help finance the project together with the British government and the World Bank. However, on July 19, 1956, Dulles announced that the United States was withdrawing its offer owing to disagreements with Nasser. Thereafter, the ball returned to the Soviet court, and Nasser decided to conclude the deal with the USSR.

In fact, since late 1953 Nasser had arrived at the conclusion that Egypt should be independent of both blocs. He believed that support from either of the two rival blocs signified Egyptian inferiority and dependency, and that in its struggle against domination, Egypt must search for new sources of political and diplomatic support. Prior to the Bandung Conference,[24] Nasser had held several meetings with the chief proponents of neutralism—Pandit Jawaharlal Nehru and Josef Tito, the Indian and Yugoslav leaders, respectively. They had convinced him then of the soundness of their "third way" of nonalignment.[25]

He now made it clear that Egypt would adopt an independent policy to serve its interests: "All we want today is to create for ourselves an independent personality which will be strong and independent, which will be free to direct its domestic policy the way it wants and direct its foreign policy in a way which serves its interests." Nasser went further to explain the logic and motives behind his policy of neutralism, stressing that "communism has been considered a danger, but I still believe that imperialism or our being dominated by the other side [the West] represents another danger."[26]

Nevertheless, this approach was not as balanced as it may have appeared. Since the formation of the Turco-Iraqi Pact of Mutual Cooperation (February 1955), Nasser's public speeches and interviews were characterized more by their anti-Western tone and less by their anticommunist content. Even before the outbreak of the Suez crisis, Nasser's interbloc policy clearly displayed intensive distrust of the West. An accurate analysis of the motives behind Egypt's anti-Western policy at the time was provided by Sir Humphrey Trevelyan, the British ambassador to Cairo, in April 1956.

> He [Nasser] thinks that we [the West] want to isolate Egypt and thus regain our old influence over Egyptian policy. He wishes to destroy our political influence in the Arab world based on special positions, since they run counter to his ambitions to make Egypt into the dominant Arab state. He distrusts the Soviet government because he knows that ultimately they are against him and want to make the Middle Eastern states into communist satellites. However, they [the Soviets] are at the moment useful to him and he will cooperate with them whenever they are prepared to help him to achieve his political and economic aims. He thinks that he can use them and remain independent of them, but he is clearly in danger of becoming dependent on them.

Trevelyan concludes this dispatch with an acknowledgment that this state of affairs regarding Egypt's troubled relations with the West could still be cured, and that as far as the East-West battle for influence over Egypt was concerned, the West could gain the advantage should it employ the right means in the economic field.[27]

Western officials continued to maintain that the Egyptian case was not totally lost even after the Suez crisis, although they acknowledged that Soviet influence in Egypt was on the rise, particularly as a result of the Soviet pro-Egypt policy during the Suez crisis. In accordance with this policy, the Soviets supported Egypt's decision to nationalize the Canal and condemned the Anglo-French-Israeli military actions against Egypt. The Soviets even went a few steps further in their reaction to the tripartite attack on Egypt, threatening that Soviet volunteers would, if necessary, join Egypt in its war against the aggressors. Notwithstanding the favorable conditions for the Soviets in Egypt, the British maintained that the West's stronghold in Egypt could still be revived: "The United States has been careful to disassociate herself from British and French policy and to act only under the aegis of the UN, [a matter which] still leaves Egypt with substantially the same field for maneuver."[28] In other words, at this stage, once the Suez crisis was over, the United States could offer Egypt economic aid and thus keep Egypt out of the Soviet camp.

Overall, it is noteworthy that during the formative phase in Soviet-Egyptian relations (1953–58), both countries, motivated by their own interests, learned to distinguish between ideology and politics. Nasser continued his harsh campaign against internal communism, while the USSR closed its eyes and declared no intentions of interfering in Egypt's internal affairs. For example, Nasser's antipathy toward communism was revealed after he accepted an invitation in August 1955 to visit the USSR for the first time; he announced frankly that "our anti-communist principles" would not be dimmed by the trip and emphasized his intention to continue to "arrest the communists and put them on trial."[29] While telling the *Sunday Times* in June 1962 his own version of the July 1952 Revolution, Nasser explained the motives behind his adverse approach to communism:

> [In my early] formative years . . . I was approached on several occasions to join the Communist Party, but although I studied Marxist doctrine and the works of Lenin with sympathy, I encountered two basic obstacles, ones that I knew could never be overcome. First, communism is in its essence atheistic; I have always been a sincere Muslim, with an unshakable belief in an outside force that we call God, who watches over all our destinies. It is quite impossible to be a good Muslim and a good communist. Second, I realized that communism necessitated certain control from Moscow and the central communist parties, and this, too, I could never accept. . . . I do not intend, while it lies in my power, to allow my country ever again to come under the power or control of any other country or bloc, whether in the East or the West.[30]

In 1956, Khrushchev was equally blunt in expressing the cynical realpolitik relations between the two countries: The USSR supported Nasser, he said, although Nasser "even put communists in jail."[31] Likewise, Dimitri Shepilov, the Soviet foreign minister, in his official visit to Cairo in June 1956, made it clear that the USSR was not going to protest against Nasser's anticommunist policy insofar as the relations between the two countries were based on "principles of equality in rights, mutual respect for sovereignty and noninterference in internal affairs."[32] This Soviet-Egyptian modus vivendi remained relevant until the late 1950s.

### The Khrushchev-Nasser Ideological Warfare, 1958–1961

Following the formation of the United Arab Republic (UAR) in February 1958, Nasser's battle against communism intensified, given the relative strength of communism in Syria at the time of unification.[33] Furthermore, Syrian communists opposed the very idea of Arab unity other than proletarian solidarity among the Arabs and association with international communism. One of Nasser's conditions for union with Syria was the dissolution of all Syrian political parties—a condition which met with the approval of the Syrian authorities and which consequently led to the abolition of the influential Syrian Communist Party (SCP). This development created friction between Nasser and the Soviets, who opposed Nasser's moves in Syria. The fact that Moscow's first response to the formation of the UAR was delayed and cool left no doubts of their reservations.

Khalid Bakdash, the SCP leader who left Syria on February 5, 1958, attacked the dissolution of all Syrian parties. While wandering from one Eastern bloc country to another, he expressed fierce criticism of the UAR's internal policies, with full backing by the Soviets for his activities and views. A U.S. State Department intelligence report noted that for the Soviets, Bakdash was the "pre-eminent communist leader in the Middle East and was thus useful to Moscow not only for what he could achieve in Syria but also as a factor in the development of other communist parties in the area." The Soviets, therefore, even allowed Bakdash to publish an anti-UAR article in the first issue of a new communist international journal, *Problems of Peace and Socialism*. The article criticized Nasser's 1958 agrarian reform in Syria, stating that the UAR government was "incapable of solving this problem." Bakdash also accused the UAR of using Soviet bloc aid "as a bargaining tool with the West." He concluded by declaring: "We shall never give up our communist party." Several months after the formation of the UAR, Nasser remonstrated strongly to the Soviets against the activities of the Soviet embassy in Syria during the pre-plebiscite period, as well as against attempts by Syrian communists to prevent the union between Egypt and Syria. In response, Khrushchev promised that such activities would be halted.[34]

A few months after the establishment of the UAR, Nasser was invited to visit the USSR, a tour which was supposed to mark the pinnacle of Soviet-Egyptian relations. However, despite the efforts by both hosts and guests to create an atmosphere of cordiality and understanding, certain signs of discord were evident during Nasser's visit (April 29–May 16, 1958). It was apparent that the Soviets were disappointed by Egypt's declared policy of neutralism. The Soviets expected Nasser to take a more radical anti-Western stand and were concerned over prospects for improved UAR–U.S. relations. Furthermore, they expressed indignation over Nasser's friendly relations with Tito. Khrushchev was displeased with Nasser's forthcoming visit to Yugoslavia and severely attacked Tito's policies.[35] Nevertheless, Nasser showed himself, throughout the visit, to be a self-confident and seasoned leader. Despite his gratitude for Soviet military, economic, and diplomatic support, he displayed no obsequiousness and made it clear that he was not only Egypt's leader but also the leader of an Arab nationalist movement as well as a practicing representative of Islam.[36]

Nasser's visit to Yugoslavia in July 1958 shed more light on Soviet-Egyptian frictions. According to Yugoslav sources, Nasser told Tito that the

USSR "was pressing hard for 'independent apparatuses' in Syria in both the military and political fields, including special privileges for the Soviet military personnel there and special liaison arrangements between the Soviet embassy and the SCP."[37]

Qassem's coup of July 1958, which raised expectations that Iraq would soon join the UAR, soon led to bitter disappointment inside the UAR.[38] Qassem's alliance with the Iraqi communists and his rapprochement with the USSR changed Nasser's approach to communism. He now blamed international communism for interference in Arab domestic affairs and thus created tension in relations with the Soviets and, subsequently, the mutual conduct of ideological warfare.

The Kurdish question was another source of contention in Soviet–UAR relations. Following Qassem's takeover, the Soviets altered their traditional approach regarding the Kurds—from firmly backing the "long-standing Kurdish aspiration for an independent Kurdistan" to fully supporting Qassem's efforts to play down Kurdish separatism and to secure Iraqi independence outside the UAR. Nasser's position toward the Kurds also wavered. Several weeks before Qassem's coup, Egyptian propaganda broadcasts called for Kurdish independence, possibly in response to the Iraqi alliance with the West.

In September 1958, in an attempt to win Iraqi support and especially to encourage those pro-UAR elements within the new Iraqi regime, Nasser accused the USSR of "continuing support of Kurdish separatism." Nasser was obviously angry with the Soviets because two influential pro-Soviet political factions in Iraq—the communists and the Kurdish Democratic Party (KDP)—supported the anti-UAR group within the Iraqi ruling elite, led by Qassem. Both the communists and the KDP agreed on September 6 to support the Iraqi Republic if Iraq preserved its independent identity, that is, refused to join the UAR, and if the Iraqi Kurds were recognized as a nation linked to Arab Iraq—a condition which was provided for by the new Iraqi constitution. Having been given the green light to act by Qassem, the Iraqi communists stepped up their activities, directing their attacks at Nasser and the UAR. Qassem, who opposed union with the UAR, found the communists to be temporarily reliable partners.[39]

In an effort to ease tensions and disagreements, the Soviet leadership sent Nureddin Mukhitdinov, a member of the Presidium of the USSR Communist Party, to Cairo for an extended visit (September 17–26, 1958). In the course of Mukhitdinov's meetings, Nasser complained, "Communists in the Arab world were receiving liberal financing from the Soviet embassy in Baghdad. In Syria the local communists were cooperating with conservative elements in obstructing the implementation of Syrian-Egyptian unification." In reply to Nasser's accusations, Mukhitdinov denied the "existence of any link between the USSR and national communist movements." He went even further, saying that Soviet support of the Syrian communists was impossible, as such a move "would be contrary to Khrushchev's policy of helping Nasser wherever possible."[40]

However, in spite of Mukhitdinov's words, Bakdash continued with his harsh criticism of the UAR, while enjoying the hospitality of Eastern bloc countries, which gave him free rein to direct his anti-Nasser campaign. On March 17, 1959, while delivering a speech to the Polish United Workers Party Congress, he accused the UAR of making imperialist attacks on Iraq. Moreover, he charged: "The attempts of the imperialists to break up the friendly relations between the Arab countries and Russia coincided with the position taken by certain Arab circles." Bakdash's general reference to "Arab circles" did not remain obscure. He clearly pointed to "certain determined circles in the UAR," that is, Nasser and his inner circle. They, stated Bakdash, were utterly responsible for the current tension in UAR–Soviet relations. Bakdash quoted Khrushchev's indirect advice to Nasser not "to trust false friends" and fall into the American trap of "hypocritical smiles," and to remember that the USSR was the Arabs' tried and true friend. Bakdash concluded his attack by slandering Nasser's slogan of Arab unity, describing him as a representative of the Egyptian bourgeoisie who "aspired to achieve unity in conformity with their own class interests." In contrast, the "Arab liberation movement," of which Bakdash saw himself a part, sought to unify the "Arab world in the struggle against imperialism."[41]

It would seem that both the Soviets and Nasser were playing a power game, aimed at testing each other's limits while knowing that they were not willing to break the rules of the game at that stage. For his part, Nasser estimated that the Soviets were not likely to threaten him, nor would they withdraw economic, military, or any other types of aid to the UAR. From the Soviet viewpoint, there was nothing to be gained by doing so because, as they were well aware, an open rift with Nasser could have negative implications on their relations with other Afro-Asian states that followed Nasser's policy of nonalignment. As Patrick Reilly, the British ambassador to Moscow, suggested correctly, the Soviet government "would probably prefer to bide their time until the situation in Iraq has become clearer and they have a better idea of future possibilities there and in Syria." Taking into consideration the leaders' personal characteristics, Reilly concluded that "Nasser's propensity for speech-making, and Khrushchev's unwillingness to leave attacks unanswered, may make this difficult, and the Soviet aim will probably be to 'keep Nasser in play' with continued aid spiced with vague threats."[42]

The Soviet-Egyptian ideological disagreements culminated during a two-week tour of the USSR in April-May 1961 by a UAR parliamentary delegation, led by Anwar al-Sadat. When the delegation met Khrushchev on May 3, he seized the opportunity to rail against the UAR's socialist ideology and domestic measures:

> [Y]ou say you want Arab nationalism and also socialism. We have different views on many issues. . . . [W]e are communists and you are not connected with this word. But history will teach you. . . . If our people live better than you under the communist banner, then how can you declare yourselves adverse to communism? The people will tell you to go out. . . . Communism consists of ideas and ideas cannot be buried in prisons. . . . You [Arabs] say that you seek socialism. But you do not know much about the socialism which leads to communism. As a scientific phenomenon, socialism is the first step to communism. You are still in the first stage of your thinking, if you want to build up socialism.[43]

Sadat responded to Khrushchev's attacks only after he returned to Egypt and consulted with Nasser. While emphasizing in his reply to Khrushchev the basic differences between Soviet communism and Arab socialism, Sadat said:

> The socialism we believe in is based . . . on the liberation and freedom of the individual. We aim at the destruction of exploitation and work for the elimination of class differences. . . . [W]e believe that the bloody character of the inter-class struggle can be avoided and that the imperative elimination of social anomalies can be accomplished within the framework of national unity. We also believe that there are a number of spiritual factors, including religion, which have their effects in addition to the accepted basis of material development.[44]

For his part, Nasser explained the reasons for the anticommunist campaign in the UAR: "We have not permitted the establishment of a communist party in Egypt because we are sure that it cannot act in conformity with its own will or work for the interest of the country." Communism in the UAR, Nasser concluded, would mean that "the country would have no will of its own, and we would follow the line of international communism and receive directions from it."[45]

## Nasser's Socialism and the Upgrading of Soviet-Egyptian Relations

The ideological warfare came to an end soon after the introduction of Nasser's Socialist Laws of July 1961. These laws marked the beginning of Nasser's Arab socialism—an idea that constituted a basic principle in his political credo. There are several reasons why Nasser decided to take such a step at this particular time. One of them, according to Western diplomats in Cairo, is that Nasser was sensitive to Soviet criticism of his social policy following the measures taken against communism—a policy that had cooled relations between the two countries. Nasser, they suggested, was dependent on Soviet arms supplies and financial support and therefore could not afford such a rift. He seems to have believed, they concluded, that the introduction of socialist measures at this particular time might appease Soviet anger over his anticommunist campaign. However, it is noteworthy that his decision to embark on the socialist route was actually consolidated and determined earlier, in the late 1950s. This decision had, in fact, almost nothing to do with either Soviet influence or pressure. In any case, the shift to socialism was warmly received by the Soviets, albeit with certain reservations.[46]

The National Charter (al-Mithaq al-Watani), which Nasser presented on May 21, 1962, to the 1,750 members of the National Congress of the Popular Forces, was Nasser's most comprehensive and precise statement of Egyptian policy and Arab socialist ideas since he seized power. This document was indeed regarded by the Soviets as another positive step on Egypt's fitful road to socialism. In his analysis of the intellectual structure of the National Charter, Georgiy Mirskiy, a top Soviet Middle East expert, established that "the influence of the world system of socialism [and] the influence of socialist ideology is being felt [in that document]."[47]

Relations between the two countries significantly improved during Khrushchev's final years in power (1962–64), culminating in his visit to Egypt in May 1964 to celebrate the inauguration of the Aswan High Dam. Prior to Khrushchev's visit, an Egyptian high-level delegation, led by Vice President 'Abd al-Hakim 'Amr, made an extended visit (June 7–19, 1963) to the USSR. The Soviets had made great efforts to give 'Amr exceptionally special treatment, indicating to Nasser that they were interested in commencing a new chapter in relations between the two countries. This visit led to the conclusion of two agreements between Egypt and the USSR. The first was an agreement for a further credit for industrial development. The second agreement regulated "the supply of spare parts and replacements of Soviet military material already held by the UAR, and for repayments under existing arms agreements to be spread evenly over a number of years."[48]

Khrushchev's only lengthy visit to Egypt (May 9–25, 1964) was well prepared. In his speeches, Khrushchev took pains to stress the common interests and points of similarity between the two countries: They both believed in peaceful coexistence and complete disarmament; they both opposed colonialism in all its forms and supported the struggle to expel imperialism from its remaining footholds in Africa, Asia, and Latin America; and they both opposed the presence of foreign bases and aggressive pacts. He placed special emphasis on the significant Soviet assistance in the building of the Aswan High Dam, stressing the unconditional nature of Soviet aid to all countries that were "struggling to develop their resources after freeing themselves from the nightmare of colonialist domination." Soviet aid, in contrast to Western aid, was an "extension of the Soviet Union's political support for liberation movements of other peoples," whereas the latter's aid "was no more than a new form of imperialism which was selfish and rapacious and designed to exploit its recipients."[49] Nasser, for his part, was satisfied with Khrushchev's endorsement of his policy of neutralism and his promise of substantial material aid to Egypt and other anti-imperialist countries. This Soviet policy had definitely enhanced Nasser's prestige in the Afro-Asian bloc, as he had made no political or ideological concessions while sticking to his third road in international affairs.

After several years of ideological and political dispute between Egypt and the USSR, Khrushchev's visit strengthened the Soviet position in Egypt and other Arab countries in the face of both Western and Chinese competition. The fact that Egypt was perceptibly leaning once again toward the USSR had already been noted several months before Khrushchev's visit, by R.A.D. Ford, the Canadian ambassador to Cairo, who was on close terms with both Soviet diplomats in Cairo and high-ranking Egyptian officials. Ford provided his superiors with first-rate reports and analysis on social, ideological, and political developments and trends in Egypt. While analyzing Soviet-Egyptian relations in November 1963, Ford noted: "During my two and one-half years in Cairo, Soviet influence gradually declined while American influence grew, but as I prepare to leave I detect some signs that the Soviet position is beginning to improve once again."[50]

It would seem apparent that in spite of Nasser's effort to moderate his anti-Western policy, particularly his rapprochement with the United States in the early 1960s, the Soviet position in Egypt was still quite secure. The Soviets guaranteed their interests in Egypt by continuing their policy of military aid to Cairo. This included shipments of sophisticated weapons, such as jet bombers, MiG 21s, radar systems, rocket firing MTBS, and surface-to-air missiles. In order to be able to handle the Soviet weapons, Egypt permitted entry to Soviet technicians. Furthermore, the USSR supported Egypt's war efforts in Yemen by replacing destroyed military equipment. The Soviets also provided Egypt with direct assistance in the military operation in Yemen, including participation of Soviet pilots and deliveries of necessary ammunition and oil supplies.[51]

Ideologically, the Soviets could also be pleased with the social developments taking place within Egypt—the speeding up of the socialization process. In addition, a slow and gradual process of releasing Egyptian communists had begun in the early 1960s and reached its climax by the end of April 1964, when all communist parties and organizations had decided to dissolve themselves. Nasser prohibited the formation of a new communist party, but opened certain doors of his establishment, on an individual basis, to former communists who supported his socialist revolution and were willing to participate in "reestablishing" Egyptian society in accordance with his brand of socialism.[52]

In his effort to demonstrate that his decision to embrace socialism was purely motivated by Egypt's own interests, Nasser declared that Egypt's brand of socialism and its pursuit of economic development lay in nonalignment. Nasser noted that Egypt's socialism placed special emphasis on the abolition of artificial class barriers and the establishment of full liberty and democracy, including the rights of freedom of conscience and property ownership. However, this ideological nonalignment of domestic policy was in practice no more neutral than Nasser's nonalignment in foreign affairs; in other words, it was ideologically closer to Eastern European doctrine than to Western concepts. Nevertheless, Nasser's Arab socialism was a fusion of nationalist and Islamic ideas with socialism. It was a nationalist socialism in the sense that it accommodated itself to particular Arab and Egyptian circumstances. Arab socialism rejected proletarian internationalism and emphasized the distinctiveness of the Arab nation.[53]

Soviet theoreticians defended their largely positive evaluation of Arab socialism by stressing its theoretical compatibility with Marxism-Leninism, despite denials by its Arab proponents. Apparently, the Soviets calculated that they could best advance their position in Egypt and in other Arab countries by embracing Arab socialism and bestowing their approval, albeit qualified. This pragmatic Soviet approach indeed bore dividends, particularly following the June 1967 War.

The results of the June 1967 War were a hard blow for Nasser and the Soviets. Nasser needed to rebuild his military power in an effort to recapture the territories occupied by Israel, and only the Soviets were willing to provide the goods. The USSR feared a collapse of the pro-Soviet Arab regimes, whereby it would lose its influence and strategic strongholds in the Middle East after years of considerable investment in many fields in Egypt and other Arab countries.[54]

The ascendancy of Sadat marked the beginning of the end of a long-standing friendship and close relations between Egypt and the USSR. In July 1972, Sadat expelled thousands of Soviet military experts and technicians from Egypt. Sadat's leaning toward a free-market economy, his liberal social policy which replaced Nasser's Arab socialism, his removal of left-wing and Nasserist personnel from key positions, his reorientation toward the United

States and limitation of relations with the USSR—all left the Soviets with no influence at all in the Egyptian political arena and the loss of their main ally and stronghold in the Middle East.[55]

## Conclusion

Soviet-Egyptian relations throughout Nasser's period had many ups and downs. As we have seen, political and economic factors were the driving forces in bringing the two countries closer together in the early 1950s. At the time, both countries learned to distinguish between ideology and politics. In other words, Nasser continued with his harsh campaign against internal communism, while the USSR ignored it and declared no intentions of interfering in Egypt's internal affairs. This was the case until the late 1950s, when this Soviet-Egyptian modus vivendi was to change thereafter.

The years 1958–61, in contrast, witnessed an intense ideological warfare for two main reasons. First, following the formation of the UAR, Nasser stepped up his battle against communism. Second, Qassem's coup boosted Nasser's expectations that Iraq was on its way to join the UAR, but soon changed to bitter disappointment inside the UAR. Qassem's alliance with the Iraqi communists and his rapprochement with the USSR changed Nasser's approach to communism. He now blamed international communism for interference in Arab domestic affairs, a matter which created tension in relations with the Soviets and subsequently the mutual conduct of ideological warfare.

However, this state of affairs changed following the introduction of Nasser's Arab socialism. The shift to socialism was warmly received by the Soviets, and the relations between the two countries significantly improved, thus culminating in Khrushchev's visit to Egypt in May 1964 to celebrate the inauguration of the Aswan High Dam. The socialist revolution of the early 1960s was followed by Nasser's declaration that his brand of socialism lay in nonalignment. However, this was not quite accurate because his socialist doctrine was ideologically closer to East European socialism than to Western socioeconomic concepts. Although domestically Nasser remained persistent in his strict anticommunist measures, the shift toward socialism was still a great ideological victory for the Soviets. By the mid-1960s, many communists had joined Nasser's establishment and held key positions, mainly in the press and ideological forums, aimed at guiding the state and nation on their route to socialism.

Nasser's self-confidence and sense of independence in conducting Egypt's foreign policy affairs during the 1960s were weakened significantly in comparison with the situation in the mid-1950s. His firm policy of neutralism, which characterized his first years in power, increasingly turned to one of "pro-Soviet neutralism." Good evidence to support this argument can be seen by his decision to support the Soviet invasion of Czechoslovakia in 1968 contrary to the position of Tito and his other allies within the camp of the nonaligned countries.[56]

The growing Soviet influence in Egypt was halted by the death of Nasser. This dramatic development marked the demise of Nasser's socialist revolution and the termination of Soviet hegemony over Egypt. Sadat embraced an utterly different agenda in all areas and speeded up the process of de-Nasserization. One may say, in conclusion, that the Soviet failure in Egypt can be seen as one of the earlier stops of the speeding Soviet train as it headed to its final destination—that of the total disintegration of the USSR in late 1991.

## Notes

1. See, e.g., Walter Laqueur, *The Soviet Union and the Middle East* (London: Routledge and Kegan Paul, 1957); George Lenczowski, *Soviet Advances in the Middle East* (Washington, D.C.: American Enterprise Institute for Public Policy Research, 1971); David Dallin, *Soviet Foreign Policy after Stalin* (Philadelphia: Lippincott, 1961); Galia Golan, *Soviet Policies in the Middle East from World War Two to Gorbachev* (Cambridge: Cambridge University Press, 1990); Uri Ra'anan, *The USSR Arms the Third World* (Cambridge: MIT Press, 1969); Yaacov Ro'i, *From Encroachment to Involvement: A Documentary Study of Soviet Policy in the Middle East, 1945–1973* (Jerusalem: Israel Universities Press, 1974); and Aryeh Yodfat, *Arab Politics in the Soviet Mirror* (Jerusalem: Israel Universities Press, 1973).

2. See, e.g., Yaacov Ro'i, *Soviet Decision Making in Practice* (New Brunswick, N.J.: Transaction Books, 1980); and Rami Ginat, *The Soviet Union and Egypt, 1945–1955* (London: Frank Cass, 1993). See also Mohrez Mahmoud El-Hussini, *Soviet-Egyptian Relations, 1945–85* (Basingstoke: Macmillan Press, 1987); however, only a small part of this book was based on archival material. As a former senior officer in the Egyptian navy, El-Hussini managed to gain access to the navy's archives, and most of the files deal with the purchase of military equipment. The parts that deal with the social and political aspects of Soviet-Egyptian relations are mainly based on sources belonging to the first group.

3. See, e.g., Yaacov Ro'i, *Islam in the Soviet Union: From World War II to Perestroika* (London: Hurst, 2000).

4. See, e.g., Rami Ginat, "Soviet Policy towards the Arab World, 1945–1955," *Middle Eastern Studies* 32, no. 3 (1996): 321–35.

5. See, e.g., Yodfat, *Arab Politics in the Soviet Mirror*; Muhammad Hasanayn Haykal, *Milaffat al-Suways* (Cairo: Markaz al-Ahram, 1986); Haykal, *Nasser: The Cairo Documents* (London: New English Library, 1972); Oles Smolansky, *The Soviet Union and the Arab East under Khrushchev* (New Brunswick, N.J.: Associated University Press, 1974); Golan, *Soviet Policies in the Middle East*; Aaron S. Klieman,

*Soviet Russia and the Middle East* (Baltimore: Johns Hopkins University Press, 1970); Harry Hanak, *Soviet Foreign Policy since the Death of Stalin* (London: Routledge and Kegan Paul, 1972); John M. Mackintosh, *Strategy and Tactics of Soviet Foreign Policy* (London: Oxford University Press, 1962); Adam Ulan, *Expansion and Coexistence: The History of Soviet Foreign Policy, 1917–1967* (New York: Praeger, 1968).

6. See Rami Ginat, "British Concoction or Bilateral Decision: Revisiting the Genesis of Soviet-Egyptian Diplomatic Relations," *IJMES* 31, no. 1 (1999): 39–60.

7. See Ginat, *The Soviet Union and Egypt,* 76.

8. On the visit of the Egyptian military mission to Prague, see PRO, letter no. 126/19/48 from Sir R. Campbell, British ambassador to Egypt, March 18, 1948, FO371/69200, J2003/46/16; secret letter from FO to British embassy, Cairo, April 19, 1948, FO371/69200, J2003/46/16; minute by R. Jones from the Egyptian Department in the FO, May 7, 1948, FO371/69200, J3064/46/16; secret letter no. 126/33/48 from British embassy, Cairo, May 3, 1948, ibid. On arms selling from the Eastern bloc to Arab countries, see also the report of the CIA entitled "Probable Effects on Israel and the Arab States of a UN Arms Embargo," August 5, 1948, President's Secretary's Files, File Subject: Central Intelligence Reports—ORE 48-8, box 255, Truman Library; CIA report "Possible Developments from the Palestine Truce," July 27, 1948, in *U.S. Declassified Documents Reference System,* 1975, 4F. On the deal and on Soviet-Egyptian commercial relations in the period 1948–49, see Ginat, *The Soviet Union and Egypt,* 103–7.

9. Ginat, *The Soviet Union and Egypt,* 104.

10. Salah al-Din was the deputy foreign minister in Nahhas's previous government (1942–44) and was involved in the process of establishing relations with the Soviets in 1943. The prime minister, Nahhas Pasha, also undertook the position of foreign minister.

11. This information was given to the American embassy in Cairo by a source classified as highly confidential. See USNA, dispatch 325 from Caffery, Cairo, August 10, 1951, RG 59, 661.741/8–1051. The Egyptian press had called for the strengthening of relations with the USSR and fighting by all means to expel "British imperialism." See *Al-Sha'b al-Jadid* (the weekly of the Socialist Party), May 10, 1951. The paper said that Britain should know that the Egyptian government was not afraid to conclude a nonaggression treaty with the USSR. "If Britain itself had such a treaty with the Soviets, why should Egypt hesitate to conclude a similar pact?" Words in the same spirit were uttered by the *Al-Musawwar,* May 10, 1951. On September 20, 1951, *Al-Ahram* declared: "We must not limit our national struggle to Britain but should enlarge it to include the allies of Britain as well." The paper suggested that Britain's argument that the USSR was attempting to create another Korea in the Middle East was false.

12. On the relations between the two countries under the Wafdist government (1950–1952), see Ginat, *The Soviet Union and Egypt,* 107–43.

13. See TASS report, July 24, 1952, SWB, USSR, 12; Ivanov, TASS International Review, August 1, 1952, SWB, USSR, 3–4.

14. On the Soviet approach see Ginat, *The Soviet Union and Egypt,* 157–58.

15. Papers of Matthew J. Connelly, Set I, file subject: cabinet meeting, Friday, September 19, 1952, box 1, Truman Library. See also report by Lakeland, American embassy, Cairo, November 5, 1952, RG 84, Cairo-Embassy-General Documents, file subject: 320 U.S./Egypt, box 219.

16. Telegram 730 from Caffery, September 18, 1952, *FRUS,* vol. 9, 1952–1954, 1860–61. See also a statement made by Nagib, in reply to the first installment of Faruq's memoirs, in which the former king accused the Free Officers of being communists; in dispatch 728 from Caffery, October 20, 1952, RG 59, 774.00/10–2052.

17. See Ginat, *The Soviet Union and Egypt,* 159–60.

18. Ibid., 170–76.

19. Muhammed Abd al-Wahab Sayed Ahmed, "Relations between Egypt and the USA in the 1950s," in Charles Tripp, ed., *Contemporary Egypt: Through Egyptian Eyes: Essays in Honour of P. J. Vatikiotis* (London: Routledge, 1993), 92.

20. See Ginat, *The Soviet Union and Egypt,* 207–19. See also Central Intelligence report, "The Soviet Arms Offer to Egypt," in *CIA Research Reports: The Middle East, 1946–1976,* reel 2, M5617, SOAS Library.

21. Letter from Dulles to Nasser, September 27, 1955, John Foster Dulles Papers, 1951–59, File Subject: John Foster Dulles Chronological, September 1955 (1), box 12, Eisenhower Library.

22. This information was given to the American embassy on February 11, 1954, by an Egyptian official, described as reliable. See USNA, dispatch 902 from Caffery, Cairo, February 12, 1954, RG 59, 661.74/2–1254.

23. "Soviet Bloc Economic Activities in the Near East and Asia as of November 25, 1955," report, Office of Research, Statistics, and Reports, Clarence Francis Papers, Eisenhower Library. See also CIA Intelligence Memorandum, "The Communist Economic Campaign in the Near East and South Asia," November 30, 1955, in *Declassified Documents Reference System,* United States, 1986, 002516.

24. The Asian-African conference, known as the Bandung Conference, was held in Bandung, Indonesia, on April 18–24, 1955.

25. See Ginat, *The Soviet Union and Egypt,* 191.

26. Nasser addressed this speech to Egyptian army officers on March 28, 1955. See the text of the speech in USNA, dispatch 1899 from Henry Byroade, British embassy, Cairo, April 4, 1955, RG 59, 674.00/4–455.

27. PRO, dispatch 56 from Humphrey Trevelyan, British ambassador, Cairo, April 19, 1956, FO371/118846, JE1024/1. On Nasser's policy of neutralism, see a broad discussion in Elie Podeh, "The Drift towards Neutrality: Egyptian Foreign Policy during the Early Nasserist Era, 1952–1955," *Middle Eastern Studies* 32, no. 1 (1996): 159–78.

28. PRO, minute by P. Dean, Foreign Office, November 16, 1956, FO371/118853, JE10338/1.

29. Laqueur, *The Soviet Union and the Middle East,* 219–20.

30. *Sunday Times,* magazine section, June 17, 1962.

31. Ro'i, *From Encroachment to Involvement,* 204.

32. PRO, telegram 1054 from Trevelyan, Cairo, June 17, 1956, FO371/118847, JE1025/4. Shepilov visited Egypt from 16 to 22 of June 1956 to attend the celebra-

tion held to mark the completion of the withdrawal from Egypt of the British forces in the Suez Canal zone. On the visit, see dispatch (S) 96 from Trevelyan, Cairo, June 28, 1956, FO371/118847, JE1025/10.

33. On the communist factor and its role in bringing Egypt and Syria closer in late 1957 and early 1958, see Elie Podeh, *The Decline of Arab Unity: The Rise and Fall of the United Arab Republic* (Brighton: Sussex Academic Press, 1999), 34–48; Gordon H. Torrey, *Syrian Politics and the Military, 1945–1958* (Columbus: Ohio State University Press, 1964), 360–81.

34. Intelligence report 7848, State Department, October 22, 1958, in OSS/State Department Intelligence and Research reports, 12, Middle East, 1950–1961, reel 2, M5618, SOAS Library.

35. On Nasser's visit, see intelligence report 7738, State Department, June 16, 1958, SOAS Library; intelligence report 7848, State Department, October 22, 1958, SOAS Library.

36. PRO, dispatch 105 from D. P. Reilly, British embassy, Moscow, May 24, 1958, FO371/131336, JE10338/26.

37. Intelligence report 7848, State Department, October 22, 1958.

38. See Podeh, *The Decline of Arab Unity,* 60–64.

39. Intelligence report 7851, State Department, October 22, 1958, reel 3, SOAS Library.

40. See the record of conversation between Mukhitdinov and Nasser in intelligence report 7848, State Department, October 22, 1958, SOAS Library.

41. See more on Bakdash's speech in the *Times* (London), March 17, 1959.

42. PRO, letter 10342/26/3 from Patrick Reilly, British embassy, Moscow, March 26, 1959, FO371/141914, VG10338/3.

43. See quotation in Rami Ginat, *Egypt's Incomplete Revolution: Lutfi al-Khuli and Nasser's Socialism in the 1960s* (London, Frank Cass, 1997), 41.

44. Ibid.

45. Ibid., 40–41.

46. On Nasser's route to socialism, see Ginat, *Egypt's Incomplete Revolution,* chaps. 1–3, 8–10. On the Soviet view of the July 1961 Laws, see record of conversation between R. A. Ford and Vladimir Erofeev, Soviet ambassador in Cairo, in PRO, dispatch 537 from British embassy, Cairo, August 3, 1961, FO371/158822, VG1102/83.

47. Georgiy Mirskiy, *Arabskie Narody Prodolzhayut Bor'by* (Arab peoples continue the struggle) (Moscow: Mezhdunarodnye Otnosheniya, 1965), 51 (Russian).

48. The details and information about the visit and its results were given to the British ambassador to Moscow by his Egyptian counterpart. See PRO, dispatch 80 from British embassy, Moscow, June 20, 1963, FO371/172863, VG103138/9. The Soviet signatories were respectively, I. V. Arkhipov, first deputy chairman of the State Committee for Foreign Economic Relations attached to the Council of Ministers of the USSR, and Marshal R. Ya. Malinovsky, minister of defense of the USSR. The Egyptian signatory was 'Abd al-Hakim 'Amr. See an attached translation of TASS communiqué on the visit in dispatch 80.

49. See full account of Khrushchev's visit in PRO, dispatch 24 from H. Beeley,

British ambassador to Cairo, June 4, 1964, FO371/178589, VG103138/19. See also a minute by H.F.T. Smith, Foreign Office, May 27, 1964, FO371/178589, VG103138/18.

50. PRO, letter 530 from R.A.D. Ford, Canadian ambassador, Cairo, November 12, 1963, in FO371/172863, VG103138/17.

51. Ibid.

52. See more on this subject in Ginat, *Egypt's Incomplete Revolution*, 26–29, 54–59.

53. On Nasser's Arab socialism, its ideological sources, theoretical tenets, and the differences between socialism and Marxism/communism, see ibid., 9–29, 35–40.

54. The literature on Soviet-Egyptian relations from the mid-1960s onward can be placed in the "first group," the so-called contemporary research works. Works that can be classified within the second and the third groups and cover this period have not yet been published. The first group, however, offers a large number of works on that subject and period. See, e.g., Walter Z. Laqueur, "The Deepening of Dependency upon the USSR," in Shimon Shamir, ed., *The Decline of Nasserism, 1965-1970: The Waning of a Messianic Movement* (Tel-Aviv: Mif'alim Universitayim, 1978), 297–309 (Hebrew); Ro'i, *From Encroachment to Involvement*, 447–96, 528–36; Shimon Shamir and Michael Confino, eds., *The USSR and the Middle East* (Jerusalem: Israel Universities Press, 1973); El-Hussini, *Soviet-Egyptian Relations, 1945-85*, 151–88; Mohamed Heikal, *The Sphinx and the Commissar* (New York: Harper and Row, 1978), 172–214.

55. On Soviet-Egyptian relations under Sadat, see El-Hussini, *Soviet-Egyptian Relations, 1945-85*, 191–211. On Sadat decision of July 1972 and its effects on the two countries' relations, see Yaacov Ro'i, *The USSR and Egypt in the Wake of Sadat's "July Decisions"* (Tel-Aviv: Russian and East European Research Center, 1975); and Talal Nizameddin, *Russia and the Middle East: Towards a New Foreign Policy* (London: Hurst, 1999), 30–33.

56. Ro'i, *From Encroachment to Involvement*, 490–91.

# IV.

**Nasser's Socioeconomic Policies and Achievements**

# 10

# An Assessment of Egypt's Development Strategy, 1952–1970

M. Riad El-Ghonemy

## Introduction

The term *development strategy* refers here to the set of policies and declared objectives expressing the approach followed to tackle Egypt's underdevelopment problems between 1952 and 1970. During this period, the strategy was characterized by two major features: One was the gradual shift toward a central design of development, which provided the role of government (and its public sector) with prominent supremacy over that of the market (and its private sector). The second was a fundamental change in the institutional framework of the economy to bring about sustained economic growth, rapid employment expansion, and equitable distribution of income and wealth in favor of low-income groups.

In order to understand the process of national development, two periods (1952–55 and 1956–70) are distinguished in terms of the initial development objectives regarding the roles of government and the market in shaping the structure of the economy and the distribution of income. However, there is a possible misinterpretation of the development objectives expressed in general terms both in Nasser's 1954 book, *The Philosophy of the Revolution* (*Falsafat al-Thawra*), and in his May 1962 National Charter (al-Mithaq al-Watani).

Throughout the entire Nasserite period, historical experience suggests that, with the exception of the September 1952 Land Reform and the post-1957 rapid industrialization, policy choice was largely in response to both internal and external events. A good example of this is the nationalization of the Suez Canal in July 1956 in response to the refusal of the World Bank and the United States to finance the construction of the Aswan High Dam upon

Egypt's conclusion in September 1955 of an arms purchase deal with Czechoslovakia and its negotiations with the Soviet Union for financial aid. Another example is the absence of investment provisions in the preparation of the Five-Year Development Plan of 1959/60–1964/65, for the 1961–63 massive nationalized foreign and domestic enterprises, suggesting that nationalization was not predetermined.

### The Period of Private Enterprise Economy, 1952–1956

Apart from government control of irrigation, main railways, and a few imports, this period featured a private property and free enterprise economy, representing a continuation of the pre–July 1952 situation. Despite budget and balance of payments deficits and the effects of the Korean War on cotton prices (1950–52), this first period of Nasser's development strategy witnessed a remarkable economic stability in terms of national output growth, total investment, price levels, and low inflation rate. This stability was realized through a series of regulations, including the closure of the Alexandria cotton exchange for two years and an increase in direct government revenues through higher direct taxation and increased import duties on competing manufactured commodities and nonessential consumer goods. Increasing import tariffs was also intended to protect domestic industry.

Furthermore, measures conducive to macroeconomic stability included the promotion of exports by way of concluding several bilateral agreements and the facilitation of direct foreign capital investment by granting investors generous incentives and concessions in 1953–54, particularly in the oil industry. At the same time, multisectoral projects, covering a wide range of activities, were prepared by the newly created National Production Council. Examples of these projects were land development for creating new rural communities (for example, Tahrir Province), transport, major roads, electricity, and schemes for manufacturing iron, steel, paper, and fertilizers that later contributed toward the expansion of the public industrial sector.

The major policy enacted to address inequality and poverty reduction was the 1952 Land Reform. Supplemented by the reform laws of 1961 and 1969, it redistributed 13 percent of total agricultural land among small tenants, in family units of two *feddans*,[1] on average, representing only 10 percent of total agricultural households. In addition to the redistribution of land above an established maximum limit of private ownership, the reform program confiscated the royal family estates and substantially reduced land rental values in real terms by fixing them at seven times the already low land tax. For the first time in Egyptian history, a maximum limit on private landownership was established at 200 feddans in 1952, reduced in 1961 to 100 feddans per person, and reduced even further to 50 feddans in 1969.

Though partial in its scale of redistribution, the land reform program introduced a fundamental change in Egypt's sociopolitical power structure, moving away from a policymaking apparatus dominated by the landlords and toward an equity-oriented policy intended to benefit the peasants and landless workers. Combined with other income-raising sources, such as remittances of migrant workers and subsidization of basic consumer goods, land reform reduced inequality in distribution of both landholdings and personal income/expenditure. It reduced absolute poverty in rural areas from my estimate of 56.1 percent in 1950 to 27.4 percent in 1958/59. The pre–July 1952 conditions of poverty, inequality, and overall population pressure on the limited cultivable land justify the speedy implementation of land reform and the urgency in the construction of the Aswan High Dam.[2] Furthermore, Nasser and his fellow members of the Revolutionary Command Council (RCC) wanted to deliver tangible results at an early stage. They maintained the traditional private property rights in land, and consequently agriculture was—and still is—the major private enterprise sector of the Egyptian economy.

### Predominant State Intervention in a Mixed Economy, 1956–1970

The success of the land reform, the nationalization of the Suez Canal, and the sequestration of British and French properties encouraged the Nasser administration to extend government control over the whole economy. The major features of this expanded role were tightly planned investment allocations, administered pricing, control of foreign trade, tighter control of farming, and the adoption of a welfare-oriented strategy in which private and public ownership of assets coexist. The pattern of development gradually shifted away from a profit-making liberal capitalist system toward a welfare-oriented distribution of wealth and economic growth benefits among the social classes, with a preference for the poorer class.

The National Charter stressed the concept of "Arab socialism," to be created in a "socialist, co-operative, and democratic society." This broad concept aimed at such ambiguous ends as social solidarity, social justice, and raising the living standard along a socialist path, permitting private enterprise and ownership to function under "guided capitalism" free of monopoly (*ihtikar*). It also emphasized the elimination of exploitation in transactions (*istighlal*) within the domestic market through the dominance of a large public sector and regulation of profit margins, wage rates, and consumer prices, as well as through the protection of tenants and the substantial reduction of rental values both in farming and in housing.

The continued emphasis on "elimination of exploitation" in the development strategy since the July 1952 Revolution seems to be more of an expression of the violation of Islamic moral principles in business conduct (what is permitted, *halal,* and what is prohibited, *haram*) than of Karl Marx's conception of exploited and exploiter in terms of his notion of surplus value accumulation. In fact, I find it difficult to discern precisely, from available sources, what the socialist aims of the 1956–70 policy were and what was meant by "socialism." In operational terms, the "elimination of exploitation" in the minds of ordinary people should be taken to mean rapid poverty reduction, quick gains from employment expansion, and efficient bureaucracy.

In retrospect, it seems that the design of development in 1956–70 and the models used in its comprehensive planning were also influenced by the emergence of analytical models in the 1950s and ideas of the two Nobel Prize laureates in economics, Jan Tinbergen and Roger Frisch. Also influential were Bent Hansen's technical assistance in Egypt's planning exercise, Oskar Lange's ideas on competitive socialism, and Albert Hirschman's 1958 model for a development strategy. This strategy gives industry an investment priority in order to absorb wider employed manpower, accelerate capital accumulation, and become the economy's engine of growth through its several linkages with other sectors. Accordingly, agriculture is to be kept as a reservoir of labor and food. Moreover, I may add that the leading role of the state in industrialization was seemingly a response to the failure of the 1953–54 laws to induce private investment and the inflow of foreign capital to industry.

### The Character of the Reformed Economic System

The tight planning of the Egyptian economy was made possible by an apparatus consisting of the National Planning Commission, the Institute of National Planning, and the Ministry of Planning, all of which were—and still are—well equipped with competent economists, statisticians, sociologists, and engineers. The result was the preparation—for the first time in Egypt—of a broad framework for a ten-year investment program, starting with the First Five-Year Development Plan for the years 1960–65, followed by a second plan for 1965–70.[3] A close examination of major policy statements and development plans suggests two sets of objectives: economic growth with quantifiable targets for investment allocation and national product increase, and unquantified social justice or social welfare ends.

### Economic Growth

For the periods 1960–65 and 1965–70, the average annual growth of GDP was planned at 7 percent to surpass the 4 percent realized during the initial period (1952–56). However, the average annual growth realized over 1960–70 was only 4.5 percent, falling far short of the target for the following three reasons:

a. The collapse of the cotton crop in 1961.
b. The diversion of resources away from commodity-producing investment and toward armaments purchase and the defense expenditure needed for Egypt's involvement in the Yemen Civil War (1962–67) and the June 1967 War with Israel.
c. The loss of the Suez Canal revenues during its closure in the late 1960s.

Nevertheless, an annual growth rate of 5.7 percent over the entire period of 1952–70 was still higher than the population growth rate of 2.5 percent on average. The result was a per capita annual growth of income at 3 percent, on average, during this long period of 1952–70. This sustained growth was combined with a low inflation rate of 3 percent.

### Egalitarian Measures and Massive Nationalization

The socialist pattern of development strategy was expressed in the social justice objectives of the two five-year plans between 1960 and 1970. They include such broad aims as greater equality of opportunities and income distribution, as well as rapid employment expansion. In a developing economy like that of Egypt, a rapid achievement of economic growth and reduction of income inequality requires the simultaneous institution of egalitarian measures, state control of major productive activities, and planned high saving and investment rates to be directed into channels generating vast expansion of employment.

As noted earlier, egalitarian measures began with the redistributive land reform of September 1952. These were later reinforced by the subsidization of consumer goods, introduction of tax reforms, establishment of social security schemes and pension funds, reduction of house rental values, and provision of free health care and education services. Furthermore, employment of graduates was guaranteed by the 1964 policy action, and substantial jobs were created by the construction of the Aswan High Dam and related large-scale land reclamation projects. Employment opportunities were also made available through the rapid industrialization taking place, as well as through the enormous expansion occurring in government administration and the rest of the public sector, particularly following the wave of nationalization in 1961–63. Government administration was enlarged even further for the management of the 1961 sequestration of property of nearly six hundred wealthy Egyptians, immediately after the separation of Syria from Egypt within the United Arab Republic in September 1961.

Later in 1963, the state took over half the capital of nearly eighty-two private business establishments. Through labor legislation, workers benefited a great deal from the establishment of welfare funds, a raise in the minimum daily wage, restrictions on expelling workers, representation on company boards of directors, and guaranteed transfer of one-fourth of public enterprise profits to employees. While these policies of the development strategy led to almost full employment in the 1960s, the problems of overstaffing, low productivity, and increased bureaucracy remained.

### Investment Expansion and the Leading Public Sector

In addition to the employment benefits from large-scale nationalization, the accumulation of profits for the badly needed investment expansion also had a strategic importance, especially for financing projects planned for industrialization, irrigation expansion in newly developed areas, transport, and construction. In a single decade, between 1952 and 1962, public investment increased tenfold.[4] As one would expect, increased investment was necessary in such a tightly planned economy as that of Egypt. In the 1950s and early 1960s, the belief was that—given the failure of private enterprises to increase post-1955 savings and investments—nationalization would contribute significantly to higher savings and government revenues. This belief was reinforced by Egypt's high rates of public and private consumption and the perennially very low share of savings and investment in national income, as presented in table 10.1. In fact, by 1963, the contribution of the public sector to national income (GDP) was quite high: industry and electricity (60 percent), transport (75 percent), and public utilities (100 percent). However, the public sector accounted for only 6 percent in agriculture, a sector in which private ownership of land and livestock had been maintained, even while pricing was controlled.

The pattern of investment allocation among the commodity-producing sectors (agriculture and industry, including oil) and the noncommodity-

Table 10.1. Shares of Consumption, Savings, and Investment in GDP, 1950 and 1970

| Structure of GDP (%) | 1950 | 1970 |
|---|---|---|
| Share of total consumption | 88 | 76 |
| Share of total savings | 8 | 12 |
| Share of total investment | 13 | 18 |

Source: Ministry of Planning, Cairo.

producing sectors of the economy (transport and services) was a manifestation of the priorities accorded to these activities in Egypt's development strategy. At the start of Nasser's administration, the economy was overwhelmingly agricultural in terms of its share in total employment (60 percent), merchandise exports (85 percent), and gross national income (35 percent). Moreover, the bulk of manufacturing was in the form of processing of agricultural raw products (for example, cotton, foodstuff, hides, and skin). By the mid-1960s, this sector ranked high both in terms of resource allocations for rapid growth and in terms of the degree of equality in the distribution of income and wealth.

Nasser always stressed rapid industrialization, as recalled by his saying "To produce from the needle to the missile." In contrast to the dominant position of agriculture in the economy in the early 1950s, industry (manufacturing, electricity, and mining) accounted for only 12 percent of national income, 8 percent of the total workforce, and 9 percent of export earnings. As in other developing countries, Egypt accorded industry with the highest investment priority in 1952–70, as expressed in the First Industrial Development Plan for the years 1957–61, in the First Five-Year Development Plan of 1960–65, and in the 1956 justification for the establishment of the Ministry of Industry. For Nasser and his first minister of industry, 'Aziz Sidky, the Ministry's leading role in the public sector's huge enterprises was a conscious element of national development and import-substitution strategy. Yet, despite heavy government protection and subsidization, industrial output growth in the 1960s was low, amounting to only 5.5 percent annually or less than half of the planned rate of 11.5 percent. Various explanations for this poor performance may be offered, including government control of the production structure and wage system, and investment preference for heavy capital-intensive industry (iron, steel, aluminum, petroleum refining, petrochemicals, cars, and tires) over labor-intensive manufacturing (textiles, clothing, food products, and footwear).

To balance national development, the strategy did not neglect the other major commodity-producing sector—agriculture. As shown in table 10.2, between 1952 and 1970, the sector's investment allocations fluctuated, as did the total area of land reclaimed, increasing from 19.7 percent of total investment in 1952–60 to 23.4 percent in 1960–65, then declining to 20.1 percent in 1966–70 after the completion of the Aswan High Dam, whose costs reached £E (Egyptian pound) 260 million, including £E103 million in two loans from the USSR.[5] Additional costs of nearly £E62 million were for compensation payments to Sudan and for resettlement of the displaced Nubians in new rural areas north of Aswan, as well as for payment of interest on the Soviet loan. Another sum of £E240 million was required for irrigation works and land reclamation.

Table 10.2. Investment, GDP Growth, Inequality, and Poverty Estimates in Agriculture, 1952–1970

|  | 1952–1960 | 1960–1965 | 1966–1970 |
|---|---|---|---|
| 1. Average investment in agriculture (% of total investment) | 19.7 | 23.4 | 20.1 |
| 2. Total land reclaimed (feddans) | 116,499 | 558,000 | 272,000 |
| 3. Agriculture—GDP annual growth % | 2.0 | 3.3 | 2.5 |
| 4. Degree of inequality [a] |  |  |  |
| Land ownership distribution | 0.61 (1951) | 0.38 (1965) |  |
| Rural income/expenditure | 0.65 (1947) | 0.29 |  |
| 5. Rural poverty estimate (% of total rural households) | 56.1 (1950) | 27.4 (1959) |  |

[a] Degree of inequality is measured in terms of the Gini Coefficient, ranging from an absolute equality value of zero to a maximum value of absolute inequality of one.
Sources: M. Riad El-Ghonemy, *The Political Economy of Rural Poverty: The Case for Land Reform* (London: Routledge, 1990), and "The Egyptian State and Agricultural Land Market, 1810–1986," *Journal of Agricultural Economics* 43, no. 2 (May 1992).

However, there is a consensus among researchers with respect to the high cost per feddan and the loss of some areas of intensively cultivated land to rapid urbanization.[6] Due to a time lag of 5–8 years between the investment in land reclamation (soil treatment, leveling, and irrigation and drainage systems) and the realized economic benefits, average annual growth of agricultural GDP over the period of 1960–70 was below expected level, estimated by the World Bank at 2.9 percent.

### Investing in Human Capital

A striking feature of the development strategy during the Nasserite period was the use of economic growth benefits to raise the living standard of the low-income population in terms of infant mortality, illiteracy, life expectancy at birth, nutritional standards, and access to safe drinking water. It was realized that these improvements must be combined with deliberate efforts to slow down population growth through greater public spending on basic social services and an official family planning campaign. The relationship between these forms of human capital investment and economic growth was suggested in the first development plan for 1960–65 and rhetorically in the National Charter. The assumption was that greater access to education and primary health care would result in a healthier and better educated workforce—an investment that raises their productivity and in turn the national income.

Accordingly, 35–40 percent of the total planned investment in 1960–70 was allocated to health care, education, safe drinking water, subsidized transport, public utilities, construction of dwellings for low-income workers, and investment in infrastructure, especially paved roads between cities and in rural areas. The most important gain was the substantial decline in the infant (0–1) mortality rate from 130 per 1,000 live births in 1952 to 103 in 1970, leading to increased longevity. During the same period, government expenditure on health and education, as a percentage of the GDP, increased nearly fourfold. The length of paved roads, as an important aspect of infrastructure, increased fivefold, from 2,800 kilometers to 13,890 kilometers during the same period. However, the adult illiteracy reduction in 1952–70 fell short of expectations; the national average declined from 76 percent to 65 percent, but it was much higher, at 80 percent, among adult females in 1970, despite a considerable expansion in free compulsory primary education.

Raising the educational level and other well-being components in a poor developing country, whose population was growing fast, increasingly requires heavy public expenditure. The concern over the links between demography and the development process in general, and raising the living standard in particular, was clearly pronounced in 1953 when the National Population Commission was established as an integral part of the Permanent Council of Public Services. In 1957, the Population Commission became part of the official apparatus for national planning. In his public speeches, Nasser stressed the seriousness of the population problem, and after securing *fatwas* from al-Azhar that family planning (*tanzim al-usra*) was permissible, Nasser himself launched a massive family planning campaign, with active participation of nongovernmental organizations.[7] Birth control services were provided by local community development centers, free of charge to persons voluntarily accepting contraception methods. An important aim of these efforts was to create public awareness about families' welfare needs and the pressing urgency of confronting the population pressure problem.[8]

## Conclusion: Rethinking Development Priorities

Under tight planning and administered pricing, the sustained economic growth of total and per capita income, combined with effective poverty-reducing egalitarian measures in 1952–70, represent important achievements of Nasser's administration in a historical perspective. However, the several measures for social justice that were actually implemented to redistribute income and property rights in favor of low-income groups do not warrant the exaggerated title of "socialism."

Rethinking industrialization strategy with regard to directing the tenfold increase in public investment, labor-intensive textiles, and food manufacturing should *not* have been neglected in favor of the capital-intensive heavy industry shielded from competition (e.g., steel and aluminum). In their production, the state acted as the sole entrepreneur, and they were granted domestic monopolies.

In the overpopulated and capital-scarce Egypt that has rich experience in cotton production and manufacturing, giving top priority to the industrial expansion of manufacturing resulted in high social opportunity costs. In fact, during the two development plans in 1957–70, the textiles and food industries enjoyed a domestic comparative advantage and a global competitive advantage that justified preferential investment in their modernization, industrial expansion, and export promotion. This distorted investment priority during that period represents a missed opportunity that has disadvantaged labor absorption in industrial development.

Lastly, despite some unsatisfactory development consequences of massive nationalization, the pattern of development established during the Nasser administration has, in the 1990s, brought rewards in terms of human capital investments. Life expectancy at birth has risen steadily, reaching sixty-five in 1999, that is, twenty-four years longer than in 1952. I believe that this is the true meaning of development.

## Notes

This chapter was an invited lecture given at the University of Haifa on December 16, 1999.

1. One feddan equals nearly one acre or 0.42 hectare.

2. In "The Egyptian State and Agricultural Land Market, 1810–1986," *Journal of Agricultural Economics* 43, no. 2 (May 1992), I examined the implications of the scarcity of and the increasing demands for land. Cultivable area is the amount of land available for farming, irrespective of its intensive use. Cropped area is the area of different crops cultivated in one feddan during the same year. Poverty estimate for 1958/59 is that of Richard H. Adams Jr., "Development and Structural Change in Rural Egypt," *World Development* 13, no. 6 (1985): table 1. See details of my poverty study in M. Riad El-Ghonemy, *The Political Economy of Rural Poverty: The Case for Land Reform* (London: Routledge, 1990), 247 and table 6.11.

3. Several criticisms were made of the plan preparations and its assumptions for planned investment. See Bent Hansen and Girgis A. Marzouk, *Development and Economic Policy in the UAR (Egypt)* (Amsterdam: North-Holland, 1965), chap. 11; Patrick Karl O'Brien, *The Revolution in Egypt's Economic System: From Private Enterprise to Socialism, 1952–1965* (London: Oxford University Press, 1966), 156–64; Robert Mabro, *The Egyptian Economy, 1952–1972* (Oxford: Clarendon Press, 1974), 120–24.

4. Hansen and Marzouk, *Development and Economic Policy in the UAR*, 254–56.

5. The £E was equal to US$4.13 up until September 1949 and thereafter was devalued to US$2.87 until 1977.

6. See El-Ghonemy, "The Egyptian State and Agricultural Land Market"; 'Ali Ahmad al-Jiritli, *Khamsa wa-'Ishruna 'Aman: Dirasa Tahliliyya lil Siyasat al-Iqtisadiyya fi Misr, 1952–1977* (Cairo: al-Hay'a al-Misriyya al-'Amma lil-Kitab, 1977), 26–30; and National Bank of Egypt, *Economic Bulletin* 19, no. 4 (1966).

7. Al-Azhar and the Egyptian Ministry of Wakfs compiled all fatwas related to birth control. See Arab Republic of Egypt, Ministry of Waqfs and Ministry of Information, State Information Service, *Islam's Attitude toward Family Planning* (Cairo, 1994), which was issued on the occasion of the 1994 World Population Conference in Cairo.

8. On the family planning program in Egypt under Nasser, see chapter 12 of this volume.

# 11

## Nasser's Egypt and Park's Korea

A Comparison of Their Economic Achievements

Paul Rivlin

### Introduction

This chapter compares the economic policies of Egypt in the 1960s with those of South Korea, both of which were ruled by military regimes. Although the two regimes had different ideologies, President Park of South Korea, who came to power in a coup in 1961, acknowledged the influence of Gamal 'Abd al-Nasser in his work. He was said to have been a student of Korean and world history, and he compared South Korea under his rule to the Meiji reform in Japan, the modernization of China under Sun Yat-sen, Kemal Atatürk's development of Turkey, and Nasser's Egypt.[1] The purpose of the comparison is to better understand some of the options that were available to Nasser in the economic field and the role of what might be called "exogenous factors" in the development process. Both Egypt and South Korea launched industrialization programs in the early 1960s. Although these were not their first attempts to industrialize, they had certain features in common, including the use of import-substitute industrialization.

By the late 1950s and early 1960s, Nasser had nationalized the Suez Canal and other foreign property, as well as major sectors of the economy. In 1960, he introduced the First Five-Year Development Plan for the entire country, modeled on Soviet experience. Egypt was then at the height of its Arab socialist phase (al-Ishtirakiyya al-'Arabiyya). The regime was trying to mobilize the economy for a huge development effort and, in many respects, to break with the past. The 1950s would seem, at first sight, to have been an auspicious prelude to the Egyptian industrialization drive of the 1960s, but, as will be shown, this is too superficial a view. As in South Korea, growth rather than stability was the order of the day.

Table 11.1. Population, Total GDP, and GDP per Capita in Egypt and South Korea, 1960–1998 (current prices)

|  | 1960 | 1970 | 1980 | 1990 | 1998 |
|---|---|---|---|---|---|
| **South Korea** | | | | | |
| Population (millions) | 24.7 | 32.2 | 38.1 | 42.9 | 46.4 |
| Total GDP (US$ billion) | 4.6 | 8.9 | 63 | 254 | 320 |
| GDP per capita (US$) | 185 | 276 | 1,643 | 5,921 | 6,842 |
| **Egypt** | | | | | |
| Population (millions) | 25.9 | 33.3 | 42.1 | 52.7 | 62.0 |
| Total GDP (US$ billion) | 3.9 | 6.8 | 10.8 | 38.4 | 82.7 |
| GDP per capita (US$) | 151 | 205 | 257 | 729 | 1,304 |

*Source*: International Monetary Fund, *International Financial Statistics Yearbook*, 1987, 1995, October 1999 (Washington, D.C.).

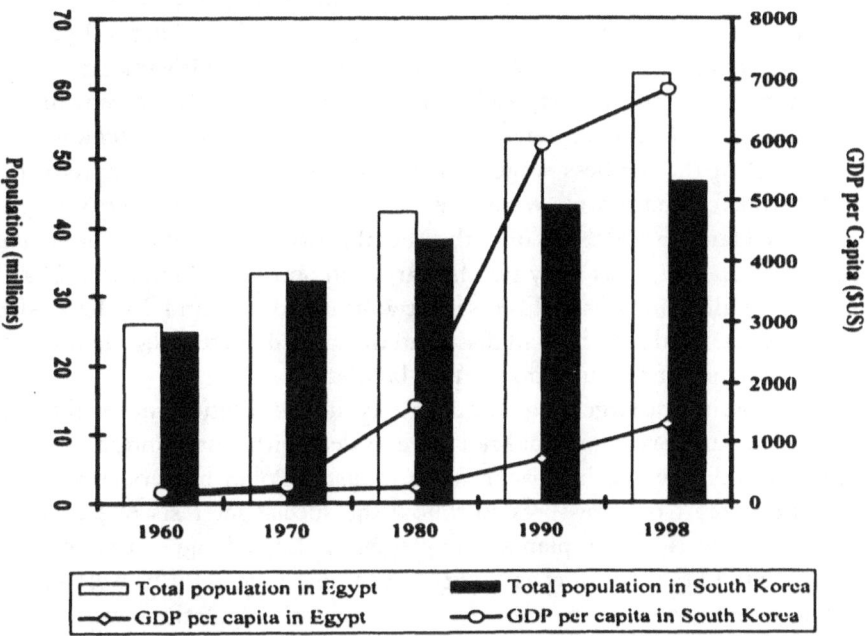

Fig. 11.1. Total population and GDP per capita in Egypt and South Korea, 1960–1998.

As shown in table 11.1, the gross domestic product (GDP) per capita in South Korea in 1960 was $185, as compared with $151 in Egypt. Although these figures should be treated with caution, they do provide a general guide. GDP, population, and GDP per capita were at similar levels in the two countries in 1960. By 1998, South Korea's GDP was almost four times that of

Egypt, but its population was only two-thirds as large. As a result, its GDP per capita was five times that of Egypt.

## Initial Conditions for Economic Development

The initial conditions that have been identified in economic growth theory as necessary for economic development cannot be summarized only in terms of GDP per capita. In East Asia they included the high quality of basic education, which meant that skilled labor was available. Another initial condition was the relative equality in income distribution. The importance of these factors has been recognized both by the World Bank and by its critics in the debate about growth in East Asia.[2]

In terms of economic parameters, some direct comparisons between South Korea and Egypt are possible. Around 1960, the Gini coefficient for land distribution in South Korea was 0.39, while in Egypt it was 0.67.[3] The coefficient for income in South Korea was 0.34 and for Egypt, 0.42.[4] In Egypt, between 1952 and 1961, 14 percent of total cultivable land was redistributed, with property rights transferred to only 10 percent of the population. Each family received one hectare.[5] Two-thirds of the tenants and nearly all of the landless wage earners were excluded from the reforms, although excluded tenants were given security of tenure and were charged low, fixed rents in real terms until the liberalization of the 1990s. The ceiling for landownership was forty-two hectares.[6] In South Korea in the 1930s, 3 percent of all farm households owned two-thirds of the land. By the 1940s, however, the land reforms had dissolved the landed aristocracy, leaving less than 7 percent of the rural population landless.[7]

The absence of large inequalities in income distribution meant that the South Korean government did not have to deal with vested interests of the wealthy and powerful in agriculture or industry. Policy makers were therefore insulated from pressures to follow the special interests of particular sectors and were able to plan and implement policies designed to maximize the growth of the economy as a whole. Administrative reforms were undertaken without outside interference, and economic regulations were generated in the technocratic elite, with politicians, especially President Park in South Korea, acting to prevent such interference. Given relatively equal income distribution in South Korea, authorities were not under pressure to redistribute income.[8] They were also less concerned about the consequences of growth on distribution than would otherwise have been the case. It should be noted that this equality was in large part the result of action in the United States, rather than deliberate decisions in South Korea. Between 1945 and 1953, war and revolution resulted in the redistribution of wealth.[9]

During the 1960s, a transition to lower population growth took place in South Korea and Taiwan, thereby reducing the pressure to generate employment over time. It also reduced the burden of education and health services and permitted resources to be allocated to improving the quality of those services, which in turn yielded further economic benefits. In 1960, the South Korean crude birth rate was 43 per 1,000 people and the crude death rate was 14 per 1,000. By 1970, the crude birth rate had fallen 25 percent to 30 per 1,000 and the crude death rate had dropped 36 percent to 9 per 1,000. These trends continued in the 1970s and 1980s, and by 1991 the crude birth rate was 16 per 1,000 and the crude death rate was 6 per 1,000.

Egypt did not experience such a demographic transition in the 1960s, and progress in the 1970s and early 1980s was much slower. In 1960, the country had a crude birth rate of 44 per 1,000 and a crude death rate of 19 per 1,000. In 1970, the crude birth rate declined to 40 per 1,000 and the crude death rate to 17 per 1,000. Given these modest declines, the Egyptian population growth rate in the 1960s and 1970s thus remained unchanged at about 2.5 percent.[10] In the 1980s, Egypt's population increased by an annual average of over 2.4 percent.[11] In contrast, South Korea's population grew annually by only an average of 1.1 percent.[12] Between 1992 and 1998, Egypt's population rose by an annual average of 1.9 percent, while South Korea's rose only 1 percent.[13]

In educational terms, initial conditions were better in South Korea, where primary school enrollment in 1960 was 94 percent, as compared with 66 percent in Egypt (see table 11.2). Between 1960 and 1997, primary school enrollment rates improved in Egypt, and the literacy rate doubled. Despite such progress, almost half of the Egyptian population over fifteen years of age was still illiterate in 1995. Thus, Egyptian literacy rates were much lower than South Korea's throughout the period examined (see table 11.3). The main obstacle to increasing the literacy rate in Egypt was the high population growth rate, although there was also evidence of declining effective-

Table 11.2. Primary Educational Enrollment Ratio in Egypt and South Korea, 1960–1997

|  | 1960 | 1978 | | | 1997 | | |
| --- | --- | --- | --- | --- | --- | --- | --- |
|  | Total | Male | Female | Total | Male | Female | Total |
| Egypt | 66 | 80 | 52 | 74 | 88 | 58 | 96 |
| South Korea | 94 | 99 | 89 | 111 | 112 | 111 | 92 |

Source: World Bank, World Development Report, various issues (New York: Oxford University Press).

Table 11.3. Literacy Rates in Egypt and South Korea, 1960–1997*

|  | 1960 | 1976 | 1997 | |
|---|---|---|---|---|
|  | Total | Total | Male | Female |
| Egypt | 26 | 44 | 65 | 40 |
| South Korea | 71 | 93 | 99 | 96 |

\* Percentage of population over fifteen years of age.
*Source*: World Bank, *World Development Report,* various issues (New York: Oxford University Press).

ness of Egyptian education.[14] Another initial condition favoring development was strong growth in agricultural production.[15] South Korean agricultural production rose by an annual average of 4.5 percent in the 1960s and by 5 percent in the period of 1970–77. By contrast, agricultural production in Egypt rose by an annual average of 2.9 percent in the 1960s and by 3.1 percent between 1970 and 1977.[16]

### Political and Economic Development in South Korea

Korea was ruled by the Yi dynasty from 1392 until it was overthrown by the Japanese in 1910. The extraordinary longevity and stability of the Yi dynasty was, according to J. B. Pallais, a result of the equilibrium between different social forces in the country. This equilibrium helped to maintain political stability, but it was not a system that could respond effectively to the foreign challenges facing Korea in the twentieth century. The Yi in Korea relied on the Ming dynasty and then on the Ching dynasty in China to supply luxury goods and to help suppress peasant uprisings in 1894. In 1910, Japan formally annexed Korea after declaring it a protectorate, and Japan's rule continued until 1945. The Japanese abolished slavery, codified civil law, and introduced a tax system based on cash payments rather than payments in kind. They created an independent court system and separated the judiciary from the executive branch of government.[17] They also reformed the land-ownership system and taxed landlords who collected rents from their tenants. Although the system was highly exploitative, it introduced market relations into agriculture.

However, the Japanese legacy left Korea at the mercy of outside powers in 1945. Between the end of World War II and the outbreak of the Korean War in 1950, Korea was polarized between right and left, with the Soviet Union and the United States taking increasing interest in the country as the Cold War proceeded. The United States backed the Korea Democratic Party, which safeguarded remnants of the feudal dynasty. American forces stationed in Korea relied on the same Korean civil servants who had served the Japanese. The United States also extended the land reforms that the Japanese had introduced. This served to further reduce the power, influence, and wealth of the landlords; encouraged funds to move from speculation in land to investment in manufacturing; and increased food production. Finally, it helped to develop the Korean army, which numbered 600,000 by 1953, when the war ended.

The period of the first republic, 1948–60, was one in which sales of confiscated Japanese property and U.S. aid provided a gravy train of benefits for those with political connections to the regime, including subsidized loans and rights to import commodities that were in short supply. This did permit industrialization and rapid economic growth, but it was not sustainable, and in 1959 the economy went into recession. The 1950s were marked by war and corruption under the regime of President Syngman Rhee. With only limited emphasis on development, the South Korean economy grew in the 1950s, but the pattern of growth was less stable and the rate was slower than in the 1960s.

## South Korea in the 1960s

In April 1960, the army refused to suppress a student revolt, and Syngman Rhee was removed from office. The party that succeeded him in the general elections was ideologically similar. In 1961, a military coup brought General Park Chung Hee to power. The military's main claim to power was its ability to create a sustainable mechanism to raise national income. Whereas the United States, South Korea's main aid donor, favored policies aimed at stabilizing the economy, the military believed that only economic growth would provide stability.[18]

Park, who ruled South Korea until his assassination in 1979, placed the need for economic growth at the center of his policy prescription.[19] Within one hundred days of assuming power, the military government announced that it would launch a five-year development plan. The policy emphasis was on large-scale enterprises and long-term planning, though the latter would not be allowed to stifle creativity or private enterprise.

The military managed to play a dominant, almost entrepreneurial, role in the economy because of the weakness of other social classes. Workers were small in number, and the capitalists relied on the state for monetary aid and other forms of assistance. One month after the 1961 coup, a law against illicit wealth accumulation was passed, and a number of profiteers were arrested. They were threatened with the confiscation of their assets, but the threat was not carried out. Instead, they were allowed to take a central part in the economy by promising to invest sums in industry equal to those that they were alleged to have gained through corruption under the previous regime. In this way, an alliance was formed between the industrialists and the military government, which was to form the backbone of the investment boom that followed.[20] Land reform during the period of the U.S. occupation from 1945 to 1948 had dissolved the aristocracy, and peasants who were, or had recently become, small holders did not form a homogeneous social class. The military government was also influenced by a powerful student movement that had played a major part in the downfall of Syngman Rhee in 1960 and was now acting as a watchdog to keep the military government honest.[21]

The presence of the U.S. occupation forces pushed the Korean military toward an activist economic policy as a means of reducing reliance on U.S. aid, which amounted to $270 million a year and equaled 15 percent of the GDP.[22] South Korea benefited in a more general sense from its strategic relationship with the United States. It was an ally of the United States in the struggle against communism in Asia, and it received large amounts of economic aid that helped it to maintain a healthy balance of payments. During the Vietnam War (1965–75), the United States bought agricultural and industrial goods from South Korea for its war effort, and the country was used as a rest and recreation center for U.S. troops. Moreover, South Korean companies won large construction contracts in Vietnam. This massive, localized demand was a major factor in the expansion of industry and the economy as a whole.

### Economic Policies in South Korea

Two types of conclusions can be drawn from the experience of South Korea. The first relates to the economic policies followed, and the second comprises the reasons why those policies were followed. The economic policies followed had a number of positive features. Investments in human capital and infrastructure increased the private sector's rate of return on investment and thus promoted economic growth. Investment in real estate was discouraged, making more resources available for other sectors.[23] Economic policy was pragmatic and adaptable; it changed as circumstances changed and as the economy developed. Policies were designed to complement or enhance markets rather than replace them. They neither abandoned the market (through central planning) nor were slaves to it. The policy interventions were designed to fill the gaps where there were market imperfections. Exports were encouraged after import substitution had been successfully used to create domestic competitive advantages.

Why were these particular policies followed? Both the World Bank and its critics agree on the importance of strong, effective, and inclusive leadership by government. The state in South Korea, as well as elsewhere in Southeast Asia, was strong and often led by virtual dictators. It used its powers to develop the economy and had an effective bureaucracy to implement its policies, which were intended to yield widespread benefits. Although income distribution became less equal over time, it remained much more equitable than in many other developing countries.[24] Initial conditions were built upon; they were not considered a given or immutable external factor. In South Korea, the state even subsidized school meals and uniforms. Between 1960 and 1989, the share of government spending devoted to education rose from 11 percent to 20 percent.[25] The importance of equality as a policy goal was reflected in the emphasis placed on primary education.[26]

Strong and effective government, however, did not mean that there was no corruption or favoritism in South Korea. Alice H. Amsden noted that "for all the venality . . . beginning in the 1960s, the government's favorite pets—the big business groups that came to account for so large a share of GNP—were outstanding performers. What with export targets—an objective, transparent criterion by which firm performance is easily judged—price controls, restrictions on capacity expansions, limits on market entry, prohibitions on capital flight, restraint on tax evasion, and a government control over the banking system, the big business groups had to deliver."[27]

Discipline in South Korea and its absence elsewhere were due to differences in state power rather than in differential abilities among policy makers.[28] To this should be added the effects of the Confucian tradition with its emphasis on discipline—something which applied elsewhere in East Asia as well. According to the World Bank, in each of the high-performing Asian economies, new leaders faced an urgent need to establish their political viability before economic takeoff. The Republic of Korea was threatened by invasion from the north, Taiwan from China, and Thailand from Vietnam and Cambodia. In Indonesia, Malaysia, Singapore, and Thailand, leaders faced formidable communist threats. In addition, leaders in Indonesia, Korea, and Taiwan, having taken power, needed to prove their ability to govern. Others in Malaysia and Singapore had to contend with ethnic diversity and attendant questions of political representation. Even in Japan, leaders had to earn public confidence after the debacle of World War II. In all cases, leaders were compelled to answer a basic question: Why should they, rather than others, lead their countries? They hoped that rapid, widely shared improvement in economic welfare would bring the legitimacy they needed.[29]

The traditional agrarian elite of South Korea was wiped out after World War II, and its industrialists were, as a group, unorganized and reliant on the state for capital. External resources (U.S. aid) were channeled to the state, but the ideological environment forced it to rely on private capital, despite the fact that the position of the state in U.S.–occupied Korea had been enhanced.[30]

South Korea sought to create competitive advantages where none existed. The South Korean steel industry was a classic example of this. In the 1960s, a team of advisors from the World Bank suggested that the creation of an integrated steel mill in South Korea was premature and that it was not economically feasible. The industry was capital intensive, a resource that South Korea lacked at the time; costs were sensitive to scale, and its domestic market was small. Furthermore, it also lacked raw materials. Its nearest substantial market, Japan, had an efficient industry. Finally, South Korea lacked the skills needed to produce steel. These factors constituted a lack of comparative advantage. Yet, by 1986, the Pohang Iron and Steel Company (POSCO) had become one of the lowest-cost steel producers in the world, and it had entered into a joint venture with U.S. Steel (USX) to modernize the latter's Pittsburgh plant. POSCO supplied capital, training, and technology for its U.S. partner. As POSCO was owned by the state, the Korean government played a central role in its success. Among other factors, the government subsidized the development of the infrastructure, provided POSCO with long-term, low-interest loans in foreign currency to buy imports of machinery, and subsidized loans for building purposes. However, subsidies for water supply facilities, roads, and rent were not high enough to account for all of POSCO's early profitability. Assistance was also received in the form of capital and up-to-date technology from Japan under the latter's reparations scheme for South Korea.[31]

A more significant feature of industrial policy in South Korea involved the private sector. The South Korean automobile industry provides an interesting example of the success of industrial policy. In 1962, the first state-owned car plant was established in cooperation with the Japanese company, Nissan. Tight controls were imposed on imports of finished vehicles, whereas components were allowed in, duty free, and tax exemptions were provided for local products. In 1965, the plan was transferred to the private sector, and a new technology agreement was signed with Toyota of Japan. The agreement provided for a minimum domestic content of 50 percent, which was rigorously enforced.

### The "Hard State" in South Korea

The concept of the "soft state" was developed by Gunnar Myrdal in the 1960s in his *Asian Drama: An Inquiry into the Poverty of Nations,* which dealt with the problems of development in South Asia. The "soft state" was defined as one which demanded very little of its citizens.[32] The East Asian states have been called "hard states" because they have been effective in carrying out their economic objectives. "Soft states" register demands by different groups but are unable to do much more. "Hard states" not only resist private demands but enforce their will. To use one of the favored terms among political scientists, these are states which penetrate their societies, regulate social relations, extract resources, and then use them effectively.[33]

South Korea has experienced massive dislocation in war, has been threatened from outside, and has suffered (as well as benefited) from colonization. These factors have provided symbols for unity and incentive for the leadership to succeed. The same was true for Japan in the second half of the nineteenth century.[34] Such developments were preconditions for the creation of strong states with a concentration of social control in the hands of the government. War and/or revolution swept away existing systems of social control, enabling new regimes to mobilize the country behind programs designed to stimulate economic development.[35]

A second factor present in the so-called "hard states" was the existence of an independent, skilled, and effective bureaucracy.[36] The bureaucracy has also been successfully isolated from excessive politicization or association with private-sector interest groups. These factors were, however, present in other countries which did not experience such fast rates of economic growth. India provides an excellent example of a merit-based, professional civil service, with highly selective entry. Conversely, South Korea was not immune to corruption.[37] When a regime interprets its survival in terms of the need to provide economic results, then it has motivation; when it has political power and an effective bureaucracy to carry out its instructions, then it has capacity. The combination of these factors constitutes the key component of a "hard state," helping to bring about major economic achievements. The success of this formula in South Korea was measured by the fact that between 1960 and 1985, GDP per capita rose by an annual average of 3.5 percent.[38] By 1998, South Korea had a population 46 million, a GDP of $320 billion, and a GDP per capita of $6,840.[39] In 1996, the country was admitted into the "rich man's club," the Organization for Economic Cooperation and Development (OECD).

### Egypt's Economy under Nasser

In 1952, the new regime in Egypt, which took power in a military coup, made it clear that the state would have to play a major role in the economy by building the infrastructure and mobilizing capital. Industrialization would be achieved through import substitution, but neither the private sector nor foreign investment were to be discouraged. In agriculture, which was recognized to be the backbone of the economy, a major land reform was introduced during the 1950s to bring an end to the feudal ownership patterns and also to encourage large landowners to invest in industry. Funds would come from the forced sale of land holdings over the limit.

In practice, as has been shown, the agricultural reforms had limited effects in terms of redistribution. No significant investment in industry resulted, and political tensions between the military regime and civilian political parties increased, with negative consequences for private sector investment. In 1953, the Parliament was disbanded, the Constitution was suspended, and political parties were banned. In this environment, private industrial investment declined by 25 percent, from Egyptian pounds (£E) 28 million a year in 1952/53 to £E23 million in the fiscal years of 1953/54 and 1956/57.[40] In 1953 and 1954, measures were taken to encourage private sector and foreign investment, with virtually no effect.

The nationalization of the Suez Canal in 1956 was carried out in response to Western refusals to finance the Aswan High Dam project. This, in turn, led to the nationalization in 1957 of other foreign assets in Egypt, including banks, insurance companies, and foreign trade agencies. These measures provided assets for the public sector and a stream of income that could be used when and where the government wanted. At the same time, however, the private sector felt even more threatened by the increase in state power and the growth of the public sector at the expense of the private sector.

In 1958–59, it was decided to draw up the First Five-Year Development Plan for 1960–65. In 1958, Egypt negotiated its first twelve-year loan for economic development from the USSR, worth $126 million.[41] In 1958, the USSR agreed to provide financing for the Aswan High Dam project, which was designed to provide an assured water supply and an increase in electricity production. However, there was a serious imbalance between the intentions of the First Five-Year Plan and the politico-economic realities then developing in Egypt.

### Egypt's Economy in the 1960s

The First Five-Year Plan stated that 55 percent of locally funded investment was to come from the private sector. This meant that private sector savings would have to increase from £E87 million in 1959/60 to £E157 million in 1960/61 and to £E214 million in 1964/65, in constant 1959/60 prices.[42] The forecast for private sector savings was unrealistic, even in more harmonious conditions than those prevailing in Egypt in the late 1950s and early 1960s. In 1959, laws were enacted that forced joint-stock companies to invest 5 percent of their net distribution to stockholders in state banks and to limit profit distribution to 10 percent of the nominal value of company shares. This caused a collapse of share prices on the stock market.[43] In February 1960, two major Egyptian banks were nationalized. One of them, the Misr

Bank, owned much of the country's textile industry. In July 1961, a year after the First Five-Year Plan was launched, the remaining banks were nationalized, as were insurance companies, heavy and basic industries, and shipping companies. Many firms were forced to sell 50 percent of their shares to the public sector, and others were subject to partial sell-over to the public sector. Public utilities, foreign trade, and the Alexandria Cotton Exchange were also nationalized.

The implied marginal savings rate for households in the First Five-Year Plan was 16 percent, as compared with an actual rate of 3 percent in 1959/60. There was virtually no discussion in the plan of how the savings rate was to be increased so radically.[44] The failure of the private sector to mobilize its share in investment in the first year of the plan was one of the factors that provoked the nationalization measures of 1961.[45]

The period of 1960–65 did, however, bring a number of accomplishments. The consensus in the literature is that the economy grew by an average annual rate of 5.5 percent, although this figure was partly inflated by the growth of civil service and public sector payrolls.[46] A massive employment drive led to the creation of 1 million jobs.[47] A total of £E1.7 billion was invested, of which 25–28 percent went into industry. About 94 percent of planned investment was carried out, although industrial investment fell 10 percent below target, electricity 22 percent, and housing 20 percent. The Achilles' heel was the balance of payments. Imports rose much faster than had been planned, and exports grew much more slowly. Instead of falling by 6 percent between 1960/61 and 1964/65, imports rose by 80 percent, mainly because agriculture failed to grow as planned and because imports of intermediate goods for industry were much higher than expected.[48] As a result, there was a balance of payments crisis as early as 1962. On the other hand, the 5.5 percent annual GDP growth rate was 1.5 percent lower than the planned rate. Agricultural production increased by 3.3 percent, as compared with a planned rate of 5.1 percent. All other sectors, with the exception of electricity and construction, fell behind their target growth rates.[49]

There were three main problems with the policies adopted under the First Five-Year Plan:

a. First, the main policy adopted in Egypt in the period of the plan was one that had been implemented there since the 1930s: import substitution. Its main weakness was that it reduced imports of one kind, only to increase those of another. The new industries developed in the 1960s were designed to supply local markets; they lacked the economies of scale and the marketing expertise needed to export. Most significantly, they required imports, but were not able to finance them through exports.

b. The second problem was the reliance on private sector investment at a time when private sector activity was being strongly discouraged. In the end, this meant that the plan was doomed. It could have been saved had the public sector been able to raise the funds instead, but there was no mechanism in place for this and no adjustments were made to the plan to allow for the radical changes in ownership that occurred. The plans and the nationalization had different origins.[50] This was part of a more serious problem—the separation of planning from the policy-making system. In July 1961, the finance minister was abroad when he heard, to his surprise, of Nasser's nationalization announcement.[51]

c. The third major problem was, ironically, a result of the achievements. The employment drive that created 1 million jobs resulted in the public sector and the civil services becoming dumping grounds for graduates who received guarantees of employment. This had major negative effects on the efficiency of various enterprises, but managers of companies that had protected markets and a guaranteed source of raw material had few incentives to protest. Nor did the repressive political environment encourage debate, let alone protest.

Egyptian planners wanted progress on all fronts. They wanted heavy industry and an increasing supply of consumer goods. They designed import substitution projects that were expected to increase their exports in a short time. They planned to reach full employment and efficiency, to finance the Aswan High Dam project, and to invest in massive horizontal expansion in agriculture.[52] The economy, however, could not meet all the demands, and by 1964–65, it came to a standstill.

### Nasser's Political Priority over Economic Development

The political leadership wanted all that the planners advocated and more. During the 1960s, Egypt was involved in a war in Yemen (1962–67); this increased the defense burden. Defense spending, as a share of GNP, rose from 8 percent to 12 percent between 1963 and 1965. This was precisely the period in which the trend should have been downward or at least stable. That it rose was a reflection of the fact that the political leadership, much of whose power was concentrated in the hands of Nasser, had a huge noneconomic agenda. In 1965, the economy was in crisis, negotiations were going on with the International Monetary Fund (IMF), and the government was considering how to raise revenues to fund the Second Five-Year Plan for 1966–70.

In the domestic political arena, there were allegations of plots and rivalries in the army, the ruling party, and the government. Internationally, Nasser witnessed the overthrow of major international allies. U.S. wheat supplies were suspended, while the king of Saudi Arabia announced in 1966 the formation of an Islamic Alliance with the unspoken aim of opposing Nasser. Finally, the fighting in Yemen intensified with military, political, and economic consequences for Egypt. In this context, Nasser had little time for economic details, and he announced a gradual exit from what was called "Arab socialism" toward *infitah*, or economic liberalization.

In early 1965, there was a fall in imports as the means to finance them dried up. Factories began to close. In June 1965, austerity measures were announced. A stabilization program was worked out between the government and the IMF, including familiar measures: devaluation, cuts in public investment, and price and tax increases. Nasser, however, rejected the proposals. Assistance was obtained from the USSR, but even Soviet leaders called for austerity measures in Egypt.[53] In April 1965, it was announced that the Second Five-Year Plan would be extended to seven years. Nevertheless, the First Five-Year Plan was abandoned before it ended, and the second was abandoned before it even started.

As a result of the prevailing economic conditions and the tensions that had built up between the regime and the private sector, by the early 1960s, Nasser was fearful of potential threats to his regime. In September 1961, the union with Syria collapsed when an army/business alliance took power there. Nasser feared that the Syrian example might be followed in Egypt. Therefore, the appointment of officials in the government and in the Arab Socialist Union (ASU) and, perhaps most significantly from an economic perspective, the selection of managers in the public sector became a matter of political loyalty. In this regard, Nasser placed political loyalty above all else, even efficiency. No clear distinction was drawn between the political level and the bureaucratic one. In the end, his fear that managers in the public sector and officials in the ASU would form an independent base overrode his desire for efficient production and an increase in output. Managers and workers were "contained" in a bureaucratic web that prevented further political development.[54] The leadership's consciousness of the suffering of the masses was such that it could not and did not ask for sacrifices. Not only this, but it pushed for the production of consumer goods as well as heavy industrial products. This was the implication of Nasser's May 1962 National Charter.

## Conclusions

The first and uncontroversial conclusion is the importance of initial conditions to the relative economic achievements of Nasser's Egypt and Park's

Korea. As has been shown, positive demographic trends during the 1960s, high educational levels, and relatively strong agricultural performance were present in South Korea. Income and land distribution were much more equal in South Korea than in Egypt. The absence of these initial conditions in Egypt, even after the implementation of the agrarian reform, in parallel to the lack of attention accorded the demographic issue until the mid-1960s,[55] may be a sufficient explanation for the failure of the economy to take off or move into sustained growth.

The second and more controversial set of conclusions relates to factors identified in new growth models, which stress the link between macroeconomic variables and their microeconomic foundations, namely, the institutions that support them. Savings, for example, are a function of the financial and business systems that exist in an economy. All banks in South Korea during the 1960s and 1970s were in the public sector. The implication for other countries is that the institutions which served growth so well in East Asia need to be analyzed along with the performance of the economy in macroeconomic terms.[56]

The final conclusion is that the leadership in South Korea (and elsewhere in East Asia) gave priority to economic growth, while that in Egypt did not. It was more determined and, by the start of the 1960s, became significantly disengaged from regional military struggles. Egypt increased its defense spending during the period of the First Five-Year Plan, and its leadership was preoccupied with noneconomic developments inside and outside the country. The Egyptian regime failed to create an effective civil service and failed to give economic issues an absolute priority. The first can be seen as part of the second. The regime did not see economic success as vital to its own survival. This is not to say that Nasser and others did not want the best for their people; indeed, their concern for the citizenry was demonstrated in their unwillingness to impose burdens. They managed to maintain basic consumption levels, and this was enough to keep them in power.

Expectations of major economic improvements, which the regime had promised, were apparently not taken seriously by the population; otherwise, frustration at the failure to achieve them would have been greater. The net effect of their policies was, therefore, to leave the country in severe difficulties in the mid-1960s, even before the June 1967 War broke out.[57] By the late 1960s, Egypt's economy was in stagnation and Arab socialism was being reconsidered. South Korea was by then experiencing rapid growth, and the gap between the two countries widened dramatically.

## Notes

1. Alice H. Amsden, *Asia's Next Giant: South Korea and Late Industrialization* (Oxford: Oxford University Press, 1989), 51.

2. World Bank, *The East Asian Miracle* (Oxford: Oxford University Press, 1993); Dani Rodrik, "King Kong Meets Godzilla: The World Bank and the East Asian Miracle," Centre for Economic Policy Research Papers, no. 944 (London, 1994), 9–10.

3. The closer the Gini coefficient is to zero the greater the level of equality.

4. Rodrik, "King Kong Meets Godzilla," 5, table 2.

5. One hectare = 10,000 square meters.

6. M. Riad El-Ghonemy, *Affluence and Poverty in the Middle East* (London: Routledge, 1998), 160.

7. Amsden, *Asia's Next Giant*, 28, 52, 203.

8. Dani Rodrik, "Getting Interventions Right: How South Korea and Taiwan Grew Rich," *Economic Policy* 10, no. 2 (April 1995): 55–107.

9. Dwight H. Perkins, "There Are at Least Three Models of East Asian Development," *World Development* 22, no. 4 (1994): 655–61.

10. World Bank, *World Development Report* (New York: Oxford University Press, 1981–82, 1993).

11. Galal Amin, *Egypt's Economic Predicament: A Study in the Interaction of External Pressure, Political Folly, and Social Tension in Egypt, 1960–1990* (Leiden: E. J. Brill, 1995), 28.

12. World Bank, *East Asian Miracle*, 40.

13. World Bank, *Country Data* (www.worldbank.org/data/countrydata).

14. Nader Fergany, "Egypt 2012 Education and Employment," *Economic Research Forum for the Arab Countries, Iran, and Turkey*, 1995, Economic Research Forum (www.erf.org.eg).

15. Walt Whitman Rostow, *The Stages of Economic Growth* (Cambridge: Cambridge University Press, 1960), 17–36.

16. World Bank, *World Development Report, 1979*.

17. Amsden, *Asia's Next Giant*, 29–32.

18. Ibid., 49.

19. Ibid.

20. Ibid., 72.

21. Ibid., 52.

22. Ibid., 39.

23. Joseph E. Stiglitz, "Some Lessons from the East Asian Miracle," *World Bank Research Observer* 11, no. 2 (August 1992): 151–77.

24. Robert Wade, *Governing the Market: Economic Theory and the Role of the State in East Asian Industrialization* (Princeton: Princeton University Press, 1990), 180; World Bank, *East Asian Miracle*, 43–47.

25. World Bank, *East Asian Miracle*, 31, fig. 1.3.

26. "The Evolving Role of the World Bank: The East Asian Miracle," World Bank report (n.d.), 6.

27. Amsden, *Asia's Next Giant*, 146–47.
28. Ibid., 147.
29. World Bank, *East Asian Miracle*, 157.
30. Peter Evans, "The State as Problem and Solution," in Stephen Haggard and Robert R. Kaufman, eds., *The Politics of Economic Adjustment* (Princeton: Princeton University Press, 1992), 161–62; Wade, *Governing the Market*, 80.
31. Amsden, *Asia's Next Giant*, 127.
32. Gunnar Myrdal, *Asian Drama: An Inquiry into the Poverty of Nations*, vol. 2 (New York: Random House, 1968), 895–96.
33. Joel S. Migdal, *Strong Societies and Weak States* (Princeton: Princeton University Press, 1988), 4.
34. Wade, *Governing the Market*, 328.
35. Migdal, *Strong Societies and Weak States*, 262, 269–71.
36. Wade, *Governing the Market*, 338–39; World Bank, *East Asian Miracle*, chap. 4.
37. Rodrik, "King Kong Meets Godzilla," 32–33.
38. World Bank, *East Asian Miracle*, 2, fig. 2.
39. In late 1997 and early 1998, there was a huge devaluation of the Korean won against the U.S. dollar, while prices rose by an annual rate of about 8 percent. If the devaluation had been at the same rate as inflation, then GDP would have equaled $437 billion and GDP per capita of $9,427.
40. John Waterbury, *The Egypt of Nasser and Sadat: The Political Economy of Two Regimes* (Princeton: Princeton University Press, 1983), 62.
41. Ibid., 70.
42. Patrick O'Brien, *The Revolution in Egypt's Economic System* (London: Oxford University Press, 1966), 333.
43. Waterbury, *The Egypt of Nasser and Sadat*, 72.
44. Donald Mead, *Growth and Structural Change in the Egyptian Economy* (Homewood, Ill.: Richard D. Irwin, 1967), 242.
45. Alan Richards and John Waterbury, *A Political Economy of the Middle East* (Boulder: Westview Press, 1990), 195.
46. Waterbury, *The Egypt of Nasser and Sadat*, 89.
47. Richards and Waterbury, *A Political Economy of the Middle East*, 196.
48. Mead, *Growth and Structural Change*, 242–43.
49. Mourad Wahba, *The Role of the State in the Egyptian Economy, 1945–1981* (Reading: Ithaca Press, 1994), 92.
50. Paul Rivlin, *The Dynamics of Economic Policy Making in Egypt* (New York: Praeger, 1985), 40.
51. 'Abd al-Mun'im Qaysuni, interviewed by the author in 1980.
52. Waterbury, *The Egypt of Nasser and Sadat*, 84.
53. Ibid., 97.
54. Ibid., 75, 122; Migdal, *Strong Societies and Weak States*, 230–32.
55. See chapter 12 in this volume.
56. Alice H. Amsden, "Why Isn't the Whole World Experimenting with the East Asian Model to Develop? A Review of the East Asian Miracle," *World Develop-*

*ment* 22, no. 4 (1994): 627–33; Joseph Stiglitz, "Comment on 'Towards a Counter-Counterrevolution in Development Theory,' by Krugman," in *Proceedings of the World Bank Annual Conference on Development Economics, 1992* (Washington D.C.: World Bank, 1993), 39–49.

57. These issues are discussed more fully in Paul Rivlin, *Economic Policy and Performance in the Arab World* (Boulder: Lynne Rienner, 2001).

# 12

# Nasser's Family Planning Policy in Perspective

Gad G. Gilbar and Onn Winckler

## Introduction

During the twentieth century, Egypt's population increased almost sevenfold, reaching 67.9 million by mid-2000.[1] This rapid population growth was an outcome of the high rates of natural increase of the Egyptian population, which rose from less than 2 percent in 1907 to a peak of 3 percent in the mid-1980s. The rise was the result of high fertility levels and declining death rates. However, in the past fifteen years, crude birth rates have declined from 39.8 per 1,000 in 1985 to 27.5 in 1998. Similarly, total fertility rates have decreased substantially from 5.2 in 1980 to 3.3 in 1998. The decline in crude death rates during this period, in contrast to the 1960s and 1970s, was slower: from 9.2 per 1,000 in 1986 to 6.5 in 1998. As a result of these changes, the rates of natural increase fell from over 3 percent in 1985 to 2.1 percent in 1998 (see table 12.1).

Egypt's long-standing demographic problem has three interrelated dimensions: high rates of natural increase, unbalanced spatial distribution of the population, and low levels of income. The socioeconomic effects of Egypt's rapid population growth and the unbalanced spatial distribution of its population have already been extensively studied. Hence this chapter will focus on the dimension of high rates of natural increase. Specifically, the study aims to reevaluate 'Abd al-Nasser's family planning policy. This evaluation has three aspects. The first is a comparison of Nasser's family planning policy with that of his successors, Anwar al-Sadat and Husni Mubarak. The second is an examination of the overall contribution of family planning policy to the process of fertility decline. The third is a comparison of Egypt's family planning policy with that of Tunisia, which, like Egypt, began implementing a national family planning program in the mid-1960s.

Table 12.1. Egypt's Rates of Natural Increase, 1907–1998

| Year | Crude birth rate (per 1,000) | Crude death rate (per 1,000) | Natural increase (per 1,000) |
|---|---|---|---|
| 1907 (c) | 45.9 | 28.4 | 17.5 |
| 1917 (c) | 40.1 | 29.4 | 10.7 |
| 1927 (c) | 44.0 | 25.2 | 18.8 |
| 1937 | 43.4 | 27.1 | 16.3 |
| 1940 | 41.3 | 26.3 | 15.0 |
| 1942 | 37.6 | 28.3 | 9.3 |
| 1943 | 38.7 | 27.7 | 11.0 |
| 1944 | 39.8 | 26.0 | 13.8 |
| 1947 | 43.8 | 21.4 | 22.4 |
| 1952 | 45.2 | 17.8 | 27.4 |
| 1953 | 42.6 | 19.5 | 23.1 |
| 1954 | 42.6 | 17.8 | 24.8 |
| 1955 | 40.3 | 17.5 | 22.8 |
| 1956 | 40.7 | 15.3 | 25.4 |
| 1957 | 38.0 | 17.7 | 20.3 |
| 1958 | 41.1 | 16.5 | 24.6 |
| 1959 | 42.8 | 16.3 | 26.5 |
| 1960 (c) | 42.9 | 16.9 | 26.0 |
| 1961 | 44.1 | 15.8 | 28.3 |
| 1962 | 41.5 | 17.9 | 23.6 |
| 1963 | 43.0 | 15.5 | 27.5 |
| 1964 | 42.3 | 15.7 | 26.6 |
| 1965 | 41.7 | 14.1 | 27.6 |
| 1966 (c) | 40.9 | 15.8 | 25.1 |
| 1967 | 39.2 | 14.2 | 25.0 |
| 1968 | 38.2 | 16.1 | 22.1 |
| 1969 | 37.0 | 14.5 | 22.5 |
| 1970 | 35.1 | 15.1 | 20.0 |
| 1971 | 35.5 | 13.2 | 21.9 |
| 1972 | 34.4 | 14.5 | 19.9 |
| 1973 | 35.8 | 13.0 | 22.8 |
| 1974 | 35.8 | 12.7 | 23.1 |
| 1975 | 36.1 | 12.1 | 24.0 |
| 1976 (c) | 36.6 | 11.8 | 24.8 |
| 1977 | 37.5 | 11.8 | 25.7 |
| 1978 | 37.4 | 10.5 | 26.9 |
| 1979 | 40.2 | 10.9 | 29.3 |
| 1980 | 37.5 | 10.0 | 27.5 |
| 1981 | 37.0 | 10.0 | 27.0 |
| 1982 | 36.2 | 10.0 | 26.2 |
| 1983 | 36.8 | 9.7 | 27.1 |
| 1984 | 38.6 | 9.5 | 29.1 |
| 1985 | 39.8 | 9.4 | 30.4 |
| 1986 (c) | 38.6 | 9.2 | 29.4 |

(*continued*)

Table 12.1—continued

| Year | Crude birth rate (per 1,000) | Crude death rate (per 1,000) | Natural increase (per 1,000) |
|---|---|---|---|
| 1987 | 37.4 | 9.1 | 28.3 |
| 1988 | 36.6 | 8.1 | 28.5 |
| 1989 | 32.1 | 7.7 | 24.4 |
| 1990 | 30.9 | 7.1 | 23.8 |
| 1991 | 29.2 | 6.9 | 22.3 |
| 1992 | 26.2 | 6.6 | 19.6 |
| 1993 | 27.4 | 6.4 | 21.0 |
| 1994 | 27.0 | 6.4 | 20.6 |
| 1995 | 27.9 | 6.7 | 21.2 |
| 1996 (c) | 28.3 | 6.5 | 21.8 |
| 1997 | 27.5 | 6.5 | 21.0 |
| 1998 | 27.5 | 6.5 | 21.0 |

(c) = census year

Sources: Arab Republic of Egypt, Central Agency for Public Mobilisation and Statistics, *Statistical Yearbook*, various issues (Cairo); A. M. Abdelghany, "Evaluating the Application of the Stable Population Model of the Population of Egypt," *Population Bulletin of ECWA*, no. 21 (December 1981): 109, table 3; Robert Mabro, *The Egyptian Economy, 1952–1972* (Oxford: Clarendon Press, 1974), 29, table 2.2; James Coyle and John Parker, *Urbanization and Agricultural Policy in Egypt* (Washington, D.C.: Agriculture Department, 1981), 8, table 4.

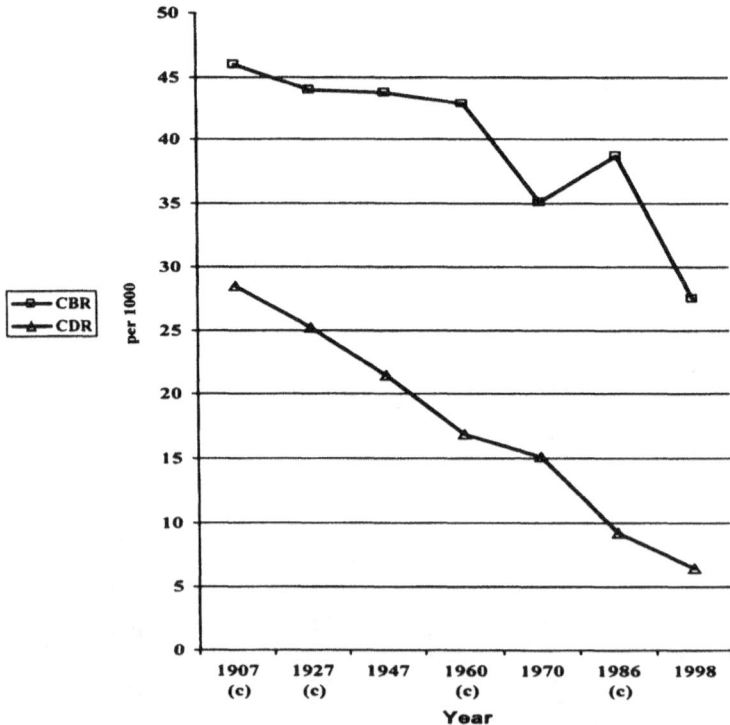

Fig. 12.1. Egypt's crude birth and death rates, 1907–1998.

## Nasser's Demographic Policy

Nasser's remarks about Egypt's demographic policy in speeches and interviews during his early years in power indicated his awareness that the country's rapid population growth constituted a major hindrance to rapid economic development.[2] For example, in a speech delivered to the Liberalization Organization in November 1953 he stated: "The total number of Egyptians is 22 million. Our national income is 660 million Egyptian Pounds. This means that the annual per capita income is about 30 Egyptian Pounds. Three hundred fifty thousand people are added annually. In fifty years the population of Egypt will reach 44 million. . . . If we are earnest about raising our standard of living we should not be forgetful of this fact."[3]

In early 1953, the new regime established a parliamentary Committee for Population Affairs, a move that reflected official recognition of the existence of a demographic problem in Egypt. However, five years passed before any concrete step was taken. In 1958, twenty experimental family planning clinics were established.[4] A voluntary family planning association, the Egyptian Association for Population Studies, had been established at an earlier stage.[5]

Toward the end of the 1950s, Nasser appeared to have adopted the view that rapid economic growth could raise Egypt's low standard of living without the need for direct governmental involvement in family planning. This approach was evident in an interview he gave to the *Christian Science Monitor* in October 1959:

> I am not a believer in calling on people to exercise birth control by decrees or persuasion. . . . Instead of teaching people how to exercise birth control, we would do better to teach them how to increase their land production. . . . In my opinion, instead of concentrating on birth control, we would do better to concentrate on how to make use of our own resources. We live in and make use of only 4 percent of the area of our country. The rest is all neglected and desert. If we direct our efforts to expanding the area in which we live instead of concentrating on how to reduce the population, we will soon find the solution.[6]

Apparently, a reliance on rapid economic development, combined with a decision not to further antagonize the Muslim Brothers, led to Nasser's "economic-oriented approach" as the proper way to confront demographic pressures.[7] Reflecting this attitude, government efforts were concentrated in the economic arena during the late 1950s and the first half of the 1960s. Specifically, the focus was on the construction of the Aswan High Dam, land reclamation programs, and massive industrialization projects. Notably, other leaders of developing countries during the 1950s, such as Pandit Jawaharlal Nehru of India and Ferdinand Marcos of the Philippines, also shared the belief that rapid economic development would make direct government involvement in family planning unnecessary.[8]

By 1965, however, it became apparent that the strenuous efforts to bring about a major change in Egypt's path of economic growth could not be sustained and that a different approach was needed to cope with the country's growing economic difficulties. Even earlier, at the Congress of Popular Forces on May 21, 1962, in the midst of the implementation of the Five-Year Development Plan (1960–65), Nasser stated that "the rapid population growth is the most dangerous obstacle facing Egyptians in their attempts to increase the production level in their homeland."[9]

A major change in Nasser's demographic policy took place in February 1966 with the formation by presidential decree of the Higher Council for Family Planning (al-majlis al-aʿla li-tanzim al-usra), headed by Prime Minister Zakariyya Muhi al-Din. The primary aims of the council were to set up a comprehensive family planning program, conduct and encourage demographic research, and coordinate the governmental departments dealing with the various aspects of family planning and related issues. This new program was based on the assumption that decreased fertility could be attained by supplying low-priced contraceptives, since young couples were interested in having smaller families but simply did not have the means to do so. The basic approach of the program was "technical."[10] The overall goal of the program was to reduce the crude birth rate from around 42 per 1,000 to 30 per 1,000 by 1978.[11]

That same year, the Egyptian General Family Planning Association, supported by the Ministry of Social Affairs, was established to coordinate all nongovernmental organizations (NGOs) dealing with family planning and promote collaboration with the International Planned Parenthood Federation.[12] The premise was that the most convenient way to expand family planning services rapidly was by utilizing the mother-and-child clinics and the Ministry of Social Affairs units, both of which were widespread throughout most regions in the country, including the remote countryside. This would enable the authorities to save both time and money, as well as benefit from the established relationship of confidence between the community and the health staff. These clinics, under the jurisdiction of the Executive Board of Family Planning, generally consisted of a physician and a nurse who provided information and supplied contraceptives.[13] In August 1966, a few months after the adoption of the national family planning program, the Egyptian authorities announced that family planning services were available at 2,850 mother-and-child clinics throughout the country.[14]

Nasser was aware that most ʿulama, and large segments of the lower stratum were opposed to family planning from an Islamic point of view. The authorities therefore attempted to weaken resistance to the antinatalist policy through *fatwas* and newspaper articles proving that the use of contraceptives was not contradictory to the Shariʿa. The government also instructed the *imams* employed by the Ministry of Awqaf to make the public, and particularly the rural population, aware of these Islamic legal opinions. During the late 1960s and early 1970s, crude birth rates in Egypt declined considerably (see table 12.1). By 1970, Egypt's crude birth rate of 35 per 1,000 was the lowest among Arab countries, as compared with 48 per 1,000 in Syria, Jordan, and Saudi Arabia and 41 per 1,000 in Tunisia (see table 12.2). In Nasser's last years (1968–70), Egypt's rates of natural increase were the lowest since the Free Officers came to power and lower than in any other Arab country.[15]

The correlation between the decline in Egypt's fertility rate and the period of heightened family planning activity during the late 1960s and early 1970s cannot be taken for granted. By comparison, in the early 1940s, and again in the mid-1950s, crude birth rates in Egypt declined substantially, apparently due to economic hardships. Hence scholars are divided over the causes of the sharp reduction in fertility levels in the late 1960s and early 1970s. While some attribute the decline to the new demographic policy adopted by the Egyptian government,[16] most attribute it to the severe political and economic crisis that paralyzed Egypt following the June 1967 War. Notably, over a million Egyptians were in military service at that time. Thus fertility reduction was probably "an achievement by default, and not the result of a policy."[17] An official report published in the late Sadat period by the Egyptian Supreme Council for Population and Family Planning attributed the fertility decline during the late 1960s and early 1970s to the "intensive socioeconomic change which started in the early 1950s continuing till the mid-1960s, the launching of a national program for family planning and the war situation involving massive mobilization from 1967 to 1973."[18]

Whatever the reasons for the fertility decline in the late 1960s and early 1970s, the implementation of the first family planning program then faced many difficulties: a shortage of contraceptive supplies, inadequate services in the family planning clinics, overconcentration on supply factors at the expense of focusing on information and awareness, and the absence of a well-defined target for the program.[19] Moreover, even after the government decided to adopt a formal family planning policy, it failed to direct sufficient resources or adequate public attention to the implementation of an efficient national family planning program. The end result was a poor public response. With the improvement in the country's economic and political situation following the October 1973 War, fertility levels began to rise again (see table 12.1).

Table 12.2. Demographic Variables for Egypt and Several Middle Eastern, Asian, and Latin American Countries, 1960–1998

| Country | 1960 | | | 1970 | | |
|---|---|---|---|---|---|---|
| | CBR[a] | CDR[b] | TFR[c] | CBR | CDR | TFR |
| Egypt | 43 | 17 | 6.1 | 35 | 15 | 5.2 |
| **Middle Eastern Countries** | | | | | | |
| Jordan | 48 | 20 | 6.8 | 48 | 16 | 7.1 |
| Syria | 48 | 18 | 7.3 | 48 | 16 | 7.6 |
| Tunisia | 49 | 21 | 7.1 | 41 | 15 | 6.5 |
| Morocco | 52 | 23 | 7.2 | 47 | 17 | 7.1 |
| Saudi Arabia | 49 | 23 | 7.2 | 48 | 18 | 7.3 |
| **Asian and Latin American Countries** | | | | | | |
| Turkey | 45 | 18 | 6.3 | 37 | 12 | 5.6 |
| South Korea | 43 | 14 | 5.6 | 30 | 10 | 4.2 |
| Brazil | 43 | 13 | 6.2 | 35 | 10 | 5.0 |
| Mexico | 46 | 12 | 6.8 | 45 | 10 | 6.6 |
| Pakistan | 49 | 24 | 7.5 | 48 | 19 | 7.1 |

a. Crude birth rate per 1,000 people.
b. Crude death rate per 1,000 people.
c. Total fertility rate.

Sources: Arab Republic of Egypt, Central Agency for Public Mobilisation and Statistics, *Statistical Yearbook*, 1984–99, various issues (Cairo); Hashemite Kingdom of Jordan, Department of Statistics, *Statistical Yearbook*, 1970–99, various issues (Amman); Syrian Arab Republic, Office of the Prime Minister, Central Bureau of Statistics, *Statistical Abstract*, 1960–98, various issues (Damascus); World Bank, *World Tables*, 1984–95, various issues

## Egypt's Family Planning Policy under Sadat and Mubarak

While Sadat's ascent to power in late 1970 did not bring about an immediate change in Egypt's socioeconomic policies, including in the demographic area, a slow and unstated shift away from the supply-oriented approach to fertility reduction occurred during the early 1970s.[20] Instead, new thinking regarding family planning programs held that they should be included in broader socioeconomic development plans, rather than concentrating on the "unmet need" of contraceptives alone. In 1973, the Supreme Council for Population and Family Planning (al-majlis al-aʿla lil-sukan wa-tanzim al-usra) announced a new national family planning program, namely, the "Socioeconomic Approach to Fertility Reduction."[21] According to the new plan, heightened demand for contraceptives would be achieved mainly through indirect measures, namely, by developing health care services that would

|  | 1980 |  |  | 1990 |  |  | 1998 |  |
|---|---|---|---|---|---|---|---|---|
| CBR | CDR | TFR | CBR | CDR | TFR | CBR | CDR | TFR |
| 38 | 10 | 5.2 | 31 | 7 | 4.3 | 28 | 7 | 3.3 |
| 47 | 11 | 7.3 | 39 | 6 | 5.8 | 35 | 5 | 4.8 |
| 46 | 8 | 7.3 | 44 | 6 | 6.5 | 30 | 5 | 4.0 |
| 35 | 10 | 5.3 | 29 | 7 | 3.7 | 20 | 7 | 2.5 |
| 44 | 12 | 6.9 | 34 | 9 | 4.5 | 26 | 7 | 3.0 |
| 46 | 14 | 7.3 | 42 | 7 | 7.1 | 34 | 4 | 5.4 |
| 32 | 10 | 4.4 | 28 | 8 | 3.5 | 22 | 6 | 2.5 |
| 24 | 7 | 3.0 | 16 | 6 | 1.7 | 15 | 6 | 1.7 |
| 30 | 9 | 4.1 | 27 | 8 | 3.3 | 20 | 7 | 2.3 |
| 37 | 7 | 5.1 | 28 | 6 | 3.3 | 24 | 5 | 2.7 |
| 44 | 24 | 6.1 | 44 | 12 | 6.2 | 36 | 8 | 5.0 |

(Baltimore); World Bank, *World Development Report*, 1978–1999/2000, various issues (New York); United Nations, *Demographic Yearbook*, 1970–99, various issues (New York); United Nations, *Population and Vital Statistics Report*, Statistical Papers, series A, vol. 51, no. 2 (New York, 1999); ECWA/ESCWA, *Demographic and Related Socio-Economic Data Sheets for Countries of the Economic and Social Commission for Western Asia*, 1978–99, various issues (Beirut, Baghdad, and Amman); ECWA/ESCWA, *Statistical Abstract of the ECWA/ESCWA Region*, 1970–2000, various issues (New York, Baghdad, and Amman); UNICEF, *The State of the World's Children*, 1984–2000, various issues (New York: Oxford University Press).

reduce the high infant and child mortality rates;[22] raising the educational level of the entire population, particularly that of women; increasing employment opportunities for women to increase their labor force participation; and enhancing agricultural mechanization in order to diminish the need for child labor. The new plan also called for improving family planning services throughout the country, particularly in rural areas, where fertility rates were much higher than in the urban centers.[23]

This change in the Egyptian family planning approach during the 1970s was in line with the concept adopted in the 1974 World Population Conference held in Bucharest: "Development is the best contraceptive."[24] In other words, economic development would naturally bring about a reduction in fertility.[25] Broadly, the shift from a direct to an indirect family planning approach under Sadat was the outcome of both political and economic considerations. Politically, Sadat preferred an indirect approach mainly because of his policy of rapprochement toward the Muslim Brothers.[26] Sadat released Brothers' leaders from jail.[27] He also made a point of paying greater tribute to Islamic traditions in his public appearances.[28] Economically, the notion of solving the problem of high fertility rates through the free play of socioeconomic factors appeared feasible, given the high growth rates achieved by the Egyptian economy during the second half of the 1970s and the early 1980s.[29]

Furthermore, the massive migration of Egyptian workers to the major Middle Eastern oil-exporting countries following the October 1973 oil boom led to a reduction in employment pressure in Egypt to some extent, as the remittances transferred by these workers created a boost in the number of new work opportunities in Egypt.[30] Another new element in Sadat's demographic policy was the establishment by the Egyptian authorities of new cities in the desert (*al-mudun al-jadida fil-sahra*).[31] The thinking that underlay this program was that a better geographic distribution of the urban population would reduce many of the negative consequences of rapid urbanization.

Ultimately, under Sadat, economic growth had again become the focus of socioeconomic policy. An explicit indication of this approach was given in 1975 by Hilmi ʿAbd al-Rahman, advisor to the prime minister: "The development of the population for the next 25 years has already been determined. . . . Our population will double in the next 25 years with only a 20 percent possibility of variation. . . . Therefore, for the next 20 or 25 years the problem in Egypt is mainly to meet the requirements of an increase in population."[32] Rapid population growth by itself was relegated to the fringe of the regime's priorities.[33] Indeed, the issue of family planning was not even mentioned in the *October Working Paper* of 1974.[34]

As in the case of Sadat, Mubarak's ascent to power, in October 1981, did not bring about an immediate change in the government's family planning policy.[35] Presumably, Mubarak was not compelled to tackle the problem of high fertility rates, in view of the ongoing economic growth that had begun in the second half of the 1970s.[36] However, the halt in economic growth in 1984–85, combined with a rate of natural increase that had reached a new peak—estimated at over 3 percent in 1985—led Mubarak to change his attitude radically regarding the demographic situation. The indirect approach to overcoming Egypt's demographic plight, he realized, was inadequate.

A National Population Council, headed by Mubarak himself, was established in January 1985,[37] and a new family planning policy was announced a year later. Although it included many elements from the previous plans, the new policy reflected change in two critical areas: The demographic development of the country was given top priority, and in recognition of the inadequacy of previous family planning perceptions, emphasis was placed on both the supply and the demand measures simultaneously.[38]

In the area of demand, the new policy aimed at changing attitudes toward reproductive behavior. Direct appeals were made to the public by Mubarak himself on various occasions, calling for the practice of birth control and emphasizing the negative consequences of rapid population growth for both the nation and the family. *Fatwas,* articles, and interviews were published by leading religious authorities, both Muslim and Coptic, emphasizing that no religious prohibitions existed regarding the use of contraceptives. Articles written by well-known journalists stressed the negative results of rapid population growth in the social and economic arenas. Caricatures illustrating the consequences of the population explosion appeared frequently in the Egyptian press.[39]

In the area of supply, the Ministerial Committee for Social Services decided in early 1987 to establish additional family planning units so that there would be one unit per 2,000 families in order to improve the quality of, and access to, medical and family planning services, particularly in rural areas.[40] By 1991, 4,115 family planning units operated throughout the country, 63.1 percent of them in rural areas.[41] By 1996, the number of units had risen to 4,733, with 62.1 percent in rural areas.[42] Following the United Nations International Conference on Population and Development (ICPD), which convened in Cairo in September 1994, another element was added to the Egyptian national family planning program: governmental support for NGOs active in the area of family planning.[43] Overall, between 1980 and 2000, the contraceptive use levels have more than doubled, from 24 percent to 56 percent.[44]

### The Contribution of the Family Planning Programs to Reduced Fertility

One of the most important questions regarding reduced fertility in developing countries worldwide, including those of the Middle East, is whether this reduction should be attributed to the various family planning programs implemented since the mid-1960s, or whether it is the outcome of prolonged processes of socioeconomic and cultural change in these societies. Such change has included the sharp decline in infant and child mortality rates; accelerated urbanization process; changes in occupational structure, particularly the increase in the rate of participation of women in the labor force; and, most important, the improvement in women's educational level. Simply put, the issue centers on whether developing countries should invest their limited resources in expensive national family planning programs or concentrate their efforts on improving the socioeconomic conditions of the population, particularly of women, in the expectation that contraceptive prevalence rates will increase without direct governmental intervention.

The latter, indirect approach views fertility as determined mainly by the desire for children; the value attached to children and family; the economic costs and benefits of children; the status of women; and other societal aspects of the family. Access to family planning services and the cost of contraception are not considered major factors in determining fertility levels.[45] The direct approach holds that well-designed family planning programs can effectively reduce unwanted childbearing, which, in turn, can contribute significantly to reducing fertility in developing countries.[46] In this view, the issues of availability and costs of contraceptives are considered crucial to facilitating fertility decline.[47]

Clearly, these two approaches—the direct and the indirect—are not mutually exclusive. The "economic growth approach" does not negate the "active family planning" attitude. Quite simply, politicians in developing countries, where societal norms rejected state intervention in the issue of reproduction, found it convenient to promote the indirect ("economic growth") approach as an adequate solution to demographic pressures. Indeed, a 1994 World Bank demographic study of the various attitudes concluded, "The answer is not 'either/or' but rather 'both' and, even better, a balance of both that is responsive to the specific needs and conditions of different countries at different levels of the demographic transition and socioeconomic development."[48]

An evaluation of the impact of Egypt's family planning policies, and particularly the results of Mubarak's efforts to bring down rates of natural increase, have become a subject of disagreement among demographic and social historians in recent years. Analyzing Mubarak's family planning policy (the "demand-oriented direct approach"), and based on data on Egypt's crude birth rate and total fertility rate, Gad Gilbar reached the conclusion in 1993 that the sharp drop in fertility rates in the late 1980s should indeed be regarded as a significant achievement of this policy. Moreover, laudably, it was attained by persuasion and not by coercion.[49]

Saad Eddin Ibrahim regarded Mubarak's family planning policy from the late 1980s onward as a success, writing in 1994 that "the results [of Egypt's population policy] of the last five years are quite impressive."[50] Mona Khalifa expressed a similar view in 1994, arguing that the decline in fertility since the mid-1980s "would not have been possible in the absence of active family planning."[51] In a similar vein as Gilbar, Steven Wisensale and Amany Khodair concluded, in a 1998 study, that Egypt's successful experience in family planning "represents one model from which other nations can learn."[52] Based on anthropological research in the area of family planning in Egypt, Kamran Ali claimed in 2002 that "family planning programs do not just reduce the number of children and regulate reproduction. Rather, they also introduce or foster notions of individual choice and responsibility."[53]

Not all scholars, however, accept this positive evaluation of Mubarak's policy and its implementation. Philippe Fargues, in contrast, wrote in 1996: "No causal relationship has ever been established between the direct action of the Egyptian state to reduce the birth rate and its actual reduction."[54] Fargues claimed that the downward trend in the birth rate beginning in 1985 was a response to two social and economic developments: increased education for women, and a deteriorating standard of living for a large proportion of the population. Explaining the impact of the economic factor, he stressed the cuts in government subsidies to health services and schools, leading to the increased cost of supporting children.[55]

The existence of a high correlation between the educational level of women and fertility rates is well known and goes back to demographic studies of the 1960s. The correlation has been demonstrated in almost all demographic and health surveys conducted in developing countries, including Egypt. The problem with Fargues's argument regarding the impact of women's educational level on fertility is that he fails to show the extent, or rate, of influence of this factor. Even according to Fargues's presentation, the educational level of women ("mean number of years at school") increased in certain years—in fact, during most of the 1970s—while the birth rate did not decrease. Rather, it increased sharply. With regard to the impact of the economic factor, an increase in the cost of raising children indeed affects a downward trend in fertility rates. Again, however, Fargues does not show to what extent this factor influenced Egyptian birth rates or fertility rates in the late 1980s and early 1990s. In summary, while social and economic developments in Egypt since Nasser's time affected fertility rates, these developments by themselves do not explain the dramatic change in crude birth rates in the late 1980s and early 1990s. The conclusion to be drawn is that Mubarak's family planning policy (1985 onward) played a central role in the process of fertility decline in Egypt.

Viewed more broadly, data from other Arab countries confirm the existence of a high correlation between declining fertility and governmental family planning programs. Moreover, a high correlation is discernible between the extent of family planning efforts and the rate of fertility decline: the more intensive the governmental efforts and the more organized and broad-based the family planning program, the greater the rate of fertility decline. This was also the conclusion of several scholars. Alan Richards and John Waterbury wrote that "family planning programs have an independent impact on fertility."[56] Valentine M. Moghadam stated that "state policy, including population or family planning policies, affect women's productive and reproductive choices."[57] Abdel R. Omran and Farzaneh Roudi claimed that the fertility decline in Egypt, Turkey, and Iran in recent decades came as a result not only of increases in the educational level of women but also of the availability of family planning services.[58]

If, as Fargues argues, the major reason for declining fertility in Egypt was changing socioeconomic conditions, then arguably the process of fertility reduction should have begun earlier in Iraq, Syria, and Jordan, which had a better record in both women's educational level and infant and child mortality rates than Egypt, Morocco, or even Tunisia during the 1970s and the early 1980s.[59] Conversely, throughout the second half of the twentieth century, female enrollment ratio in the tertiary educational level (higher education) in Egypt was higher than in any other Arab country except Kuwait.[60] Hence, according to Fargues's perception, the fertility rates in Egypt should have been considerably lower than in Tunisia and Morocco. However, this was not the case (see table 12.2). Another comparison may be made in this context with the capital-rich Arabian Gulf oil states, which achieved the highest per capita income and the lowest infant and child mortality rates all over the Middle East, along with a significant improvement in women's educational levels, particularly during the 1980s and 1990s. Fertility rates there, however, remained high. This can only be explained by the pronatalist policies implemented by the governments of these countries, which in the case of Saudi Arabia included the prohibition of distributing and use of contraceptives.[61]

### Egypt and Tunisia: Different Approaches, Different Results

The evaluation of Egyptian family planning policies may benefit from a comparison with other Arab countries. Space limitations compel us to concentrate on one country—Tunisia—for three reasons: First, Tunisia was the only Arab country, besides Egypt, to adopt an official family planning policy as early as the mid-1960s. Second, the two countries shared several significant socioeconomic characteristics in the early 1960s, for example, percentage of urban population within total population, female illiteracy rate, and standard of living (see table 12.3). Third, Tunisia's fertility rate was much higher than that of Egypt in the early 1960s, yet by the end of the twentieth century, Tunisia's total fertility rate was much lower than that of Egypt, a difference that makes the comparison striking.

During the late 1950s and early 1960s, in line with the prevailing socioeconomic approach of international institutions, the Tunisian authorities, as

Table 12.3. Selected Socioeconomic Data for Egypt and Tunisia, 1960 and 1998

| Socioeconomic Characteristics | 1960 | | 1998 | |
| --- | --- | --- | --- | --- |
| | Egypt | Tunisia | Egypt | Tunisia |
| GNP per capita (US$ market prices) | 179[a] | 215[a] | 1,290 | 2,050 |
| Percentage of manufacturing/GDP | 20 | 9[a] | 26 | 18 |
| Urban population (% of total population) | 38 | 36 | 45 | 64 |
| Life expectancy (years) | 46 | 51 | 67 | 70 |
| Infant mortality rate (per 1,000 live births) | 128 | 159 | 51 | 28 |
| Population per physician | 2,550 | 10,030 | 495[d] | 1,429[e] |
| Female illiteracy rate, age fifteen and over (%) | 80[b] | 83[b] | 62[c] | 47[c] |
| Female students per 100,000 people | 246[a] | 45[a] | 1,472[c] | 1,110[c] |
| Female labor force (% of workforce) | 7 | 6 | 23 | 24 |

a. Relates to 1965
b. Relates to 1970
c. Relates to 1995
d. Relates to 1996
e. Relates to 1997

Sources: World Bank, *World Tables*, 3d ed., vols. 1 and 2 (Baltimore: Johns Hopkins University Press, 1984); World Bank, *World Development Report—1999/2000* (New York: Oxford University Press, 2000); UNICEF, *The State of the World's Children*, various issues (New York: Oxford University Press); United Nations, *Statistical Yearbook—1967* (New York, 1968); United Nations, *Demographic Yearbook—1998* (New York, 2000); United Nations, *The World's Women, 1995: Trend and Statistics* (New York, 1995); UNESCO, *Statistical Yearbook*, various issues (Paris); World Health Organization, *WHO Estimate of Health Personnel* (http://www-nt.who.int).

the Egyptians, became convinced that rapid economic development would bring about a spontaneous fertility reduction. When the opposite occurred, and its crude birth rate peaked at 46.2 in 1964, the Tunisian authorities began advocating a national family planning policy. Tunisia thus became the first Arab country to officially adopt a family planning policy on a pilot basis in 1964. Two years later, the government began to implement this policy nationwide on a permanent basis.[62]

The direct measures of the Tunisian program included the provision of family planning information and services within the existing network of the mother-and-child health care clinics. In 1973, a National Office of Family Planning and Population was established as a semiautonomous agency of the Ministry of Health. Since then, there has been a continuous expansion of the program. According to the Tunisian Maternal and Child Health Survey, the percentage of women ever married (ages 15–59) between November 1994 and January 1995 who ever used contraception was 77.3 percent,[63] increasing from 13.5 percent in 1976.[64] Data for 1994 showed that three out of five married women used contraceptives. This represented the highest contraceptive prevalence rate in Arab countries.[65]

From its inception, the Tunisian family planning effort was accompanied by promoting the status of women.[66] The first step in this direction was the abolishment of polygamy in 1956 within the framework of the new Code of Personal Status (*al-majalla*), which also abrogated the family law of the Shariʻa. This was followed, in 1964, by revising the legal age for marriage from fifteen to seventeen for females and from eighteen to twenty for males.[67] Of great importance was the government's decision concerning the availability of abortion. In September 1973, a previous law that permitted abortion at government health facilities for mothers with five children was liberalized to apply to mothers with two children.[68] This was followed, in 1988, by reduced financial allowances to families, as an incentive for small families. Family allowances were limited to the first three children instead of the first four children as stipulated in the regulations dating back to 1960. Maternity leave of two months at full pay followed by four months at half pay was also limited to the first three offspring only.[69]

Based on current forecasts, Tunisia is expected to reach the replacement-level fertility of 2.1 children per woman in the early 2000s,[70] while in Egypt this rate will probably remain around 3.0. Viewed retrospectively, the difference in the fertility decline between the two countries is striking, especially since Tunisia's total fertility rate in 1960 was much higher than that of Egypt: 7.1 and 6.1, respectively. A series of factors may explain the difference between Egypt's and Tunisia's demographic positions at the end of the twentieth century:

1. *The low priority given by the Egyptian government to family planning before 1985*, as against the high priority given to fertility reduction in Tunisia. From the mid-1960s onward, the program was given considerable attention in Tunisia's development plans.[71]
2. *The "soft approach" of Egypt's family planning programs until the mid-1980s.* This approach was part of a broader phenomenon that Gunner Myrdal called "the soft state."[72] Instead of taking advantage of his enormous popularity and the support of the masses, particularly during the period between the Suez War and the June 1967 War, to implement socioeconomic changes crucial to Egypt's future development, Nasser chose the "soft" approach, namely, gaining wide public support for his socioeconomic moves without imposing any economic demands. The high rates of economic growth achieved by Egypt during the early 1960s were the outcome of capital import rather than domestic savings,[73] and once capital imports declined, economic growth rates decreased accordingly. By 1965,

when Egypt's debt burden had grown so heavy that international banks were no longer prepared to provide new loans, the Second Five-Year Plan, for the period of 1965–70, never took off.[74] Egypt continued to be a "soft state" under Sadat as well, with rapid economic growth in the second half of the 1970s and the early 1980s resulting primarily from rental sources, mainly foreign aid, revenues from the Suez Canal, oil exports, and workers' remittances, rather than from increased output in the main production sectors. A major characteristic of the "soft approach" in the concept of family planning was the avoidance by the authorities of taking the appropriate steps against those who violated laws that discouraged high fertility. Although violations of state regulations concerning the minimum age at marriage for girls and the prohibition against child labor declined, they were present still in the 1990s, mainly in rural areas. One result of early marriage is high fertility levels at earlier ages. According to the *1995—Egypt Demographic and Health Survey*, the age-specific fertility rate for the 15–19 age group (per 1,000 women) in rural districts was 80,[75] declining to 65, according to the *2000—Egypt Demographic and Health Survey*. In the rural areas of Upper Egypt, the age-specific fertility rate for the 15–19 age group (per 1,000 women) remained high at 77 in 2000.[76] In the area of child labor, according to World Bank figures, 18.3 percent of all Egyptian children in the 10–14 age group were working in 1980, and an estimated 10.8 percent in this age group still worked in 1996.[77]

3. *Islamic opposition.* The unwillingness to confront the Muslim Brothers' opposition to family planning led both Nasser and Sadat to tackle the demographic problem mainly through indirect measures. Notably, the inclination of these two leaders to avoid confrontation with the Muslim Brothers on family planning issues was not unique to Egypt; it was prevalent in other Arab countries as well.[78] In Tunisia, however, the Islamic opposition never constituted a real threat to the stability of the regime. Hence the Tunisian authorities, under the leadership of Habib Bourguiba, were able to adopt a comprehensive family planning program, under the assumption that attacks by Islamic militants would not be effective. In this they were correct. Muslim Brothers' opposition to the Tunisian antinatal policy did not gain wide public support.[79] This was clearly illustrated from the 1983 fertility survey conducted in Tunisia by Roderic Beaujot and Mongi Bchir in which "only a few of our survey respondents, usually men, expressed religious opposition in response to questions on the family planning program or on contra-

ceptive experience." They noted that "there is no organized opposition among the public [to the governmental family planning program]."[80]
4. *The position of women in society.* Women's personal status, economic independence, educational level, and access to abortion are significant factors in determining fertility levels. Significantly, the improvement in the position of women in Tunisia since the 1960s in terms of all four of the above-mentioned variables has been markedly greater than in Egypt, namely, in higher enrollment rates in education, higher participation rates in the labor force,[81] greater accessibility to legal abortion, and other measures of personal status.
5. *Positive and negative financial incentives.* These are important factors in a couple's decision concerning desired number of children. The Egyptian government made only limited use of these tools. By contrast, the Tunisian authorities were more daring in this respect. Their antinatal policy included several components that were either totally absent in Egypt's demographic policy (e.g., differential transfer payments in line with number of children) or only loosely implemented (e.g., the prohibition of child labor).

### Conclusions: Egypt's Demographic Challenge

Almost all the Arab countries have experienced fertility decline during the past two decades, many of them without adopting family planning policies. However, fertility fell more rapidly in those countries that implemented a national family planning program. Indeed, the more comprehensive the program, the faster fertility declined. A comparison of the Egyptian and the Tunisian family planning policies supports this conclusion. The fact that a comprehensive family planning policy was not implemented under Nasser and Sadat, despite their awareness of both the short- and long-term consequences of rapid population growth, contributed to Egypt's rapid population growth of over threefold during the second half of the twentieth century.

Moreover, due to the prolonged high rates of natural increase, according to the 1996 census, 83.4 percent of Egypt's total population was under the age of 45.[82] This means that the vast majority of Egyptians are either currently in their reproductive period or about to enter it. Such a wide-based age pyramid has had two major impacts on the demographic profile of Egyptian society. First, despite a decline in fertility, in absolute terms the country's population growth in the late 1990s was similar to that which prevailed in the mid-1980s—approximately 1.3 million annually.[83] Second, it appears that Egypt's population will continue to grow rapidly in the coming decades. According to the 2000 edition of the United Nations *World Population Prospects* (medium-level projection), Egypt's population will reach 94.8 million by the year 2025 and 113.8 million by the year 2050,[84] an increase of almost 70 percent from its size in 2000. Only a more extensive and comprehensive antinatal policy can slow down Egypt's ongoing population growth.

## Notes

1. United Nations, Department of Economic and Social Affairs, *World Population Prospects: The 2000 Revision* (New York, 2001), 24, table 1. (http://www.un.org/esa/population/wpp2000at.pdf).

2. The section dealing with Nasser's family planning policy relies heavily on Gad G. Gilbar, "Ägypten auf dem Wege von Laisser Faire zur 'Soft Revolution,'" *Orient* 31, no. 1 (1990): 97–109. Also on the translation of this article in Shimon Shamir, ed., *Egypt: From Monarchy to Republic* (Boulder: Westview Press, 1995), 67–71; and Gad G. Gilbar, *Population Dilemmas in the Middle East* (London: Frank Cass, 1997), 81–86.

3. Cited in Saad M. Gadalla, *Is There Hope? Fertility and Family Planning in a Rural Egyptian Community* (Cairo: American University in Cairo Press, 1978), 212.

4. J. Mayone Stycos, Hussein Abdel Aziz Sayed, Roger Avery, and Samuel Fridman, *Community Development and Family Planning: An Egyptian Experiment* (Boulder: Westview Press, 1988), 14.

5. Khalid Ikram, *Egypt: Economic Management in a Period of Transition* (Baltimore: Johns Hopkins University Press, 1980), 110.

6. Cited in Gadalla, *Is There Hope?* 212.

7. Hussein Abdel-Aziz Sayed, "The Population Family Planning Program in Egypt: Structure and Performance," *Population Studies* (Dirasat Sukaniyya) 11, no. 70 (July–September 1984): 6–8.

8. John W. Thomas and Merilee S. Grindle, "Political Leadership and Policy Characteristics in Population Policy Reform," in Jason L. Finkle and C. Alison McIntosh, eds., *The New Politics of Population,* a supplement to vol. 20 of the *Population and Development Review* (New York: Population Council, 1994), 57.

9. *Al-Ahram* (Cairo), May 22, 1962.

10. Charles F. Gallagher, "Population and Development in Egypt, Part I: Birth and Death on the Nile," *American University Field Stuff Report,* no. 31 (1981): 10.

11. Steven K. Wisensale and Amany A. Khodair, "The Two-Child Family: The Egyptian Model of Family Planning," *Journal of Comparative Family Studies* 29, no. 3 (autumn 1998): 505.

12. Ikram, *Egypt,* 110.

13. Sayed, "The Population Family Planning Program in Egypt," 9–12.

14. *Al-Ahram,* August 6, 1966.

15. For comparison with other developing countries worldwide, see World Bank, *World Tables,* 3d ed., vol. 2, *Social Data from the Data Files of the World Bank* (Baltimore: Johns Hopkins University Press, 1984).

16. See Wisensale and Khodair, "The Two-Child Family," 505.

17. Saad Eddin Ibrahim, "State, Women, and Civil Society: An Evaluation of Egypt's Population Policy," in Carla Makhlouf Obermeyer, ed., *Family, Gender, and Population in the Middle East* (Cairo: American University in Cairo Press, 1995), 60.

18. Supreme Council for Population and Family Planning, "National Strategy Framework of Population, Human Resource Development, and the Family Planning Program," *Population Studies* 8, no. 56 (January–March 1981): 35.

19. Gadalla, *Is There Hope?* 215–19; Mahasen Mostafa Hassanin, Amany Mousa Mohamed, and Galaa Helmy Selem, "Estimating Family Planning Target Population of Egypt in 1997," in *CDC 24th Annual Seminar on Population Issues and the Challenges of the Twenty-first Century in the Middle East, Africa, and Asia*, Research Monograph Series, no. 24 (Cairo: Cairo Demographic Center, 1995), 441.

20. The discussion of Sadat's and Mubarak's family planning policies relies on Gad G. Gilbar, "Population Growth and Family Planning in Egypt, 1985–92," *MECS* 16 (1992): 335–48, and Gilbar, *Population Dilemmas*, 113–36.

21. See Allen C. Kelley, Atef M. Khalifa, and M. Nabil El-Khorazaty, *Population and Development in Rural Egypt* (Durham, N.C.: Duke Press Policy Studies, Studies in Social and Economic Development, 1982), 40–41.

22. In 1970, the infant mortality rate in Egypt was estimated at 158 per 1,000 live births. See World Bank, *World Tables,* 1989–90 ed., 226. See also United Nations, Department of International Economic and Social Affairs, "Mortality of Children under Age Five: World Estimates and Projections, 1950–2025," *Population Studies,* no. 105 (1988).

23. Gallagher, "Population and Development in Egypt," 11.

24. World Bank, *Population and Development: Implications for the World Bank* (Washington, D.C., 1994), 51–52.

25. This concept gained support from several Western studies showing that increased income and improved standard of living are generally accompanied by reduced fertility, without the need for direct governmental intervention. See Richard Anker and Ghazi M. Farooq, "Population and Socio-Economic Development: The New Perspective," *International Labour Review* 117, no. 2 (March/April 1978): 143–55; United Nations, Department of International Economic and Social Affairs, *Demographic Transition and Socio-Economic Development* (New York, 1979); Gilbar, *Population Dilemmas,* 119.

26. Meir Hatina, *Islam in Modern Egypt: Studies in the Writings of Faraj Fuda* (Tel Aviv: Hakibutz Hameuhad, 2000), 34 (Hebrew).

27. On the relationship between Sadat and the Islamic movement, see Raymond A. Hinnebusch, *Egyptian Politics under Sadat: The Post-Populist Development of an Authoritarian-Modernizing State* (Cambridge: Cambridge University Press, 1985), 206–8.

28. Martin Kramer, "The Egyptian Religious Establishment in Crisis," in Ami Ayalon, ed., *Regime and Opposition in Egypt under Sadat* (Tel Aviv: Hakibutz Hameuhad, 1983), 94–96 (Hebrew).

29. Between 1973 and 1984, the average annual GDP growth rate was 8.5 percent, while real per capita income was almost double. See Galal A. Amin, *Egypt's*

*Economic Predicament: A Study in the Interaction of External Pressure, Political Folly, and Social Tension in Egypt, 1960–1990* (Leiden: Brill, 1995), 138. According to the World Bank figures, the per capita GNP in Egypt increased from $420 in 1974 to $540 in 1981 (in current prices). World Bank, *World Tables,* 1989–90 ed., 224–25.

30. By 1980, the number of Egyptians working abroad was estimated at over 800,000. On Egyptian labor migration during the 1970s, see Central Agency for Public Mobilisation and Statistics, *External Migration as a Demographic Phenomenon* (Cairo, September 1994); J. S. Birks, C. A. Sinclair, and J. A. Socknat, "The Demand for Egyptian Labor Abroad," in Alan Richards and Philip L. Martin, eds., *Migration, Mechanization, and Agricultural Labor Markets in Egypt* (Boulder: Westview Press and Cairo: American University in Cairo Press, 1983), 117–34; Gil Feiler, "The Number of Egyptian Workers in the Arab Oil Countries, 1974–1983: A Critical Discussion," *Occasional Papers,* Dayan Center for Middle Eastern and African Studies, Tel Aviv University, October 1986.

31. On this subject, see Onn Winckler, "The Challenge of Internal Migration in Egypt: Tendencies in Urban and Village Development, 1974–1990," M.A. thesis, University of Haifa, March 1992, 125–76 (Hebrew).

32. John Waterbury, *The Egypt of Nasser and Sadat: The Political Economy of Two Regimes* (Princeton: Princeton University Press, 1983), 44.

33. Thomas Lippman described Sadat's family planning approach as follows: "Sadat and his prime ministers hardly even gave lip service to birth control, despite all their speeches about the demands posed by the rising population. They did not hide their embarrassment at the dogged, outspoken support for family planning by the only prominent figure to make that commitment—Sadat's wife, Jihan." Thomas W. Lippman, *Egypt after Nasser: Sadat, Peace, and the Mirage of Prosperity* (New York: Paragon Press, 1989), 162.

34. Sadat presented his major concepts and policies in the *October Working Paper,* issued by the Egyptian Ministry of Information in June 1974.

35. In fact, during the first four years of his presidency, the demographic issue was almost totally ignored. See Ami Ayalon, "Demography, Politics, and Tradition in Mubarak's Egypt," in Ami Ayalon and Gad G. Gilbar, eds., *Demography and Politics in the Arab States* (Tel Aviv: Hakibutz Hameuhad, 1995), 32 (Hebrew).

36. By the fiscal year of 1982/83, the real GDP growth rate was 7.9 percent, meaning a net increase of more than 5 percent in per capita terms. In addition, the current account deficit narrowed from over $2 billion in the fiscal year of 1981/82 to around $1 billion in the fiscal year of 1983/84. Source: *MEED,* December 2, 1983, 10; August 10, 1984, 10.

37. *Al-Ahram,* January 24, 1985. See also ESCWA, *Population Situation in the ESCWA Region, 1990* (May 1992), 96.

38. Mona A. Khalifa, "Family Planning and Sustainable Development in Egypt," *CDC Series on Population and Development,* no. 5 (Cairo: Cairo Demographic Center, 1994), 4–5; Gilbar, *Population Dilemmas,* 120.

39. See interviews and fatwas issued by the Grand Mufti of Egypt, Dr. Nuhammad Sayd Tantawi in *Al-Ahram,* February 7 and October 22, 1989; April 20, 1990.

See also Arab Republic of Egypt, Ministry of Waqfs and Ministry of Information, State Information Service, Information, Education, and Communication Center, *Islam's Attitude toward Family Planning* (Cairo, 1994).

40. *Egyptian Gazette* (Cairo), February 11 and July 23, 1987.

41. *Al-Ahram al-Iqtisadi,* August 26, 1991, 47.

42. Naguib Ghita (consultant of statistics and information at the National Population Council), "A Seminar on the Preliminary Results of the 1996 Census on Population, Housing, and Establishments in the Light of the National Population Strategy," *Population Studies* 16, no. 81 (January–March 1998): 103.

43. National Population Council and Macro International, Inc. (Calverton, Md.), *Egypt Demographic and Health Survey—1995* (Cairo, September 1996), 4.

44. Arab Republic of Egypt, Ministry of Health and Population, National Population Council, and ORC Macro, *Egypt Demographic and Health Survey—2000* (Cairo, 2001), xxi.

45. See Lant H. Pritchett, "Desired Fertility and the Impact of Population Policies," *Population and Development Review* 20, no. 1 (1994): 1–55.

46. See John Bongaarts, "The Impact of Population Policies: Comment," *Population and Development Review* 20, no. 3 (1994): 616–20.

47. See Robert J. Lapham and Parker Mauldin, "Family Planning Program Effort and Birthrate Decline in Developing Countries," *International Family Planning Perspectives* 10, no. 4 (1984): 109–18; Susan H. Cochrane and David K. Guilkey, "The Effects of Fertility Intensions and Access to Services on Contraceptive Use in Tunisia," *Economic Development and Cultural Change* 43, no. 4 (1995): 779–804.

48. World Bank, *Population and Development,* 2, 6.

49. Gilbar, *Population Dilemmas,* 132–33.

50. Saad Eddin Ibrahim, "State, Women, and Civil Society," 77.

51. Khalifa, "Family Planning and Sustainable Development in Egypt," 26.

52. Wisensale and Khodair, "The Two-Child Family," 513.

53. Kamran Asdar Ali, *Planning the Family in Egypt: New Bodies, New Selves* (Austin: University of Texas Press, 2002), 1.

54. Philippe Fargues, "State Policies and the Birth Rate in Egypt: From Socialism to Liberalism," *Population and Development Review* 23, no. 1 (1997): 115.

55. Ibid., 126–27.

56. Alan Richards and John Waterbury, *A Political Economy of the Middle East,* 2d ed. (Boulder: Westview Press, 1996), 78.

57. Valentine M. Moghadam, *Modernizing Women: Gender and Social Change in the Middle East* (Boulder: Lynne Rienner, 1993), 120.

58. Abdel R. Omran and Farzaneh Roudi, "The Middle East Population Puzzle," *Population Bulletin* 48 (July 1993): 7.

59. By 1980, according to World Bank figures, the infant mortality rate was 63.4 per 1,000 live births in Syria, 58.4 in Jordan, and 78.0 in Iraq, as compared with 90.0 in Tunisia and 108.0 in Egypt. See World Bank, *World Tables,* various issues.

60. UNESCO, *Statistical Yearbook, 1965–99,* various issues, (Paris); ESCWA, *Statistical Abstract of the ESCWA Region, 1984–99,* various issues (New York).

61. On the Gulf oil countries' pronatalist policies, see Onn Winckler, "Gulf Mon-

archies as Rentier State: The Nationalization Policies of the Labor Force," in Joseph Kostiner, ed., *Middle East Monarchies: The Challenge of Modernity* (Boulder: Lynne Rienner, 2000), 242–44. In an earlier article, Fargues indeed mentioned that in the Gulf oil-exporting countries the fertility level remained high despite the sharp improvement in economic condition. "The lack of household taxes, the meeting of the costs of childhood from public funds, and keeping women at home thanks to imported female domestic staff have prevented any change in the birth rate." Philippe Fargues, "Demographic Explosion or Social Upheaval?" in Ghassan Salamé, ed., *Democracy without Democrats? The Renewal of Politics in the Muslim World* (London: I. B. Tauris, 1994), 166. However, Fargues argued, "In all Arab countries, female education is now the most important factor in differing birth rates" (167).

62. International Planned Parenthood Federation—Middle East and North Africa Region, "Family Planning and Population Policies in the Middle East and North Africa," in James Allman, ed., *Women's Status and Fertility in the Muslim World* (New York: Praeger, 1978), 42.

63. League of Arab States, Pan Arab Project for Child Development, Republic of Tunisia, Ministry of Public Health, Office National de la Famile et de la Population, *Tunisian Maternal and Child Health Survey, Summary Report* (Tunis, 1997), 20.

64. Roderic Beaujot and Mongi Bchir, *Fertility in Tunisia: Traditional and Modern Contrasts* (Washington, D.C.: Population Reference Bureau, August 1984), 33, table 4.

65. *Tunisian Maternal Child Health Survey Summary Report*, 20–27. According to United Nations data, the average contraceptive prevalence rate between 1990 and 1999 was 36 percent in Syria, 40 percent in Oman, 53 percent in Jordan, 55 percent in Egypt, 57 percent in Algeria, 59 percent in Morocco, and 60 percent in Tunisia. See UNICEF, *The State of the World's Children, 2000* (New York, 2000), 108–11, table 7.

66. See Kelley Lee, Gill Walt, Louisiana Lush, and John Cleland, *Population Policies and Programmes: Determinants and Consequences in Eight Developing Countries* (London: London School of Hygiene and Tropical Medicine and United Nations Population Fund, 1995), 41.

67. Harold D. Nelson, ed., *Tunisia: A Country Study* (Washington, D.C.: Foreign Area Studies, American University, 1979), 86.

68. International Planned Parenthood Federation, Middle East and North Africa Region, "Family Planning and Population Policies in the Middle East and North Africa," 43.

69. Ghazi Duwaji, *Economic Development in Tunisia: The Impact and Course of Government Planning* (New York: Praeger, 1967), 167–70; United Nations, Department of International Economic and Social Affairs, "World Population Policies," *Population Studies* no. 102, vol. III (New York, 1990), 159–60. See also Muhammad Faour, "Fertility Policy and Family Planning in the Arab Countries," *Studies in Family Planning* 20, no. 5 (September/October 1989): 260.

70. United Nations, *World Population Prospects: The 2000 Revision*, 34, table 3.

71. K. L. Brown, "The Campaign to Encourage Family Planning in Tunisia and Some Responses at the Village Level," *Middle Eastern Studies* 17, no. 1 (1981): 73.

72. Myrdal wrote, "When we characterize . . . countries as 'soft states' we mean that . . . national governments require extraordinarily little of their citizens." *Asian Drama: An Inquiry into the Poverty of Nations,* vol. 2 (New York: Twentieth Century Fund, 1968), 895–96. See also chapter 11 in this volume and John Waterbury, "The 'Soft State' and the Open Door: Egypt Experience with Economic Liberalization, 1974–1984," *Comparative Politics* 18, no. 1 (October 1985): 69.

73. The Aswan High Dam, the establishment of heavy industry, and other development projects were financed by imported capital and foreign aid.

74. Gad G. Gilbar, "Egypt from Laissez-Faire to 'Soft Revolution': Birthrates, Saving Patterns, and Economic Growth," in Shamir, ed., *Egypt from Monarchy to Republic,* 74.

75. *Egypt Demographic and Health Survey—1995,* 38, table 3.1.

76. *Egypt Demographic and Health Survey—2000,* 44, table 4.1.

77. World Bank, *African Development Indicators, 1998/99* (Washington, D.C., 1998), 284, table 11.2; Hayam El-Beblawi and Azza Mohamed Abedo, "Some Aspects of Child Labour in Egypt," *CDC Working Paper,* no. 41 (1999). See also the wide discussion on the scale and characteristics of child labor in Egypt in Mohamed Abdel Rahman, "Socio-Demographic Aspects of Child Labour in Egypt," in *Population and Sustainable Development,* Research Monograph Series, no. 5 (Cairo: Cairo Demographic Center, 1998), 349–68.

78. See Joseph Chamie, "Trends, Variations, and Contradictions in National Policies to Influence Fertility," in Finkle and McIntosh, eds., *The New Politics of Population,* 45; Onn Winckler, *Demographic Developments and Population Policies in Ba'thist Syria* (Brighton: Sussex Academic Press, 1999), 138.

79. Brown, "The Campaign to Encourage Family Planning in Tunisia," 82; Beaujot and Bchir, *Fertility in Tunisia,* 36–37. See also Kenneth J. Perkins, *Tunisia: Crossroads of the Islamic and European Worlds* (Boulder: Westview Press, 1986), 118.

80. Beaujot and Bchir, *Fertility in Tunisia,* 36–37.

81. Since the early 1980s, the Tunisian women have had the highest labor force participation rates among all Arab countries. See Moghadam, *Modernizing Women,* 43–53.

82. Central Agency for Public Mobilisation and Statistics, *Statistical Yearbook, 1992–1998,* 20, table 1.9.

83. Ibid., 26, table 1.13.

84. United Nations, *World Population Prospects: The 2000 Revision,* 28, table 2.

# V.

## Cultural Aspects of Nasserism

# 13

## The Nightingale and the Ra'is
'Abd al-Halim Hafiz and Nasserist Longings

Joel Gordon

### Introduction

Egyptians have taken their grief into the streets three times in the past thirty years: first for Gamal 'Abd al-Nasser ("Ra'is," September 28, 1970), then for Umm Kulthum, Star of the East ("Kawkab al-Sharq," February 3, 1975), and finally for 'Abd al-Halim Hafiz, the Dark Nightingale ("Al-'Andalib al-Asmar," March 30, 1977).[1] The age of titans having passed, it is not likely they will ever mourn so publicly again. Of the three, it is the Nightingale's passing, not that of the Ra'is or the Star of the East, that is still regularly marked. 'Abd al-Halim's persona has transcended politics, music, even stardom itself, to bridge a gap between political and artistic fame, to serve as a symbol to a generation that has grown deeply nostalgic for the lost innocence of Nasserism, an era of social-political dreams that are deeply enmeshed in his music, whether love songs or socialist-nationalist anthems, and his screen performances, whether comic or tragic, whether the fresh, sweet face of his early films or the creased, battered features of his final works.

Two decades later, the anniversary of the Nightingale's death remains a phenomenon. Tributes pour out on radio, television, and in print media, lasting virtually an entire month. The text has changed little over time. With the exception of recycled rumors (primarily concerning a "secret marriage" to actress Su'ad Husni in the early 1960s), the tone is hagiographic.[2] This is the story of a poor country boy whose talent eclipsed all others but who still needed the melodramatic lucky break, the beautiful young man who captured the affection of a nation, brought down by bilharzia, an insidious disease that devoured him as he struggled, ever the perfectionist, to perform one more time, record one more song, film one more movie. It is an Egyptian story. 'Abd al-Halim is a son of the soil, not the progeny of the cosmopolitan Hollywood on the Nile, and his ailment is rooted right in the rich, muddy waters of his native Delta.

Nostalgia for the Nasser era is not hegemonic. Thirty years since the Ra'is's passing, Nasser's legacies remain hotly contested, and those who claim to carry the torch find that the "Nasserist tradition, once official public culture, has become just another vernacular tradition competing for public memory."[3] Or traditions in the plural, for as something called "Nasserism" has been remembered and commemorated, it has been renarrated on both individual and communal levels. One resilient aspect of the Nasserist legacy is that of a forward-looking, optimistic, unified society not rent by internecine strife. Another is the recollection by the "Nasser generation," those who came of age during the Nasser years, of a golden age of the cinema and broadcast media.[4] 'Abd al-Halim Hafiz is not the only bridge between Nasserist civic culture and the arts. But he is far and away the most canonized. And whereas Nasserist politics or civics are barely commemorated officially, 'Abd al-Halim is the vehicle through which artists and intellectuals (and others) may signal their own personal commemoration of a particular era that represents to them the "good old days."[5]

'Abd al-Halim Hafiz continues to personify the archetypical Nasser-era hero. His ongoing stature as the dominant cultural icon of postwar Egypt cannot be divorced from his chronological and ideological positioning in Egyptian political or cultural history. That positioning has always been an important part of the memorialization of his life and achievements, however those in power have tried to edit or truncate his memory. Shortly after Anwar al-Sadat's ascension (October 1981), the famed nationalist anthems were banned from the radio. Husni Mubarak's censors, not without misgivings, allowed the anthems to be released on cassette; they have more recently been performed on television to bolster national pride and civic purpose.[6]

'Abd al-Halim has always been more than a recorded voice. It was on the silver screen where he sang his most popular love songs and where he fashioned a persona that, combined with the beauty and pathos of voice and face, touched the heart of a nation. Successive generations have encountered him first on television, both from frequent broadcasts of movies (in full or snippets) and recorded concert footage and, more recently, from home video screenings (all of his films and a number of concerts are available on video for rental or purchase). It is also on screen—through movies that work their way onto television and video—that a younger generation of filmmakers has utilized the Nightingale as a symbol of long-lost Nasser-era (if not Nasserist) aspirations, as an unassailable icon—which Nasser is not—by which to decry the predicaments of post-Nasserist Egypt.

## Son of the Revolution

'Abd al-Halim Hafiz was born 'Abd al-Halim 'Ali Isma'il Shibana on June 20, 1929, in the West Delta town of al-Halawat.[7] Orphaned young, he and his three siblings were raised by an uncle in Zagazig. At sixteen he followed an older brother, Isma'il, to the music academy in Cairo, where he specialized in stage music and the oboe. In music school he met Kamal al-Tawil and Muhammad al-Mugi, lifelong friends who would be among his primary collaborators in succeeding years. To make ends meet, he taught in a primary school for girls. Summers were spent with his musical cohort at the Tawil family house in Alexandria. In a scene replete with cinema clichés, 'Abd al-Halim Shibana first took the microphone to sing when the vocalist scheduled to sing Tawil's song "Liqa'" for a radio session failed to show.[8] Rechristened 'Abd al-Halim Hafiz in order to distinguish him from his brother Isma'il, who had become a successful vocalist, he soon made his first headline recording. Unfortunately, "Liqa'" was not a success.

It is hard to believe in retrospect—as hard in real life as in several of his best film roles—that the Nightingale's newfound career as a crooner foundered. The hagiography highlights his self-doubt, thoughts of bowing out, which are no doubt credible. Reading between the lines, a somewhat different character also emerges—however vindicated by posterity—of a stubborn perfectionist with a clear sense of artistic self. 'Abd al-Halim would not take the easy path by singing old standards the old way. He bombed during a ten-night run in Alexandria in August 1952; it was a week after the Free Officers' coup, but the beach crowd was obviously not ready for an artistic revolution.[9]

His career took off over the course of the following year. In November 1952 he was summoned to the headquarters of the military junta, where Nasser spoke to the importance of art in building a new society and anointed him the voice of the new era.[10] Eight months later, he performed at a concert honoring the abolition of the monarchy. There, and again a month later at the first annual Revolution Day gala, famed actor-director Yusuf Wahbi introduced 'Abd al-Halim to the nation as the new star to usher in the birth of the republic, proclaimed on June 18, 1953. Astutely conscious of his image, 'Abd al-Halim had declined an invitation to open the later show, preferring to wait until the audience grew more attentive.[11] The Nightingale never looked back. In 1955 star musician Muhammad 'Abd al-Wahhab signed him to a two-year recording contract that included the production of two films.

Three years after the Free Officers' coup, and a year before the Suez War, 'Abd al-Halim had established himself as the most prominent vocalist of his generation. His reputation as the bard of the revolution was solidified by his collaboration with the best nationalist lyricists and composers.[12] Everyone sang nationalist anthems (*wataniyyat*) in the heady first years of the revolution—Layla Murad, Shadia, Farid al-Atrash, Sabah, and the great Umm Kulthum. Leading composers and lyricists competed to capture the spirit of the times.[13] But 'Abd al-Halim's anthems were in a league of their own. By the onset of the socialist decrees, Egyptians eagerly awaited his annual collaboration with Salah Jahin (lyrics) and Kamal al-Tawil (music).[14] He continued to insist on headlining nationalist galas, not fearful of ruffling the feathers of even the powerful Umm Kulthum. The Star of the East sang at Revolution Day fêtes, but his was the awaited thematic highlight. When she tried to bump him from prime time in 1964, he refused to appear on the gala stage until Revolutionary Command Council (RCC) members interceded to restore his position.[15]

In her mannerism and fashion consciousness, the great lady evoked a sense of earthy propriety and modesty.[16] By contrast, the Nightingale personified a nation of smiles as well as tears, hand slaps, practical jokes, triumphs over social adversity and, ultimately, ever-present mortality. If the tabloids still chided—Was his recurrent illness feigned or hyped to outdo Farid al-Atrash? Which leading lady had he secretly married this time, Shadia or Su'ad?—it was a vain attempt to bring the Nightingale down from his soaring heights. Whatever acrimony might exist between artistic competitors, whatever tensions among creative collaborators, the love affair with the public remained unabated. We may never be able to touch the real 'Abd al-Halim, except perhaps by scratching between the lines of hagiography. What we have is the screen persona, so seemingly natural that we would not want to believe otherwise.

### Screen Persona

'Abd al-Halim Hafiz made sixteen films between 1955 and 1969 (for a complete listing, see the filmography). His first three films screened in 1955. In *Ayyamna al-Hilwa* (Our sweet days), for the first and only time, he played second male lead (to Omar Sharif and in tandem with another newcomer, Ahmad Ramzi).[17] The remaining films were all his, even *Al-Banat wal-Sayf* (Girls and summer, 1960), a compilation of three one-acts in which he only appeared in one segment. He completed eleven movies between 1956 and 1962. A five-year absence was broken by the appearance of *Ma'budat al-Jamahir* (People's idol, 1967), which was followed a year later by *Abi Fawq al-Shajara* (Father's up a tree). There were other planned projects, including perhaps a nonmusical role, but poor health intervened.[18]

The films are all musical romances, some lighter, some more somber, in which 'Abd al-Halim played essentially the same role: a sensitive youth struggling to achieve some combination of financial and romantic success, fame and fortune beyond his social means. Stardom, a comfortable station in life, and romantic fulfillment are all precluded either by class and connections or by his heartthrob's own aspirations to do better than the gentle, unassuming boy on the next balcony. Whether a struggling student, artist, journalist, or teacher, he lives at home (with mother and younger siblings) or shares quarters with a flatmate or two. The studio settings are never as dreary as the story line would suggest. In some cases, the family appears to be comfortably middle class: In *Banat al-Yawm* (Today's girls, 1957), he shares a flat in Ma'adi and can afford membership at the Club; in *Al-Banat wal-Sayf,* his family summers in Alexandria. Wherever he fits in a real sociological hierarchy, he is always a figure for mass identification in clear contradistinction to his sociological betters. His often marginal existence is underscored by scenes in which he borrows—or playfully swipes from a flatmate—suitable courting clothes, eats beans cooked over a kerosene primus stove, washes his clothes in a metal basin, slips out past landlords to avoid rent queries, and gets around town by bicycle.

Costars and directors have all claimed that he was a natural screen talent. Critics insist that his films broke new ground in screen musicals; rather than cutting the action or relying primarily on stage revues, his songs complemented the scenario, and he never lip-synched.[19] He wonderfully played off comic sidekicks and convincingly romanced the leading ladies of his day (for female costars, see filmography). He played loveable trickster as well as forlorn victim and often a combination of the two. Personal ambition was ever tempered by compassion, and his triumphs were always the victory of social justice and propriety over narrow-minded social conservatism and excess.

His movies are derivative of earlier films that celebrated middle- and lower-middle-class virtue.[20] They are not ideologically forthright revolutionary epics, but do nonetheless exude the optimism of early Nasserist social reformism. They draw upon prerevolutionary melodramatic tropes, but carry them a step further to meet the clarion call of the "new" postmonarchical era in which class boundaries fall to true romance.[21] In films that are less overtly socially conscious, true love is often frustrated by social conventions, parental interference, or adolescent romantic ambition.[22]

Whatever the social setting, however explicit the reformist strain, 'Abd al-Halim always represents his generation, one that "trembled with feeling, anxiety, love, and vigor, welcoming life and striving for perfection."[23] He reflects the anguish that was so often the product of romantic love, the aspiration of the new middle class. No one in Egyptian film ever exuded more powerfully the pain of rebuffed affection, the long dark night of the soul following an unkept rendezvous, an unanswered, curtly answered, or abruptly ended phone call, or a glimpse of his intended riding past in another man's car. The one early film in which he broke character, playing a somewhat hedonistic child of privilege, *Fata Ahlami* (My prince charming, 1957), was his only box office disappointment. Then there is the explosive *Abi Fawq al-Shajara,* in which he flees the chaste good girl for the arms of the dancer. Despite a somewhat conventional ending, the film might well have become transitional had it not been his final production.

The last film in which 'Abd al-Halim imprinted his classic character is his penultimate work, *Ma'budat al-Jamahir.* As if time has stood still, this film re-creates all the key symbols of his early work. The Nightingale is still the struggling artist living on the edge, getting by on extended credit from supportive neighbors, and pining for the unattainable rich girl, a beautiful stage star (Shadia, 'Abd al-Halim's leading lady in his first star performance twelve years earlier) in whose play he has a bit part. If there is one enduring screen image of 'Abd al-Halim in this film (and others), it is of him riding a bicycle, singing, through the not yet crowded streets of Cairo. The bicycle is his personal badge of honor—as a teenager he had apprenticed in a repair shop—and has been a key symbol of the people in Egyptian cinema.[24] While rich girls have cars and drivers, poor boys take public transportation and ride bikes.[25]

'Abd al-Halim is often painfully aware that not having access to a vehicle puts him at a terrible disadvantage. In *Al-Wisada al-Khaliya* (1957), he misses Lubna 'Abd al-'Aziz on their daily walk, only to see her in her fiancé's convertible. In *Hikayat Hubb,* he trudges home from a disastrous debutante gig along the Alexandria corniche until the lovely heiress (Maryam Fakhr al-Din) pulls up in her limo. He sings to her under the moon and wins her heart, but later frets that he cannot meet her out at the pyramids on his bicycle. In *Ma'budat al-Jamahir,* he takes Shadia for a spin, and in the most enduring bicycle scene he rides home from the theater, singing as he pedals through the city, enters the alley, interacts playfully with kiosk vendors and cafe denizens, and then climbs the stairs to his lonely flat. This scene contrasts sharply with Shadia's later unannounced arrival in a chauffeured limousine.

## Neo-Halim

'Abd al-Halim's films are replete with images that are ingrained in the minds of successive generations, no less than his lyrics and tunes. He is at once part of Egypt's collective memory and a living interface with the nation's collective present. Forever rescreened on television and video, his films—along with the larger canon of pre-1970s black-and-white classics—serve to remind viewers of a far more liveable environment, a nation of manners, a Cairo of wide, uncrowded, often tree-lined boulevards that you could navigate on bicycle while singing your heart out.[26] Viewers may well recall the political and military prices that the nation paid under Nasserist authoritarianism, and some surely recognize the romantic unreality of much that they see on the screen. Yet, amid the soundstages and studio sets, key scenes were in fact filmed out on the street, and present-day Cairo/Egypt cannot compare with the look of the golden oldies.

Since the mid-1970s, a younger generation of directors, many the products of Nasser's state-owned film sector, have taken their cameras into the streets to film a far more "real" society than that ever portrayed in the older corpus, producing powerful "new" films in which "yesterday's filmic conventions are no longer valid."[27] While their deliberate neorealist bent has always been in some respects a response to, if not criticism of, the film canon that preceded them, leading filmmakers also invoke a great degree of nostalgia for the Egypt that "was." Not surprisingly, the key symbol in some of their most powerful manifestations of nostalgia is 'Abd al-Halim Hafiz. In the new cinema, he becomes and remains the personification of lost innocence, shattered dreams, and a particular era that, whatever its warts, was far better than the present.

The films that I highlight below treat a number of issues, evoke a variety of moods, and speak in varying degree to matters of past and present. Each posits a dreary today in relationship to a romantic—and romanticized—yesterday. Each utilizes 'Abd al-Halim in a different fashion. In the first two films, he serves as symbolic backdrop, through music, film clips, and newsreel. The second two films are more pointed efforts to revive the spirit of his films, one an affectionate homage to a particular musical genre, the other a pointed overturning of plot and mood. Although each film establishes the link through the utilization of text, lyric, and image, all ultimately rely on the high degree of pop-cultural literacy, the "encyclopedic knowledge of Egyptian films and serials . . . and private lives and previous roles of actors and actresses" that Egyptians of all social classes and ages command.[28]

### *Sawwaq al-Autobis* (The Bus Driver) ('Atif al-Tayyib, 1983)

The story of Hasan (Nur al-Sharif), a combat veteran of the October 1973 War, *Sawwaq al-Autobis* is an archetypical "new" *infitah* film, critical of Sadat's post-Nasserist economic liberalization. In these movies, protagonists—here driver and close friends—recall the triumphal "crossing" of the Suez Canal, the expiation of 1967 now undone by economic speculation, rampant corruption, and a general lack of civic compass. In recurring scenes that provide a jarring lyrical refrain, Hasan guides his packed bus through interminable traffic, just as his conductor weaves his way from front to back, collecting fares. Incongruously, yet true-to-life, 'Abd al-Halim sings

314 | Joel Gordon

over the radio, folding recollected images of wide-open, easily navigable thoroughfares onto the harsh visual realities of a jammed bus, parasitical pickpockets, and the chaos of the streets.

The all-too-obvious choreography of life on the streets masks deeper social ills. Hasan's sisters and their husbands, engaged in speculative business ventures, have allowed his father's wood shop to fall into arrears so that they can sell it to speculators. To help pay off the debt, Hasan takes a second job as a cab driver and enlists moral and financial support from his army buddies. They save the business, but not in time to revive his father's dashed spirit. The film ends on a redemptive note: The bus driver is finally able to nab the pickpocket who eluded capture in the opening scene. What lingers, however, is the ultimate futility of the lone virtuous actor. A common thief gets pummeled in full view of passersby, but the decay of middle-class family values remains chronic.[29]

### Zawjat Rajul Muhim (Wife of an Important Man) (Muhammad Khan, 1987)

Muhammad Khan's troubling story of a young woman, who leaves university studies to marry an "important" security police officer, moves 'Abd al-Halim Hafiz from background soundtrack to the forefront of dramatic action.[30] The film opens with a nostalgic cinema flashback: A young schoolgirl runs to catch an afternoon matinee. The film is *Banat al-Yawm,* and the scene is that in which 'Abd al-Halim sits at the piano to sing "Ahwak" (I love you), his signature tune. As Magda swoons in the screened film, our heroine sits transfixed. Suddenly (as Khan's credits end) time spins forward, and a young adult Mona watches an older Nightingale sing the same song in a televised concert clip.

'Abd al-Halim will become the movie's coda and the mirror to the downward spiral of Mona's life and marriage, with her husband's increasing brutality at home and on the job, and to the parallel crisis of Egyptian being. Mona (Mervat Amin) first encounters Hisham (Ahmad Zaki) in a neighborhood shop when she runs down, midconcert, to buy a blank cassette. When Hisham later discovers his bride's obsession with the Nightingale, he chides her—an omen of their not being kindred spirits—but also plays a tape to gently wake her in the morning. As the marriage decays, Mona takes increasing refuge in her tape player. When she attempts to walk out on Hisham, he crassly tries to seduce her by invoking the Nightingale.

*Zawjat Rajul Muhim,* an important political work, openly treats the abuse of power by those with no regard for common aspirations. There is no mistaking the symbolic utilization of 'Abd al-Halim as a marker of lost innocence, common (rather than personal) aspirations, and Nasser-era ambitions to create a just, modern society. At a contentious 1977 New Year's gathering of high police officials, Mona defends the Aswan High Dam—a key symbol of Nasserism and the subject of a popular Nightingale anthem, "Hikayat Shaʿb" (The people's story). When the country erupts in violence —the January 1977 bread riots—and Hisham disappears for days, busy restoring order, Mona reaffirms Nasser's Suez promise to carry on the struggle. The symbolism is accentuated by the casting (whether deliberately or not) of Mervat Amin as Mona. She had, after all, played Amal, ʿAbd al-Halim's girlfriend in *Abi Fawq al-Shajara*, first spurned for Nadia Lutfi, then reunited for the longest and most famous series of screen kisses in Egyptian cinema. The "double level of the articulation of fame," the intersection of "star-as-self/star-as-role," linking Amal to Mona and both to ʿAbd al-Halim, makes Mona's descent into depression and her undying fantasy-love for the Nightingale all the more poignant.[31]

That fantasy ends with the Nightingale's death, which Mona learns of after observing a schoolgirl—reminiscent of her youth—running hysterically through the street, tearing at her hair. Snippets of the funeral follow, with throngs of common Egyptians accompanying the body, while the soundtrack plays another early love song, "Ana Lak ʿala Tul" (I will always be yours), then cuts to a quick view of a young woman leaping from a balcony. Hisham remains dismissive. He is fired for his handling of the disturbances; as his world crashes down around him, he ejects a cassette from the player and yanks out the tape. When, in the climactic scene, he shoots Mona's father, then turns the gun on himself, her silent screams are covered by strains of "Ahwak," the song that opened the film.

### *Ice Cream fi Glim* (Ice Cream in Gleem) (Khayri Bishara, 1992)

Khayri Bishara's hip revival of the musical, out of fashion for nearly two decades, is an ʿAbd al-Halim film updated for the MTV generation. Not a remake of any particular film, it is a general homage to the singer, star, and film genre that recalls the classic Nightingale scenario. Sayf (pop-singer ʿAmr Diab) lives in a converted Maʿadi garage, delivers videos for an unscrupulous music producer, and dreams of true love and stardom. He exercises with an old spring chest extender, bathes in a bathtub rigged with a bucket shower, and boils water for tea with an electric coil. His entire persona, from his black leather jacket to his wall posters of 1950s Hollywood icons (Marilyn Monroe, James Dean, Paul Newman) to the Elvis Presley tunes he plays on his Walkman while riding his motorcycle around Cairo invoke a transplanted Western-inspired nostalgia. Concurrently, these symbols also conjure up more culturally rooted images. Sayf, as the first Elvis-snippet reminds us, is a "poor boy." His beat-up Jawa is like an updated bicycle, in sharp contrast to the open Jeep driven by the rich kids who harass him for attracting the girls.

As in many of the ʿAbd al-Halim musicals, the mood remains light and optimistic, although tinged with sadness, and ends on a note of romantic and artistic triumph. Sayf, a recent migrant from the countryside, has been smitten on the Alexandria corniche by a chicly dressed beauty he sees fleetingly at an ice cream bar. She remains his creative muse as he struggles to get by, to keep his upwardly mobile girlfriend (she eventually rides off in a sports car with a rich older man), to express himself musically, and to maintain a positive love for homeland amid the grumblings of his outwardly mobile band buddies. The Nightingale allusions are ever-present, from plot convention to mood to the prominent photos in the video shops where Sayf makes his drops. Although Sayf cruises to Elvis, his friend Nur, a leftist poet with a *kufiya* draped over his shoulders, rides behind him listening to the Nightingale's wataniyyat. As in *Sawwaq al-Autobis,* the optimism of the Nasser-era anthems rings hollow against the gloomy vision of the streets.

Although Sayf rejects ideology, opting to follow an apolitical path, Khayri Bishara does not intend his audience to reject the leftist poet's politics and certainly not the Nasser-era anthems. Their one collaborative song, "Rasif Nimra Khamsa" (Platform #5), despite its comical performance—Sayf plays a cripple while the band members feign blindness—is a good number, reminiscent of the underground political collaborations of Shaykh Imam and Ahmad Fu'ad Nagm. Sayf and Nur quarrel over romantic jealousies, yet Nur always comes back, and Sayf sticks up for him against his manager. Nur is there on the sidelines when Sayf wins true love and finally scores commercial success. That success takes place on the same Alexandria beach where Sayf first found artistic inspiration and, more importantly, where ʿAbd al-Halim found his voice and where his screen persona repeatedly suffered romantic anguish and found true love.

### *Lay ya Banafsij* (Violets Are Blue) (Radwan al-Kashif, 1993)

If Khayri Bishara paid doting homage to the ʿAbd al-Halim film as genre, Radwan al-Kashif's directorial debut took a more hard-boiled approach, cynically reworking *Ayyamna al-Hilwa,* one of the Nightingale's debut films, in order to underscore the contrast between a sweet past and a sour present.[32] In the earlier film, ʿAbd al-Halim, Omar Sharif, and Ahmad Ramzi play struggling students who share a flat, as well as a romantic interest in Hoda (Fatin Hamama), who rooms below. The competition, initially good-natured, turns serious. Hoda's engagement to Omar precipitates a split, until her life-threatening illness draws the friends back together in a desperate effort to raise money for her operation: Ramzi takes a beating in the boxing ring, and 'Abd al-Halim returns to his village to wed a cousin whom he does not love. The operation is a success, but Hoda, despairing of a projected future as an invalid, disobeys her doctor's orders to remain in bed, then falls dead as the three friends, unaware of the severity of her condition, walk off arm in arm.

Kashif's version turns the story on its head. His trio lives not in a respectable student flat but in a one-room hovel on an unpaved back alleyway in a slum on the edge of Cairo. They share the meager profits of a *kushari* (rice-pasta-lentils) cart, a double bed, and the goodwill of a close-knit community. Unfortunately, they also share affections for the beautiful but opportunistic Nadia (Lucy). Rather than fall for Ahmad (Faruq al-Fishawi), who most approximates Omar Sharif in the original, she weds 'Abbas (Nagah al-Mugi), a crass reworking of the muscle-bound Ramzi character, who commandeers the flat and, at Nadia's prodding, siphons off the business. The strained friendship is not helped by her sexual overtures to Ahmad, unthinkable in the earlier version. When 'Abbas attempts to steal the cart, his friends expel him from the flat.

Allusions to *Ayyamna al-Hilwa* are not veiled. On the two occasions when Ahmad visits a friend in the projection room of a local theater, an 'Abd al-Halim film is being screened. The second time the film is *Ayyamna;* a brief snippet shows the jealous rivals reconciled.[33] Sa'id (played by the diminutive Ashraf 'Abd al-Baqi) incorporates the 'Abd al-Halim persona. He suffers most from unrequited love and the loss of brotherly camaraderie, and in one scene he roams along the Nile corniche as an 'Abd al-Halim tune plays in the background. Later, after he and Ahmad have fallen out over sexual jealousy for another local girl, Ahmad torches the food cart and abandons the neighborhood. In a moving scene near the end, Sa'id and 'Id, the blind conscience of the neighborhood, visit 'Abd al-Halim's grave. They lean a picture of the Nightingale against the tombstone and seat themselves before it. 'Id beseeches God to "open the gates of opportunity as you did for 'Abd al-Halim Hafiz." The atmosphere in the tomb is blessed, as "the beautiful sounds of his songs swirl around us . . . magical, like something sweet."

In the background, a young man sits reverentially, clutching a tape player to his chest. Two young women stand off to the other side, swaying in silent grief. As in the original film, death serves to reunite the three friends. This time it is not the tragic mortality of the beloved but rather the intrusion of ultimate social corruption. Sa'id finds 'Abbas mopping floors at the neighborhood café after Nadia has dumped him, and he brings him home. Ahmad returns carrying his dying brother, who was lured from the neighborhood by illicit profit and who has now been wounded in a business-related shoot-out.

*Lay ya Banafsij* is a difficult film to categorize, for it is at once reverential and deconstructive. In its deconstruction of the mid-1950s melodrama—and by implication an entire genre—it reflects the cynicism, prevalent in an entire corpus of remakes produced since the 1970s, that speaks to the shattered dreams of a cosmopolitan modernist ethos rooted in the early decades of the twentieth century. That lost world was personified by another popular singer and film star, Muhammad 'Abd al-Wahhab, who became 'Abd al-Halim's great patron. Since 1977, however, the ethos that has been increasingly recalled on film is not that exemplified by 'Abd al-Wahhab's cosmopolitan modernism but rather that of his young protégé's social revolution.

As in the screen personification of the middle-class son, 'Abd al-Wahhab aspired for more; when he attained higher social status, he wore it well. In his wide-lapelled suits and tilted *tarbush* (fez), he was as dapper as Fred Astaire. 'Abd al-Halim, on the other hand, may attain success, but he does not wear it well. Success does not spoil him; he never abandons his modest roots, his friends, or his fundamental *baladi* (native/indigenous) tastes. When he makes it—as in *Ma'budat al-Jamahir*—leaving the alley for an elegant villa, trading in his threadbare suit for silk robes and his modest repast for an elaborate buffet, he still prefers to hang out with old chums and eat from the common *ful* (bean) pot.

In this respect, the Nightingale's persona corresponds to ever-present populist images of the Ra'is. Nasser is fondly recalled by many, whether in the street or in the halls of influence, as a figure who tempered success and power with modest appetite and the common touch. That persona, so vivid in the popular memory of the Nasser generation, has been recaptured with striking impact in the recent hit film *Nasir 56* (1996), a clarion call to counter post-Nasserist efforts to officially erase the Ra'is.[34] The positioning of 'Abd al-Halim/Nasser in the films described above is clearly marked by textual and/or visual juxtaposition: the anthems, the references to Nasser-era projects, and even pictures of the two side by side (in *Lay ya Banafsij*).

### Postscript: "'Abd al-Halim Is Always with Us"

To the generation that both rules and struggles against the constraints of a state that is still too dominant, 'Abd al-Halim personifies the idealistic dreams of lost youth. No one personifies contemporary cynicism better than master comic 'Adil Imam. For over two decades, on screen and stage, Imam has been the most satirically vocal and physically comical exponent of commoner outrage. No wonder he has played the downtrodden everyman in the most successful and illuminating, cynically altered remakes of the optimistic classics of the pre-Nasserist cinema.[35] Imam's movies—especially his recent collaborations with director Sharif ʿArafa and scenarist Wahid Hamid—speak forthrightly, if always in comic mood, to the disjunctures of a society whose social revolution, for all its faults, has been systematically dismantled since the infitah.

In his most enduring work, *Al-Irhab wal-Kabab* (Terrorism and Shish Kabob, 1992), he and his collaborators took on the behemoth symbol of all that has gone wrong in Egypt, the towering bureaucratic nerve center—and nervous breakdown—of internal affairs, the Mugamaʿ.[36] The story revolves around how an average Egyptian—as he describes himself to the press at the end of the movie—inadvertently seizes the building and takes its thousands of occupants hostage. He does this after returning every working day for a full week to join the chaotic parade of fellow citizens passing from one office to the next in search of an official signature to effect what should be a simple action (in his case, the transfer of his two children to a nearby neighborhood school). He never does find the elusive Mr. Midhat—only his phone-bound secretary and eternally-at-prayer subordinate. Confronted by an insensitive, faceless bureaucracy, the Imam character loses his temper and winds up holding a security guard's Kalashnikov.

The ensuing pathos-tinged comedy bears little resemblance to anything produced by ʿAbd al-Halim. With his comically expressive face, ʿAdil Imam in no way recalls the Nightingale. Yet here, too, ʿAbd al-Halim lurks in the wings. He croons in the background when our hero tries to grab a few moments of peace at a local sandwich shop. Returning home to a sleeping flat on a Thursday night—with a weekly Friday respite upcoming—Imam turns to the Nightingale, first singing love lyrics ("Ahwak" again) while undressing (albeit noisily and increasingly irritated), then resorting to the tape player to set a romantic mood. Alas, he fails to rouse, let alone arouse, his sleeping wife. "What's with the ʿAbd al-Halim at this hour?" she complains, finally awake. "ʿAbd al-Halim is always with us in our thoughts," he protests. "Life's pressures make us forgetful, but we remember him as soon as things are not so bad."

If the Nightingale's love songs fail to spark passion, what hopes for society remain? This is where nostalgia and cynicism converge: in the playful romantic antics of a downtrodden husband, the daydreams of a depressed wife, the souring memories of combat veterans who find national triumph undone by corruption, the sexual jealousy of bosom buddies, the reverence of disconsolate youth who sit at the feet of the dead star, hoping to soak up the *baraka* of a bygone era. ʿAbd al-Halim Hafiz cannot be appreciated outside the Nasser-era context. The films I have referenced all make serious statements of social criticism directed at what has followed. ʿAtif al-Tayyib and Radwan al-Kashif target the pervasive corruption that invades the *baladi* quarter, undermining communal values. Muhammad Khan looks up the ladder at officialdom to find the same decay. Khayri Bishara, with his humor-laced contempt for the nouveau elite,[37] provides the most upbeat finale. His hero stays true to friends and class, and his ending, against the grain of contemporary social cinema, is happy. Yet by trying to re-create the conventional feel-good musicals of a bygone era, his homage, too, reminds historically conscious viewers that their "sweet days" ended so long, long ago.

### Filmography

Films of 'Abd al-Halim Hafiz (in order of release)

1955. *Lahn al-Wafa'* (Faithful tune), dir. Ibrahim 'Imara; female lead, Shadia.

1955. *Ayyamna al-Hilwa* (Our sweet days), dir. Hilmi Halim; female lead, Fatin Hamama.

1955. *Layali al-Hubb* (Nights of love), dir. Hilmi Rafla; female lead, Amal Farid.

1956. *Ayyam wa-Layali* (Days and nights), dir. Henry Baracat; female lead, Ayman.

1956. *Maw'ud Gharam* (Rendezvous of love), dir. Henry Baracat; female lead, Fatin Hamama.

1956. *Dalila*, dir. Muhammad Karim; female lead, Shadia.

1957. *Banat al-Yawm* (Today's girls), dir. Henry Baracat; female lead, Magda.

1957. *Al-Wisada al-Khaliya* (The empty pillow), dir. Salah Abu Sayf; female lead, Lubna 'Abd al-'Aziz.

1957. *Fata Ahlami* (My prince charming), dir. Hilmi Rafla; female lead, Mona Badr.

1958. *Shar'i al-Hubb* (Love Street), dir. 'Izz al-Din Zulficar; female lead, Sabah.

1959. *Hikayat Hubb* (Love story), dir. Hilmi Halim; female lead, Maryam Fakhr al-Din.

1960. *Al-Banat wal-Sayf* (Girls and summer), dir. Fatin 'Abd al-Wahhab; female lead, Zizi al-Badrawi.

1961. *Yawm min 'Umri* (A day in my life), dir. 'Atif Salim; female lead, Zubayda Tharwat.

1962. *Al-Khitaya* (The sin), dir. Hasan al-Imam; female lead, Nadia Lutfi.

1967. *Ma'budat al-Jamahir* (The people's idol), dir. Hilmi Rafla; female lead, Shadia.

1968. *Abi Fawq al-Shajara* (Father's up a tree), dir. Husayn Kamal; female lead, Nadia Lutfi.

## Other Films Cited (alphabetical)

1949. *Al-'Aysh wal-Milh* (Bread and salt), dir. Husayn Fawzi.
1954. *Bint al-Akabir* (Daughter of nobility), dir. Anwar Wagdi.
1992. *Ice Cream fi Glim* (Ice cream in Gleem), dir. Khayri Bishara.
1992. *Al-Irhab wal-Kabab* (Terrorism and shish kabob), dir. Sharif 'Arafa.
1990. *Kaburya* (Crabs), dir. Khayri Bishara.
1993. *Lay ya Banafsij* (Violets are blue), dir. Radwan al-Kashif.
1996. *Nasir 56* (Nasser 56), dir. Muhammad Fadil.
1983. *Sawwaq al-Autobis* (The bus driver), dir. 'Atif al-Tayyib.
1957. *Sijin Abu Za'bal* (The prisoner of Abu Za'bal), dir. Niyazi Mustafa.
1987. *Zawjat rajul Muhim* (Wife of an important man), dir. Muhammad Khan.

## Songs (sung by 'Abd al-Halim Hafiz unless otherwise noted)

"Ahwak" (I love you); lyrics by Husayn al-Sayyid; music by Muhammad 'Abd al-Wahhab.

"Ana lak 'ala Tul" (I will always be yours); lyrics by Ma'mun al-Shinawi; music by Muhammad 'Abd al-Wahhab.

"Bil-Ihdan" (Embrace); lyrics by Salah Jahin; music by Kamal al-Tawil.

"Hikayat Sha'b" (The people's story); lyrics by Ahmad Shafiq Kamil; music by Kamal al-Tawil.

"Lay ya Banafsij" (Why, O violet?); lyrics by Bayram al-Tunsi; music by Riyad al-Sunbati, sung by Salih 'Abd al-Hayy.

"Liqa'" (Encounter); lyrics by Salah 'Abd al-Sabur; music by Kamal al-Tawil.

"Al-Mas'uliya" (Responsibility); lyrics by Salah Jahin; music by Kamal al-Tawil.

"Rasif Nimra Khamsa" (Platform #5); lyrics by Midhat al-'Adil; music/performance by 'Amr Diab.

"Sura" (Picture); lyrics by Salah Jahin; music by Kamal al-Tawil.

"Al-Watan al-Akbar" (The greater nation); lyrics by Ahmad Shafiq Kamil; music by Muhammad 'Abd al-Wahhab.

## Notes

1. For the origin of the nickname "Nightingale," see Majdi al-'Imrusi, *A'azz al-Nass* (Cairo: 'Adil al-Balak, 1994), 105.

2. The list of popular books about 'Abd al-Halim is ever-growing. Only the most helpful are cited in this essay. The most visible tell-all text is Munir 'Amr, *Al-Nisa' fi Hayat 'Abd al-Halim Hafiz* (Cairo: Madbuli al-Saghir, 1995).

3. Joel Gordon, "Secular and Religious Memory in Egypt: Recalling Nasserist Civics," *Muslim World* 87, no. 2 (April 1997): 107.

4. Joel Gordon, "*Nasser 56*/Cairo 96: Reimaging Lost Community," in Walter Ambrust, ed., *Mass Mediations: New Approaches to Popular Culture in the Middle East and Beyond* (Berkeley: University of California Press, 2000), 161–81.

5. Gabriel Rosenbaum's contribution to this volume raises similar comparisons and makes a nice companion piece to this essay.

6. When Arab leaders gathered in Egypt to assess the election of Israeli prime minister Benjamin Netanyahu in 1996, the theme song for official radio and television coverage was the 1958 anthem of Egyptian-Syrian unity, "Al-Watan al-Akbar" (The greater nation). Egyptian television broadcast footage of gala performances of Egyptian singers, with 'Abd al-Halim as the featured lead, singing under Muhammad 'Abd al-Wahhab's stiff baton. For the rerelease of 'Abd al-Halim's anthems, see Wa'il Qandil, "Aghani al-Thawra fi Mabahith Amn al-Dawla," *Al-'Arabi* (Cairo), July 24, 1995.

7. For 'Abd al-Halim's biography, see 'Adil Hasanayn, *Ayyamna al-Hilwa: 'Abd al-Halim Hafiz* (Cairo: Amadu, 1995); and 'Imrusi, *A'azz al-Nass*.

8. He was urged forward by Tawil, who had long tried to convince 'Abd al-Halim to focus on vocals; see 'Imrusi, *A'azz al-Nass*, 65.

9. 'Imrusi, *A'azz al-Nass*, 54–64.

10. 'Abd al-Halim Hafiz, *Hayati* (Cairo: Ruz al-Yusuf, 1977), 147–48.

11. 'Imrusi, *A'azz al-Nass*, 73; Hasanayn, *Ayyamna al-Hilwa*, 31.

12. Ibid., 93–127.

13. Lyricist Ahmad Shafiq Kamil to author, 22 May 1996.

14. The most often recalled are *Bil-Ihdan, al-Mas'uliyya,* and especially *Sura*.

15. 'Imrusi, *A'azz al-Nass*, 287–88.

16. Virginia Danielson, *The Voice of Egypt: Umm Kulthum, Arabic Song, and Egyptian Society in the Twentieth Century* (Chicago: University of Chicago Press, 1997).

17. Fatin Hamama received a top billing, Sharif was second, and Ramzi was listed among the supporting players. 'Abd al-Halim received special billing as a featured player. The film, his first, is often listed second because it opened four days after *Lahn al-Wafa'* (Faithful Tune) in March 1955.

18. Kamal al-Shaykh (personal conversation with author, 23 January 1996) recalled engaging in serious discussions with 'Abd al-Halim but did not remember details of the project.

19. Kamal al-Malakh and 'Abd al-Mun'im Sa'd, *'Abd al-Halim Hafiz wal-Sinima* (Cairo: n.a., 1977), 46–47; 'Imrusi, *A'azz al-Nass*.

20. Walter Ambrust, *Mass Culture and Modernism in Egypt* (Cambridge: Cambridge University Press, 1996).

21. Joel Gordon, "Class-Crossed Lovers: Popular Film and Social Change in Nasser's New Egypt," *Quarterly Review of Film and Video* 18, no. 4 (2001): 385–96. Classic examples in the 'Abd al-Halim canon are *Layali al-Hubb, Hikayat Hubb,* and *Yawm min 'Umri*.

22. Here the classics are *Al-Wisada al-Khaliya, Al-Banat wal-Sayf,* and *Al-Khitaya*.

23. Malakh and Saʿd, *ʿAbd al-Halim Hafiz*, 47.

24. Egyptian films are replete with images of honorable, modest heroes riding bicycles. Examples include *Al-ʿAysa wal-Milh,* in which the young alley lawyer proudly owns a bike; *Bint al-Akabir,* in which phone repairman Anwar Wagdi and comic sidekick Ismaʿil Yasin ride to a house call; and *Sijin Abu Zaʾbal,* in which the good-hearted Muhsin Sirhan is framed by having drugs planted on his bicycle.

25. In ʿAbd al-Halim films, good girls also take public transportation (Fatin Hamama in *Ayyamna al-Hilwa*) or ride bikes (Magda in *Banat al-Yawm,* Nadia Lutfi in *Al-Khitaya*).

26. Egyptians commonly draw a dividing line between the films made before 1970, which were with only a few exceptions in black and white, and those which followed, when color became the dominant mode of film production.

27. Lizbeth Malkmus, "The 'New' Egyptian Cinema: Adapting Genre Conventions to a Changing Society," *Cineaste* 16 (1988): 30–33.

28. Lila Abu Lughod, "The Objects of Soap Opera: Egyptian Television and the Cultural Politics of Modernity," in Daniel Miller, ed., *Worlds Apart: Modernity through the Prism of the Local* (New York: Routledge, 1995), 204.

29. Kamal Ramzi, "*Sawwaq al-Autobis:* Injaz Jil al-Shabab fi Majal al-Sinima," *Al-Funun* (Cairo), May/June 1984, 65–67. This moral decay is represented most poignantly by Hasan's sister and brother-in-law in Port Said, black marketeers in the city that had steadfastly resisted British invasion in 1956.

30. Khan cowrote the original story for *Sawwaq al-Autobis.*

31. For the notion of star power and fame, see George Custen, *Bio/Pics: How Hollywood Constructed Public History* (New Brunswick, N.J.: Rutgers University Press, 1992), 34, 47.

32. Kashif's dedication is "To the writers of the '60s and the joy of composition," but his plot inspiration is clearly rooted a decade earlier. The title refers to a song performed by Salih ʿAbd al-Hayy.

33. The first clip is the famous slap delivered by ʿImad Hamdi in *Al-Khitaya,* and one of ʿAbd al-Halim's most famous scenes.

34. See Gordon, "*Nasser 56*/Cairo 96."

35. Ambrust, *Mass Culture,* 165–73, 206–12, 214–17.

36. Although built before the Free Officers' coup, and already a disaster by July 23, 1952, the Mugamaʿ is often taken to be symbolic of the public sector state.

37. See especially in his earlier *Kaburya.*

# 14

## Nasser and Nasserism as Perceived in Modern Egyptian Literature through Allusions to Songs

Gabriel M. Rosenbaum

### Introduction

Gamal ʿAbd al-Nasser and the period of his rule left such an impact on modern Egyptian society that it is not surprising to find allusions to both in Egyptian literature.[1] Such allusions are often made through the use of songs that are identified with Nasser and his era. Songs play an important role in modern Egyptian culture; composers and singers who are considered great are admired in all strata of society, and their lyrics are memorized by people of all ages.[2] Allusions to songs are very common in modern Egyptian literature, as well as in conversation.[3] In the early 1990s, journalist Lutfi al-Khuli told me that in his opinion many stanzas from Egyptian songs expressing certain truths and a kind of wisdom enjoy a status similar to popular proverbs. In his opinion, an allusion to such a stanza is equivalent to using a proverb, since it delivers the same kind of message.

The Nasser period generated a wave of patriotic songs praising the achievements of the July 1952 Revolution, the new regime, and Nasser himself. These songs, known as *wataniyyat,* became part of the cultural heritage. Many have remained in the Egyptian collective memory and are often used to allude to Nasser and his time. Notwithstanding their central position in modern Egyptian culture and the attention they receive from critics and scholars in Egypt and the Arab world, these songs have not enjoyed the attention they merit from Western historians of modern Egypt.[4] I hope that this study will demonstrate the role that these songs and their performers played in Nasserite Egypt and continue to play in modern Egyptian literature.

In Egypt today, many literary and nonliterary texts are written in colloquial Arabic ('Ammiyya) as opposed to standard literary Arabic (Fusha). Most songs are also written and performed in the colloquial, thus facilitating the incorporation of elements of such songs into Egyptian literature. This is especially true for modern drama, which is written mostly in colloquial Arabic.[5] The stage offers numerous possibilities for creating an allusion: The actors may sing the song, or its tune may be played under the dialogue that alludes to the song, or a recording of the original performance of the song may be played, with or without the actors joining in.

Nasser was the dominant political figure in the 1950s and 1960s; to this day, Egyptians find it difficult to talk about him with equanimity. Many still remember him with admiration or with anger and bitterness. Nasser had a magnetic personality and was an inflammatory speaker. He was the first Arab leader to speak publicly in 'Ammiyya or to purposefully insert elements of 'Ammiyya into his speeches.[6] His voice is familiar to Egyptians to this day. Volumes of his speeches were published during his lifetime, and tapes are still sold in local shops and stands. Nasser and his era often serve as the background or even the pivot on which a certain literary text is based.[7] References to both the man and the period are often made through allusions to songs and sometimes to their performers. In this chapter, I shall discuss this kind of allusion and its function in modern Egyptian literature.

### The Revolution's Singers

The most popular singers in Egypt during the second half of the twentieth century were Umm Kulthum (1898–1975), Muhammad 'Abd al-Wahhab (1901–91), and 'Abd al-Halim Hafiz (1929–77). Of the three, Umm Kulthum was regarded as the greatest, and 'Abd al-Halim was the most popular and undoubtedly the one most closely associated with the revolution.[8] 'Abd al-Wahhab also enjoyed recognition as a composer. He and Umm Kulthum were popular before the revolution, whereas 'Abd al-Halim Hafiz grew with the revolution.

Although all three performed songs in the service of the revolution, 'Abd al-Halim is the one most identified with its messages. He performed most of the popular songs of that period, making him "the voice of the revolution" and "the voice of the president."[9] Nasser called him a national treasure (*tharwa qawmiyya*), and more than twenty years after his death, he is still regarded as the most popular Egyptian singer.[10] Although young Egyptians may not be familiar with Nasserite ideology, they do know 'Abd al-Halim's songs, which convey elements of that ideology.

Two cartoons reflect the position of 'Abd al-Halim Hafiz in modern Egyptian culture. In the first, the singer is shown hovering in the sky like an angel, while Egyptian Song is depicted as a woman leaning on a crutch, symbolizing its sad state, who says to him, "Ahwak, bahlam bik, khusara" (I love you, I dream about you, it is pity).[11] These three short sentences are all allusions to "sentimental" songs that ʿAbd al-Halim made famous, and they convey the idea that the Egyptian Song was not the same without him, eleven years after his death. In the second cartoon, a father, holding an issue of *Al-Ahram* whose headline reads "History Is an Elective Subject," angrily rebukes his son: "Izayy ya wad mish fakir di sawrit min, di bitaʿit ʿAbd al-Halim, ya hmar!" (Son, why don't you remember whose revolution it is? It is of ʿAbd al-Halim, you ass!)[12]

Most of the leading writers, composers, and singers of that time took part in creating the wataniyyat, but the most dominant ones were ʿAbd al-Halim, poet Salah Jahin, and composer Kamal al-Tawil.[13] ʿAdil Hasanayn, who has devoted several books to Egyptian songs and singers, calls these three "al-thaluth al-mubdiʿ lil-wataniyyat" (the creative trinity of the wataniyyat), and the critic Sami al-Salamuni calls them "thulathi Jahin Kamal al-Tawil ʿAbd al-Halim" (the Jahin Kamal al-Tawil ʿAbd al-Halim trio).[14]

Nasser had a special relationship with the three leading singers and regularly invited them to his table for the annual celebration of the July 1952

"I love you, I dream about you, it is pity." *Al-Akhbar,* March 29, 1988.

"Son, why don't you remember whose revolution it is? It is of 'Abd al-Halim, you ass!" A tribute to 'Abd al-Halim Hafiz in Ra'uf 'Iyad, *'Alam Ra'uf 'Iyad* (Cairo: Mirit, 2000), 21.

Revolution.[15] This close relationship is mentioned in numerous books and articles published in Egypt in recent years. According to Virginia Danielson, "Friendship developed between Umm Kulthum and 'Abd al-Nasir during the 1950s, and the connection between the two figures remains strong in the collective memory to the present day. 'She was a powerful weapon for him,' people said, suggesting that he made political use of her performances." Danielson also quotes Ni'mat Ahmad Fu'ad, who said, "President 'Abd al-Nasser gained much from his association with her. He always liked her and he took the opportunity to befriend her." She describes the close personal relations between the two and points out that "Umm Kulthum supported the policies of the revolutionary government and cultivated friendships with a number of the new national leaders."[16] The singer also had a close relationship with Nasser's wife.[17]

The report about the conflict between Umm Kulthum and 'Abd al-Halim Hafiz demonstrates the power of Umm Kulthum and the influence that she had over Nasser. Umm Kulthum was furious with 'Abd al-Halim, who not only dared to criticize a new song of hers but also refused to retract his criticism and to apologize. A few days later, he found that Egyptian radio was no longer broadcasting any of his songs. One minister, a friend of 'Abd al-Halim, promised him that he would speak with the president and solve the problem, but a few days later he reported that he had failed. 'Abd al-Halim had no choice but to go to Umm Kulthum and apologize. Umm Kulthum, who had awaited that act, accepted his apology, and immediately after that 'Abd al-Halim could again be heard on Egyptian radio. When Nasser himself called and told him that the problems with Egyptian radio were over, 'Abd al-Halim then realized that Umm Kulthum had asked Nasser to ban him and later to lift the ban and call him.[18]

On October 21, 2001, I interviewed an old musician in Cairo who used to work with both Umm Kulthum and 'Abd al-Halim Hafiz. This musician told me some amazing stories about Umm Kulthum's powerful personality and the influence she had in Egypt. As an example, he told me that once he was on his way with 'Abd al-Halim to Syria, where they were planning to perform. Before the airplane took off, the doors opened and he and several of his colleagues were asked to leave the plane. It appeared that Umm Kulthum was about to give her monthly performance on Egyptian radio, and she would not consent to perform without these musicians. She was influential enough to stop the plane and take the musicians out of the orchestra of 'Abd al-Halim Hafiz, who could not protest. Another story he told me was that Umm Kulthum and 'Abd al-Halim were supposed to sing at the Officers' Club on the occasion of the Revolution Day celebration. At that time Umm Kulthum was angry at 'Abd al-Halim because he had criticized her. She declared that he must wait outside the club until she finished singing, as she did not want him present. Then she stood up and sang for more than seven hours, preventing him from performing that night.

In his book *Sirri Giddan!* Yusri al-Fakhrani shows that Nasser and 'Abd al-Halim Hafiz were particularly close. Nasser saw to it that 'Abd al-Halim, suffering from bilharzia, was sent abroad for treatment at state expense (39). 'Abd al-Halim referred to Nasser as *baba,* meaning daddy (39). According to al-Fakhrani, Nasser used to call 'Abd al-Halim, listen to him sing through the telephone, and ask for his opinion about his ideas; the singer always responded as cautiously as possible (109–10). Nasser could appreciate the influence of 'Abd al-Halim's songs because he himself would become so excited when he heard these songs that his eyes were wet with tears (110). Al-Fakhrani compares Nasser and 'Abd al-Halim Hafiz, finding similarities in their personalities and activities, particularly in the realms of politics and art: "For eighteen years Nasser practices art for the sake of politics, and 'Abd al-Halim practices politics for the sake of art!" (13).

Al-Fakhrani also compares the singer to Muhammad Hasanyn Haykal, who reflected the regime's policy in his weekly articles: "Haykal writes and 'Abd al-Halim Hafiz sings"; "Haykal builds a wall around the press and controls it, and 'Abd al-Halim builds a wall around singing and controls it" (109). In al-Fakhrani's opinion, 'Abd al-Halim's songs were equal to Nasser's speeches and Haykal's articles in their power to influence the masses (110). Al-Fakhrani compares 'Abd al-Halim and Haykal to two train rails on which Nasser rapidly rode to establish his leadership (110). Because of his activity, al-Fakhrani describes 'Abd al-Halim as "the real information ministry of Nasser" (50) and even defines him as a "political party" (45).

Umm Kulthum saw 'Abd al-Wahhab and 'Abd al-Halim as her rivals. Nasser regarded himself as a patron of all three and interfered in their private and artistic lives. For example, a story well known in Egypt is Nasser's role in creating one of the most popular Arab songs ever. Nasser decided that 'Abd al-Wahhab would compose for Umm Kulthum, and he was very persistent about it. The first result of this effort was the song "Inta 'Umri" (You are my life),[19] which became one of the most popular songs in the history of Arab culture. There is practically no Arabic-speaking adult in the Middle East who does not know this song, both lyrics and melody.

### Allusions to Songs from the Nasserite Period

In Egyptian literature, occasional references to the quality of Egyptian songs and singers can be found. Listening to songs of Umm Kulthum and 'Abd al-Halim not only is a sign of good musical taste but also proves something about the quality of the listener. For example, in the play *Crazy Sa'dun* (Sa'dun al-Magnun), by Lenin al-Ramli, when Sa'dun appears before a medical committee, it turns out that on the day he was committed he walked the streets and sang one of the songs of 'Abd al-Halim Hafiz. One of the doctors reacts, "So he has good taste."[20] In another play by the same author, when a young man asks a father for his daughter's hand, the father asks him, "Do you listen to the Lady?" meaning Umm Kulthum.[21] In the play *Ma'rakat Marid al-Edz* (The struggle of the man sick with AIDS), by Galal Muhammad, Hamida describes her meeting with a police officer at the police station: "I found the officer sitting, listening intently to the radio playing a song of Umm Kulthum. I felt I could trust him when I found out that he listens to Umm Kulthum."[22]

In an early short play by Tawfiq al-Hakim, *Al-Zammar* (The piper, 1932), Umm Kulthum is one of the characters.[23] In one scene, her fans gather to listen to her records.

In a short story by Ihsan ʿAbd al-Quddus, "Allah Allah ... ya Sitt" (God, how wonderful, lady), friends gather to listen to Umm Kulthum's weekly broadcast.[24] "Is-Sitt" (the lady) is a general reference in Egypt to either Saint Sayyida Zaynab or Umm Kulthum. Umm Kulthum has several admiring ephitets, like "Sitt il-Kull" (the best of all ladies) and "Sayyidat al-Ghina al-ʿArabi" (the lady of Arab singing). Fans at her performances used to exclaim, "Allah Allah ... ya Sitt," to express admiration.

The attitude of the older generation toward the emergence of the young ʿAbd al-Halim in the world of singing is reflected in the words of Saniyya al-Mahdi in Nagib Mahfuz's story "Al-Baqi min al-zaman saʿa" (There is one hour left). Saniyya, who is upset because her grandson is "indifferent to ʿAbd al-Wahhab and Umm Kulthum while he is enthusiastic about ʿAbd al-Halim," says about the new singers: "They are annoying, but every generation has its own interest."[25] This attitude, of course, changed rapidly.[26]

ʿAbd al-Halim is so identified with the revolution that in Mahfuz's novel *Yawm Qatl al-Zaʿim* (The day the leader was killed), he is mentioned by ʿIlwan Fawwaz Muhtashimi on the same level as Nasser: "We have lost our first leader and our first singer."[27] The same Muhtashimi, who is not happy with Anwar al-Sadat, Nasser's successor, compares Sadat not to Nasser but to ʿAbd al-Halim, as a representative of the revolution, referring to ʿAbd al-Halim's famous nickname, the "Dark Nightingale" (al-ʿAndalib al-Asmar) as opposed to "the dark crow," here a reference to the dark complexion of Sadat. The two figures are not mentioned by their names, but the allusion would immediately be identified by any Egyptian:

> la yugad shakhs yastahiqq al-ihtiram wala fiʾl yastahiqq al-thiqa wala waʿd yastahiqq al-tasdiq. dhalika al-taʾrikh al-munhadir ma bayna al-ʿandalib al-asmar wal-ghurab al-asmar.

> There is no person who deserves respect nor an action that deserves trust nor a promise that deserves credence. That history descends between the dark nightingale and the dark crow.[28]

When "Ilwan Fawwaz Muhtashimi, in the above-mentioned novel, describes the beautiful days of Nasser's period, two short sentences in colloquial Arabic are integrated into the description, which is otherwise written in Fusha. These sentences, which contradict the style of the text as well as the principles of Mahfuz, who was always against writing in the colloquial, are in fact an allusion to one of the revolution's songs, "Ihna -sh-Shaʿb" (We are the people), which was first performed by "Abd al-Halim Hafiz in July 1958, after Nasser was elected president.[29]

Ayna al-ayam al-hilwa? kanat tugad ayam hilwa la shakka fi dhalika
... wakan yugad hiwar wadihk wahamas al-dirasa wasatwat al-butula.
ihna -sh-shaʿb. ikhtarnak min ʿalb-i sh-shaʿb. wal-hubb kan baqa min
al-ward fi qirtas min al-amal.

Where are the good old days? There were, no doubt, good days ... and there were, in those days, a dialogue, a laughter, the enthusiasm of studies and the power of heroism. **We are the people. We chose you from the very heart of the people.** And love was a bouquet of flowers wrapped up in hope.[30]

Some literary works are replete with allusions to songs that become a dominant element in the text. Such are the novel *The Time of ʿAbd al-Halim Hafiz* (Zaman ʿAbd al-Halim Hafiz) and the plays *Bus Station* (Mahattit Utubis), *Crazy Saʿdun* (Saʿdun al-Magnun), and *The Problem, the Shame, and the Rescue* (al-Qadiyya wal-ʿAr wal-Khalas). Many events from the Nasser period are recalled in these texts, and there are numerous allusions to songs identified with the events mentioned in the plays.

*The Time of ʿAbd al-Halim Hafiz,* by Mahmud Qasim, is a nostalgic novel that depicts the Nasser period through the songs of ʿAbd al-Halim. This novel contains many allusions to these songs, both the patriotic and the sentimental ones. I will quote only one example here, in which the path of Egypt with Nasser from 1952 to 1967 is depicted by a joke that creates puns through allusions to five songs of ʿAbd al-Halim. Three of these are wataniyyat ("Sura," "Ya Ahlan bil-Maʿarik," and "Idrab") and two are sentimental ("Gana -l-Hawa" and "Wayl"):

saʾaltu:

— hal samiʿtum akhir nukta?

— lam antazir hatta yuʿdhan li an aqul al-nukta.

— fi al-bidaya ahassu bil-ghurur faghannu "**sura kullina kida ʿayzin sura**" waʿindama badat al-sura gamila waqafu yughannuna "**ya ahlan bil-maʿarik**" wabisurʿa gaʾat al-maʿraka, wabisurʿa ghannu "**idrab ... idrab. lagl-i -l-kubar ... lagl-i s-sighar**" wi-hoba ... gaʾa yadribu faduriba madha yafʿal? lam yakun amamahu siwa ann yaqul "**illi shabakna yikhallisna.**" lakin man shabakhum lam yukhallishum ... faqal "**il-wayl il-wayl ... ya -[Yu] mmah ... il-wayl.**"

I asked:

Have you heard the latest joke?

I did not wait until I would be permitted to tell the joke.

In the beginning they felt pride so they sang, "**Picture, we all want a picture,**" and when the picture seemed beautiful they stood up singing, "**Welcome, you wars,**" and quickly the war did come, and quickly they sang, "**Shoot, shoot, for the sake of the older ones, for the sake of the young ones.**" And all of a sudden, he who came to shoot was himself shot. What could he do? He had no choice but to say, "**The one who got us involved will rescue us.**"[31] But the one who got them involved did not rescue them, so he said, "**Woe is me, woe is me, oh Yumma.**"[32]

*The Problem, the Shame, and the Rescue* traces the history of Egypt from the June 1967 War to the October 1973 War, through the story of a young Egyptian couple.[33] Throughout the play, the appropriate atmosphere is created through allusions to songs performed by ʿAbd al-Halim Hafiz and other singers. In most cases, as is clear from the stage directions, these songs are played in the background. For example, "We listen to one of the songs of the year 1967" (74); "We see on the screen and listen to the song by Fayda Kamil: I will fight to the last drop of my blood, like my father said to my uncle" (90). On a few occasions, lyrics are integrated into the dialogue, as in the following example:

Sadiq: id-darb-i lissa mustamirr..

[*ughniyyat ʿAbd al-Halim: "khalli -s-silah sahi."*]

Sadiq: aywa.. brafu.. ʿalek.. **khalli -s-silah sahi..** iwʿa yinam ya wlad abadan.. [*yughanni ʿAbd al-Halim.*] khalli -s-silah sahi.

Sadiq: The shooting continues.

[ʿAbd al-Halim's song: "Let the Weapon Be Awake."]

Sadiq: Yes, well done. **Let the weapon be awake.** Do not let it ever fall asleep, boys. [*ʿAbd al-Halim sings.*] Let the weapon be awake. (127)

Military songs constitute part of the wataniyyat. When Egypt's wars are mentioned in plays, military songs identified with those wars may be heard in the background, helping to create a warlike atmosphere. In the play *Mahattit Utubis,* when Safiyya, Kamal, and Bilya reminisce about the Sinai War, one hears in the background the war song "Wallah Zaman ya Silahi" (It's been a long time, my weapon), performed by Umm Kulthum. This song served under Nasser as the national anthem. Its opening lines are integrated into the dialogue in such a way that lyrics (whose textual order is kept intact) alternate with lines spoken by the characters. In the printed text, the name of

Umm Kulthum appears in this scene as one of the figures, although it is clear that the song is meant to be heard from a recording, since she is not a character in the play:

Umm Kulthum: **wallah zaman ya silahi.**

Kamal: hanihzimhum..

Umm Kulthum: **ishta't-i lak fi kifahi.**

Bilya: nazlin bil-barashut..

Safiyya: yib'a kalb-i ibn-i kalb-i minhum yigi 'uddami wa-na a'ta'u hitat!

Umm Kulthum: **iz'aq wiqul ana sahi ya harb wallah zaman..**

Umm Kulthum: **By God, it has been a long time, my weapon.**

Kamal: We shall defeat them.

Umm Kulthum: **I have missed you in my struggle.**

Bilya: They are coming down with parachutes,

Safiyya: If just one of those dogs, sons of dogs, comes at me, I will tear him to bits!

Umm Kulthum: **Shout and say: "War, I am awake, so much time has passed."**[34]

The Nasser period is further evoked in this play by an allusion to 'Abd al-Halim's sentimental song "'Ala Add ish-Sho' (illi fi 'iyuni)" (According to the longing [in my eyes]) (99). Later, the song "Sura" is heard (100), and Nasser's death and funeral are hinted at by 'Abd al-Halim's 1958 song "Ya Gamal ya Habib al-Malayin" (Oh, Gamal, beloved by the millions) (104).

In *The Problem, the Shame, and the Rescue,* the change from Nasser's era to Sadat's, from defeat to victory and from despair to pride, is marked several times through allusions to "Let the Weapon Be Awake," identified with the period after the October 1973 War and performed by 'Abd al-Halim.[35]

The 1992 play *Crazy Sa'dun* is replete with allusions, mostly to songs from the Nasser period. The atmosphere of that era is re-created with the help of familiar songs, by playing recordings of them, mentioning their names, and actually performing parts of them. The following are some typical examples; the first one is heard when Sa'dun mentions the union between Egypt (the southern region) and Syria (the northern region):

Sa'dun: kanit ayamha -l-wahda mawguda ben il-iqlim ish-shimali wil-iqlim il-ganubi! (ughniyyat min il-muski lisu' il-hamidiyya ana 'arfa -s-sikka liwahdiyya).

Sa'dun: In those days there was a union between the northern region and the southern region! [*Song "From al-Muski to al-Hamidiyya Market, I know the way by myself."*] (87)

This is an allusion to a song performed by the Lebanese singer Sabah from the time of the union between Syria and Egypt. Al-Muski is a famous market in Cairo, and al-Hamidiyya is a famous market in Damascus. When Sa'dun tells Wafa that his brother Hagras went to participate in building the Aswan High Dam, he and Wafa sing the opening line of the song "Al-Sadd al-'Ali" (The high dam, also known as "Hikayit Sha'b," The story of a people), which tells the story of building the dam:

Sa'dun: wa-khuya hagras rah yishtaghal fi -s-sadd il-'ali wimshina nihtif.

Al-ithnan: 'ulna hanibni wa-adi ihna banena is-sadd il-'ali.

Sa'dun: And my brother Hagras went to work on the high dam and we walked shouting.

Both: **We said we shall build, and here we are, we did build the high dam.** (87)

In several places in the play, when wars are mentioned, 'Abd al-Halim's song "ya Ahlan bil-Ma'arik" (Welcome, battles) is integrated in various ways. In the following example, the song may either be heard on the radio or sung by the actor, or both:

Sa'dun: ir-radyu biyzi' marshat aho. [*yagri nahwa al-gihaz.*] ya ahlan bil-ma'arik ya bakht-i min yisharik.

Sa'dun: The radio is playing martial music. [*He runs toward the receiver.*] **Welcome, battles, lucky are those that take part in you.** (90)

In the second example, the song is performed by the actor alone:

Sa'dun: [*yughammid 'aynayhi wayutamtimu hamisan ka'annahu yaqra'u ta'widha.*] ya ahlan bil-ma'arik.. ya bakht-i min yisharik.

Sa'dun: [*Closes his eyes and murmurs quietly, as if mouthing an incantation.*] **Welcome, battles, lucky are those that take part in you.** (97)

And in the third example, only a recording is used:

[*nasma' bidayat ughniyyat "ya ahlan bil-ma'arik" bisawt khafid.*]

Al-sawt: ya ahlan bil-ma'arik.. ya bakht-i min yisharik.

[*We hear the beginning of the song "Welcome, battles," in a low voice.*]

The voice: Welcome, battles. Lucky are those that take part in you. (101-2)

The role of 'Abd al-Halim as Nasser's "real information ministry" can be seen, for example, in the songs "al-Mas'uliyya" (The responsibility) and "ya Ahlan bil-Ma'arik," in which the singer gives a simple explanation of the May 1962 National Charter of Nasser. Allusions to this charter are made several times in the play (51, 56–57, 129).

Allusions to the Nasser period are occasionally also made in order to illuminate issues in contemporary Egypt, by linking them with Nasserite Egypt. Such is the case of the song "Sura, Sura" (Picture, picture) in the title of a short play by Lenin al-Ramli, *Kullina 'Ayzin Sura* (We all want a picture).[36] The title is, of course, an allusion to the famous song. The background of the play is contemporary post-Nasserite Egypt. The main character is an Egyptian who is taking pictures in a poor neighborhood, to the indignation of the local inhabitants. The allusion makes the reader think simultaneously of the play's plot as well as of the song, its period, and its message.

A reference and a pun based on this song are made in a recent satirical story by 'Ali Salim, entitled "Shura Shura Shura Kullina 'Awzin Shura" (Shura, Shura, Shura, we all want Shura). Shura (close in sound to sura) is here Maglis al-Shura, the upper house of Parliament, and the story criticizes the special privileges that members of Parliament misuse.[37]

The satirical story "Ihtifaliyyat Watani Habibi" (The celebration of my beloved fatherland), by Is'ad Yunis, criticizes various aspects of behavior in Cairo. Cairo here is nicknamed "Watani Habibi" (my beloved fatherland), and the humor is largely based on allusions to the patriotic song "Il-Watan il-Akbar" (The great fatherland), performed by 'Abd al-Halim Hafiz. This song opens with the line "watani habibi il-watan il-akbar" (my beloved fatherland, the great fatherland) and praises the glories of the Arab world. Several times, while describing Cairene scenes, with both its local inhabitants and visitors from the Arab world, the author cynically refers to Cairo with the opening line of the song. For example, when describing the way in which taxi drivers treat Egyptians and then Arab tourists, she says, "innahu yahraʿ bikull al-himma lil-tarhib biʾabna **watani habibi** illi **yom wara yom amgadu bitikbar**" [and he (the taxi driver) hurries with utmost care to welcome the sons of my beloved fatherland whose glories increase day after day].[38]

## Conclusion

In 1998, I edited the Hebrew translation of the play *Saʿdun al-Magnun*. I found it necessary to add more than one hundred footnotes, mainly referring to the numerous allusions to songs mentioned in the play. Without notes, such texts would remain incomprehensible to the Israeli (as well as to the Western) reader. When rethinking Nasserism, it should thus be borne in mind that a large part of the legacy of the revolution is preserved in the Egyptian collective memory by the songs of that period. These songs also serve as a literary stock from which writers can take materials that create an intimate dialogue with the Egyptian reader. This dialogue may seem like a code to the non-Egyptian, and if we want to decipher it, we must not ignore the key to the cipher: the wataniyyat by ʿAbd al-Halim Hafiz, Umm Kulthum, Muhammad ʿAbd al-Wahhab, and other singers of their time.

### Songs Recorded by ʿAbd al-Halim Hafiz

"ʿAla Add ish-Shoʾ (illi fi ʿiyuni)" [According to the longing (in my eyes)]. Lyrics: Muhammad ʿAli Ahmad. Music: Kamal al-Tawil. EMI/Sawt al-fann, 0946 31821–2 2 (compact disc).

"Gana -l-Hawa." Lyrics: Muhammad Hamza. Music: Baligh Hamdi. EMI/Sawt al-fann, 0946 310519–2 0 (compact disc).

"Khalli -s-Silah Sahi." Lyrics: Ahmad Shafiq Kamil. Music: Kamal al-Tawil. New Sound (audiocassette).

"Hikayit Shaʿb." Lyrics: Ahmad Shafiq Kamil. Music: Kamal al-Tawil. Hafni, *ʿAbd al-Halim Hafiz*, pp. 76–78.

"Khusara Furaʾik ya Gara." Lyrics: Maʾmun al-Shinawi. Music: Baligh Hamdi. New Original (audiocassette).

"Ihna -sh-Shaʿb." Lyrics: Salah Jahin. Music: Kamal al-Tawil. Sawt al-fann, T.C. 156 (audiocassette).

"Al-Masʾuliyya." Lyrics: Salah Jahin. Music: Kamal al-Tawil. Sawt al-fann, T.C. 145 (audiocassette).

"Sura." Lyrics: Salah Jahin. Music: Kamal al-Tawil. Sawt al-fann, T.C. 146 (audiocassette).

"Il-Watan il-Akbar." Lyrics: Ahmad Shafiq Kamil. Music: Muhammad ʿAbd al-Wahhab. EMI/Sawt al-fann, 0946 310547–2 3 (compact disc).

"Il-Wayl il-Wayl." Lyrics: Salih Gawdat. Music: Muhammad ʿAbd al-Wahhab. New Original (audiocassette).
"Ya Ahlan bil-Maʿarik." Lyrics: Salah Jahin. Music: Kamal al-Tawil. Sawt al-fann, T.C. 156 (audiocassette).
"Ya Gamal ya Habib al-Malayin." Lyrics: Ismaʿil al-Habruk. Music: Kamal al-Tawil. Sawt al-fann, T.C. 156 (audiocassette).

## Notes

1. Allusion in a work of literature is defined as a reference, explicit or implicit, to another literary work or passage or to a person, place, or event. See M. H. Abrams, *A Glossary of Literary Terms*, 7th ed. (Philadelphia: Harcourt Brace College, 1999), 9–10; Karl Beckson and Arthur Ganz, *Literary Terms: A Dictionary* (New York: Farrar, Straus and Giroux, 1983), 9. An allusion, however, is not a mere reference; it "may enrich the work by association and give it depth. When using allusions, a writer tends to assume an established literary tradition, a body of common knowledge with an audience sharing that tradition, and an ability on the part of the audience to 'pick up' the reference." John A. Cuddon, *A Dictionary of Literary Terms and Literary Theory*, 4th ed., rev. Claire E. Preston (London: Blackwell, 1998), 27. "Since allusions are not explicitly identified, they imply a fund of knowledge that is shared by an author and the audience for whom the author writes. Most literary allusions are intended to be recognized by the generally educated readers of the author's time, but some are aimed at a special coterie." Abrams, *Glossary*, 10. For a detailed discussion of the literary allusion, see Ziva Ben-Porat, "The Poetics of Literary Allusion," *Journal for Descriptive Poetics and Theory of Literature* 1 (January 1976): 105–28; Ziva Ben-Porat, "Reader, Text, and Literary Allusion: Aspects in the Actualization of Literary Allusions," *Ha-Sifrut* 26 (April 1978): 1–25 (Hebrew).

2. Books and articles that deal with the musical activities and biographical details of singers who are considered great, especially Umm Kulthum, ʿAbd al-Wahhab, and ʿAbd al-Halim Hafiz, as well as anthologies of their songs, are constantly being published in Egypt and in the Arab world. The items mentioned below are only a few examples.

About Egyptian songs and Egyptian music in general, see Virginia Danielson, "The Arab Middle East," in Peter Manuel, ed., *Popular Musics of the Non-Western World: An Introductory Survey* (Oxford: Oxford University Press, 1988), 141–60, 256–59; Mustafa Fathi Ibrahim and Armand Pignol, *l'Extase et le Transistor: La Chante Égyptienne* (Cairo: Centre d'Études et de Documentation Économiques Juridiques et Sociales, 1987); Kamal al-Nagmi, *Al-Ghina al-Misri: Mutribun Wamustamiʿun* (Cairo: Dar al-Hilal, 1993); Kamal al-Nagmi, *Turath al-Ghina al-ʿArabi* (Cairo and Beirut: Dar al-Shuruq, 1993); Muhammad Qabil, *Mawsuʿat al-Ghina al-Misri fi al-Qarn al-ʿIshrin* (Egypt: al-Hay'a al-Misriyya al-ʿAmma lil-Kitab, 1999); Ali Jihad Racy, "Music in Contemporary Cairo: A Comparative Overview," *Asian Music* 13, no. 1 (1981): 4–26; Qastandi Rizq, *Al-Musiqa al-Sharqiyya wal-Ghina al-ʿArabi* (Cairo: Maktabat al-Dar al-ʿArabiyya lil-Kitab, 1993); Salwa A. El-Shawan,

"Al-Musiqa al-ʿArabiyya: A Category of Urban Music in Cairo, Egypt, 1927–1977," Ph.D. diss., Columbia University, 1980; ʿAbd al-Hamid Tawfiq Zaki, *Aʿlam al-Musiqa al-Misriyya ʿIbra 150 Sana* (Egypt: al-Hayʾa al-Misriyya al-ʿAmma lil-Kitab, 1990); ʿAbd al-Hamid Tawfiq Zaki, *Al-Tadhawwuq al-Musiqi wa-Taʾrikh al-Musiqa al-Misriyya* (Egypt: al-Hayʾa al-Misriyya al-ʿAmma lil-Kitab, 1995).

On Umm Kulthum in Western languages, see Hammadi Ben Hammed, *Oum Kalthoum* (Paris: Alif Les Éditions de la Méditeranée, 1997); Gabriele Braune, *Umm Kulthum: Ein Zeitalter der Musik in Ägypten* (Frankfurt: Peter Lang, 1994); Virginia Danielson, *The Voice of Egypt: Umm Kulthum, Arabic Song, and Egyptian Society in the Twentieth Century* (Cairo: American University in Cairo Press, 1997); Stefanie Gsell, *Umm Kulthum: Persönlichkeit und Faszination der ägyptischen Sängerin* (Berlin: Das Arabische Buch, 1998); Samir Mégally, *L'Égypte Chantée: 2—Oum Kalthoum* (Paris: Éditions Samir Mégally, 1994); Ysabel Saïah, *Oum Kalsoum: L'étoile de l'Orient* (Paris: Denoël, 1985). See also Sélim Nassib's novel *Oum* (Paris: Éditions Balland, 1994), which tells the story of Umm Kulthum and the love of poet Ahmad Rami for her. On Umm Kulthum in Arabic, see Suhayr ʿAbd al-Fattah, *Hayat Sawt Umm Kulthum* (Jidda and Cairo: Manshurat al-Khazindar); ʿAbdallah Ahmad ʿAbdallah, *Umm Kulthum* (Cairo: Markaz al-Raya lil-Nashr wal-Iʿlam, 1995); ʿAdil Hasanayn, *Sirat al-Hubb: Umm Kulthum* (Cairo: Amadu, 1999); ʿAdil Hasanayn, *Wataniyyat Umm Kulthum wa-ʿAbd al-Halim Hafiz* (Cairo: Amadu, 1999); *Hayat wa-Aghani Kawkab al-Sharq Umm Kulthum* (Beirut: Dar Maktabat al-Hayat, n.d.); Khalil al-Misri and Mahmud Kamil, eds., *Al-Nusus al-Kamila liGamiʿ Aghani Kawkab al-Sharq Umm Kulthum* (Cairo: Muhammad al-Amin, 1975); Saʿd Sami Ramadan, *Umm Kulthum: Sawt fi Taʾrikh Umma* (Lebanon: al-Sharika al-ʿAlamiyya lil-Kitab, 1997); Muhammad Rifʿat, *Mudhakkirat Kawkab al-Sharq Umm Kulthum kama Rawatha Binafsiha* (Beirut: Muʾassasat ʿIzz al-Din, 1990). On the relations between Umm Kulthum and the Free Officers, see Hanafi al-Mahallawi, *ʿAbd al-Nasir wa-Umm Kulthum: ʿAlaqa Khassa Giddan* (Cairo: Markaz al-Qada lil-Kitab wal-Nashr, 1992); Saʿid al-Shahhat, *Umm Kulthum waHukkam Misr* (Cairo: Dar al-Fursan, 2000).

On ʿAbd al-Wahhab, see Mustafa ʿAbd al-Rahman, *Al-Shiʿr fi Musiqa ʿAbd al-Wahhab* (Egypt: Akhbar al-Yawm, 1989); Nabil Salim Azzam, "Muhammad ʿAbd al-Wahhab in Modern Egyptian Music," Ph.D. diss., University of California, 1990; Ratiba al-Hafni, *Muhammad ʿAbd al-Wahhab: Hayatuhu waFannuhu* (Cairo and Beirut: Dar al-shuruq, 1991); ʿAdil Hasanayn, *ʿAbd al-Wahhab* (Cairo, n.d.); Samir Mégally, *L'Égypte Chantée: 1—Mohammed Abdel Wahhab* (Paris: Éditions Samir Mégally, 1992); ʿAdil Nashid, "Muhammad ʿAbd al-Wahhab: Fannan al-Qarn al-ʿIshrin," *Sabah al-Kher,* May 15, 2001, 39–46; Muhammad Rifʿat, *Mudhakkirat Musiqar al-Gil Muhammad ʿAbd al-Wahhab Kama Rawaha Binafsihi* (Beirut: Muʾassasat ʿIzz al-Din, 1990); Mahmud Sultan, *ʿAbd al-Wahhab: Muʿgizat al-Zaman fi al-Fann al-Musiqi wal-Ghinaʾi* (Egypt: al-Hayʾa al-Misriyya al-ʿAmma lil-Kitab, 1986). *Al-Nahr al-Khalid* (Kuwait and Cairo: Dar Suʿad al-Sabah, 1992) contains conversations between ʿAbd al-Wahhab and the playwright Saʿd al-Din Wahba, presented in a series on Egyptian television (these conversations were published in colloquial Egyptian).

On 'Abd al-Halim Hafiz, see *'Abd al-Halim Hafiz* (Cairo: Markaz al-Raya lil-Nashr wal-I'lam, 1999); Samir Mégally, *L'Égypte Chantée: 3—Abd El-Halim Hafez* (Paris: Éditions Samir Mégally, 1998); 'Adil al-Balk, *'Abd al-Halim Hafiz* (Cairo: Dar al-Ma'arif, 1993); 'Abd al-Karim 'Abd al-'Aziz al-Gawadi, *'Abd al-Halim Hafiz: Damir al-Hubb al-Mutakallim* (Beirut and Baghdad: Dar al-Kitab al-'Ilmi and Maktabat al-Iishtiraki, 1992); 'Adil Hasanayn, *'Abd al-Halim Hafiz: Aghani wa-Ash'ar* (Cairo: Amadu, 1997); 'Isam Hafni, *'Abd al-Halim Hafiz Dhalika al-Ustura* (Egypt, 1999); 'Adil Hasanayn, *Ayyamuna al-Hilwa: 'Abd al-Halim Hafiz* (Cairo: Amadu, 1995); 'Adil Hasanayn, *Wataniyyat;* 'Ali Nagi, *Sinima 'Abd al-Halim Hafiz: Bayna Sidq al-Ihsas.. wa-'Abqariyyat al-Ada!—Mishwar al-'Andalib al-Asmar ma'a al-Sinima al-Misriyya min "lahn al-Wafa" ila "Abi Fawqa al-Shagara," 1954–1969* (Tanta: Dar Nagi lil-Nashr wal-Tawzi', 1989); Muhammad Rif'at, *Mudhakkirat al-'Andalib al-Asmar 'Abd al-Halim Hafiz kama Rawaha Binafsihi* (Beirut: Mu'assasat 'Izz al-Din, 1990); al-Sayyid al-Shorbagi, *'Abd al-Halim Hafiz: Mishwar al-Magd wal-'Adhab* (Cairo: al-Dar al-'Arabiyya lil-Kitab, 2000); Majid Tarad and Rabi' Muhammad Khalifa, *'Abd al-Halim Hafiz: Hayatuhu wa-Fannuhu* (Tripoli, Lebanon: al-Mu'assasa al-Haditha lil-Kitab, 1999).

Articles about these singers constantly appear in the Egyptian press, especially on the anniversaries of their deaths. 'Abd al-Halim Hafiz receives most of the attention, with whole issues of weekly magazines replete with articles, interviews, and pictures devoted to him, his career, and his personality. See *Al-Kawakib; Akhbar al-Nugum; Sabah al-Kher; Al-Sinima wal-Nas*. Cheap editions of pocket books containing biographies and lyrics of the great singers, many of which are edited by Ahmad, are sold in stands and on the street, e.g., Muhammad 'Ali Ahmad, *'Abd al-Halim Hafiz: Hayatuhu wa-Rawa'i' Aghanihi Kamila* (Egypt: Maktabat Ragab, n.d.); Muhammad 'Ali Ahmad, *'Abd al-Wahhab: Rawa'i' Aghani 'Abd al-Wahhab al-Qadima wal-Haditha* (Cairo: Maktabat Kusta, n.d.); Muhammad 'Ali Ahmad, *Al-'Andalib al-Asmar 'Abd al-halim* (Cairo: Maktabat Kusta, n.d.); Muhammad 'Ali Ahmad, *Sayyidat al-Ghina al-'Arabi Umm Kulthum: Hayatuha wa-Aghaniha* (Cairo: Maktabat Nasir, n.d.).

A series of three programs produced in France in 1990 offers interesting testimony to the attitude of Egyptian culture (and Arab culture in general) toward Umm Kulthum, Muhammad 'Abd al-Wahhab, and Farid al-Atrash. The series, *Les grandes voix de la chanson arabe*, cites prominent Egyptian cultural figures, such as Nagib Mahfuz, as well as the man on the street. Produced by Arcadia Films, La Septe, and Institut national de l'audiovisuel. Written by Simone Bitton. Directed by Claude Guisard.

A 1996 American film about Umm Kulthum, *A Voice like Egypt*, directed by Michal Goldman, is based on Danielson's book, *The Voice of Egypt*. In addition, an Egyptian television series about Umm Kulthum has recently been released. Songs of Umm Kulthum, distributed in Egypt by Sawt al-Qahira (Sono-Cairo), and of 'Abd al-Wahhab and 'Abd al-Halim Hafiz, distributed in Egypt by Sawt al-Fann, are available on audiocassettes and compact discs.

3. See Gabriel M. Rosenbaum, "Allusions to Popular Songs in Modern Egyptian Drama," in Clive Holes, ed., *Proceedings of the Second International Conference of*

*l'Association Internationale pour la Dialectologie Arabe* (Cambridge University, 1995), 197–206.

4. There are a few exceptions. See Yoram Meital, "Revolutionizing the Past: Historical Representation during Egypt's Revolutionary Experience, 1952–1962," *Mediterranean Historical Review* 12, no. 2 (December 1997): 60–77, in which he describes the role of Egyptian songs and singers in spreading the ideas of the revolution. See also "The National Songs and Rabi'a al-'Adawiyya," in Danielson, *Voice*, 164–67.

5. See Gabriel M. Rosenbaum, "The Language of Dialogue in Modern Egyptian Drama (Mainly since 1952)," Ph.D. diss., Tel-Aviv University, 1994 (Hebrew).

6. On Nasser's speeches, see Clive Holes, "The Uses of Variation: A Study of the Political Speeches of Gamal 'Abd al-Nasir," *Perspectives on Arabic Linguistics* 5 (1993): 13–45; Nathalie Mazrani, *Aspects of Language Variation in Arabic Political Speech-Making* (Richmond, U.K.: Curzon, 1997).

7. On this kind of literature, see Mustafa Bayumi, *Burtireh: Gamal 'Abd al-Nasir fi 'Uyun al-Adab al-'Arabi* (Cairo: Dar al-Huda lil-Nashr wal-Tawzi', 1998). For allusions to Nasser in the writings of Nagib Mahfuz, see Mustafa Bayumi, *Mu'gam A'lam Nagib Mahfuz* (Cairo: Matabi' al-Ahram, 1997), 92–104. On allusions to Nasser and the revolution in Egyptian and Arab films, see Ziyad Fayid, *Al-Thawra fi al-Sinima al-Misriyya: Yulyu 1952–Uktubar 1973* (Egypt: al-Hay'a al-Misriyya al-'Amma lil-Kitab, 1999).

8. For example, Tariq al-Shinawi reports in *Ruz al-Yusuf,* no. 3283 (May 13, 1991), 3–7, that when the *Sawt al-Fann* record company released a few years earlier two cassettes of patriotic songs, one by 'Abd al-Halim Hafiz and one by 'Abd al-Wahhab, the tape by 'Abd al-Halim sold far better. See Walter Armbrust, *Mass Culture and Modernism in Egypt* (Cambridge: Cambridge University Press, 1996), 73.

9. On the reasons for preferring 'Abd al-Halim to Umm Kulthum as the leading singer of the revolution, see Yusri al-Fakhrani, *Sirri Giddan! 'Abd al-Nasir, 'Abd al-Halim* (Cairo: Matabi' al-Ahram, 1993), 37.

10. Shorbagi, *'Abd al-Halim,* 100.

11. Cartoon entitled "An evening with 'Abd al-Halim Hafiz, 1045 p.m. (first channel)," *Al-Akhbar,* March 29, 1988. Allusions are printed in boldface; on transliterating *'Ammiyya* and *Fusha,* see note 20 below.

12. Cartoon entitled "Memorial of the July Revolution," in Ra'uf 'Iyad, *'Alam Ra'uf 'Iyad* (Cairo: Mirit, 2000), 21.

13. On Salah Jahin, see Marilyn Booth, "Jahin, Salah," in Julie Scott Meisami and Paul Starkey, eds., *Encyclopedia of Arabic Literature,* vol. 1 (London: Routledge, 1998), 407–8; Marilyn Booth, "Poetry in the Vernacular," in Muhammad Mustafa Badawi, ed., *Modern Arabic Literature* (Cambridge: Cambridge University Press, 1992), 463–82, 474–76; Gabriel M. Rosenbaum, "*The Big Night*: A Popular Play in Colloquial Egyptian Arabic," *Jerusalem Studies in Arabic and Islam* 23 (1999): 228–93. For references to sources on Jahin, see ibid., 229 n. 5. On Kamal al-Tawil, see Qabil, *Mawsu'a,* 223–24.

14. Hasanayn, *Wataniyyat,* 142; Sami al-Salamuni quoted in ibid., 144, and Hasanayn, *Ayyamuna,* 102.

15. See Balk, *'Abd al-Halim*, 61.

16. Danielson, *Voice*, 166. On Umm Kulthum as a national singer, see 'Abdallah, *Umm Kulthum*, 33–34.

17. Shahhat, *Umm Kulthum*, 130.

18. Shorbagi, *'Abd al-Halim*, 91–101.

19. On this matter see Shahhat, *Umm Kulthum*, 120–21; Hafni, *'Abd al-Wahhab*, 94–95.

20. Lenin al-Ramli, *Sa'dun al-Magnun* (Kuwait and Cairo: Dar Su'ad al-Sabah, 1992), 22. The transliteration represents literary or colloquial Egyptian Arabic, depending on the text quoted. Both are written in the same Arabic characters; the differences between the two varieties are reflected in the transliteration.

21. Lenin al-Ramli, *Inta Hurr* (Egypt: Matabi' Ruz al-Yusuf, 1982), 71.

22. Galal Muhammad, "Ma'rakat Marid al-Edz," in Galal Muhammad, *Ma'rakat Marid al-Edz/ Fazlaka fi al-Mustawayat* (Cairo: Distributed by Maktabat al-Nahda al-Misriyya, 1991), 30.

23. Tawfiq al-Hakim, "Al-Zammar," in Tawfiq al-Hakim, *Al-Masrah al-Munawwa'* (Egypt: Maktabat al-Adab, 1966), 653–690. Her nickname was often spelled Thuma but was pronounced Suma in colloquial Arabic.

24. Ihsan 'Abd al-Quddus, "Allah Allah . . . ya Sitt," in Ihsan 'Abd al-Quddus, *'Ilba min Safih* (Cairo: Maktabat Misr, n.d.), 61–67.

25. Nagib Mahfuz, *Al-Baqi min al-Zaman Sa'a* (Cairo: Maktabat Misr, 1982), 58, 59.

26. The younger generation debated who was better, 'Abd al-halim Hafiz or Farid al-Atrash, the sentimental singer and musician of Druze origin. Both were popular, but the popularity of 'Abd al-Halim overshadowed (and still overshadows) any other Egyptian singer.

27. Nagib Mahfuz, *Yawm Qatl al-Za'im* (Cairo: Maktabat Misr, n.d.), 23; cf. cartoon 1 above.

28. Mahfuz, *Yawm*, 35.

29. Hasanayn, *Wataniyyat*, 74.

30. Mahfuz, *Yawm*, 23. Later, as mentioned above, a comparison is made between Nasser and 'Abd al-Halim Hafiz, without their names being mentioned.

31. This is a line from the song "Gana -l-Hawa" (Love came to us). The other allusions here are to the opening lines.

32. Mahmud Qasim, *Zaman 'Abd al-Halim Hafiz* (Saudi Arabia and Cairo: al-Dar al-Wataniyya al-Jadida lil-Nashr wal-Tawzi' and al-Markaz al-Faddi lil-Ma'lumat, 1995), 34–35.

33. 'Abd al-Mun'im Salim, *Al-Qadiyya wal-'ar wal-Khalas* (Egypt: al-Hay'a al-Misriyya al-'Amma lil-Kitab, 1977). Page numbers are cited in text.

34. Nihad Gad, *Mahattit Utubis*, in Nihad Gad, *'Adila: Mahattit Utubis* (Cairo: Maktabat Gharib, 1985), 100–101. For the full lyrics, see Misri and Kamil, *Nusus*, 390. The recorded version of this song (lyrics: Salah Jahin; music: Kamal al-Tawil) is no longer on sale in Egypt. Subsequent pages are cited in text.

35. Salim, *Qadiyya*, 127, 133, etc. See example quoted above.

36. Lenin al-Ramli, *Kullina ʿAyzin Sura*," in Ramli, *Al-Aʿmal al-Kamila*, vol. 2 (Cairo: al-Hayʾa al-Misriyya al-ʿAmma lil-Kitab, 2002).

37. ʿAli Salim, "Shura Shura Shura Kullina ʿAwzin Shura," in Salim, *Hal Ladayka Aqwal Ukhra?* (Cairo: Akhbar al-Yawm, 1999), 19–24.

38. Isʿad Yunis, "Ihtifaliyyat Watani Habibi," in Yunis, *Al-Mutasawwilun* (Cairo: Dar al-Huda lil-Nashr wal-Tawziʿ, 1995), 39.

# Selected Bibliography

## Works in European Languages

Abdel Fadil, Mahmoud. *The Political Economy of Nasserism: A Study in Employment and Income Distribution Policies in Urban Egypt, 1952–1972*. Cambridge: Cambridge University Press, 1980.

Abdel-Khalek, Gouda, and Robert Tignor, eds. *The Political Economy of Income Distribution in Egypt*. New York: Holmes and Meier, 1982.

Abdel-Malek, Anouar. *Egypt Military Society: The Army Regime, the Left, and Social Change under Nasser*. Translated by Charles Lam Markmann. New York: Random House, 1968.

Abu Izzeddin, Nejla M. *Nasser of the Arabs: An Arab Assessment*. London: Third World Centre for Research and Publication, 1981.

Abu-Lughod, Ibrahim. "The Mass Media and Egyptian Village Life." *Social Forces* 42 (1963).

Abu-Lughod, Janet. "Migrant Adjustment to City Life: The Egyptian Case." *American Journal of Sociology* 67 (1961).

———. "Rural Migrations and Politics in Egypt." In Richard Antoun and Iliya Harik, eds., *Rural Politics and Social Change in the Middle East*. Bloomington: Indiana University Press, 1972.

Ajami, Fouad. *The Arab Predicament: Arab Political Thought and Practice since 1967*. Cambridge: Cambridge University Press, 1981.

———. *The Dream Palace of the Arabs: A Generation Odyssey*. New York: Pantheon Books, 1998.

———. "The End of Pan-Arabism." *Foreign Affairs* 57, no. 2 (winter 1978–1979).

———. "The Open-Door Economy." In Gouda Abdel-Khalek and Robert Tignor, eds., *The Political Economy of Income Distribution in Egypt*. New York: Holmes and Meier, 1982.

Amin, Galal A. *Egypt's Economic Predicament: A Study in the Interaction of External Pressure, Political Folly and Social Tension in Egypt, 1960–1990*. Leiden: E. J. Brill, 1995.

Ansari, Hamied. *Egypt: The Stalled Society*. Albany: State University of New York Press, 1986.

———. "Sectarian Conflicts in Egypt and the Political Expediency of Religion." *Middle East Journal* 38, no. 3 (summer 1984).

Antoun, Richard, and Iliya Harik, eds. *Rural Politics and Social Change in the Middle East*. Bloomington: Indiana University Press, 1972.

Armbrust, Walter. *Mass Culture and Modernism in Egypt*. Cambridge: Cambridge University Press, 1996.

———, ed. *Mass Mediations: New Approaches to Popular Culture in the Middle East and Beyond*. Berkeley: University of California Press, 2000.

Ashton, Nigel John. *Eisenhower, Macmillan, and the Problem of Nasser: Anglo-American Relations and Arab Nationalism, 1955–1959*. Basingstoke: Macmillan Press, 1996.

'Awad, Louis. "Cultural and Intellectual Developments in Egypt since 1952." In P. J. Vatikiotis, ed., *Egypt since the Revolution*. New York: Praeger, 1968.

Ayubi, Nazih N. *Bureaucracy and Politics in Contemporary Egypt*. London: Ithaca Press, 1980.

———. *Over-Stating the Arab State: Politics and Society in the Middle East*. London: I. B. Tauris, 1995.

Badeau, John S. "The Role in Search of a Hero: A Brief Study of the Egyptian Revolution." *Middle East Journal* 9 (fall 1955).

Baker, Raymond W. *Egypt's Uncertain Revolution under Nasser and Sadat*. Cambridge: Harvard University Press, 1978.

Baraka, Magda. *The Egyptian Upper Class between Two Revolutions, 1919–1952*. Reading: Ithaca Press, 1998.

Beattie, Kirk J. *Egypt during the Nasser Years: Ideology, Politics, and Civil Society*. Boulder: Westview Press, 1994.

Be'eri, Eliezer. *Army Officers in Arab Politics and Society*. Jerusalem: Israel Universities Press, 1969.

Beinin, Joel. "The Communist Movement and Nationalist Discourse in Nasirist Egypt." *Middle East Journal* 41, no. 4 (1987).

———. "Labor, Capital, and the State in Nasserist Egypt, 1952–1961." *IJMES*, 21, no. 1 (1989).

Beinin, Joel, and Zachary Lockman. *Workers on the Nile: Nationalism, Communism, Islam, and the Egyptian Working Class, 1882–1954*. Princeton: Princeton University Press, 1987.

Ben-Dor, Gabriel. *State and Conflict in the Middle East*. New York: Praeger, 1983.

Berger, Morroe. *The Arab World Today*. Garden City, N.Y.: Doubleday, 1962.

Berque, Jacques. *Egypt: Imperialism and Revolution*. Translated by Jean Stewart. London: Faber and Faber, 1972.

Bill, James A., and Carl Leiden. *The Middle East: Politics and Power*. Boston: Allyn and Bacon, 1974.

Binder, Leonard. *In a Moment of Enthusiasm: Political Power and the Second Stratum in Egypt*. Chicago: University of Chicago Press, 1978.

———. "Nasserism: The Protest Movement in the Middle East." In Leonard Binder, ed., *The Ideological Revolution in the Middle East*. New York: John Wiley, 1964.

———, ed. *The Ideological Revolution in the Middle East*. New York: John Wiley, 1964.

Black, Cyril E., and L. Carl Brown, eds. *Modernization in the Middle East: The Ottoman Empire and Its Afro-Asian Successors*. Princeton: Darwin Press, 1992.
Botman, Selma. *Engendering Citizenship in Egypt*. New York: Columbia University Press, 1999.
Boutros-Ghali, Boutros. "The Foreign Policy of Egypt." In Joseph E. Black and Kenneth W. Thompson, eds., *Foreign Policies in a World of Change*. New York: Harper and Row, 1963.
Bowie, Leland. "Charisma, Weber, and Nasir." *Middle East Journal* 30, no. 2 (1976).
Brown, Carl. *International Politics and the Middle East*. London: I. B. Tauris, 1984.
Brown, Nathan J. "Judicial Review in the Arab World." *Journal of Democracy* 9, no. 4 (October 1998).
———. *Peasant Politics in Modern Egypt: The Struggle against the State*. New Haven: Yale University Press, 1990.
———. *The Rule of Law in the Arab World: Courts in Egypt and the Gulf*. Cambridge: Cambridge University Press, 1997.
Burns, William J. *Economic Aid and American Policy toward Egypt, 1955–1981*. Albany: State University of New York Press, 1985.
Cady, Barbara. *Icons of the Twentieth Century: Two Hundred Men and Women Who Have Made a Difference*. Photography edited by Jean-Jacques Naudet. Woodstock, N.Y.: Overlook Press, 1998.
Campbell, John C. *Defense of the Middle East: Problems of American Policy*. New York: Praeger, 1960.
Cooper, Mark Neal. *The Transformation of Egypt*. London: Croom Helm, 1982.
Copeland, Miles. *The Game of Nations: The Amorality of Power Politics*. New York: Simon and Schuster, 1969.
Crabbs, Jack, Jr. "Politics, History, and Culture in Nasser's Egypt." *IJMES* 6, no. 4 (1975).
Cremeans, Charles Davis. *The Arabs and the World: Nasser's Arab Nationalist Policy*. New York: Published for the Council on Foreign Relations by Praeger, 1963.
Danielson, Virginia. *The Voice of Egypt: Umm Kulthum, Arabic Song, and Egyptian Society in the Twentieth Century*. Chicago: University of Chicago Press, 1997.
Dawisha, Adeed I. *Egypt in the Arab World: The Elements of Foreign Policy*. New York: John Wiley, 1976.
———. "Intervention in Yemen: An Analysis of Egyptian Perception and Policies. *Middle East Journal* 29, no. 1 (1975).
Dekmejian, R. Hrair. *Egypt under Nasir: A Study in Political Dynamics*. Albany: State University of New York Press, 1971.
———. "Marx, Weber, and the Egyptian Revolution." *Middle East Journal* 30, no. 1 (1976).
Dessouki, Ali E. Hillal. "Nasser and the Struggle of Independence." In William Roger Louis and Roger Owen, eds., *Suez 1956: The Crisis and Its Consequences*. Oxford: Clarendon Press, 1989.
Doran, Michael. *Pan-Arabism before Nasser: Egyptian Power Politics and the Palestine Question*. New York: Oxford University Press, 1999.

Erlich, Haggai. *Students and University in Twentieth-Century Egyptian Politics.* London: Frank Cass, 1989.

Eveland, Wilbur Crane. *Ropes of Sand: America's Failure in the Middle East.* London: W. W. Norton, 1980.

Farah, Tawfic E., ed. *Pan-Arabism and Arab Nationalism: The Continuing Debate.* Boulder: Westview Press, 1987.

Fargues, Philippe. "State Policies and the Birth Rate in Egypt: From Socialism to Liberalism." *Population and Development Review* 23, no. 1 (March 1997).

Fawzi, Mahmoud. *Suez 1956: An Egyptian Perspective.* London: Shorouk International, 1987.

Gadalla, Saad M. *Is There Hope? Fertility and Family Planning in a Rural Egyptian Community.* Cairo: American University in Cairo Press, 1978.

Gallagher, Charles E. "Population and Development in Egypt, Part I: Birth and Death on the Nile." *American University Field Staff Report,* no. 31 (1981).

———. "Population and Development in Egypt, Part II: New Hopes for Old Problems." *American University Field Staff Reports,* no. 32 (1981).

Gerges, Fawaz A. *The Superpowers and the Middle East: Regional and International Politics, 1955–1967.* Boulder: Westview Press, 1994.

El-Ghonemy, M. Riad. *Affluence and Poverty in the Middle East.* New York: Routledge, 1998.

Gilbar, Gad G. *Population Dilemmas in the Middle East.* London: Frank Cass, 1997.

Ginat, Rami. "British Concoction or Bilateral Decision: Revisiting the Genesis of Soviet-Egyptian Diplomatic Relations." *IJMES* 31, no. 1 (1999).

———. *Egypt's Incomplete Revolution: Lutfi al-Khuli and Nasser's Socialism in the 1960s.* London: Frank Cass, 1997.

———. "Soviet Policy towards the Arab World, 1945–1955." *Middle Eastern Studies* 32, no. 3 (1996).

———. *The Soviet Union and Egypt, 1945–1955.* London: Frank Cass, 1993.

Gordon, Joel. "Film, Fame, and Public Memory: Egyptian Biopics from Mustafa Kamil to Nasser 56." *IJMES* 31 (1999).

———. "Nasser 56/Cairo 96: Reimaging Lost Community." In Walter Armbrust, ed., *Mass Mediations: New Approaches to Popular Culture in the Middle East and Beyond.* Berkeley: University of California Press, 2000.

———. *Nasser's Blessed Movement: Egypt's Free Officers and the Revolution.* New York: Oxford University Press, 1992.

———. *Revolutionary Melodrama: Popular Film and Civil Identity in Nasser's Egypt.* Chicago: University of Chicago Press, 2002.

———. "Secular and Religious Memory in Egypt: Recalling Nasserist Civics." *Muslim World* 87 (April 1997).

Hahn, Peter L. *The United States, Great Britain, and Egypt, 1945–1956.* Chapel Hill: University of North Carolina Press, 1991.

Al-Hakim, Tawfiq. *Return of the Spirit.* Trans. William M. Hutchins. Washington, D.C.: Three Continents Press, 1990.

Halpern, Manfred. *The Politics of Social Change in the Middle East and North Africa.* Princeton: Princeton University Press, 1963.

Hansen, Bent, and Girgis A. Marzouk. *Development and Economic Policy in the UAR (Egypt)*. Amsterdam: North-Holland, 1965.

Harik, Iliya. *The Political Mobilization of Peasants: A Study of an Egyptian Community*. Bloomington: Indiana University Press, 1974.

Harkabi, Yehoshafat. *Arab Attitudes to Israel*. Jerusalem: Israel Universities Press, 1971.

Hasou, Tawfig Y. *The Struggle for the Arab World: Egypt's Nasser and the Arab League*. London: KPI, 1985.

Hatem, Abdel-Kader M. *Information and the Arab Cause*. London: Longman, 1974.

Hatina, Meir. "On the Margins of Consensus: The Call to Separate Religion and State in Modern Egypt." *Middle Eastern Studies* 36, no. 1 (January 2000).

Haykal, Muhammad Hasanayn [Heikal, Mohamed Hassanein]. *Autumn of Fury*. New York: Random House, 1983.

———. *The Cairo Documents: The Inside Story of Nasser and His Relationship with World Leaders, Rebels, and Statesmen*. New York: Doubleday, 1973.

———. *Cutting the Lion's Tail: Suez through Egyptian Eyes*. New York: Arbor House, 1987.

———. *The Road to Ramadan*. London: Collins, 1975.

———. *The Sphinx and the Commissar*. New York: Harper and Row, 1978.

Hilmi, Ibrahim M., and Askar F. Nahed. "Ideology, Politics, and Sports in Egypt." *Leisure Studies* 3, no. 1 (1984).

Hinnebusch, Raymond A., Jr. *Egyptian Politics under Sadat: The Post-Populist Development of an Authoritarian-Modernizing State*. Cambridge: Cambridge University Press, 1985. 2d ed. Boulder: Lynne Rienner, 1988.

Hiro, Dilip. *A Dictionary of the Middle East*. Houndmills, Basingstoke: Macmillan, 1996.

Hopkins, Harry. *Egypt, the Crucible: The Unfinished Revolution of the Arab World*. London: Secker and Warburg, 1969.

Hopwood, Derek. *Egypt Politics and Society, 1945–1990*. 3d ed. London: Routledge, 1993.

Hudson, Michael C. *Arab Politics: The Search for Legitimacy*. New Haven: Yale University Press, 1977.

———, ed. *Middle East Dilemma: The Politics and Economics of Arab Integration*. London: I. B. Tauris, 1998.

Hussein, Mahmoud. *Class Conflict in Egypt, 1945–1970*. New York: Monthly Review Press, 1973.

El-Hussini, Mohrez Mahmoud. *Soviet-Egyptian Relations, 1945–1985*. Basingstoke: Macmillan Press, 1987.

Ibrahim, Saad Eddin. "A Socio-Cultural Paradigm of Pan-Arab Leadership: The Case of Nasser." In Fuad I. Khuri, ed., *Leadership and Development in Arab Society*. Beirut: American University of Beirut, 1981.

———. "State, Women, and Civil Society: An Evaluation of Egypt's Population Policy." In Carla Makhlouf Obermeyer, ed., *Family, Gender, and Population in the Middle East*. Cairo: American University in Cairo Press, 1995.

Ikram, Khalid. *Egypt: Economic Management in a Period of Transition*. A World

Bank Country Economic Report. Baltimore: Johns Hopkins University Press, 1980.
Ismael, Tareq Y. *The Arab Left.* Syracuse: Syracuse University Press, 1976.
———. *The U.A.R. in Africa: Egypt's Policy under Nasser.* Evanston: Northwestern University Press, 1971.
Issawi, Charles. *Egypt in Revolution.* London: Oxford University Press, 1963.
Jankowski, James. "Arab Nationalism in 'Nasserism' and Egyptian State Policy, 1952–1958." In James Jankowski and Israel Gershoni, eds., *Rethinking Nationalism in the Arab Middle East.* New York: Columbia University Press, 1997.
———. "Egyptian Responses to the Palestine Problem in the Interwar Period." *IJMES* 12, no. 1 (1980).
———. *Nasser's Egypt, Arab Nationalism, and the United Arab Republic.* Boulder: Lynne Rienner, 2002.
Karnouk, Liliane. *Contemporary Egyptian Art.* Cairo: American University in Cairo Press, 1995.
Karpat, Kemal, ed. *Political and Social Thought in the Contemporary Middle East.* New York: Praeger, 1982.
Kaufman, Burton I. *The Arab Middle East and the United States: Inter-Arab Rivalry and Superpower Diplomacy.* New York: Twayne, 1996.
Kazziha, Walid. *Revolutionary Transformation in the Arab World.* London: Croom Helm, 1975.
Kelley, Allen C., Atef M. Khalifa, and M. Nabil El-Khorazaty. *Population and Development in Rural Egypt.* Durham, N.C.: Duke Press Policy Studies, Studies in Social and Economic Development, 1982.
Kerr, Malcolm. *The Arab Cold War: Gamal 'Abd al-Nasir and His Rivals, 1958–1970.* Oxford: Oxford University Press, 1971.
———. "Coming to Terms with Nasser." *International Affairs* 43, no. 1 (1967).
———. "Egypt." In James S. Coleman, ed., *Education and Political Development.* Princeton: Princeton University Press, 1965.
———. "The Emergence of a Socialist Ideology in Egypt." *Middle East Journal* 16, no. 2 (1962).
———. *Regional Arab Politics and the Conflict with Israel.* Santa Monica: Rand, 1969.
Khadduri, Majid. *Arab Contemporaries: The Role of Personalities in Politics.* Baltimore: Johns Hopkins University Press, 1973.
Khuri, Fuad I., ed. *Leadership and Development in Arab Society.* Beirut: American University of Beirut, 1981.
Kienle, Eberhard. "Arab Unity Schemes Revisited: Interest, Identity, and Policy in Syria and Iraq." *IJMES* 27, no. 1 (1995).
Klein, Menachem. "*Ikhtarna Laka* (We Have Selected for You): A Critique of Egypt's Revolutionary Culture." *Orient* 38, no. 4 (1997).
Korany, Bahgat, and Ali E. H. Dessouki, eds. *The Foreign Policies of Arab States.* Boulder: Westview Press, 1984.
Lacouture, Jean. *The Demigods: Charismatic Leadership in the Third World.* Trans. Patricia Wolf. New York: Knopf, 1970.

———. *Nasser: A Biography.* Trans. Daniel Hofstadter. New York: Knopf, 1974.
Laqueur, Walter Z., ed. *The Middle East in Transition.* New York: Praeger, 1958.
———. *The Soviet Union and the Middle East.* London: Routledge and Kegan Paul, 1957.
Le Gassick, Trevor. "Mahfouz's *al-Karnak:* The Quiet Conscience of Nasir's Egypt Revealed." In Le Gassick, ed., *Critical Perspectives on Naguib Mahfouz.* Washington D.C.: Three Continents Press, 1991.
Lenczowski, George. "The Objects and Methods of Nasserism." In Jack H. Thompson and Robert D. Reischauer, eds., *Modernization of the Arab World.* Princeton: D. Van Nostrand, 1966.
———. *Soviet Advances in the Middle East.* Washington, D.C.: American Enterprise Institute for Public Policy Research, 1971.
Lerner, Daniel. *The Passing of Traditional Society: Modernizing the Middle East.* London: Free Press, 1958.
Lesch, David W. "Gamal 'Abd al-Nasser and an Example of Diplomatic Acumen." *Middle Eastern Studies* 31, no. 2 (1995).
———, ed. *The Middle East and the United States: A Historical and Political Reassessment.* 3d ed. Boulder: Westview Press, 2003.
Lorenz, Joseph P. *Egypt and the Arabs: Foreign Policy and the Search for National Identity.* Boulder: Westview Press, 1990.
Louis, William Roger, and Roger Owen, eds. *Suez 1956: The Crisis and Its Consequences.* London: Clarendon Press, 1989.
Mabro, Robert. *The Egyptian Economy, 1952–1972.* Oxford: Clarendon Press, 1974.
Mansfield, Peter. *Nasser's Egypt.* London: Methuen Educational, 1965, 1969.
Mayfield, James B. *Rural Politics in Nasser's Egypt: A Quest for Legitimacy.* Austin: University of Texas Press, 1971.
Mead, Donad. *Growth and Structural Change in the Egyptian Economy.* Homewood: Richard D. Irwin, 1967.
Meital, Yoram. "The Aswan High Dam and Revolutionary Symbolism in Egypt." In Haggai Erlich and Israel Gershoni, eds., *The Nile: Histories, Cultures, Myths.* Boulder: Lynne Rienner, 2000.
———. "The Khartoum Conference and Egyptian Policy after the 1967 War: A Reexamination." *Middle East Journal* 54, no. 1 (winter 2000).
———. "Revolutionizing the Past: Historical Representation during Egypt's Revolutionary Experience, 1952–62." *Mediterranean Historical Review* 12, no. 2 (1997).
Meyer, Gail E. *Egypt and the United States: The Formative Years.* Rutherford, N.J.: Fairleigh Dickinson University Press, 1980.
Milson, Menahem. *Najib Mahfuz: The Novelist-Philosopher of Cairo.* New York: St. Martin's Press, 1998.
Mufti, Malik. "The United States and Nasserist Pan-Arabism." In David W. Lesch, ed., *The Middle East and the United States: A Historical and Political Reassessment.* 3d ed. Boulder: Westview Press, 2003.
Najjar, Fauzi M. "The Egyptian Press under Nasser and al-Sadat." In George N.

Atiyeh and Ibrahim M. Oweiss, eds., *Arab Civilization: Challenges and Responses.* Albany: State University of New York Press, 1988.

Nasser, Gamal Abdul. "The Egyptian Revolution." *Foreign Affairs* 33, no. 2 (January 1955).

Nasser, Munir K. *Press, Politics, and Power: Egypt's Heikal and* al-Ahram. Ames: Iowa State University Press, 1979.

Nutting, Anthony. *Nasser.* New York: E. P. Dutton, 1972.

O'Brien, Patrick. *The Revolution in Egypt's Economic System: From Private Enterprise to Socialism, 1952–1965.* London: Oxford University Press, 1966.

Oren, Michael B. *Six Days of War: June 1967 and the Making of the Modern Middle East.* Oxford: Oxford University Press, 2002.

Owen, Roger. *State, Power, and Politics in the Making of the Modern Middle East.* London: Routledge, 1992, 2000.

Palmer, Monte. "The United Arab Republic: An Assessment of Its Failure." *Middle East Journal* 20, no. 1 (1966).

Paterson, Thomas G., ed. *Kennedy's Quest for Victory: American Foreign Policy, 1961–1963.* New York: Oxford University Press, 1989.

Podeh, Elie. "The Big Lie: Inventing the Myth of British–U.S. Involvement in the 1967 War." *Review of International Affairs* 2, no. 1 (2002).

———. *The Decline of Arab Unity: The Rise and Fall of the United Arab Republic.* Brighton: Sussex Academic Press, 1999.

———. "The Drift towards Neutrality: Egyptian Foreign Policy during the Early Nasserist Era, 1952–1955." *Middle Eastern Studies* 32, no. 1 (1996).

———. *The Quest for Hegemony in the Arab World: The Struggle over the Baghdad Pact.* Leiden: E. J. Brill, 1995.

———. "Regaining Lost Pride: The Impact of Suez Affairs on Egypt and the Arab World." In David Tal, ed., *The 1956 War: Collusion and Rivalry in the Middle East.* London: Frank Cass, 2001.

———. "Suez in Reverse: The Arab Response to the Iraqi Bid for Kuwait, 1961–1963." *Diplomacy and Statecraft* 14, no. 1 (2003).

———. "To Unite or Not to Unite; That Is *Not* the Question: The 1963 Tripartite Unity Talks Reassessed." *Middle Eastern Studies* 39, no. 1 (2003).

Posusney, Marsha Pripstein. *Labor and the State in Egypt: Workers, Unions, and Economic Reconstructing.* New York: Columbia University Press, 1997.

Ra'anan, Uri. *The USSR Arms in the Third World.* Cambridge: MIT Press, 1969.

Rabinovich, Itamar, and Haim Shaked, eds. *From June to October.* New Brunswick, N.J.: Transaction Books, 1978

Rejwan, Nissim. *Nasserist Ideology: Its Exponents and Critics.* New York: John Wiley, 1974.

Richards, Alan, and John Waterbury. *A Political Economy of the Middle East.* 2d ed. Boulder: Westview Press, 1996.

Rivlin, Benjamin, and Joseph S. Szyliowicz, ed. *The Contemporary Middle East: Tradition and Innovation.* New York: Random House, 1965.

Rivlin, Paul. *The Dynamics of Economic Policy Making in Egypt.* New York: Praeger, 1985.

———. *Economic Policy and Performance in the Arab World.* Boulder: Lynne Rienner, 2001.
Ro'i, Yaacov. *From Encroachment to Involvement: A Documentary Study of Soviet Policy in the Middle East, 1945–1973.* Jerusalem: Israel Universities Press, 1974.
Safran, Nadav. *Egypt in Search of Political Community: An Analysis of the Intellectual and Political Evolution of Egypt, 1804–1952.* Cambridge: Harvard University Press, 1961.
Salem, Paul. *Bitter Legacy: Ideology and Politics in the Arab World.* Syracuse: Syracuse University Press, 1994.
Sayed, Hussein Abdel-Aziz. "The Population Family Planning Program in Egypt: Structure and Performance." *Population Studies (Dirasat Sukaniyya)* 11, no. 70 (July–September 1984).
Sayyid-Ahmad, Muhammad Abd al-Wahab. *Nasser and American Foreign Policy, 1952–1956.* Cairo: American University in Cairo Press, 1991.
Seale, Patrick. *The Struggle for Syria: A Study of Post-War Arab Politics, 1945–1958.* Oxford: Oxford University Press, 1965.
Sela, Avraham. *The Decline of the Arab-Israeli Conflict: Middle East Politics and the Quest for a Regional Order.* Albany: State University of New York Press, 1998.
———, ed. *Political Encyclopedia of the Middle East.* New York: Continuum, 1998.
Shaked, Haim, and Itamar Rabinovich, eds. *The Middle East and the United States.* New Brunswick, N.J.: Transaction Books, 1980.
Shamir, Shimon, ed. *Egypt: From Monarchy to Republic.* Boulder: Westview Press, 1995.
Shamir, Shimon, and Michael Confino, eds. *The USSR and the Middle East.* Jerusalem: Israel Universities Press, 1973
Sharabi, Hisham. *Nationalism and Revolution in the Arab World.* Princeton: D. Van Nostrand, 1966.
———, ed. *Theory, Politics, and the Arab World: Critical Responses.* New York: Routledge, 1990.
Shemesh, Moshe. *The Palestinian Entity, 1959–1974: Arab Politics and the PLO.* London: Frank Cass, 1988, 1996.
Silbermann, Gad. "National Identity in Nasserist Ideology." *Asian and African Studies* 8, no. 1 (1972).
Springborg, Robert. "Professional Syndicates in Egyptian Politics, 1952–1970." *IJMES* 9, no. 3 (1978).
Stephens, Robert. *Nasser: A Political Biography.* London: Allen Lane, Penguin Press, 1971.
Stycos, J. Mayone, Hussein Abdel Aziz Sayed, Roger Avery, and Samuel Fridman. *Community Development and Family Planning: An Egyptian Experiment.* Boulder: Westview Press, 1988.
Tripp, Charles, ed. *Contemporary Egypt through Egyptian Eyes: Essays in Honour of Professor P. J. Vatikiotis.* London: Routledge, 1993.
Vatikiotis, P. J. *Arab and Regional Politics in the Middle East.* London: Croom Helm, 1984.

———. *The Egyptian Army in Politics: Pattern for New Nations?* Bloomington: Indiana University Press, 1961.
———. *The History of Egypt from Muhammad Ali to Sadat.* London: Wiedenfeld and Nicolson, 1983.
———. *The Modern History of Egypt.* London: Weidenfeld and Nicolson, 1969.
———. *Nasser and His Generation.* London: Croom Helm, 1978.
———, ed. *Egypt since the Revolution.* New York: Praeger, 1968.
Vaucher, Georges. *Gamal Abdel Nasser et son Equipe.* Paris: R. Julliard, 1959.
Wahba, Mourad. *The Role of the State in the Egyptian Economy, 1945–1981.* Reading: Ithaca Press, 1994.
Warburg, Gabriel R., and Uri M. Kupferschmidt, eds. *Islam, Nationalism, and Radicalism in Egypt and the Sudan.* New York: Praeger, 1983.
Waterbury, John. *Burdens of the Past, Options for the Future.* Bloomington: Indiana University Press, 1978.
———. *The Egypt of Nasser and Sadat: The Political Economy of Two Regimes.* Princeton: Princeton University Press, 1983.
———. "The 'Soft State' and the Open Door: Egypt Experience with Economic Liberalization, 1974–1984." *Comparative Politics* 18, no. 1 (October 1985).
Wheelock, Keith. *Nasser's New Egypt.* Westport, Conn.: Greenwood Press, 1975.
Wikan, Unni. *Life among the Poor in Cairo.* London: Tavistock, 1980.
Wilson, Rodney. *Economic Development in the Middle East.* London: Routledge, 1995.
Woodward, Peter. *Nasser: Profiles in Power.* London: Longman, 1992.
Wynn, Wilton. *Nasser of Egypt.* Cambridge: Arlington Books, 1959.
Yodfat, Aryeh. *Arab Politics in the Soviet Mirror.* Jerusalem: Israel Universities Press, 1973.
Yousif, Mona Tawfik. "History of Egyptian Demography: Multimedia Representation." In *Twentieth-eighth Annual Seminar on Population Issues in the Middle East, Africa, and Asia.* Cairo: Cairo Demographic Center, 1999.

## Works in Arabic and Hebrew

'Abd al-Nasser, Gamal. *Falsafat al-Thawra.* Cairo: Dar al-Ma'arif, 1954.
'Abd al-Rahman, 'Awatif. *Misr wa-Filastin.* Kuwait: al-Majlis al-Watani lil-Thaqafa wal-Funun wal-Adab, 1980.
Ahmad, Rif'at Sayyid. *Thawrat al-Jinaral.* Cairo: Dar al-Huda lil-Nashr wal-Tawzi', 1993.
Ahmad, Salah Zaki. *Qamus al-Nasiriyya.* Cairo: Dar al-Mustaqbal al-'Arabi, 1985.
Ahmad, Yusuf Ahmad, ed. *Al-Majmu'a al-Kamila li-Khitab wa-Ahadith wa-Tasrihat Gamal 'Abd al-Nasir.* Beirut: Markaz al-Dirasat al-Wahda al-'Arabiyya, 1995.
'Allush, Naji. *Al-Thawra wal-Jamahir.* Beirut: Dar al-Tali'a lil-Tiba'a wal-Nashr, 1973.
'Awad, Louis. *Aqni'at al-Nasiriyya al-Sab'a.* Beirut: Dar al-Qadaya, 1975.
Ayalon, Ami, and Gad G. Gilbar, eds. *Demography and Politics in the Arab States.* Tel Aviv: Hakibutz Hameuhad, 1995 (Hebrew).

Baghdadi, 'Abd al-Latif. *Mudhakkirat 'Abd al-Latif al-Baghdadi*. 2 vols. Cairo: al-Maktab al-Misri al-Hadith, 1977.
Al-Dawla, Mustafa Sayf. *Hal Kan 'Abd al-Nasir Diktaturan?* N.p, n.d.
Erlich, Haggai. *Youth and Politics in the Middle East: Generations and Identity Crises*. Tel Aviv: Ministry of Defense, 1998 (Hebrew).
Fa'iq, Muhammad Muhammad. *'Abd al-Nasir wal-Thawra al-Ifriqiyya*. Beirut: Dar al-Wahda, 1980.
Fawzi, Mahmud. *Al-Baba Qirilus wal-'Abd al-Nasir*. Cairo: al-Watan lil-Nashr, 1993.
Fawzi, Muhammad. *Harb al-Thalath Sanawat, 1967–1970*. Cairo: Dar al-Mustaqbal al-'Arabi, 1986.
Hamrush, Ahmad. *Qisat Thwrat 23 Yuliyah*. Beirut: al-Mu'asasa al-'Arabiyya lil-Tiba'a wal-Nashr, 1978.
———. *Thawrat Yuliyah wa-'Aql Misr*. Cairo: Maktabat Madbuli, 1985.
———. *Thawrat 23 Yuliyah*. Cairo: al-Hay'a al-Misriyya al-'Amma lil-Kitab, 1992.
Al-Hakim, Tawfiq. *'Awdat al-Wa'y*. 2d ed. Beirut: Dar al-Shuruq, 1975.
Hatina, Meir. *Islam in Modern Egypt: Studies in the Writings of Faraj Fuda*. Tel Aviv: Hakibbutz Hameuchad, 2000 (Hebrew).
Haykal, Muhammad Hasanayn. *Azmat al-Muthaqafin*. Cairo: al-Sharika al-'Arabiyya al-Muttahida lil-Tawzi', 1961.
———. *Bayna al-Sahafa wal-Siyasa*. 3d ed. Beirut: Sharikat al-Matbu'at lil-Tawzi' wal-Nashr, 1984.
———. *al-Infijar 1967*. Cairo: Markaz al-Ahram lil-Tarjama wal-Nashr, 1990.
———. *Kharif al-Ghadab*. Beirut: Sharkat al-Matbu'at lil-Tawzi' wal-Nashr, 1983.
———. *Li-Misr la li-'Abd al-Nasir*. Cairo: Markaz al-Ahram lil-Tarjama wal-Nashr, 1987.
———. *Ma-Aladhi Jara fi Suriya*. Cairo: Dar al-Qawmiyya lil-Tiba'a wal-Nashr, 1962.
———. *Milaffat al-Suways: Harb al-Thalathin 'Ama*. Cairo: Markaz al-Ahram, 1986.
———. *Nahnu wa-Amrika*. Cairo: Dar al-'Aser al-Hadith, 1965.
———. *Qissat al-Suways: Akhir al-Ma'arik fi 'Asr al-'Amaliqa*. 5th ed. Beirut: Sharkat al-Matbu'at lil-Tawzi' wal-Nashr, 1977.
———. *Sanawat al-Ghalayan*. Cairo: Markaz al-Ahram, 1988.
———. *Al-'Uqad al-Nafsiyya allati Tahkum al-Sharq al-Awsat*. 'Aka: Maktab al-Aswar, 1970, 1958.
———. *Waqa'i Tahkik Siyasa Amama al-Mudda'i al-'Amm al-Ishtiraki*. 2d ed. Beirut: Sharkat al-Matbu'at lil-Tawzi' wal-Nashr, 1982.
Ibrahim, Hasanayn Tawfiq. *Al-Nizam al-Siyasi wal-Ikhwan al-Muslimun fi Misr*. Beirut: Dar al-Tali'a, 1998.
Imam, 'Abdallah. *'Abd al-Nasir wal-Ikhwan al-Muslimun*. Cairo: al-Qahira lil-Thaqafa al-'Arabiyya, 1987.
———. *Madhbahat al-Qada*. Cairo: Maktabat Madbuli, 1976.
Al-'Imrusy, Majdi. *A'azz al-Nass*. Cairo: 'Adil al-Balak, 1994.
Al-Khuli, Lutfi, ed. *Harb Yunyu 1967 Ba'da 30 Sana*. Cairo: Markaz al-Ahram, 1997.

Karum, Hasanayn. *'Abd al-Nasir Bayna Haykal wa-Mustafa Amin*. Cairo: Dar A'mun lil-Tiba'a, 1975.

Mahfuz, Najib. *Hawla al-Taharrur wal-Taqaddum*. Cairo: al-Dar al-Misriyya al-Lubnaniyya, 1996.

Mansur, Anis. *'Abd al-Nasir al-Muftara 'Alyhi wal-Muftari 'Alayna*. 4th ed. Cairo: al-Maktab al-Misri al-Hadith, 1994.

Mattar, Fu'ad. *BiSaraha 'an 'Abd al-Nasir: Hiwar ma'a Muhammad Hasanayn Haykal*. Beirut: Matba'a al-Sharq al-Ta'awuniyya, 1975.

Ramadan, 'Abd al-'Azim. *Al-Haqiqa al-Ta'rikhiyya Hawla Ta'mim Sharikat Qanat al-Suways*. Cairo: al-Hay'a al-Misriyya al-'Amma lil-Kitab, 2000.

Riad, Magdi. *Hiwar Shamil ma'a Jamal al-Atasi 'an al-Nasiriyya wal-Nasiriyyin*. Cairo: Markaz al-Khadara al-'Arabiyya lil-I'lam wal-Nashr, 1992.

Rif'at, Kamal. *Nasiriyyun? Na'am*. Cairo: Markaz al-Kahirah lil-Thaqafa al-'Arabiyya, 1976.

Riyad, Mahmud. *Mudhakkirat Mahmud Riyad, 1948–1978*. 3 vols. Cairo: Dar al-Mustaqbal al-'Arabi, 1985.

Al-Sa'id, Rif'at. *Ta'mmalat fi al-Nasiriyya*. 3d ed. Cairo: al-Mada, 2000.

Al-Saydawi, Riyad. *Haykal: Aw al-Milaff al-Siri Lil-Zakirah al-'Arabiyya*. Cairo: Maktabat Madbuli, 1999.

Shamir, Shimon, ed. *The Decline of Nasserism, 1965–1970: The Waning of a Messianic Movement*. Tel Aviv: Mif'alim Universitayim, 1978 (Hebrew).

Al-Shelby, Gamal. *Muhammad Hasanayn Haykal: Istimrariyya am Tahawwul*. Beirut: al-Mu'asasat al-'Arabiyya lil-Dirasat wal-Nashir, 1999.

Shuqair, Labib, ed. *Hadith al-Batal al-Za'im Jamal 'Abd al-Nasir Ila al-Umma*. Cairo: Dar al-Tahrir, 1965.

Sivan, Emmanuel. *Arab Political Myths*. 2d ed. Tel Aviv: 'Am Oved, 1997 (Hebrew).

'Umran, Muhammad. *Tajribaty fi al-Thawra*. Damascus, 1970.

Vered, Yael. *Coup and War in Yemen*. Tel Aviv: 'Am Oved, 1967 (Hebrew).

Yahya, Jalal. *Misr al-Ifriqiyya*. Alexandria: Dar al-Ma'arif, 1967.

Zaki, Salah Ahmad. *Qamus al-Nasiriyya*. Cairo: Dar al-Mustaqbal al-'Arabi, 1985.

# Contributors

Gabriel Ben-Dor is professor of political science at the University of Haifa and head of national security studies at the university. His publications include *The Druzes in Israel: A Political Study* (1979), *Confidence Building in the Middle East* (with David B. Dewitt, 1995), and *Minorities and the Arab States* (edited with Ofra Bangio, 1999).

Leonard Binder is professor of political science at UCLA. He is the author or editor of *The Ideological Revolution in the Middle East* (1964), *In a Moment of Enthusiasm: Political Power and the Second Stratum in Egypt* (1978), *Islamic Liberalism: A Critique of Development Ideologies* (1988), *Ethnic Conflict and International Politics in the Middle East* (1999), and *Politics in Lebanon* (1963).

Nathan J. Brown is professor of political science and international affairs at George Washington University. He has written *Peasant Politics in Modern Egypt* (1990), *The Role of Law in the Arab World* (1997), and *Constitutions in an Unconstitutional World: Arab Basic Laws and the Prospects for Accountable Government* (2001).

Yoav Di-Capua is a Ph.D. candidate at Princeton University. He is writing a dissertation titled "Historians and Historiography of Twentieth-Century Egypt," and his publications include "Embodiment of the Revolutionary Spirit: The Mustafa Kamil Mausoleum in Cairo," *History and Memory* (2000).

Mohamed Riad El-Ghonemy is a senior research associate at the International Development Center, Oxford University. He is a fellow of the Department of Economics of the American University in Cairo and professor emeritus at the University of El-Shams. His publications include *Mafhum al-Islah al-Zira'i wal-Tanmiya al-Rifiyya* (1980), *The Political Economy of Rural Poverty* (1990), *Land, Food, and Rural Development in North Africa* (1993), and *Affluence and Poverty in the Middle East* (1998), and *Egypt in the Twenty-first Century: Challenges for Development* (2003).

Gad G. Gilbar is a professor in the Department of Middle Eastern History at the University of Haifa. He is the author or editor of *Economic Development of the Middle East in Modern Times* (Hebrew, 1990), *Population Dilemmas in the Middle East* (1997), *The Middle East Oil Decade and Beyond* (1997), *Ottoman Palestine, 1800–1914: Studies in Economic and Social History* (1990), and *Demography and Politics in the Arab States* (Hebrew, edited with Ami Ayalon, 1995).

Rami Ginat is a senior lecturer in the Department of Middle Eastern History at Bar-Ilan University. His publications include *The Soviet Policy towards the Middle East* (1993) and *Egypt's Incomplete Revolution* (1997).

Joel Gordon is associate professor of history and associate director of Middle East and Islamic studies at the University of Arkansas. He has written *Nasser's Blessed Movement: Egypt's Free Officers and the July Revolution* (1992) and *Revolutionary Melodrama: Popular Film and Civic Identity in Nasser's Egypt* (2002).

Meir Hatina is a lecturer in the Department of Middle Eastern and African History at Tel Aviv University. He is the author of *Islam in Modern Egypt* (Hebrew, 2000) and *Islam and Salvation in Palestine* (2001).

Uri M. Kupferschmidt is a senior lecturer in the Department of Middle Eastern History at the University of Haifa. His publications include *Henri Naus Bey: Retrieving the Biography of a Belgian Industrialist in Egypt* (1999) and *Islam, Nationalism, and Radicalism in Egypt and the Sudan* (edited with Gabriel W. Warburg, 1983).

David W. Lesch is professor of Middle Eastern history at Trinity University, San Antonio, Texas. He is the author or editor of *Syria and the United States: Eisenhower's Cold War in the Middle East* (1992), *1979: The Year That Shaped the Middle East* (2001), *The Middle East and the United States: A Historical and Political Reassessment* (1996) and *History in Dispute: The Middle East since 1945* (2003).

Elie Podeh is a senior lecturer in the Department of Islam and Middle Eastern Studies at the Hebrew University of Jerusalem. His publications include *The Quest for Hegemony in the Arab World: The Struggle over the Baghdad Pact* (1995), *The Decline of Arab Unity: The Rise and Fall of the United Arab Republic* (1999), and *The Arab-Israeli Conflict in the Israeli History Textbooks, 1948–2000* (2001).

Contributors | 357

Paul Rivlin is a senior research fellow at the Moshe Dayan Center for Middle Eastern and African Studies and at the Jaffee Center for Strategic Studies, Tel Aviv University. He is the author of *The Dynamics of Economic Policy Making in Egypt* (1985), *The Israel Economy* (1992), and *Economic Policy and Performance in the Arab World* (2001).

Gabriel Rosenbaum is a senior lecturer in the Department of Arabic Language and Literature at the Hebrew University of Jerusalem. He has published articles and chapters in numerous journals and edited collections.

Avraham Sela is a senior lecturer in the Department of International Relations at the Hebrew University of Jerusalem. He is the author or editor of *The Decline of Arab-Israeli Conflict: Middle East Politics and the Quest for Regional Order* (1998), *The Palestinian Hamas: Vision, Violence and Adjustment* (with Shaul Mishal, 2000), and *Political Encyclopedia of the Middle East* (1999).

Onn Winckler is a senior lecturer in the Department of Middle Eastern History, University of Haifa. His publications include *Population Growth and Migration in Jordan, 1950–1994* (1997) and *Demographic Developments and Population Policies in Ba'thist Syria* (1999).

# Index

'Abbud, Ahmad Pasha, 148
'Abd al-Nasser, Gamal. *See* Al-Nasser, Gamal 'Abd
'Abd al-Quddus, Ihsan, 330
'Abd al-Wahhab, Muhammad, 23, 309, 318, 325, 329–30, 336
Abrahamian, Ervand, 7
Acheson, Dean, 233
Agrarian Reform. *See* Egypt; Syria
Al-Ahali, 148, 150, 153, 156
*Al-Ahram*, 169. *See also* Egypt: media
Ajami, Fouad, 1, 4, 189
Algeria, 47, 198
Al-'Alim, Mahmud Amin, 62
Alpha Plan, 211
'Amaleq, 92
Amit, Meir, 88
'Amr, 'Abd al-Hakim, 24, 46, 60, 150, 156, 242
Anderson, Robert, 79–80
Anglo-Egyptian Treaty (1936). *See* Egypt
Anglo-Egyptian Treaty (1954). *See* Egypt
Arab Cold War, 200
Arabism. *See* pan-Arabism
Arab-Israeli conflict, 73–94, 192–95, 197–200. *See also* War
Arab League, 184, 186–87, 190, 195–96
Arab Legion, 191
Arab Nationalist Movement (al-Qawmiyyun al-Arab), 191, 203
Arab oil. *See* Oil
Arab socialism, 1, 17, 25, 27–28, 41, 55–57, 66, 127–29, 241–45, 255–62, 264, 277–78; and authoritarian regime, 129–31; and Islam, 63–64; and law, 131–34, 139, 141–42. *See also* Egypt: economy
Arab Socialist Union (ASU), 6, 19, 21, 51–53, 56–57, 60, 132, 134, 137, 277
Arab summits, 195–200

'Arafat, Yasir, 47, 65, 92
Argentina, 7. *See also* Perón; Perónism
'Arif, 'Abd al-Salam, 86
Al-Asad, Hafiz, 199
Aswan High Dam, x, 17, 109, 169, 235, 242–43, 245, 253, 255, 257, 259, 274, 276, 285, 334; symbol of Nasserism, 315
Ataturk. *See* Kemal, Mustafa
Al-Atrash, Farid, 310
'Awad, Louis, 6
Al-Azhar, 61–63, 123, 167, 170, 173, 261, 263
Al-'Azm, Khalid, 213
'Azzam, 'Abd al-Rahman Pasha, 184

Badeau, John, 216
Baghdadi, 'Abd al-Latif, 57, 59
Baghdad Pact (1955), 18, 45, 191, 209–12, 234–35; and Nasser, 78, 184, 188, 209–12, 234–35; U.S. position, 209–10, 234
Bakdash, Khalid, 213, 238–40
Bandung conference (1955), 78–79, 184, 235
Al-Baquri, Shaykh Hasan, 63, 69
Bar-Tal, Daniel, 74
Bat-Galim affair (1954), 76
Ba'th Party, 27, 185, 191; Syria, 45, 86, 191, 228; in Iraq, 86, 191, 194, 228
Ben-Gurion, David, 74–75, 229; perception of Nasser, 75–94, 223
Birth control. *See* Egypt: family planning; Al-Nasser, Gamal 'Abd: family planning
Al-Bizri, Afif, 213
Black September (Jordan, 1970), 199
Bodnar, John, 100–101
Bourguiba, Habib, 27, 198, 204, 297. *See also* Tunisia
Bowles, Chester, 216

Caffery, Jefferson, 207, 233
Cambodia, 271
Canada, 169
Capitulations: abolition of, in Egypt (1937), 131, 133
Central Intelligence Agency (CIA), 207, 216, 220
Child's Day, 22
China, 164, 208, 264, 268, 271
Cold War, 5, 26, 45, 49, 73, 78, 205–6, 208, 210, 212, 214, 224, 231, 268. *See also* United States: and Soviet Union
Colonialism, 4–5, 8, 9, 12, 145–48, 243, 273
Communism, 1, 12, 235. *See also* United States: and Soviet Union
Copts, 113, 166, 170
Crabbs, Jack, 23
Czech arms deal (September 1955), 18, 78–79, 91, 104, 234, 254
Czechoslovakia, 169, 246, 254

Dayan, Moshe, 74, 77–78
Decolonization, 4, 8, 28, 182
De Lespes, Ferdinand, 17
de-Nasserization. *See* Nasserism
Dulles, John Foster, 209, 214–15, 219, 226, 234–35
Durkheim, Émile, 152

Eban, Abba, 99
Eden, Anthony, 48
Egypt: agrarian reform (September 1952), x, 21, 57, 103–4, 108–9, 132, 164, 253–55, 266, 273, 278; agriculture, xi, 259–60, 268–74, 276; Alexandria Cotton Exchange, 275; Anglo-Egyptian Treaty (1936), 104, 232; Anglo-Egyptian Treaty (1954), 25, 76, 184; armed forces, 168–69; birth control policy, 21, 164, 171–72, 260–62, 267, 278, 282–94; Bonaparte's occupation (1798), 13, 113; British colonialism, 13–15, 103–4, 234; capitalism, 254–55, 274–75; Communist Party, 51; Constitution (1956), 22–23, 50, 60, 133, 135; Constitution (1971), 37, 140; corporatism, 19; democratic regime, 50–51, 108, 110–12, 115; demography (population growth), 15, 30, 171–72, 175, 257, 267, 278, 282–99; economy, 14–15, 20–21, 27–30, 41, 108, 110, 116, 130, 253–62, 264–68, 273–78, 285; education, 22–23, 104, 110, 130, 164, 167–68, 253–57, 261, 267, 274, 293; *effendiyya*, 14, 25–26, 28, 207 (*see also* Middle class); elite, 163–72; employment, 20, 22, 30, 256–58, 276; family planning (*tanzim al-usra*), 21, 164, 171–72, 260–62, 267, 278, 282–94; Five-Year Development Plans (First, 1960–1965), 254, 256–62, 264, 274–78, 286, 297 (Second, 1966–1970), 276–77; guided capitalism, 255; health, 261–62, 282; hegemony, 29, 76, 181, 183, 187–88, 195–200; import substitution (ISI), 259, 264, 273, 275–76, 295; industry, 254, 256–57, 259, 262, 264, 273–76, 285; infrastructure, 261; International Monetary Fund (IMF), 276–77; and Iraq, 189 (*see also* Iraq; Qassem, 'Abd al-Karim); Islam, 60–64, 113 (*see also* al-Azhar); and Israel, 75–94, 118, 181–83, 192–95, 210–11; Kuwaiti episode (1961), 190; legal system, 127–42; media, 19, 38, 169–70, 191; migration, 14–15, 37; National Production Council, 254; nationalism, 25, 66, 182–83; nationalization, 257, 262, 274–75; Ottoman rule, 13; Palestine conflict, 183, 186–87 (*see also* Arab-Israeli conflict); peasants, 132 (*see also* Nasserism: peasants); sequestration of foreign property, 255, 257, 274; social changes, 255; "soft state," 296–97; sports, 24, 145–58; State Council, 135–36, 140, 143; Supreme Court, 136–37, 139; Supreme Constitutional Court, 139; and Syria, 189–90, 211–14 (*see also* United Arab Republic; Syria); trade unions, 20, 132 (*see also* General Federation of Trade Unions); *'ulama*, 170; universities, 167–68; women in, 22, 169, 172–73, 292–93, 297–98
Eisenhower, Dwight D., 209–15, 219, 226–27
Eisenhower Doctrine (1957), 18, 45, 211, 213

*Elath* (destroyer), 222
Eliav, Benjamin, 85–86, 98
Eshkol, Levi, 74, 88–91, 98–99
Étatism, 5, 12, 27. *See also* Al-Nasser, Gamal 'Abd: economy
Eveland, Wilbur Crane, 225

Faisal, Crown Prince, 228
Farid, Muhammad, 116
Faruq (football club), 148–50
Faruq, King, 184, 207, 225, 232
Fatah, 194
*Fellahin. See* Nasserism: and peasants
Fertile Crescent, 179–81, 183–91
Ford, R.A.D., 243
Frisch, Roger, 256
Fu'ad, King, 148
Fuda, Faraj, 113, 123

Gawhar, Sami, 57–58
Gaza Raid (1955), 77, 193, 210
Gazira Club, 146, 158–59
General Federation of Trade Unions (GFTU, Egypt), 20
George, Alexander, 72–73
Germany, West, 169

Al-Hadi, Ibrahim 'Abd, 62
Hafiz, 'Abd al-Halim, 23–24, 307–20, 325–31, 333, 335–36; and Haykal, 329; and Nasser, 309, 318, 325, 326–30, 335; and Umm Kulthum, 327–28
Al-Hakim, Tawfiq, 31, 46, 53–56, 69
Halim, 'Abbas Ibrahim, 148
Harel, Isser, 78, 88
Hashemites: Iraq, 83, 187, 227; Jordan, 187, 227
Hatem, Mervat, 22
Haykal, Muhammad Hasanayn (Heikal, Mohamed Hassanein), 46, 54–55, 76, 109–10, 213, 226, 329
Higher Council of Arts, Letters, and Social Sciences (Egypt), 23. *See also* Nasserism: popular culture
Hijji, Tariq, 114
Holocaust, 74, 87–88, 92
Al-Hudaybi, Ma'mun, 166
Husayn, King (of Jordan), 83, 198

Husayn, Saddam, 47, 65, 92, 105
Husni, Su'ad, 307

Ibrahim, Hasan, 58–59
Idris, Yusuf, 24
Al-Ikhwan al-Muslimun. *See* Muslim Brothers
Imam, 'Abdallah, 61–64
Imam, 'Adil, 318–19
India, 273. *See also* Nehru; Neutralism
Indonesia, 271
International Monetary Fund (IMF), 276–77
Iran, 7, 216, 294
Iraq, 47, 65, 191, 194, 209–10, 212, 214, 226, 239–40, 294; Communist Party, 239–40; Kurdish problem, 239; Revolution of 1958, 83–85, 214, 239; and UAR, 239
Islamism, 221
Israel, 3, 6, 168, 221–22, 234; and establishment of UAR, 81–83; and Iraqi coup (1958), 83–85; perceptions of Nasser and Nasserism, 6, 72–94. *See also* Egypt; Al-Nasser, Gamal 'Abd

Japan, 164, 268–69, 271–73
Johnson, Joseph, 217
Johnson, Lyndon, 89, 215, 219–23; and Nasser, 219–23
Johnson Plan (1962), 217
Jordan, 83–85, 127, 190–91, 199, 212, 217–18, 294; Western intervention (1958), 191
Jordan River, 219

Kamal al-Din, Husayn, 57–59
Kamel, Mustafa, 2, 17, 116
Kemal, Mustafa (Ataturk), 75, 83, 90–91, 264
Kemalism, 12, 27
Kennedy, John F., 192, 205, 215–20, 227–28; assassination of, 219; and Nasser, 216, 218–19
Khartoum Arab Summit (1967), 198, 222
Khashaba, Ahmad Muhammad, 232
Khomeini, Ayatollah, 7
Khomeinism, 12, 27

362 | Index

Khrushchev, Nikita, 215, 231, 237–38, 241–43, 245
Al-Khuli, Lutfi, 55, 62, 324
"Kol Israel" (Voice of Israel), 98
Korea, South, 20–21, 264–78; agrarian reform, 266, 268–270; agriculture, 268; army, 269; Cold War, 268; demography, 267; economy, 266, 269–73, 278; education, 267, 271; employment, 267; "hard state," 272–73; health, 267; history, 268–69; import substitution, 270; industry, 269–70, 272, 278; and Japan, 268–69, 272; law system, 268; and Nasser, 264–78; tax system, 268; and U.S., 269–72; Vietnam war, effect of, 270. *See also* Korean War
Korean War, 208, 268; impact on Egypt's economy, 254
Kurdish Democratic Party (KDP), 239
Kuwait, 190, 217

Land reform. *See* agrarian reform under: Egypt; Korea; Syria
Larson, Deborah, 73
Latin America. *See* Populism
Lawzi, Salim, 24
League of Nations, 13
Lebanon, 47, 83–85, 191, 226; Civil War, 46; Western intervention (1958), 191
Liberal Party, 102, 192
Liberation Rally (1953), 18, 52, 58
Libya, 47

Mahfuz, Nagib, 46, 67–69, 71, 103, 106–8, 116, 121, 330
Malaysia, 271
Marcos, Ferdinand, 285
Meir, Golda, 74, 80; and Nasser, 80, 83–84, 87–88, 90–91
Middle class, 25–26, 28, 207; economy, 14; Nasserism, 67, 164; populism, 9–10, 12, 21, 29, 57. *See also* Egypt: economy
Middle East Command (MEC, 1951), 208, 232
Middle East Defense Organization (MEDO, 1952), 209, 233
Middle East Supply Center, 208
Mishap (1955), 76–77, 91
Modernization, 3, 4, 6, 8, 10–11, 13, 28, 48, 50, 61, 145–46, 151, 157

Monroe, Marilyn, 65
Montreau Conference (1937), 131
Morocco, 127
Mubarak, Husni, 31, 69, 165–66, 282, 308; democracy, question of, 114–16, 130; demographic policy, 290–94; Nasser's legacy, 100–118; political system, 114–16
Muhammad, 'Ali, 3, 115
Muhammad (the Muslim Prophet), 75, 154
Muhi al-Din, Khalid, 55–57, 62, 109
Muhi al-Din, Zakariyya, 60, 219–20, 286
Mukhitdinov, Nureddin, 239–40
Munich agreement (1938), 73, 92
Muslim Brothers, 46, 69, 112–13, 117, 122, 124, 166, 183; and Nasser, 57–64, 112, 120, 180, 184, 210, 220, 285, 290, 297
Myrdal, Gunnar, 272, 296

Nagib, Muhammad, 49, 58–59, 75–76, 116, 151, 200, 225, 233; role in sports, 145, 150–54
Nahhas, Mustafa, 104, 116, 232, 247
*Nasser 1956* (film), 31, 69, 105–6, 318
Al-Nasser, Gamal 'Abd: allusions to, in songs and plays, 324–36; Arab socialism, 241–45, 250, 255–62; arts, 309; assassination attempt, 61–62; Ataturk, perceived as, 75, 83, 90, 264; balance of achievements and failures, ix-xii, 199–200; Bismarck, perceived as, 75, 86, 91; charisma, x, 2, 9–10, 13, 15–18, 26, 45, 47–51, 180, 184–85, 191; and children, 22–23; death, 16, 31, 46, 51–53, 67, 90, 103, 106, 199, 246, 307, 333; demographic perception, 285–87; economic policy, 20, 27–28, 30, 41, 241–42, 253–62, 273–78 (*see also* Egypt); education, 21–23 (*see also* Egypt); the elite, 163–73; family planning, 20–21, 261, 285–88 (*see also* Egypt); father figure (*baba*), 15, 31; hegemony of Arab world, 25–26, 29, 76–77, 81, 84, 88–89, 181–82, 188, 193–95, 197, 199; Hitler, perceived as, 6, 48, 78–79, 81, 83–89, 92; al-Husayni, Hajj Amin, perceived as, 92; iconography, 64–67; Kuwait, 190, 217; and Israel, 181, 191–95, 198 (*see also* Israel); as leader,

Index | 363

ix-x, 2, 13, 45, 59, 75–94, 116, 179–81, 195, 211, 215, 238, 308, 325; legacy, ix-x, 31, 46–47, 50–53, 100–118, 140, 179–80, 308, 325 (*see also* Mubarak, Husni); March Manifesto (1968), 22, 46, 51–52, 56; media, use of, 17, 19–20; Mussolini, perceived as, 85, 92; nationalization of Suez Canal, 81, 253, 255, 274 (*see also* Suez Canal); neutralism, 26–27, 234–37, 243–44; Palestine problem, 180, 185, 188, 192–95, 199; pan-Arabism, 17, 25–26, 29, 76–77, 81, 179–81, 187–92, 199–200, 212, 223, 238, 240; Perón, comparison with, 86; personality, xiii, 49; *Philosophy of the Revolution*, 1, 56, 76, 81–85, 88, 90, 92, 181, 253; rule of law, 127–42; and Qassem, 191, 194, 214, 239, 245; and sports, 24, 150, 156–57; and Soviet Union, 26–27, 230–46; and students, 21–22; and Syria, 212–13; UAR breakup, 189, 191–92, 277; UAR formation, 82–86, 187–89, 192, 199, 213, 237, 245; and universities, 21–22; and U.S., 26, 205–25, 226, 228, 233–35, 236–38, 240, 243; "welfare state," 30; Yemen War, 192, 194, 199, 218–19, 233, 243, 257; 1967 War, 46, 59–60, 88–89, 106, 197–99, 210, 244
Al-Nasser, Hoda 'Abd, xiv
Nasserism (al-Nasiriyya), x, xiii, xiv, 1–2, 5–6, 12, 50, 54, 165, 184, 200, 211–12, 214, 219, 221; authoritarianism, 19, 28, 129, 131, 134, 142; cultural revolution, 23–24, 145, 150; decline, 86–90; definition, 1–7; de-Nasserization, 5–6, 31, 46–47, 53, 100, 119, 246; failure, 29–31; ideology, 1–3, 6, 24–28, 45; Israeli perception of, 82, 84 (*see also* Al-Nasser, Gamal 'Abd: and Israel); legal legacy, 127–42; Marxist interpretations, 3, 256; messianism, 4, 184; mobilization techniques, 18–24; modernization project, 2–3, 13; and peasants (*fellahin*), 21, 29, 31, 52, 132–33, 153, 164; popular culture, 23–24 (*see also* literature); populism, xiv, 4–7, 12–31, 132; protest movement, 3–4; social contract, 129–30, 139; and sports, 144–58; system of politics, 18–24; and women, 155–56, 164 (*see also* Egypt: women in); and youth, 155–56

Nasserist Party, 100, 109, 117
Nasserists, xi, 46, 191, 206
National Charter (May 1962), 1, 13, 19, 27–28, 51–52, 56–57, 63, 193, 242, 253, 255, 260, 277, 266, 335
National Progressive Unionist Grouping (NPUG), 109, 112
National Union (1957), 6, 18, 38, 52
National Water Carrier Project (Israel), 194
Nehru, Pandit Jawaharlal, 235, 285
Neutralism, 26–27, 29, 154, 184, 232, 235–36, 238, 240, 243–48
*New Outlook*, 91, 99
Nile Valley unity, 113
Nonalignment. *See* Neutralism
North Atlantic Treaty Organization (NATO), 208–9, 212
Nuqrashi, Mahmud Fahmi, 62, 104, 232

Oil: Arab, 197; Middle East, 209; "Oil Boom," 290
Organization for Economic Cooperation and Development (OECD), 273

Palestine: Palestinian entity, 190, 194–95; refugee problem, 211, 215, 217–18. *See also* Arab-Israeli conflict; Al-Nasser, Gamal 'Abd; Egypt; Pan-Arabism
Palestine Liberation Organization (PLO), 190, 195, 198
Palestinian Authority, 128, 142
Pan-Arab games, 155, 161
Pan-Arabism, x, 1–3, 14, 17, 25–27, 29, 54, 66, 81–82, 91, 103, 109–10, 113, 141, 179–200, 212–15, 221, 223, 237, 240–41; Palestine question, 2, 186, 192–95
Park, Chung Hee, President, 264–78. *See also* South Korea
Peres, Shimon, 74
Perón, Juan, 29, 86, 154, 160
Peronism, 7, 12, 29
Populism, xiv, 1, 4–31, 149–50, 132–33; and charismatic leadership, 9–10; and democracy, 10–11, 16; and economic perception, 27; and ideology, use of, 11–12; and Latin America, 4, 6–13, 15, 25, 28–29; and mobilization techniques, 10–11; and pan-Arabism, 26

Qaddafi, Muʿammar, 47
Qassem, ʿAbd al-Karim, 189, 194, 214, 239, 245
Qutb, Sayyid, 61

Rabin, Yitzhak, 65
Rafael, Gideon, 77–80, 97
Rajab, Hasan, 234–35
Al-Ramli, Lenin, 329, 335
Al-Rashid, Harun, Caliph, 154
Reilly, Patrick, 240
Resolution 242 (UNSC), 198, 221–22
Revolution (July 1952), xiii, 6, 13–14, 45, 56, 75, 100, 103–4, 115, 131, 166–67, 183, 206, 233, 237, 255
Revolutionary Command Council (RCC), 46, 58, 153, 206–8, 255
Ried, Malcolm, 69
Rifʿat, Kamal, 62
Russia, 7, 164

Sabri, ʿAli, 60, 62, 134, 136, 180
Al-Sadat, Anwar, 5–6, 31, 46, 50–51, 53, 57, 59, 69, 100, 106, 109, 115, 118–19, 143, 156, 165, 200, 223, 241, 244–46, 282, 297, 308, 313, 330; demographic policy, 287–90 (*see also* Egypt: family planning); economic policy (*infitah*), 130, 277, 313; legal changes, 139; and Muslim Brothers, 197, 290; and Soviet Union, 244–45; and U.S., 245. *See also* Nasserism: de-Nasserization
Al-Saʿid, Nuri, 83, 184
Salah al-Din al-Ayyubi, 17, 65
Salah al-Din, Mahmud, 232, 234, 247
Sanhuri, ʿAbd al-Razzaq, 135–36, 141
Saraj al-Din, Fuʾad, 102
Saʿud, King (of Saudi Arabia), 219, 227
Saudi Arabia, 85, 190–92, 212, 214–15, 217–18, 226–28, 277, 294
Shamir, Shimon, 4, 28
Al-Shams (sports club), 156
Sharaf, Sami, 156–57
Sharett, Moshe, 74, 97–98, 193; Nasser, negotiations with, 193; Nasser, perception of, 75–82, 91
Shepilov, Dimitri, 237
Sidqy, ʿAziz, 259

Sidqy, Ismaʾil, 104
Sinai Evacuation Day, 118
Singapore, 271
Socialist Labor Party (SLA), 124
South East Asia Treaty Organization (SEATO), 208
South Korea. *See* Korea, South
Soviet Union (USSR), 78, 181, 195, 205–6, 208–9; archives, 230–31; and Egypt, 26–27, 82–83, 89, 104, 181, 198, 228, 230–47, 254, 259, 274, 277; and Iraq, 214, 239–40, 245; and Israel, 211; July 1952 Revolution, attitude toward, 233; and Syria, 237–41; and UAR, 237–42; and U.S., 45, 50, 105–6, 156, 180, 184, 193, 211, 236, 296, 332
Sports: festivals, 152–53; and Islam, 154; during monarchy in Egypt, 145–49; nationalism, 147–49, 151–56; during republic in Egypt, 149–57
Springborg, Robert, 20
Stalin, Joseph, 65, 231–32
Students: political participation of, 22, 257. *See also* Al-Nasser, Gamal ʿAbd: students
Sudan, 47, 113, 157, 259
Suez Canal, 197, 257, 297; nationalization (1956), 18, 31, 45, 50, 81, 103–6, 184, 235–36, 253, 255, 274
Suez War. *See* War: of 1956
Switzerland, 169
Syria, 47, 189–92, 198–99, 211–14, 216, 226, 237, 294 (*see also* United Arab Republic); agrarian reform (1958), 238; Communist Party (SCP), 237–41; 1957 crisis, 211–12

Tahir, ʿAdl, 155
Taiwan, 271
Al-Taliʿa Group, 51–52, 54–55, 62
Thailand, 271
Third World, 6–7, 13, 28, 212, 215, 220
Tiran Straits, 106, 193, 211
Tito, Josef, 224, 235, 238, 246
Trevelyan, Humphrey, 236
Tripartite Declaration (1950), 208
Tripartite Federation (1963), 86–88
Truman, Harry S., 206, 208, 233–34
Truman Doctrine, 208

Tunisia: and Egypt, 294–98; family planning, 21, 282, 287, 294–98; Islamic opposition, 297–98; status of, 296, 298
Turkey, 210, 212, 264, 294
Al-Tuwani, Ahmad, 150

Umm Kulthum, 16, 23, 307, 310, 325, 327–30, 332, 336; and 'Abd al-Halim Hafiz, 327–29; and Nasser, 327
United Arab Republic (UAR), 18, 25, 28, 45, 50, 69, 82–86, 103, 156, 188–89, 194, 199, 213–16, 237–40, 242, 257, 277, 333–34. *See also* Al-Nasser, Gamal 'Abd
United States: and Arab-Israeli conflict, 205, 216–17, 220–23; and Britain, 206–8; defense plans, 208–10, 226–27, 233; and Egypt, 26, 30, 181, 188, 192, 205–25, 226–28, 233–34, 236, 243, 245, 253, 277; and Iraq, 209–10; and Israel, 209–10, 215–22, 224, 226; and July 1952 Revolution, 207, 225; and Palestinians, 215–19; policy in Middle East, 205–26; and Saudi Arabia, 214–15, 218–19, 227–28; and Soviet Union, 79, 205–25; and Syria, 212–13; and UAR, 211–16; and 1967 War, 220–22; and Yemen War, 218–19
'Urabi, Ahmad, 17
Urbanization: in Egypt, 14–15; and populism, 8–9, 15

Vietnam, 271
Voice of the Arabs, 191

Wafd Party, 13, 58, 102–4, 112–13, 115, 117, 207, 232–33
Wahhabiyya Movement, 75
War: of Attrition (1969–70), 18, 46, 48, 200, 222–23; Gulf (1991), 169; *of 1948*, 17, 74, 168, 183, 186; *of 1956*, 45, 50, 105–6, 156, 180, 184, 193, 211, 236, 296, 332; *of 1967*, 18, 21, 30, 46, 55, 59–60, 88–89, 103, 106, 109, 118, 136, 183, 198–200, 219, 220–23, 244, 257, 278, 287, 332; *of 1973*, 168, 197, 287, 313, 333; Yemen, 18, 21, 30, 86, 168, 194–95, 218–19, 223, 243, 257, 276–77, 296
Warhol, Andy, 65
Wasat Party, 122–23
*Wataniyyat*, 310, 316, 324, 332, 336
Weber, Max, 2, 9, 48
World Bank, 270–72, 292

Yemen, 18, 21, 30, 47, 56, 192, 194–95, 199, 218–19, 247, 276–77. *See also* War: Yemen
Young Egypt Party, 183
Yugoslavia, 238. *See also* Tito

Zaghlul, Ahmad, 148
Zaghlul, S'ad, 17, 116
Al-Zamaleq (football club), 150, 153, 156

www.ingramcontent.com/pod-product-compliance
Lightning Source LLC
Chambersburg PA
CBHW021334230426
43666CB00006B/288